AIDS, Opium, Diamonds, and Empire

AIDS, Opium, Diamonds, and Empire

✦

The Deadly Virus of International Greed

Nancy Turner Banks, M.D.

iUniverse, Inc.
New York   Bloomington

AIDS, Opium, Diamonds, and Empire
The Deadly Virus of International Greed

Copyright © 2010 by Nancy Turner Banks

iUniverse books may be ordered through booksellers or by contacting:

iUniverse
1663 Liberty Drive
Bloomington, IN 47403
www.iuniverse.com
1-800-Authors (1-800-288-4677)

Because of the dynamic nature of the Internet, any Web addresses or links contained in this book may have changed since publication and may no longer be valid.

ISBN: 978-1-4502-0171-1 (sc)
ISBN: 978-1-4502-0602-0 (ebk)

Library of Congress Control Number: 2010900079

Printed in the United States of America

iUniverse rev. date: 05/04/10

*This book is dedicated with endless love and gratitude to my mother,
Martha Smith, who taught me the lesson of unconditional love
And to my friend Eugene Wyatt who came into my life
to share his boundless energy and joie de vivre
They both left much too soon.*

Contents

Factors Known to Cause False-Positive HIV Antibody Test Results[1]

- Anti-carbohydrate antibodies
- Naturally-occurring antibodies
- Passive immunization: receipt of gamma globulin or immune globulin (as prophylaxis against infection which contains antibodies
- Leprosy
- Tuberculosis
- Mycobacterium avium
- Systemic lupus erythematosus
- Renal (kidney) failure
- Hemodialysis/renal failure
- Alpha interferon therapy in hemodialysis patients
- Flu
- Flu vaccination
- Herpes simplex I
- Herpes simplex II
- Upper respiratory tract infection
- Recent viral infection or exposure to viral vaccines
- Pregnancy in multiparous women
- Malaria
- High levels of circulating immune complexes
- Hypergammaglobulinemia (high levels of antibodies)
- False positives on other tests, including RPR (rapid plasma reagent) test for syphilis
- Rheumatoid arthritis
- Hepatitis B vaccination
- Tetanus vaccination
- Organ transplantation
- Renal transplantation
- Anti-lymphocyte antibodies

---

[1] Christine Johnson, "Whose Antibodies Are They Anyway?" Sept./Oct., 1996, Continuum

- Anti-collagen antibodies (found in gay men, haemophiliacs, Africans of both sexes and people with leprosy)
- Serum-positive for rheumatoid factor, antinuclear antibody (both found in rheumatoid arthritis and other autoantibodies)
- Autoimmune diseases : Systemic lupus erythematosus, scleroderma, connective tissue disease, dermatomyositis
- Acute viral infections, DNA viral infections
- Malignant neoplasms (cancers)
- Alcoholic hepatitis/alcoholic liver disease
- Primary sclerosing cholangitis
- Hepatitis
- "Sticky" blood (in Africans)
- Antibodies with a high affinity for polystyrene (used in the test kits) Blood transfusions, multiple blood transfusions
- Multiple myeloma
- HLA antibodies (to Class I and II leukocyte antigens)
- Anti-smooth muscle antibody
- Anti-parietal cell antibody
- Anti-hepatitis A IgM (antibody)
- Anti-Hbc IgM
- Administration of human immunoglobulin preparations pooled before 1985
- Haemophilia
- Haematologic malignant disorders/lymphoma
- Primary biliary cirrhosis
- Stevens-Johnson syndrome,
- Q-fever with associated hepatitis
- Heat-treated specimens
- Lipemic serum (blood with high levels of fat or lipids)
- Haemolyzed serum (blood where haemoglobin is separated from the red cells)
- Hyperbilirubinemia
- Globulins produced during polyclonal gammopathies (which are seen in AIDS risk groups)
- Healthy individuals as a result of poorly-understood cross-reactions
- Normal human ribonucleoproteins
- Other retroviruses
- Anti-mitochondrial antibodies
- Anti-nuclear antibodies
- Anti-microsomal antibodies
- T-cell leukocyte antigen antibodies

- Proteins on the filter paper
- Epstein-Barr virus
- Visceral leishmaniasis
- Receptive anal sex

Soft Money Contributions by Anti-HIV Medication Producers to the Democratic and Republican Parties in the 1997-1999 Election Cycle [1]

Pharmaceutical Company	Democratic Party	Republican Party
Abbott Laboratories	0	$166,250
Aventis	$156,785	$395,945
Bristol-Myers Squib	$253,300	$686,418
Eli Lilly	$181,500	$375,644
Glaxo Wellcome	$55,250	$477,875
Hoffman-LaRoche	$20,000	$100,525
Merck	0	$102,825
Pfizer	$175,000	$979,496
Pharmacia-Upjohn	$60,000	$135,000
Schering-Plough	$166,000	$513,500
Total:	**$1,067,835**	**$3,933,478**

2. Herron, Robert, Why Are The NSC and CIA Managing America's Global Campaign Against Aids?
"The US Government's Worldwide Campaign Against AIDS Will Kill Millions of People with the Side Effects of Highly Toxic Anti-HIV Drugs," Oct. 2001, www.virusmyth.com

AIDS: A Small Timeline
of a Large Syndrome

adapted from the <u>German version at Ummafrapp.de</u>

1931:	<u>The Nobel Prize in Biochemistry awarded to Otto Warburg</u> for his proof of the fermentative energy production of cancer cells.
1930's:	Antibiotics are manufactured for the first time.
1961:	Introduction of the birth control pill jump-starts the sexual revolution.
1966:	Otto Warburg speaks at the conference of the Nobel Prize winners in Lindau and explains that "the cause of no illness is known better than cancer..." [i.e. inhibition of the oxidative mitochondrial respiration]
Since the 1960's:	Azathioprine given after organ transplantations, in order to inhibit the cellular immunity and thus the rejection of the transplanted organ.
1961:	Azidothymidine (AZT) is found in herring sperm, with identical azide group as azathioprine.
1964:	AZT is synthetically manufactured.
1965:	AZT tested as an anti-cancer chemotherapy in rats with leukemia. The animals further developed lymphatic cancer, which made plans for clinical trials in humans grind to a halt.
mid-1960's:	Respectable cancer researchers stop their search for cancer-causing viruses.
1969:	The antibiotic Bactrim (aka Septra/Septrin) entered the pharmaceutical market, at first hailed as a miracle drug because of the dual-punch combination of trimethoprim and sulfamethoxazole, by which it was hoped to sidestep the problematic development of microbial drug-resistance.

1970:	In animal experiments it was proven that the trimethoprim in Bactrim suppresses the cellular immune function, and that this immunosuppressive power is comparable to that of Azathioprine. Additionally it was shown that after a normal therapeutic dosage and duration, systemic Candida fungal infections occurred (one of the most frequent AIDS indicator diseases).
1970:	US researchers discover the enzyme Reverse Transcriptase (RT). It was wrongly assumed to occur exclusively in RNA tumor viruses, which were subsequently called retroviruses. It was maintained that a retrovirus would transcribe its RNA into human DNA, which could then result in cancerous cellular transformations.
1971:	Just before the Watergate scandal exploded, Nixon proclaims the War on Cancer. The largest investment of funds in the history of medicine to date became focused on the hunt for cancer retroviruses
1971:	Publications of several different research groups prove that RT occurs in nearly all forms of cellular life, and is not specific to retroviruses. Under the direction of Luc Montagnier at the Pasteur Institute in Paris, accurate rules were codified for the proof and the isolation of retroviruses in human tumor cells. RT and other indirect and nonspecific markers no longer applied as proof of isolation.
1974:	The first medical cases of microbial resistance against Bactrim are published.
1975:	Bob Gallo of National Cancer Institute in the USA claims the first isolation of human retrovirus in leukemia cells, HL23V. Scientific peer-review showed that the previously codified rules had not been followed, and his proof of isolation was declared invalid. After close examination with electron microscopy, it was shown that the alleged retroviral particles emerging from the leukemia cells were nothing more than cellular waste and stress proteins. [Also the antibodies were shown to cross react with a wide variety of nonviral stimuli.] The rules of the Pasteur Institute were designed to prevent such mistakes as this. Bob Gallo was humiliated as a scientific counterfeiter, and hurried to correct his "mistake".

1977:	In the US under President Carter, and soon after in the UK, patent protection was granted for manipulations of natural cell properties. With this downfall of humankind began the race to profit from the building blocks of life itself.
Early 1980's:	Trimethoprim, azathioprine and NO gas (the active substance inhaled in 'poppers') are shown in animal experiments to have an identical immunotoxic profile, and also to be responsible for cancer cell transformation, particularly in Kaposi's sarcoma. This carcinogenic power of nitrogen derivatives is based on, amongst other things, their ability to bind to iron-containing 'heme' groups in the cell organelles of the mitochondria, with associated inhibition of ATP synthesis (H. Kremer, "The Perversions of the AIDS Medicine")
1980/81:	The billion-dollar Nixon project was terminated, as Retrovirus-Cancer researchers had nothing to show after a decade of work. For the second time Bob Gallo claims the alleged isolation of a human retrovirus (HTLV). Again the Pasteur rules were not followed, and again only surrogate markers were presented. (Two years later at the historic 1st International Symposium on AIDS, these laboratory artifacts of human leukemia cells were presented, then however "isolated" from T-cells of apparent homosexual AIDS patients. In each case only nonspecific surrogate markers were observed.)
1981:	Studies prove that Bactrim/Septra causes substantial DNA damage in human cells after even a short duration of ingestion. Nonetheless it is still prescribed to approximately 5% of the global population.
1981:	Since 1981, the distinct causal relationship between the toxic burden profile and the occurrence of the so-called AIDS-indicating diseases (opportunistic infections and Kaposi's sarcoma) was denied, albeit arbitrarily, in favor of the hypothesis of a "new type of microbe". (H. Kremer)

1981:	The historical start of the AIDS avalanche. The June 5th issue of MMWR, the monthly medical report of the CDC, outlined 5 diagnoses of pneumonia in Los Angeles. The patients did not suffer from the typical bacterial pneumonia, but rather from a rare form (PCP) caused by the pathogen Pneumocystis carinii, a ubiquitous fungal microbe that is inhaled by breathing. It has been shown that over 90% of normal children and adults have antibodies against this fungus. All of the PCP patients were treated with the chemoantibiotic Bactrim/Septra.
1982:	AIDS is introduced as clinical term, and spoken of as a gay plague: an absolutely deadly epidemic, which from homosexuals to bisexuals would spread, and then on to women and their unborn babies in the womb. Reagan exclaimed that the AIDS virus, which to date nobody had actually found, was Public Enemy #1. "It was the birth of an epidemic dictate without an epidemic agent, however its discovery was imminently expected after the allotment by the Reagan administration of the largest investment of funds in medical history." (H. Kremer)
1983:	Montagnier and Gallo maintain that they both isolated HIV independently, and with it found the AIDS agent. The French team had also not applied the rules regarding the correct isolation of retroviruses, which they made at their own Institute back in 1972. Both teams published only nonspecific surrogate markers as proof. A female employee of the Montagnier team had studied isolation techniques in the laboratories of Bob Gallo. The electron micrograph (EM) photo from the French team showed a particle budding from a fetal umbilical blood cell, not from a T-cell, yet this did not raise the eyebrows of their scientific colleagues. At this point in time the French team did not state that the AIDS virus had been found, but rather spoke of the discovery of a new human retrovirus. Today, Luc Montagnier is nevertheless considered the discoverer of HIV, in reference to this publication.

1983:	An International Symposium on AIDS was held at New York University Medical Center, during the month of March. It was distinctly dominated by Retrovirus-Cancer researchers, rather than epidemiologists. By some wondrous mutation, the alleged HTLV retroviruses from Bob Gallo's laboratories, which were previously defined as leukemia agents (and actually, as mentioned above, merely constituted transport-capsules of cellular waste), transformed into to AIDS microbes that destroy T-4 lymph cells, rather than transform them into rapidly multiplying cancer cells, as was previously published.
1983:	At the same conference, the prominent Retrovirus researcher Lewis Thomas, head of the New York Sloan Kettering Institute (of one the main profiteers of the Nixon Cancer-Virus project), gave a keynote address and literally called for "a series of human experiments, planned and executed" in order to observe whether after blocking the cellular immunity with drugs, cancer developed or already existing tumors worsened. Hence the already dying AIDS patients were surrendered without opposition into the Retrovirus-Cancer researchers' systematic experiments with immunotoxic chemotherapy.
1984:	Bob Gallo announces his creation of an HIV antibody test. Due to their short life span, the T-cells of the AIDS patients were not suitable for mass production of similar natured antigens, and an actual retrovirus could not be isolated, so immortal human leukemia cells were co-cultivated and co-stimulated with the cell culture. Gallo claimed that the allegedly isolated retrovirus had passed into the leukemia cells; the end result was that these normal human stress-proteins could be mass-produced and sold as test-kit antigens. This deceptive procedure was patented by Bob Gallo.
1985:	The HIV antibody tests were marketed worldwide by five pharmaceutical corporations, including Eli Lily with particularly close connections to President Bush Sr.

1985:	Colleagues of Bob Gallo at the US National Cancer Institute publish lab tests that showed AZT was an effective weapon against HIV. However, in accordance with Gallo's method, they had again only used overstimulated T4-lymph cells, over which they proclaimed the still unproven statement "infected with HIV". Thereafter, the first brief pilot study tested AZT on AIDS patients as "anti-HIV therapy", with further studies on AZT treatment following. As expected, a relatively small rate of opportunistic infections occurred in the medicated group, as compared to the control group--at least in the early stages of the trial. However this was not proven beyond eight weeks of drug therapy; the study was prematurely aborted due to "ethical concerns" for the control group, and no long-term effects were studied.
1986:	It was discovered that T4 cells can be separated into two types: those that produce NO gas (TH1) and those which inhibit it (TH2) [Overview iwth Mosmann and Coffman 1989]. Only a delicate balance of these sub-groups, between the cellular (inflammatory) immunity and the humoral (antibody) immunity, can guarantee an effective immune defense.
1987:	In record time, the FDA approved AZT for use in AIDS patients by the Spring. Committee members spoke of substantial political influence on the approval process.

1987:	AZT fulfilled all the requirements that the Retrovirus-Cancer researchers had sought in a substance, to enable a series of planned human experiments (L. Thomas). They needed a substance that restrained the surrogate markers provoked in the test tube, in order to be able to state that this substance was effective as an anti-HIV medicine, because this was necessarily for the permission of clinical pilot studies with patients stigmatized as "HIV positive". At the same time, this substance had to serve the actual research purpose of provoking cancer genesis via suppression of the cellular immunity. The AIDS patients should not die too rapidly from opportunistic microbes, at least not before cancer could develop. Thus this substance had to also exhibit an antimicrobial effect against opportunistic microbes, anyhow such an effect had to be at least temporarily demonstrated in clinical studies with the usual control groups. The immunotoxic, cancer-promoting effects of the substance could only be illuminated after a certain period of delay. Thus they needed a substance with an immune devastating effect similar to azathioprine, but which was not yet publicly documented. With AZT, such a substance was ripe for the picking! "The aza- group of azathioprine and the azido- group of azidothymidine (AZT) are analagous by their 3 nitrogen atoms..." (H. Kremer) After the devastating effects of AZT--which was until recently considered as the AIDS-drug par excellence and is still seen that way in Africa--had been documented, the "AIDS Cocktails" came onto the market; in which AZT is combined with a small arsenal of some 12 other substances.
1989:	AZT is approved for the preventative treatment of symptom-free "HIV positives" in the USA, and a little later in Europe.

1990's:	Fundamental research occurs outside the scope of AIDS, that corroborates the toxic origins of AIDS. Many human cell systems synthesize cytotoxic NO gas, in order to eliminate opportunistic microbes. Several groups of researchers proved that with too strong and/or prolonged stimulation of inflammatory (Th1) T4 cells, a counterregulatory inhibition of cytotoxic NO gas production occurs. The formation of these Th1 cells is inhibited and persistently switched in favor of Th2 cells, which do not produce NO gas but instead migrate from the bloodstream to the lymphoid organs in order to support the B cells in antibody production.
1991:	It was found that T4-helper cells produce NO gas via a calcium-independent method, so that it can be produced in sustained quantities for cytotoxic (cell-killing) purposes, providing that enough of the amino acid arginine is available.
1992:	Clerici and Shearer published the first paper which suggests a switch from Th1 to Th2 dominance during AIDS progression.
1993:	Kary Mullis is awarded the Nobel Prize for his invention of the Polymerase Chain Reaction (PCR), a genetic laboratory method for DNA amplification. (Later this method would be used for the construction of the alleged "viral load" assay in HIV positives, which Mullis continues to sharply reprimand. In addition, the PCR method is not suitably reproducible. Becoming conscious, he further engaged the contradictions of the HIV/AIDS medical profession and until today holds to the fact that there is no publication in the scientific literature to reference as proof that "HIV is the probable cause of AIDS.")
1996:	Sen and Packer publish an overview of research on the relationship between cell redox balance, inflammatory cytokines, and the transcription of DNA into proteins; this shows how cell stress can actually switching on or off certain genetic programs.

1997:	Two research teams [Gluschankof et al, and Bess et al], 14 years after the alleged discovery of HIV, for the first time apply the standard rules of retrovirus isolation. The published results shocked the scientific community: the EM photos of the concentrated "pure HIV" showed excessive cellular waste and some blister-like vesicles of completely different size and shape, which did not correspond with the characteristics maintained for many years by Gallo and Montagnier. To this day, no further EM photos allegedly showing an HIV concentrate have been published in the scientific literature, purified according to the standard rules of retrovirus isolation.
1997:	In an interview with Luc Montagnier, Djamel Tahi asks why he did not follow the standard rules of the retrovirus isolation. Montagnier responds that "after a Roman effort" he could only find four nonspecific surrogate markers.
1998:	The Nobel Prize in Physiology is awarded to Furchgott and Ignarro for the 1987 discovery that different body systems produce their own NO gas as a messaging chemical. Also in this same year, the Peterson/Herzenberg team discovered that the Th1/Th2 switching is controlled by intracellular glutathione (i.e. cell redox balance).
1999:	After the use of about a dozen different substances in combination therapy, those similar to AZT and an entirely new substance class, the so-called protease inhibitors, exploded into an unparalleled excess of medical intoxication; the prominent "HIV" researchers admitted that the "eradication of HIV" by means of "highly-active antiretroviral therapy (HAART)" would take 10-60(!) years. At the same time however, other HIV/AIDS researchers published that as a result of HAART itself, apart from substantial liver damage, disturbances of fat metabolism, diabetes, and various forms of multiple organ failure, above all severe DNA damage had developed within the mitochondria.
2000:	"Mythos HIV" by Michael Leitner was published: an excellent, well-readable, late-breaking book.

2001:	In November, "The Silent Revolution of Cancer and AIDS Medicine" by Heinrich Kremer comes on the scene and suddenly changes the whole situation. It is the first scientific documentation on the current status of the realization, a perhaps quiet, but nevertheless enormous revolution and a milestone of medicinal history.
2002:	Heinrich Kremer presents at the "Congreso Mundial por La Vida" (World Congress for Life) in Barcelona, before more than 60 Spanish and international groups, a critical analysis of the prior 20 years of HIV/AIDS medicine.
2002:	Meanwhile the 14th International Congress on AIDS meets in Barcelona, parallel to the alternative Congreso. It was announced that HIV could not be "defeated" by the past strategies of experimental chemotherapy. This outcome of nearly 20 years of chemotherapeutical "virus hunting" (Dr. Gallo), would only have depressed those medical doctors, who, due to lack of foundational knowledge and through the ignorance of the biotechnical lab-trickery of the inventors of the "HIV"-epidemic theory, did not see through the real intention.
2002:	Deutsches Ärzteblatt, a German doctor's newsletter, gives further misconception to their professional audience, reinforcing the HIV/AIDS assumption. Under the heading "HIV, on the track for the vaccine," the search for a so-called "naked vaccine" was publicized, a phrase that masks the fact that it is actually applied gene therapy. In popular fashion, the title photo flaunted the absence of genuine photos, instead presenting an imaginative computer graphic of the virus. Without special training, most physicians cannot recognize that the "HIV" glycoproteins and "HIV" DNA sequences are in reality laboratory constructs, accomplished via further refinement and application of the same techniques which Bob Gallo and Luc Montagnier had already applied with the alleged "HIV" isolation.

2002:	Many scandals rock the world, yet it still remains hidden to the public eye that the HIV/AIDS assumption represents a contrived house of cards that will collapse--and the sooner, the better. The knowledge around the amply investigated causes of cellular immune weakness syndromes and the knowledge around the effective balancing/compensation therapy remain suppressed. The establishment aims to mass-inoculate the globe far and wide with "HIV DNA Vaccines", with special focus on the underdeveloped nations as risk groups. In reality, contact with tuberculosis, malarial, fungal, protozoan and worm infections is endemic in these countries. After the predictable "innoculation failure" of the mass vaccination, these peoples will conveniently be the perfect candidates for treatment with the full spectrum of experimental chemotherapy.
2006:	A study is published which demonstrates a lack of correlation between so-called "viral load" and AIDS progression -- one of the most common reasons for recommending antiviral drug therapy [Cohen J. Study says HIV blood levels don't predict immune decline. Science 313(5795):1868, 2006; Rodriquez B, Sethi AK, Cheruvu VK, et al. Predictive value of plasma HIV RNA level on rate of CD4 T-cell decline in untreated HIV infection. JAMA 296(12):1498-506, 2006]. Another long-term study is released that concludes that while "viral load" is made "undetectable" by HAART medication, such numerical improvements have not translated into a decrease in mortality, thus refuting the claim that long-term treatment with the newer anti-HIV medications are the reason why people with AIDS are now living longer [Lancet 368:451-58]. A more plausible explanation is that those who were most severely ill and glutathione-depleted died the earliest, leaving a remaining population of hardier AIDS patients.

For more detailed information, please read Kremer's "The Perversions of AIDS Medicine".

Chapter 1

The Big Lie and the Art of War

o o o o o o o o o o o o o o o o o o o o o o o o o o o o o o o o

Mundus vult decipi, ergo decipiatur.
The world wants to be deceived so let it be deceived.

Racket: (a) a fraudulent scheme, enterprise, or activity;
(b) usually an illegitimate enterprise made workable by
bribery or intimidation; (c.) an easy and lucrative means of
livelihood.

A great deal of intelligence can be invested in ignorance
when the need for illusion is deep.

Saul Bellow, To Jerusalem and Back, 1976

You should never believe anyone, not even me. You can only
trust your own research. If you just comfortably lie on your
back and let people tell you everything then you'll get some
sort of answer, mostly the wrong one.

Dr. Kerry Mullis
Nobel Prize winner and inventor
of the polymerase chain reaction (PCR) test

It is a great mistake to think that wars only concern armies, regulars or
guerillas, involved in active engagement—blowing people and things to
smithereens. In today's world, nothing could be farther from the truth. The
real forces of evil wage another kind of warfare. This warfare is principally
financial. The dark princes of debt finance have gained practically unopposed
leverage over every important social, economic, and political institution,

including and especially the health care delivery system. As a result, death by iatrogenic[3] medicine kills three quarters of a million people annually--more people in a year than either cancer or heart disease.[4]

The demons of capital and "free market" ideology have created an information monopoly by gaining control of the pharmaceutical industry, the teaching of physicians, the major media, including medical journals, and the flow of research dollars. They control a clandestine intelligence agency, the Epidemic Intelligence Service, which has silently infiltrated every major health department, hospital, newspaper, and medical journal across the nation enabling its control of information and the mounting of a consolidated response at a moment's notice. The research dollars determine if there is going to be a "war on cancer," or a "war on AIDS," or the promotion of the latest viral scare to sell more vaccines or worthless "anti-viral" products such as Tamiflu[5] or Relenza.[6] Such wars are planned and mounted with the same organizational and strategic planning as the Pentagon employs. What this ultimately leads to is the development of bad science and toxic drugs that are created ostensibly to fight cancer and AIDS but in effect cause more cancer and more AIDS—which is the point of the war. People die in war, and the profiteers substantially increase their wealth and power. The object of war is twofold: to establish power relationships and profit.

A more pernicious outcome of these medical wars has been the silent loss of personal sovereignty and the loss of the most sacred and inalienable right to the sanctity and security of our own bodies and the free choice and right to select the medical treatment that we deem best. Information is power, but access to accurate medical information has become "proprietary" because of the privatizing of public resources.[7] The idea that an individual has the right to be adequately informed to make a medical decision has become an arcane notion.

---

3.   From the Greek iatros [physician] combined with genic [to induce or cause by physician or medical treatment].

4.   Gary Null et al., "Death by Medicine." They estimate that 783,936 people are killed annually by iatrogenic medicine.

5.   Jordan Lite, "Influenza drug Tamiflu ineffective against most U.S. infection," *Scientific American*, 9 Jan. 2009.

6.   Causes lung spasms, disorientation, and suicidal ideation. Not recommended for children and seniors

7.   The Stevenson-Wydler Act required that U.S. federal laboratories actively transfer technology to American private industry and the Bayh-Dole Act allowed the recipients of government grants and contracts to patent any resulting inventions.

Centralized command and control industrial cartels have mastered the art of privatizing profits and rewards and socializing risks and obligations. Over the last one hundred years, as the result of rapid industrialization combined with cartelization, and particularly during the last fifty years, we have witnessed an unprecedented event in evolutionary biology—the massive toxic poisoning on an unimaginable scale of the human metabolic system not only from industrial products but also industrial waste and increasingly from powerful electromagnetic fields generated by mobile phone towers and other electronic devices.. This pervasive human poisoning is a corporate cost that is passed on to individuals and their communities. The entire planetary biosphere is under continual siege from the widespread release of medical and industrial pollution, including heavy metals (mercury, aluminum, lead, and arsenic), carcinogens, electro-magnetic radiation and hormone disrupters. The sacred bloodstreams of our newborn infants are violated with the putrescence of contaminated vaccines of dubious effectiveness as soon as they leave the womb. This has put increasing and unremitting pressure on the human energy and immune systems and has shifted the immune system in such a way that it is less responsive to external threats and more likely to see the self as other, thus creating a rising tide of auto-immune diseases in which the body attacks itself.

Chemoantibiotics (<u>anti</u> [against], <u>bio</u> [life]), liberally given to both humans and domesticated animals, destroy the normal gut flora that aid in digestion and assimilation of our food and make it impossible to utilize the nutrition that is taken in. Many antibiotics and environmental toxins also damage a cellular organelle known as the <u>mitochondria</u>. It is in the mitochondria that our energy is produced in the form of a molecule of ATP (adenosine triphosphate). These fascinating organelles that at one time were ancient bacteria have their own DNA separate from nuclear DNA. Mitochondrial DNA is inherited through the maternal germline. Because of the intentional industrial attack of these organelles with drugs and toxins, not only is permanent genetic damage being passed on to future generations but this practice is also creating a significant rise in current chronic diseases, such as Alzheimer's, cancer and acquired immune deficiency.

Because of the inevitable rise in environmental oxidative and nitrosative stressors, most people are in need of increased intake of certain nutrients called anti-oxidants to combat this problem. This has become more of a challenge, however, because of alterations in life style, dietary habits, farming policy and animal husbandry. Farming has been seriously altered by the application of industrial methods to large agri-businesses that process and change our food until it has lost its sacred nature. Food is now genetically modified, fertilized with artificial chemicals, irradiated, and shipped unripe thousands of miles from where it was grown. It is then gassed and colored to make it look real, and then sprayed again with more chemicals in order to preserve its shelf life. In all of this processing, much nutritional value is lost.

Domesticated animals are injected with hormones to increase their growth rate and fed antibiotics to keep them from infection while they are penned into crowded stalls on factory farms and forced to live in their own excrement. They are stuffed with feed that is unnatural to their digestive systems, which leads to unnecessary illnesses. They are brutalized by their living conditions and slaughtered using the most mindless and unsanitary methods. The spirit of the animal is destroyed.

The same financiers who took control of the nation through the creation of the Federal Reserve Bank and cartelized the medical industry have done the same to agriculture. The family farm is a memory. By taking control of the food supply, they can sell genetically modified seeds and the chemical fertilizer to make the seeds grow. Their "technology agreements" have reduced many once proud and independent farmers to a state of virtual feudalism. The result of all of this adulterated food is an explosion of obesity, depression, hypertension, Alzheimer's, arthritis, and cancer. The number of chronic diseases is skyrocketing even among children.

Free capital flows, liberalization of capital markets, privatization of public assets, and debt creation are not the only weapons in the armamentarium of financial warriors. They have used the untraceable flow of commodities, oil, gold, diamonds, and drugs to amass wealth, and to buy the loyalty of enemies, the silence of friends, and mercenaries to neutralize adversaries when necessary. They strategically use the import of illicit drugs to draw community resources away from hospitals, schools, libraries, and playgrounds and toward the increasing militarization of law enforcement and an ever expanding prison population. More than anything, they have used the cumulative massive intake of environmental pollutants, of toxic drugs, both legal and illegal, and the unprecedented stressor accumulation of modern life on sub-segments of the population to create the illusion of a new disease that they call <u>AIDS</u>—acquired immune deficiency syndrome. However, AIDS is not a disease; it is a syndrome—a collection of twenty-nine old diseases, clustered together, re-branded, and given a new scary label. It is a product marketed by fear, deception, and the creation of mass hysteria. It has been selling well for twenty-five years.

AIDS is a tragedy in two parts. The first act was created by the foreign policy decisions of the state apparatus and its historical connection to the international criminal underworld. The second act was written by the pharmaceutical industry itself. The pharmaceutical industry developed several drugs designed intentionally to suppress the immune system as well as others that had the same effect because of a similar chemical configuration. Several of these drugs were released to the mass market and were used extensively and inappropriately by an underground sector of the homosexual community who were simultaneously experimenting with psychotropics and narcotics that were illegally imported and released into the general population by the clandestine agencies of the U.S. government in league with international organized crime syndicates through foreign policy initiatives.

After years of use and abuse of these environmental toxins, some of the young men began to show up in Emergency Rooms during the late 1970s and early 1980s in New York, Los Angeles, and San Francisco. Instead of using the new environmentally created mass poisoning as a clarion call to awaken the medical community to the public health threat of environmental toxins, it was used as another marketing opportunity to identify a phantom virus and create a broader market to sell more of the same kind of toxic drugs that were so harmful.

Meanwhile, on the African continent, there was a mad race for the continuing theft of her resources. Civil strife and social disruptions were created to facilitate this process. With the fall of the minority white apartheid government of South Africa, thousands of black gold and diamond miners who had sustained lung injuries because of substandard mining conditions now had the possibility of having their day in court. The mining industry led by the DeBeers Anglo-American Corporation and other extractive industries were in a panic. Reimbursing the millions of injured black workers who had developed asbestosis and silicosis and subsequently tuberculosis from unsafe mining conditions would create an enormous unfunded expense. From a financial warrior point of view, profits, which transcend human life, had to be protected. With the fall of the Botha government, pulmonary tuberculosis suddenly became an AIDS defining disease.

AIDS was created to cover both of these health crises—the toxic poisoning of young people in the West and the industrial poisoning and social disruption in Africa. It was pure insanity, but it worked. People began to die because they were toxic from a chronic onslaught of environmental oxidative stressors. Because allopathic[8] physicians are trained in recognizing and treating the infectious problems of the 19th century, the 20th century problem of systemic toxicity was misdiagnosed. What compounded the problem was an error of tragic proportions. As a result of misdiagnosis, the

---

8.   The predominant system of medicine today that uses drugs, radiation and surgery as their means of therapy. It was a term coined by Samuel Hahneman, the father of homeopathy to indicate how these doctors used methods that had nothing to do with the symptoms of disease and would be ultimately harmful

patients were then given more drugs with a similar chemical profile to those that were already poisoning them. The CDC in their infinite wisdom and eye for improving drug sales in service to big Pharma, then seized upon the excess deaths to publicize the lethality of a never isolated virus. It has been a high crime against humanity. A central player in this drama has been the British pharmaceutical concern Burroughs Wellcome.

Burroughs was the innovator of a stable of drugs that contained the nitroso chemical group structure as a common characteristic. This is a chemical compound with a nitrogen and oxygen attachment (for example, R--NO). These particular compounds can form nitrosamines that have long been known to cause oxidative and nitrosative stress and DNA damage. These compounds are also known to be both immunosuppressive and carcinogenic. One of the Burroughs' compounds, Azathioprine was used expressly as an immune suppressive drug for organ transplant patients so that they would stay sufficiently immune suppressed to accept a foreign graft without a rejection response. Azathioprine was known to trigger opportunistic infections, Kaposi's sarcoma, and lymphomas in such transplant patients. These were the same diseases that were presenting in the original cohort of AIDS patients. It was also known from the transplantation literature that these cancers can spontaneously regress and the opportunistic infections improve after cessation of the drug.[9] Since Burroughs Wellcome produced this drug and had access to some of the best chemists on the planet, it is unlikely that they were unaware of the innate nature of this particular class of compounds to produce transplantation AIDS. The literature was solid that azothioprine could cause an acquired immune deficiency syndrome and that the condition was reversible even in very ill organ transplant patients. It certainly was known by the boys and girls at the Centers for Disease Control (CDC) and the National Institutes of Health (NIH) when they released a rather macabre committee report titled Confronting AIDS that outlined the strategy for selling a new sex and blood plague to the nation and for using it as a model for developing future epidemic opportunities.

Two other nitroso compounds from Burroughs Wellcome were introduced to the market and directed largely at the homosexual community who more than willingly used these chemicals to support their lifestyle choices. One was amyl nitrite, a medication that had been released as a blood vessel dilator for patients with angina, a heart condition in which contracted blood vessels cause intermittent chest pain. This drug was used more creatively in the homosexual community as a sexual doping agent because it gave a

---

9.   L, Margoulius et al., "Kaposi's sarcoma in renal transplant recipients," South African Med J, 1994 (84):, 16–17.

transitory high, sent blood to the penis, and relaxed the rectal sphincter, facilitating anal intercourse. The other Burroughs' drug was Trimethaprim/ Sulfamethoxazole (T/S), an antibiotic that acted as both a folate and a DNA inhibitor. The drug was often used indiscriminately and prophylactically in the sexually promiscuous gay community before a night on the town in hopes of preventing sexually transmitted diseases from multiple anonymous sexual partners in one night. In essence, this community was known to have indulged over a prolonged period in lifestyle choices and activities that included the massive ingestion of immunosuppressive and carcinogenic drugs.

While the homosexual community was being flooded with Burroughs' immune suppressing drugs, the intelligence agencies of the United States government in league with international crime syndicates were flooding Western markets with heroin, cocaine, LSD, and a variety of psychotropic and immunosuppressive drugs as well as crack cocaine. When the young people who were generally born after WWII began to show up in clinics and emergency rooms, toxic and oxidized, they were traumatized with the idea of a deadly virus. Terrified and organized with money from the pharmaceutical industry, they clamored for the quick release of a drug that could save them. Violating all principles of safety in human experimentation, the FDA quickly approved azidothymidine (AZT). The young, frightened, and organized homosexuals, not being careful what they wished for, got their wish! Unfortunately, it was another drug from Burroughs Wellcome that had the same nitroso chemical configuration. The new toxin tipped thousands over the edge into irreversible pathology and left a generation of young people who spent the 1980s attending funerals, saying goodbye to friends and loved ones, and wondering if they were going to be next.

So, historically, it must be understood that the medical profession was already inducing AIDS in renal transplant patients as a "side effect" of azothioprine and that immune suppressed patients were not a medical anomaly. But within an unimaginably short time frame and without a real placebo controlled double blinded study, a shelved cancer causing drug from this same nitroso stable, azidothymidine (AZT) was approved for use in "AIDS" patients. This drug simply finished what the fast tract life style and use of amyl nitrate, T/S, and multiple other drugs these young men were taking had started—an immune imbalance as the result of an oxidative alteration in the cellular redox potential[10] and toxic suppression of their mitochondrial energy production at the cellular level. IV-drug users and hemophiliacs, both

---

10.   The electrical potential in the living cell that controls the initiation of many cellular processes.

of whom were highly toxic from the long use of oxidative stressors, were thrown in for good measure and a bit of diversion. Over a hundred years of medical literature supported the immune suppressing effects of opiates, but IV-drug users, many of whom were black, would be the gateway to target black women as an update on the eugenics agenda. Both IV-drug users and hemophiliacs were immune stressed from long-term use of foreign proteins (hemophiliacs), and the injection of foreign substances, immuno-suppressive opiates and in the case of drug addicts, poor nutrition and repeat and chronic infections. To act dumbfounded and confused by looking for a single viral etiology of multiple diseases in the face of this "new" medical crisis was a brilliant diversionary tactic. This was simply an astounding break from precedent. Viruses have very little genetic material and it was known that one virus was associated with only one disease. Now one virus would be claimed as the cause of multiple diseases—even diseases claimed to be caused by other viruses!

This is free market capitalism! This is an economic system that sells anything—people, human organs, drugs, war, and plagues. It does not matter as long as it can be done and someone can make a profit. It is the ugly underbelly of the Adam Smith philosophy of "free markets," and it needed a justification. They called it AIDS.

It has been more than two decades since the bureaucrats from the Reagan administration and the politburo at the Center for Disease Control claimed to have "isolated" a virus, the Human Immunodeficiency Virus (HIV) that was then fraudulently promoted as the cause of AIDS. They sent an ocean of fear through the universe by making an unfounded claim that AIDS was the result of this new and deadly sex and blood plague caused by HIV and was always fatal. It did not matter that the inevitability of fatality was more from a lack of medical insight than from physiological certainty. In the ensuing twenty-five years, the predicted pandemic never emerged. The theory of the virus can no longer stand up to scientific scrutiny, and in multiple studies from around the world, HIV has been shown not to be sexually transmitted. What is called *HIV* can barely be found in a white blood cell called a lymphocyte. The accurate "HIV" antibody test has been shown to cross-react with 70 different entities. More people are dying from the consequences of antiretroviral therapy than from AIDS, and the problems have remained confined to the original risks groups—polydrug users in the West and the poorest in Africa. HIV/AIDS is a failed theory.

The crisis that began in the early 1980s reached a peak a decade later. Just as the number of "classic" AIDS from the original cohort began to decline, the definition was suddenly expanded, thereby greatly enlarging the pool of targeted victims who were scared into the AIDS pharmaceutical nightmare as the result of an HIV antibody test. The release and promotion of the antibody tests have been the foundation of an unprecedented reign of medical terror. The first test was patented and quickly sent to market by Robert Gallo, a research scientist of questionable integrity who claimed he had "isolated" this new virus. The test was initially only designed to screen the blood supply, but was soon put to use in clinical application, thus enlarging the target market. It was never really important that this antibody test accurately predicted an early demise. It was only important that people were made to believe that this was so. While claiming the test was highly specific, it was found to react with more than 70 different conditions from tuberculosis, and malaria to pregnancy.[11] This information was knowingly kept from public awareness.

In retrospect, the "AIDS" crisis never seemed to be about science. It was more about human experimentation with genotoxic drugs, about creating and expanding markets, and about using AIDS as an escape valve for corporate negligence that might mount into the billions of dollars. AIDS was a created crisis that allowed the expediting and commercialization of drugs such as AZT, a known carcinogen that should never have been approved for human use to get to market. It also was the excuse to allow an unevaluated medical product—the "HIV antibody" test—to contain those who would become victims of a massive state sanctioned poisoning of millions of people. The fraud that passes for "scientific medicine" was brought to the world courtesy of the new face of the eugenics movement. Eugenics is a point of view that believes the world would be better off by culling by various means including genocide, what they consider excess population—the useless eaters. Their programs have been funded by the same foundations, financial organizations, and people who have been promoting this elitist philosophy for well over a hundred years and who totally control the medical industry.

The official public relations campaign to convince the world of this new deadly "virus" began on May 4, 1984, when the prestigious journal Science published the first of a series of four papers by a group of scientists under the leadership of Dr. Robert Gallo that claimed the probable cause of AIDS was a new retrovirus, HTLV-III, later called the Human Immunodeficiency Virus—HIV. Gallo had previously worked under contract for Litton Bionetics, a major defense contractor involved in the development of bio-weapons. He had also been part of the vainglorious virus hunters in the failed Richard Nixon "War on Cancer" project. He was one of the same geniuses who had spent years and lots of taxpayers' money claiming but never proving that retroviruses were causing massive cellular proliferation (cancer). Yet he

---

11.   Christine Johnson, "Factors known to cause false positive HIV antibody test results," Continuum, Sept.–Oct., 1996.

would turn on a dime and say that the same type of retrovirus that had never been shown to be pathogenic in humans was now causing cell death. Money and deep politics have a way of making illogical science pass muster.

The original papers published in *Science* on which rests the entire AIDS industry, were subsequently found to have a significant number of unreported deletions and alterations that made the claim of viral isolation an absolute fraud.[12] In infectious disease, the isolation of a new organism must follow precisely recognized and agreed upon protocols. Robert Koch published the basic protocols to isolate infectious bacteria in the 1890s, and they were refined in the 1960s to accommodate the isolation of viruses much smaller than bacteria that require additional isolation techniques and a photograph made by an electron microscope.

Gallo never followed these protocols. One of the project researchers, Dr. Mikulas Popovic, wisely kept a duplicate of his original typewritten paper and the handwritten changes made by Gallo, after the fact of the original research and before submitting the manuscript for publication. The original research and the typewritten duplicate were produced by Popovic while Gallo was in Europe. On his return, Gallo changed the original research document by hand a few days before it was submitted to Science on March 30, 1984. According to the Office of Research Integrity of the US Department of Health and Human Services, "Dr. Gallo systematically rewrote the manuscript for what would become a renowned Laboratory of Tumor Cell Biology paper."[13] To change information in a scientific experiment that was not actually observed is an absolute lapse of scientific integrity.

The duplicate revealed that Popovic had used the specimen sent to their lab by a French research team, Luc Montagnier and Françoise Barré-Sinoussi, of the Pasteur Institute in Paris, and renamed it Gallo's "virus," or HTLV-III (which eventually was changed to HIV). Further, the document revealed that Gallo had deleted this bit of scientific thievery. What has not been reported until recently (and this is the blockbuster), is that on page 3 of the same document, Gallo also deleted Popovic's unambiguous statement that "[d]espite intensive research efforts, the causative agent of AIDS has not yet been identified" (emphasis added) and replaced it in the published paper with a statement that said practically the opposite: "That a retrovirus of the HTLV family might be an etiologic agent of AIDS was suggested by the findings."

---

12.   Janine Roberts, Fear of the Invisible: How Scared Should We Be of Viruses and Vaccines, HIV and AIDS? (Impact Investigative Media Productions, 2008).

13.   "Offer of Proof,", Office of Research Integrity, US Dept. of Health and Human Services, 1993.

What is clear is that the rest of Popovic's typed paper is entirely consistent with his statement that the cause of AIDS had not been found. At no point in his paper did Popovic attempt to conceal that he was using the specimen obtained from the Paris lab or to prove that any virus caused AIDS. It is evident that Gallo concealed these key elements in Popovic's experimental findings.[14] Popovic's final conclusion was that the culture he produced "provides the possibility" for detailed studies. There was nothing more.

Finding and isolating a virus by the most rigorous scientific standards for making pronouncements that would have such profound life and death consequences were never the point. AIDS has become an enormous profit center buttressed by a splendid psychological operation designed to put fear into the target population and to neutralize the opposition, including injured South African mine workers who were told that the tuberculosis they suffered was the result of an acquired sexual disease instead of lung disease acquired in the mines.

In the early 1980s when a cluster of opportunistic infections and a cancer called Kaposi's sarcoma began to show up in a small group of fast-track homosexuals the medical community missed an opportunity to connect the dots because the same problems had been seen in renal transplant patients on azathioprine. Those MDs who worked in big city Emergency Rooms had also seen the immune suppressive effects in patients who were admitted with the sequelae of chronic IV drug use, and surgeons were well aware of the probability of a poor recovery in patients who had suppressed cellular immunity as demonstrated by the inability to mount a reaction to a DTH (delayed type hypersensitivity) skin test. Physicians did not ask if there was a common link between the transplant AIDS patients, the chronic IV drug users, the anergic surgical patients, and the new AIDS patients. They did not link the fundamental problem of opiate toxicity of IV drug patients with the drug toxicity of the new AIDS patients. They did not link the defect in cellular immunity of anergic surgical patients to the same defect in the new AIDS patients. The obvious links for immune suppression were in the social history—the chronic use of nitrite inhalants, antibiotics, narcotics, and a much stressed lifestyle with a history of multiple sexually transmitted infections and bowel diseases as well as a history of poor nutrition. Physicians accustomed to looking for infections missed that these patients were toxic and highly oxidized and in a hypercatabolic state. Instead of detoxifying their patients by correcting the underlying metabolic disorders while

---

14. Letter to the Editor of <u>Science</u>, Bruce Alberts, and the CEO Alan Lechner from a group of prominent and well-respected scientists and physicians. Dated December 1, 2008.

acutely attending to the various infections, the findings were seized upon by the pharmaceutical industry and the researchers from the failed "War on Cancer" to create a marketing opportunity that has successfully enriched and allowed the unthinkable—real time human experimentation with no fear of reprisal.

A targeted psychological operation was mounted that cleverly positioned AIDS as a sex and blood plague to draw attention away from "free market" policies that were allowed to develop from the aftermath of two military adventures—WWII and Vietnam[15]. It was known that these policies, once initiated, would ultimately manifest in large populations as unexplained disease clusters. The policies made exquisite "free market" financial sense, but they were divorced from any semblance of human compassion.

The baby boom generation is the last large living cohort to have grown up in an America that was relatively drug free, highly industrialized, and with a modest prison population. In the 1950s, the Dow Jones Industrials were in the 200s, drug trafficking was virtually unknown, the U.S. had the world's largest gold reserves, was the world's largest creditor nation and an unparalleled industrial giant.

This was also a time when Africa was striving for reprieve from colonial strangulation. Countries from Algeria to South Africa and Ghana to Kenya and the Congo were asserting their yearning for sovereignty and the idea of a pan-African union. The impact of WWII on Africa and WWII and Vietnam on the industrialized West would change all of that. The outcome of these two conflicts would be to set in place policies that would provoke the greatest stress on the human immune/energy systems of large populations yet seen in human evolution.

By 2007, the Dow Jones had reached 10,000, and drug use and trafficking were so common that two generations had come to believe that this was normal. The U.S. government had stopped talking about the gold at Fort Knox, the country had been systematically deindustrialized and it had become the biggest debtor nation on the planet.

By 2007, all of Africa's progressive leaders who espoused pan-Africanism had been assassinated or deposed. The continent was flooded with guns and corporate mercenaries. Her wealth was once again being systematically stolen, and externally fostered wars and genocide were the facts of life. South Africa no longer had apartheid as a social or political system, but the financial system and land wealth of the country remained solidly in the hands of the white minority.

---

15.   After the Korean War there was an up tick in heroin use that was largely concentrated in minority communities of large metropolitan areas.

How did all of this evil come to pass in the span of fifty years? An outcome of WWII was the Bretton Woods agreement that created the World Bank and the International Monetary Fund, and the National Security Act of 1947. The National Security Act created the Central Intelligence Agency and the National Security Agency. In 1951, the Epidemic Intelligence Agency was born. These institutions have largely been run as protection and extortion rackets to reduce developing nations to beggary and destitution and to transform the armed forces of developed nations into itinerant mercenaries in service to private capital expansion.

After Vietnam, the drugs formerly run into Southeast Asia since the days of the British East India Company would now, with the help of the CIA, international organized crime networks, and other international clandestine agencies, be massively imported into Western countries, the U.S. being the largest target market. The deliberate policies of creating accelerated over consumption of drugs and of other immune toxins in the West while simultaneously creating the economic conditions for the dumping of environmental pollutants and the under consumption of basic sustenance in less developed countries could not have but shocking and enormous public health and social impacts.

At the cellular level of human metabolism, the consequences of these macroeconomic policies—over consumption of drugs and environmental toxins as well as infectious and psychological stressors in the developed world and nutritional deprivation, psychological trauma, chronic infections, and miners' lung in the developing world have led to the same outcome—environmentally induced excessive reactive oxygen and nitrogen species. As a result, both nitric oxide (NO) and glutathione (the master anti-oxidant) levels were reduced leading to energy deficiency and reduced redox capacity in the cells energy factories, the mitochondria. Because nitric oxide is the poison gas produced by Th1 cells that kills intracellular parasites, patients presented commonly with opportunistic infections. These biochemical deficiencies ultimately lead to reduced energy production, immune dysfunction, and even cancer. The health consequence of cellular energy deprivation arising from parasitic macroeconomic policies is the perfect metaphor. The abject poverty on the African continent can be directly traced to the policy of structural adjustment programs as a condition for loans by the international banking houses. Both planned policies—massive illegal drug importation and economic structural adjustment programs—have had predictable physiological impacts on a subset of predisposed individuals within societies. The medical consequences arising from these physiological stressors have a rational, logical, scientific explanation that has nothing to do with a phantom virus and everything to do with what is known as deep politics.

All the conundrums of the AIDS theory, the missing virus, the nonexistent pandemic, the opportunistic infections, the Kaposi's sarcoma, and the elevated antibody titers—can be explained logically and scientifically without having to get involved in Gallo's delusional whimsy. The development of opportunistic diseases and of Kaposi's sarcoma was a predictable consequence of chronic and irresponsible use of nitroso and other immune suppressing drugs combined with a lifestyle choice. The diseases were not widespread in the homosexual community, only in a subset described as "fast track."

When there is a massive accumulation of oxidizing environmental stressors and the immune system has been depleted of the master antioxidant glutathione and other thiol-containing proteins, an evolutionary biologically programmed counterbalance will occur. As a result of the depletion of the glutathione/ thiol[16] pool in the T-helper immune cells and other cell systems, there is a switch in the biologically programmed T cell counter regulatory balance from the T cells (Th1) that produce nitric oxide—a poisonous gas that kills intracellular opportunistic infections— to the T cells (Th2) that target extra-cellular organisms with a heightened antibody response. This Th1 to Th2 counterbalance of the immune system is what the virus hunters called AIDS. The death prognosis was an expression of the limited application of knowable medical information.

The condition of acquired immune deficiency is not new. What is new is the level of destruction that globalization and "free market" policies are having on individuals, communities, countries, ecosystems, and the entire planet. Because those who institute these policies are cleverly psychopathic, they have become expert at diverting attention from the fruits of exquisite financial decisions by deftly shifting the blame from themselves, the predators, and using their vast resources to create phantom villains or to play the "Blame the Victim" game.

The villains in this war psychodrama change frequently. At one time it is communism. Next it is terrorism. It could be a War on Drugs or perhaps Cancer. One day it is Noriega, and the next it is Saddam. Perhaps it will be the impending doom of a mushroom cloud. This year it is the bird flu, last year it was SARS.[17] Who can forget the Gerald Ford swine flu fiasco? And, of course, when the drug epidemic in the West and the starvation epidemic in less developed countries exploded into collective consciousness through the speed of modern mass communications, a new villain had to be found.

---

16.   Thiols are compounds that contain a sulfur and a hydrogen molecule and are referred to as mercaptans. They maintain the redox environment that allows cellular mechanisms to function properly.

17.   Severe Acute Respiratory Syndrome, claimed to be caused by a coronavirus.

This time it was a nonexistent virus. But whether HIV exists and works as stated is not the point. Like all villains created for mobilization purposes, truth suffers the first great defeat. Selling the world on a particular point of view is what matters.

HIV fit perfectly the war model of social organization at the foundation of modern Western civilization. War, subversively, has been declared the basic social system within which other secondary modes of social organization conflict or conspire.[18] Allopathic medicine as a fundamental part of that system logically conspires. The virus was the enemy. Creating an enemy and making the people believe that they are under attack has become standard operating procedure of the massive government bureaucracies controlled by special corporate interests. Another mobilization for another profitable war could be mounted to attack this new enemy and wipe it out. That some would die was inevitable. Some always die in war, either directly or as "collateral damage". It has been twenty-five years, and the war is dragging on with no end in sight.

18.   Report from Iron Mountain on the Possibility and Desirability of Peace, 29.

Chapter 2

Silent Weapons

○ ○

...In the interest of future world order, peace, and tranquility, it was decided to privately wage a quiet war against the American public with an ultimate objective of permanently shifting the natural and social energy (wealth) of the undisciplined and irresponsible many into the hands of the self-disciplined, responsible and worthy few...In order to implement this objective, it was necessary to create, secure, and apply new weapons which...were a class of weapons so subtle and sophisticated in their principle of operation and public appearance as to earn for themselves the name "silent weapons".[19]

As the world was transformed by the utopian vision of centralized resource control and of free capital flows unrestrained by the barriers of sovereign statehood and the rule of law, it became necessary to neutralize the possibility of concerted group action against the consequences of this consolidation. With the use of strategically precise silent weapons, individuals within sovereign states were neutralized and weaned from notions of individual sovereignty. Medicine is a perfect instrument to use for this strategy because it is easy to make people believe that draconian measures are necessary to protect the public health, especially if the public is primed with the right climate of fear.

Silent weapons are tools of social engineering used by the war state that evolved from operations research in England during WWII from the master British social engineering think tank Tavistock Institute. Tavistock supports

---

19. Silent Weapons for Quiet Wars, "Operations Research Technial Manual TM-SW7905.1"

the entrenched social and economic position of the British oligarchy and their international social class. The Tavistock Institute has a long history of designing programs for control of the mass behavior of civilian populations. The Institute became expert at using psychological warfare during WWII to attack the vitality, options, and mobility of individuals within a society. A plan was developed for Britain's Royal Air Force to bomb German worker housing while leaving military targets, such as munitions plants alone. The idea behind the saturation bombing was to break the morale of the German worker. Between February 13th and February 14[th,] 1945, widely ranging estimates from 35,000 to 100,000 people were intentionally killed in a raid on the non-military target of Dresden, Germany.

Tavistock's research and access to high-speed computers has allowed members to amass a wealth of knowledge that they use to understand, manipulate, and alter the sources of natural and social energy in societies. They have mastered the art of social engineering by learning how to tap into and undermine people's physical and mental strengths and use their emotional weaknesses against them. AIDS is only one of such weapons. This book is an exploration of the history, politics, economics, science and spirituality that intersect at the junction of this disease.

The AIDS story cannot be understood without exposing the means by which Rockefeller interests cartelized and gained master control of the medical hierarchy in the early part of the 20th century. As a result, profitability and not public health drives where heavy research dollars are spent. The concentration of power and the scramble for research dollars have corrupted the medical hierarchy as it has corrupted Congress. So no one should have been surprised when a scientist who did not have the best reputation for running his research laboratories with integrity publicly proclaimed a scientific feat that he had not accomplished. What was even more outrageous, he developed an ill-conceived and intentionally fraudulent antibody test, patented it, and brought it to market before he had isolated the virus that the test is said to identify. This fraudulent antibody test has been used as the foundation for the creation of new medical profit centers—HIV tests anti-retroviral drug development and sales, and a bevy of do-gooders who work with the World Health Organization and multiple nongovernmental organizations (NGOs). Their sole mission is to run around the planet claiming the benefits of abstinence and/or "safe sex" by demonstrating how to masterfully shove condoms onto bananas. While the birth rate in Europe is declining, the birth rate in "AIDS-plagued" Africa is growing at a steady 3 percent a year although there are areas that are being depopulated for private industry.

Robert Gallo's original research that led to the development of the AIDS industry was published in the prestigious journal <u>Science</u> in 1984. These papers were used to justify the river of government money that flowed into the research and development laboratories of the same scientists who had wasted a fortune looking for a viral cause of cancer in Nixon's barren "War on Cancer" campaign. AIDS was a lifeline for those researchers whose grants would otherwise have been drastically reduced after years of effort looking for "oncoviruses." They were not about to reject the opportunity for a secure income. Failing to find a viral cause of cancer, they were more than willing to turn their attention to the new villain "HIV" to continue the influx of research money

Several years after the shock had subsided in the medical community of the premature announcement of the finding of a "probable" cause of AIDS and there was some time for sober reflection, thousands of physicians, scientists and Thabo Mbeki, former President of South Africa, openly challenged the conclusions of the viral/AIDS hypothesis. There were too many unanswered questions in this thesis. The challenge for an open scientific debate was deemed outrageous and irresponsible by those who had vested interests in the profits and the control that came with supporting the hierarchical position. The voices of those who called for transparency and open debate on the most important medical issue of the day were intentionally silenced by the usual counterinsurgency techniques of slander, derision, name calling, intentional medical perjury, and distortion of scholarly based counter-analysis. All of this was buttressed by the hysteria of the gay community who preferred to live in denial rather than face their own culpability in the self poisoning that led to the creation of the crisis.

Janine Roberts, one of today's most solidly grounded investigative journalists has uncovered incriminating evidence that clearly proves that the original papers published in <u>Science</u> in 1984 that made the world think that a terrible new sex and blood virus was poised to wipe out billions were based on fraud and unfounded conclusions.[20] Robert Gallo, the government scientist who led the team that published the original papers that spawned the AIDS industry, had never isolated a virus. Not only had Gallo not followed the standard protocols for viral isolation but what he described in those original papers were indirect surrogate markers that might indicate a viral presence but could not be conclusively proven to represent a unique virus and certainly not one that was infectious without the gold standard of isolation. There was absolutely no evidence of proof of either isolation or infectivity, yet researchers and physicians, who have never bothered to read this original research or engage themselves in the controversy that surrounds it, use it to justify all sorts of medical mischief.

---

20.   Roberts, Janine, Op. cit.

The indirect surrogate markers that they claimed indicated a unique viral presence in the blood of ill patients were an enzyme called reverse transcriptase; a few non-specific regenerative stress proteins, and some unidentifiable cellular debris on electron microscopy—none of which are viral specific. In fact, what Gallo really found were the ubiquitous cellular breakdown products of oxidative and nitrosative stress. This metabolic stress is caused by an imbalance between the production of reactive oxygen and nitrogen species and the biological system's ability to detoxify the reactive intermediates or repair the damage to cell function, structure, and organization caused by these reactive products. Gallo identified an enzyme and cellular proteins as well as "viral like particles" that can be expressed in anyone's cells that are undergoing excessive bio-electric stress. Everyone can be shown to have the so-called HIV proteins at some level depending on the arbitrary dilution of the testing reagent.[21]

The identified enzyme,[22] reverse transcriptase, is, however, not a uniquely retroviral enzyme, and for this reason cannot be used to claim the discovery of a new virus. Reverse transcriptase (RT) transcribes a single strand of RNA into DNA and helps in the helix formation of the double stranded DNA. RT is a DNA repair enzyme and can be isolated from everyone's blood. Finally, electron microscopy of cellular debris from mitogen[23] stimulated cultures is not evidence of viral isolation or infectivity. In fact, what Gallo was describing was not the cause of anything but the result of an evolutionary response against prooxidative and nitrosative stress. Gallo's limited knowledge allowed him to act as if the rules set up to define true viral isolation did not apply to him,[24] and he was clearly ignorant of the rules of evolutionary biology. By not recognizing these natural laws, he and those who support the AIDS paradigm placed themselves above the laws of nature. Millions have suffered and died because of such hubris.

Another document originating from Gallo's laboratory was a letter from Dr. Matthew A. Gonda and dated four days prior to Gallo's submission to Science. Gonda was then head of the Electron Microscopy Laboratory at the National Cancer Institute. An integral step in viral isolation is an electron

---

21. Roberto Giraldo, "Everyone Reacts Positive to the ELISA Test for HIV," Continuum Midwinter 1998/9.
22. Enzymes are proteins that speed chemical reactions in cells.
23. An oxidizing agent that stimulates mitosis or cell division.
24. In 1976, Gallo stressed that the detection of particles and RT, even RT inside particles, are not proof of the existence of retroviruses because many such particles exist that totally lack the ability to replicate. "Some evidence for infectious type C virus in humans," Animal Virology (New York: Academic Press, 1976). 385–405.

micrograph of the isolated specimen and Gallo had sent his specimens to Gonda to validate isolation. However Gonda responded to Gallo that "I do not believe any of the particles photographed are of HTLV-I, II or III (HIV)." According to Gonda, one sample contained cellular debris, while another had no particles near the size of a retrovirus. In spite of this very clear rejection of "isolation", Science published on May 4, 1984 papers attributed to Gallo et al with micrographs attributed to Gonda and described unequivocally as HTLV-III (HIV).[25] This was an outrageous scientific fraud that has created unspeakable harm.

Simply put, Gallo cheated in both claiming isolation and identification of a new virus and in the development of his antibody test that could not possibly identify a virus that he did not isolate. Concerning the antibody test; Gallo adjusted his test substrate for his patented antibody test to especially high antibody amounts. Antibody elevation is indicative of what is now known as a Type 2 (Th2) switch in the immune system, which is programmed to produce an increased antibody response. The genetic expression of pathological proteins (e.g., HIV1, TAT) by dysfunctional cells was an unrecognized symptom of intracellular/systemic imbalance. Because it was the epigenetic[26] oxidative mechanisms that resulted in unusual gene transcription, Gallo and other "HIV" researchers confused cause with effect. The "HIV" antibody test was the measurement of a particular effect of oxidative/nitrosative stress. Unfortunately it is not the optimal indicator of the functional cellular problem. More clinically relevant indicators are finding reduced glutathione (an antioxidant consisting of three amino acids) and nitric oxide levels, diminished cellular immunity as indicated by an anergic response to a DTH skin test and resultant cellular catabolism.[27]

The HIV antibody test is characterized by an arbitrary measuring threshold. In this way the test was able to identify, not HIV, but people whose immune cells form particularly high levels of antibodies; who may be undergoing an increased amount of oxidative stress from long-term drug use or from chronic exposure to environmental toxins, antibiotics, psychic trauma, vaccines, nutritional deprivation, etc. In other words, the "HIV antibody" tests measure an antibody reaction against what Gallo put into the test substrate: indeterminate proteins excreted by repeatedly stressed human immune cells that had been co-cultured with cancer cells. The proteins that Gallo identified were not the cause of immune deficiency, but

---

25. Letter dated December 1, 2008 from scientists to editors of <u>Science</u>
26. Changes in the gene expression not caused by changes in the DNA sequence.
27. Catabolism is the breakdown with a release of energy of larger molecules into smaller units.

the consequence of severe long-term immune stress that had nothing to do with an "HIV infection." Most of the original patients from Gallo's studies remained HIV negative although they developed one or more of the AIDS indicator diseases.

HIV religionists have never explained why many people who died from "AIDS" were HIV negative. How could that be—unless there really was some underlying metabolic problem that they were unable to define that had nothing to do with a virus? The people stigmatized with a positive HIV antibody test simply have higher antibody levels than the arbitrary threshold set for the test. This will become important for people of African descent who have, given the same medical history, tested positive more often than their white counterparts. This in part is due to the genetic predisposition to make more antibodies to the same stimulus than whites. There was also another genetic marker used to create the illusion of HIV being more commonly found in people of African descent and will be discussed in the chapter on HIV testing.

This does not mean that people who are HIV positive may not be ill or become ill, but the antibody test is not the determinant for the progression to disease. That determination should be made by other measurements of cellular immune Type 1 dysfunction. In addition, a positive antibody test does not mean that a person is harboring an inevitably lethal virus. This, of course, has profound implications for treatment protocols.

It is now abundantly clear, especially because of recent research into the elucidation of the mechanisms by which immune cells are counterbalanced, that AIDS is a disease of systemic toxicity from an overload of environmental stressors and not a unique retrovirus. What Gallo did in his lab was determine the antibody threshold through which people would enter the gates of hell.

The HIV antibody test is a uniquely pernicious silent weapon, and silent weapons always have two reasons: the one that will be presented to the public to make it palatable and the real social engineering reason. This book is an exploration of the less palatable option.

Giving highly toxic, experimental and carcinogenic drugs to people who were told they were going to die anyway became palatable. Giving the same drugs that were known to cause genetic damage to unborn babies also became palatable. Rushing drugs to market with poorly designed and executed clinical trials without controls became the norm. Suppressing information about drug toxicities became a matter of course. The profits generated by the pharmaceutical industry were astronomical, and the cover story for elite drug running and economic genocide became HIV/AIDS. This is the underbelly of the free market system that is precluded from examination. A few intrepid journalists have ventured into this morass and have lost not only their livelihoods but sometimes their lives. HIV is an invented virus that has served multiple purposes in much the same way that the story of the weapons of mass destruction, mushroom clouds, yellow cake uranium and "Axis of Evil" inflamed the sentiment of a nation to prosecute the ill-advised Iraq War.

Gallo's thesis of a viral cause of what became known as AIDS was given impetus by the Reagan administration, the same administration that was filled with the very players who were importing large quantities of toxic drugs into the country in what became known as the Iran-Contra affair.[28] Because of the long history of drug running of a subset of the political class, it was known that the level of newly introduced toxicants would produce a wave of illness that would require an explanation. This was not a historical surprise, nor did the idea of promoting a disease for political or profit-driven reasons begin with the Reagan administration. They were following a long tradition in certain circles of using human misery to create a profitable enterprise. Gallo's misleading antibody test and the industry it spawned were an updated version of an old and well worn medical swindle brought to perfection in the 1940s under the skillful management of Harry L. Hopkins.

In his 1940 book Your Life Is Their Toy, Dr. Emmanuel Josephson presciently observed, "An individual disease permits ruthless but effective play on human dreads and sympathies. This device is familiar to every quack. . . .The credit for the introduction of disease exploitation as a 'social service' device and a means of tapping an endless flow of alms and tribute from the public purse probably goes to Harry L. Hopkins.[29] First tried on the public on an extensive scale by the New York Tuberculosis and Health Association of which Hopkins was guiding genius and Director, it proved an instant and lucrative success for the organizers. . . .The use of the fear of disease as a political device has now become accepted practice in radical circles."[30] Josepheson revealed how the Tuberculosis Association mounted a very successful Christmas Seal campaign that netted millions of dollars, little of which went to direct care for patients with consumption. Most of the money was spent on employees' salaries and press censorship.

Press censorship of medical news was and is used to silence rational discourse for the purpose of controlling the lucrative business of medicine. This is the expertise of the Epidemic Intelligence Service—the management

---

28   Gary Webb, Dark Alliance: The CIA, the Contras, and the Crack Cocaine Explosion (New York: Seven Stories Press, 1999).

29.   Advisor to President Franklin Roosevelt and one of the architects of the New Deal.

30.   Emmanuel Josephson, Your Life Is Their Toy: Rackets, Social Service and Medical (New York: Chedney Press, 1940) .

of public perception. If AIDS can in fact be reversed with standard antimicrobials augmented by appropriate biological compensatory therapy with targeted, specific antioxidants, minerals and polyphenols[31] as well as other appropriately targeted nutrients, how much profit would have been lost to the pharmaceutical industry? Wars, including silent wars are always about power and profits.

Hopkins' Christmas seal strategy has morphed into red ribbons and red products to promote the AIDS industry. As in Hopkins' day, press censorship of those who do not harbor mainstream views, along with large doses of derision and scorn are heaped on the thousands of physicians and scientists who hold alternative views on HIV and AIDS science and therapy. The epithet denialist is used liberally as a derisive characterization. To protect a racket, the nature of public debate must be limited from access by the people whose lives are most affected. Truth becomes the first victim of a silent war. The "experts" decide the limits of debate, and no heresy is tolerated. In the meantime, people are stigmatized and dying unnecessarily while the pharmaceutical companies are making a fortune promoting HIV antibody test kits and selling "anti-retroviral" drugs. The AIDS believers are no closer to a cure than they were twenty-five years ago. AIDS has become their golden calf.

Although billions have been spent on HIV research looking for this virus, it simply cannot be found. The most obscure technology is used to dazzle the public and to hide the fact that the virus has never been isolated. Billions more have been spent on the central theory that a virus type that was said to cause cell proliferation suddenly changed its "mind" and reversed course and was now causing not proliferation but the destruction of CD4+T lymphocytes. The mechanism cannot be explained. The WHO (World Health Organization) has advised doctors to stop looking for HIV in AIDS patients consonant with the CDC (Centers for Disease Control) 1994 AIDS Testing Manual that states, "The virus cannot be detected directly by conventional molecular biology techniques." A rational scientific approach would be to suggest an alternate theory, especially if the one being used is failing to meet the bare minimum of usefulness in design and execution of effective therapy. But nothing about HIV/AIDS has been rational. It has been medicine by hysteria and decree. The medical establishment has shunned alternative theories that make scientific sense. Millions have been harmed. When the dust finally settles on this sad chapter in medical history,

---

31.   Polyphenols are a group of chemical substances found in plants known to reduce the risk of heart disease, other inflammatory diseases, and cancer.

who knows how many bodies will have fallen to the unremitting arrogance of the AIDS religion.

Although other writers have connected the development of immune deficiencies to the drug epidemic in the West, and still some others have looked at the poverty epidemic in Africa,[32] no one has considered that the immune deficiencies are medical consequences of critical historical events that have been a gradual process of global economic consolidation through free market strategies. While these strategies have brought enormous wealth to some, they have brought misery to many more. Half of the planet's six billion people go to bed hungry each night, not because the planet lacks resources but because those whom we have allowed to lead us are soulless creatures driven by greed and lack both compassion and imagination.

I will make the argument (and I am not the first)[33] that the AIDS epidemic is a subset of the drug epidemic in the West. The drug epidemic in the West has it roots in the British East India Company. It is historically myopic to consider the current drug epidemic without taking a look backward to the British East India Company (BEIC) and the profits they secured with the underlying theory of free markets. The rise of capitalism was financed by enormous <u>drug profits the BEIC "earned" from addicting the Chinese to</u> opium. Once the European and American elites entered the drug trade, they never left it. These drugs were not massively imported into the West until the Vietnam era. As a coda to the Vietnam War, the tide turned, and the drugs that formerly flowed eastward now flowed westward.

As Henry Kissinger, Nixon's Secretary of State, opened trade with China, industries that developed the middle class in the West were moved wholesale to areas where workers had been neutralized by Communism or neo-liberal shock programs developed at the University of Chicago, Harvard University, the School of the Americas and in the nation's numerous, but not exclusively, right-wing think tanks. The United States was slated for de-industrialization, and while industry was moving out to cheaper and less organized wage markets, drugs in large quantities were being shipped into the country.

Bringing drugs into this society is having the same effect they had on imperial China—an internal disintegration from the corruption that came with the opium cancer. When China finally mounted a resistance it was too late. They were overpowered twice. The free marketers in the BEIC, as all free market capitalists must do to support their economic endeavors, called

---

32.   In sub-Saharan Africa, about 60 percent of the population lives and dies without safe drinking water, adequate food, or basic sanitation.

33.   Peter H. Duesberg, <u>Inventing the AIDS Virus</u> (Washington DC: Regnery USA, 1996).

in the apparatus of the tax-supported state military to assure that their "free market" stayed open. When the dust settled, Britain was free to push dope among the Chinese and to export goods at fixed tariffs. They seized Hong Kong in the first Opium War, and the rest of that colony, Kowloon, in the second Opium War. It has been a major drug money laundering center every since.

In Africa, AIDS is an epidemic of the "structural adjustment programs" and resource wars given impetus by Western governments operating at the behest of private corporations and banking institutions using clandestine agencies and private militias to foment chaos and social disruption. The Africa story takes place against the backdrop of the WWII Bretton Woods Agreement that created the International Monetary Fund (IMF) and World Bank. The net result of bank "structural adjustment" policy is resource theft, widespread poverty, starvation, and social disruption. In the South African region, AIDS is also the cover story for the multitude of diamond and gold miners who are dying from lung diseases as a result of deliberate corporate policies to forgo the expense of handling mine dust in a responsible manner. The rise of the drug epidemic in the West and the post colonial poverty epidemic in Africa are linked inextricably to three important historical events-- the Bretton Woods Agreement negotiated by a group of international bankers who had funded both sides of the war and by the economists and accused Communist Harry Dexter White as well as John Maynard Keynes. It was signed while WWII was still being waged by soldiers on the ground; the assassination of John F. Kennedy that led to the prolongation of the Vietnam conflict that resulted in massive drug addiction of American GI's., and finally, the last but perhaps the most important was the rise of Henry Kissinger as the mastermind of U.S. foreign policy initiatives and interventions, especially prolonging the Vietnam War and the opening of trade with Communist drug-exporting China. Kissinger may still be running U.S. foreign policy.[34] Kissinger is not even the top of the pyramid. He too is merely a gopher.

---

34.   James L. Jones, "Remarks by national security adviser Jones at 45th Munich Conference on Security Policy," published Feb. 8, 2009, www.cfr.org.

Chapter 3

The Brothers Flexner, Allopathic Medicine, Lessons Learned from the British East India Company

○ ○

By 1940, the literacy figure for all states stood at 96 percent for whites, 80 percent for blacks. Notice that for all the disadvantages blacks labored under, four of five were nevertheless literate. Six decades later, at the end of the 20th century, the National Adult Literacy Survey and the National Assessment of Educational Progress say 40 percent of blacks and 17 percent of whites can't read at all. Put another way, black illiteracy doubled, white illiteracy quadrupled. Before you think of anything else in regard to these numbers, think this: we spend three to four times as much real money on schooling as we did sixty years ago, but sixty years ago virtually everyone, black or white, could read.

John Taylor Gatto, The Underground History of American Education

Three Brothers

Corruption in the medical business has been a recurrent theme throughout the course of American history. It is likely that John D. Rockefeller learned how lucrative the patent medicine business could be from his father "Old Bill" Rockefeller. "Old Bill" was a known philanderer and itinerant salesman who pawned himself off as a doctor and joined the ranks of patent medicine fakers who hawked their wares from the backs of wagons. Bill's product was a bottle of raw petroleum that he called Nujol [new oil]. He sold it to those who had cancer and those whom he could make fear they would have it. For every penny invested the return was approximately 160 times as much. These profits were breathtaking and made inevitable the addition of chemical drug trafficking business to the already vast production and sales domain of America's largest and most ruthless industrial combine (the Rockefeller Empire).[35] To consolidate the power of their pharmaceutical business and to extend their international reach, the Rockefeller cartel enlisted the support of three brothers.

As the 20th century unfolded, the three brothers, Abraham, Simon, and Bernard Flexner, were selected to represent international banking and corporate power. They were strategically placed in pivotal societal institutions to create an American counter-revolution. The idea of free people, independent of banker and state interference, was intolerable and contrary to their "free trade" philosophy. The idea was to create a society in which the development of mind and character of the young were less important than training and molding so that the young would become willing instruments for use by others. They early on envisioned turning the country from a production economy to a consuming economy that would be enfolded into a global financial network. This would be managed in stages. The first stage was to gain control of the levers of power in banking, education, including medical education, the pharmaceutical industry, and the affairs of the state.

Abraham and Simon altered and set in place the controls to direct the orientation of medical education and research away from human physiology towards pharmacology. Bernard, who is less well known, was a powerful political manipulator. He was charged with taking control of the affairs of State of the United States. Under the direction of the organization he helped found, the Council on Foreign Relations, both the vast resources and the democratic institutions of the United States have been purposely squandered and assaulted piece by piece in a lateral multi-pronged persistent attack to create a utopian dream, the new world order. This new world order was described by Georgetown Professor and historian Carroll Quigley in his 1975 book <u>Tragedy and Hope</u> as follows;

"The powers of financial capitalism had a far reaching plan, nothing less than to create a world system of financial control in private hands able to dominate the political system of each country and the economy of the world as a whole...The apex of the system was to be the Bank for International

---

35.   Morris A. Bealle, <u>Super Drug Story</u> (Washington, D. C.: Columbia Publishing Company,. 1962), 5–6.

Settlements in Basle, Switzerland, a private bank owned and controlled by the world's central banks which were themselves private corporations."

Bernard was also a representative of World Zionism at the Versailles Peace Conference following WWI. He was part of a contingent that demanded impossible financial reparations from the German people, thereby setting the conditions for WWII. However, there was another aspect to the treaty negotiations at Versailles that is seldom discussed. Germany had been winning the war until the United States entered the conflict. President Woodrow Wilson had pledged to the American people to keep them out of this uniquely European affair, but, as usual, an incident was created to inflame the people and push the President into engaging the military.

Germany was blamed for an attack on the *SS Sussex* passenger ferry plying between Dover and Calais with the loss of 38 American lives. This incident led to the declaration of war by the USA against Germany, on April 6, 1917. The *SS Sussex* had actually been concealed in a small port in the north of England, and no American lives had been lost. This intentionally staged deception aligned the USA with Great Britain in World War I and resulted in the crushing defeat of Germany in 1918.[36]

Wilson was not particularly politically astute and fearful that an illicit affair that he had while at Princeton might become common knowledge capitulated to the pressure to enter the war. With public pressure mounted in the media as the result of the Sussex "incident," Wilson was unable to resist the warmongers against the will of the American people. He took the country to war. At Versailles, when the Zionist delegation produced what has become known as the Balfour Declaration, Germany realized how she had been betrayed. British Lord Balfour (who had no conceivable right to do this), a member of the secret British Round Table group, agreed to cede Palestine to the Zionists for using their influence to bring America into the war.[37] The empire would continue.

Twelve years after the end of this first world conflict, the Bank for International Settlements (BIS) was established in Basle, Switzerland by Charles Dawes (Vice President under Calvin Coolidge), Owen D. Young (founder of RCA and GE chairman, 1922-1939) and Hjalmer Schacht, president of the German Reichsbank. The BIS is referred to by bankers as the "Central bank for the central banks"—the BIS only deals with other central banks. All of its meetings are held in secret and involve the top central bankers from around the world. Former head of the Federal Reserve, Alan

---

36.   Benjamin Friedman, "Why Congress is Crooked or Crazy or Both."
37.   Lenni Brenner, "Zionism in the Age of Dictators."

Greenspan, would go to the BIS headquarters in Basel ten times a year for these private meetings.

Louis T. McFadden, Chairman of the House Banking and Currency Committee from 1920 to 1931 commented that during the first depression, American dollars were being spent on rebuilding Germany: "After World War I, Germany fell into the hands of the German International Bankers. Those bankers bought her and now they own her, lock, stock and barrel. They have purchased her industries, they have mortgages on her soil, they control her production, they control all her public utilities…Through the Federal Reserve Board 30 billion of dollars of American money…has been pumped into Germany…the spending that has taken place in Germany…modernistic dwellings, her great planetariums, her gymnasiums, her swimming pools, her fine public highways, her perfect factories…All of this was done with our money. All this was given to Germany through the Federal Reserve Board."[38] On October 3, 1936 Congressman McFadden suddenly succumbed to an "intestinal flu". He had two previous attempts on his life. He had suffered an earlier poisoning and he had shots fired at him.

American intervention in WWI established a pattern that led America into the Second World War in 1941. If the United States had not entered the war in Europe in 1917, WWI would likely have ended in a stalemate that would have engendered a balance of power in Europe. American intervention completely shattered the old balance of power and sowed the seeds of inevitable future conflict in the dark soil of Versailles.[39] The resentment from conditions set by this treaty, the economic hardships created by the conditions of the Dawes Plan (followed by the Young Plan) and finally the financing of Hitler and the re-arming of Germany by Wall Street Bankers,[40] including Prescott Bush, the father of George H. W. Bush and grandfather to George W. Bush, led directly to the outbreak of WWII.[41] WWII led directly to more world financial consolidation that occurred at a meeting held in Bretton Woods, New Hampshire.

---

38. Andrew Carrington Hitchcock, The Synagogue of Satan (London, September 11,2006) 106-108
39. Charles Callan Tansill, Back Door to War: The Roosevelt Foreign Policy 1933-1941 (Chicago: Henry Regnery Company, 1952), 9.
40. Anthony C. Sutton, Wall Street and the Rise of Hitler (GSG Publishers, 2002).
41. Ben, Airs, Duncan and Campbell, "How Bush's Grandfather Helped Hitler's Rise to Power," www.guardian.co.uk 25 Sept. 2004.

Bretton Woods

Possibly the most significant and least discussed outcome of WWII was the Bretton Woods Agreement. Before the ink was dry on the peace treaty, 730 delegates from 44 Allied nations met at Bretton Woods, New Hampshire, to set up a structures for a central world bank that would eventually come to dominate and control the financial markets of the entire planet. The Bretton Woods Agreement established a postwar international monetary system of convertible currencies, fixed exchange rates, and "free trade." However, an underlying reason for this agreement was to build an international system for currency speculators to take advantage of interest rate differentials among nations. This open system would allow any speculator who had the means (think of George Soros) to attack and devalue the currency of any country. The agreement was set up in such a way that the institutions it established had not only enormous leverage over debtor nations but also a way to attack the sovereignty of almost any nation by providing credit financing.

To facilitate these objectives, the agreement created two international institutions: the International Monetary Fund (IMF) and the International Bank for Reconstruction and Development (the World Bank). It also established the General Agreement on Tariffs and Trade (GATT), which Congress approved in 1947. The GATT would later become known as the World Trade Organization. What the IMF and World Bank essentially did was repeat on a world scale what the Federal Reserve Act of 1913 had done in the United States.

As the old military forms of colonialism were no longer useful, the Bretton Woods Agreement put a new more sophisticated and damaging form of financial colonialism in place. These agreements were the stepping-stones to a new world economic order that would plunge formerly sovereign and emerging nations into debt slavery to the financial institutions controlled by European and American central bankers. The Bretton Woods Agreement has allowed a small number of bankers to run a worldwide fraud, extortion, and protection racket called globalization. The agreement was designed to free the international banks from the constraints of national democratic interference. Using the might of the Bretton Woods Agreement to concentrate wealth into fewer and fewer hands, the international banking institutions have come to determine the internal domestic policies of practically every nation on the globe in favor of global corporate structure.[42] What they cannot obtain by economic extortion, they use the military apparatus of states to take by

---

42.   Stephen Zarlenga, The Lost Science of Money (Valetie, NY: American Monetary Institute, 2002).

force. This international white collar crime network has become expert at propping up savage local talent such as Mobutu Sese Seko in the Congo, Suharto in Indonesia, Pol Pot in Cambodia or Pinochet in Chile, whom they have trained to carry out their will and to take the blame when their policy initiatives become intolerably oppressive. It is a cleverly ruthless system.

Bretton Woods and the Transference of Wealth

Joseph Stiglitz was chief economist of the World Bank from 1997-99. He was forced out for criticizing several key IMF-US policies. His observation on the World Bank's impact on democracy is telling: "The IMF likes to go about its business without outsiders asking too many questions. In theory, the fund supports democratic institutions in the nations it assists. In practice, it undermines the democratic process by imposing policies. Officially, of course, the IMF doesn't 'impose' anything. It 'negotiates' the conditions for receiving aid. But all the power in the negotiations is on one side—the IMF's—and the fund rarely allows sufficient time for broad consensus-building or even widespread consultations with either parliaments or civil society. Sometimes the IMF dispenses with the pretence of openness altogether and negotiates secret covenants."[43]

Stiglitz's criticism is not unfounded because the consequence of the Bretton Woods Agreement in the development of these über banking structures was the refinement of a very simple technique which has been consistently and successfully employed to transfer wealth and commonwealth into fewer hands and to ignore public needs so that the public has a negative return on investments without having participated in the decisions that directly impact their current and future lives..

The technique employed—fractional reserve banking—is fairly straightforward. Money, in the form of credit (most of which is created out of thin air), is loaned to various countries with the assumption that the money that never existed will be repaid by the countries, with interest. A portion of the money flows through a designated corrupted leader installed or controlled by the powers of the lending institution. The lending institution insists that the borrowing country use and pay for "advisors" recommended by the bank. The leaders of the various countries are drawn into the scheme by a system of kickback payments and other perks that bring them considerable wealth and an escape plan to a safe haven or an American or European jail cell when they

---

43.   MIT Press Journals, "The Insider: Joseph Stiglitz, Ex-World Bank Chief Economist, Speaks Out Against the IMF," The Ecologist, September 2000.

start skimming the profits or begin to lose control of the country as must inevitably happen because of the harsh policies they must implement.

Most of the money never goes to the borrowing country but to corporations of the "former" Western colonial power who contract to do the required work. Few of the work projects develop improvements for the ordinary citizen who pays the tab in excess taxes and fees. The penalty to leaders who refuse to cooperate is assassination, covertly initiated civil disturbances or war.[44] Such counterinsurgency techniques are masterfully orchestrated and usually successful. The ordinary people of the country receiving the loan are left to pay the debt, which becomes increasingly burdensome. The lending institutions demand that the countries institute "structural adjustment programs" to repay loans. The demand always includes the provision that the countries drastically cut social expenditures, especially in health, infrastructure, and education. A predictable downward economic spiral ensues. The IMF and World Bank have the leverage to wreck the economy of any target country, as they are currently doing to the United States[45] and as they did to Argentina in 2001. This is called "spreading democracy" or, in international terms, "the Washington consensus."

Stiglitz could have been talking about the 2008 congressional approval of the $700 billion bailout of Wall Street financial firms whose mechanisms of implementation have been shrouded in secrecy when he commented on just that problem with the World Bank:

> . . . bad economics was only a symptom of the real problem: secrecy. Smart people are more likely to do stupid things when they close themselves off from outside criticism and advice. If there's one thing I've learned in government, it's that openness is most essential in those realms where expertise seems to matter most. If the IMF and Treasury had invited greater scrutiny, their folly might have become much clearer, much earlier. Critics from the right, such as Martin Feldstein, Chairman of Reagan's Council of Economic Advisers, and George Shultz, Reagan's Secretary of State, joined Jeff Sachs, Paul Krugman, and me in condemning

---

44. William Blum, Rogue State: A Guide to the World's Only Superpower (Monroe, Maine: Common Courage Press, 2000).

45. In 1992, George H.W. Bush signed Executive Order 12803, which gave D.C. the authority to sell America's infrastructure. They called this authority "Infrastructure Privatization." E.O. 12803 tells us this power cleared the way for the "disposition or transfer of an infrastructure "asset" such as by sale or by long-term lease from a State or local government to a private party."

the policies. But, with the IMF insisting its policies were beyond reproach—and with no institutional structure to make it pay attention—our criticisms were of little use. More frightening, even internal critics, particularly those with direct democratic accountability, were kept in the dark.[46]

This scenario has been played out again and again over the last fifty years as the anticipated result of the Bretton Woods agreement that created a world economic order. This new world order has been structured in such a way that it undermines the sovereignty of every nation in their grasp. The World Bank and the IMF now dictate how public money is spent. Their structural adjustment programs have intentionally left most of the planet's people mired in abject poverty and living in shanty towns on the outskirt of Oz. Half of the planets 6 billion people go to bed hungry each night.

Scorecard of Daily Deaths:

1. Terrorism   <10
2. Starvation/malnutrition under age 5   40,000[47]

From its founding in 1920 until 1961, every Secretary of State was a member of the Council on Foreign Relations except Cordell Hull and James Byrnes. Other more recent members include, Hillary Clinton, Condeleeza Rice, Madeline Albright, Christopher Warren, James Baker, III, Lawrence Eagleberger, George Shultz, Alexander Haig, Cyrus Vance and Henry Kissinger. This list of characters goes far to explain how the United States went from the Monroe Doctrine to a world empire. It also explains why American foreign policy may meander from President to President, but its trajectory remains constant. These selected few have involved the American people in international intrigues that shocked the country out of her isolationist cocoon and robbed her of her resources. By following the policies and involving themselves in countless foreign intrigues that benefit a set of privileged utopian elitists, the United States has gone from being the biggest creditor nation to the largest debtor nation in history.

The Council on Foreign Relations has persisted in gradually advancing a globalization, capital market liberalization, and privatization agenda. They have managed to succeed by strategic deception against the American people.

---

46. Ibid.
47. Estimated during 1990 World Summit for Children at the United Nations with more than fifty heads of state in attendance

They consistently promote various trade agreements that have subverted the Constitution and neutralized the power of the representative body of the people—which is easy enough to do since the Congress has been self-emasculated by its own corruptibility. The Council has succeeded in making the idea of the sovereignty of the people an arcane notion. During the autumn of 2008, there was a collective realization in the United States that the country was in the most serious fiscal crisis since the Great Depression. The heads of countries that expanded from the G7 to the G20 descended on the capital city of this weakened nation to demand oversight of U.S. domestic financial structures. This would have been unthinkable just ten years ago.

Current financial difficulties will soon be the excuse to dismantle the social safety net of the nation, including social security and government health programs that have caused so much consternation since they were instituted under Franklin Roosevelt and Lyndon Johnson. The same structural adjustment that has hindered much of the developing world has hit the shores of the United States like a tidal wave. The people of the U.S. still think they won WWII. It has taken them sixty years and the collapse of their economy to come to an understanding that they are at the mercy of the Betton Woods Agreement and the same bankers who are killing the aspirations of developing world economies.

This is the legacy of Bernard Flexner. It will come to have great meaning once one begins to understand that the abject poverty of half of the planet's people has been systematically planned. Over 100 million Europeans were killed during the last century (and possibly twice as many other people) in the two major wars used to create the climate for the rise of these new world structures and organizational institutions. If the European elite would initiate wars that killed 100 million of their own people to establish this system, why would they not continue to eliminate others who stand in the way of their long held plans? They destroyed the city of Dresden, a nonmilitary target, and dropped two atomic bombs on Japanese civilians. More recently they have killed millions in Iraq and Afghanistan and in the ongoing wars in the Sudan and Congo.

Simon Flexner

Simon Flexner was trained as a pathologist and was installed as director of the laboratories at the newly formed Rockefeller Institute. The Rockefeller Institute, from its inception, was deeply involved in the racist and elitist eugenics movement that changed its most overt tactics (but has never ceased to exist) after the excesses of its ideology were exposed to the world in the aftermath of WWII. Rockefeller money supported the Kaiser Wilhelm

Institute for Anthropology, Eugenics and Human Heredity that spearhead the ethnic cleansing movement in Germany.

Simon was a forerunner in positioning 20th century medical research to focus on "viral" causes of disease. The obsession with viruses led directly to the failed Nixon "War on Cancer" and the failed "HIV causes AIDS" hypothesis. There will be further discussion about Simon and the men he hired to work at the Rockefeller Institute and their association with the eugenics movement in the chapter on pellagra.

The last brother, Abraham, became an education expert for the Carnegie Foundation for the Advancement of Teaching. This organization set in motion the downward spiral of the quality of U.S. education, including medical education.[48]

The Flexner Report on Medical Education

It has been almost a hundred years since Abraham Flexner, who had never set foot inside of a medical school, was called on to produce a document for Rockefeller and Carnegie interests evaluating the teaching of medicine in the U.S. He prepared a report in 1910 that is known as the Flexner Report on Medical Education in the United States and Canada: A Report to the Carnegie Foundation for the Advancement of Teaching. By 1918, of 650 medical schools, only 50 remained—mainly those that would agree to promote pharmaceutical drugs as the mainstay of therapy.

The report did point out many of the inadequacies of medical education at the time, and it proposed changes, some of which were sound. But from the beginning the emphasis was placed on pharmacology, radiation, and surgery. All other modes of therapy that would in any way compete with this model would thereafter be branded as "quackery," even when and especially if they worked. Of course, the Carnegie and Rockefeller people made sure that they only hired to the top positions of the medical campuses those who by temperament and interest were ideal propagators of the drug-oriented "science" that dominates American medicine.

The end result of this report was to congeal the "philanthropy" of the Rockefeller and Carnegie Foundations into a money mafia and radical monopoly that crushed healing modalities that would not subscribe to their use of chemical drugs and their "scientific medicine." Rockefeller and Carnegie money was used to develop medical schools that are experts at psychological conditioning of white coat repeaters who have been trained by

---

48.   John Taylor Gatto, The Underground History of American Education (New York: The Oxford Village Press, 2003).

long years of study and chronic fatigue to engage comfortably in totalitarian behaviors that would be criminal without the sanction of the State. Their role is handmaiden to the pyramidal pharmaceutical industry whose goals they are unwittingly trained to serve.

Enormous iatrogenic mischief and health damage have been caused by intentionally creating a widespread belief among ordinary people that they cannot cope with their own illnesses except by calling on the ministrations of a trained and duly state licensed medical "expert." As a result, many aspects of traditional folk medicine, homeopathy, and naturopathy are shunned by people who continually seek relief only from the neighborhood pharmacy with its various patented nostrums. The loss of faith in the healing power of nature and a dose of common sense has given the medical and pharmaceutical industries a license to kill and the money to buy get out of jail free cards. The pharmaceutical industry literally gets away with murder by spending massive amounts of excess profits lobbying politicians at every level to ensure their indemnity from adverse consequences of their products.[49] As a result, over 100,000 Americans are killed on an annual basis by their products. Over the last ten years, about 3,000 Americans have died from terrorist attacks, but during this same period over a million died as the consequence of taking a pharmaceutical drug.

The medical profession's drive to restrain people's health freedom has extended to the AMA's (American Medical Association) call for legislation that would challenge home birth (which has been proven safe) by women and could result in criminal child abuse or neglect charges leveled against them.[50] Children have been snatched from parents who refused vaccinations or a recommended medical therapy, especially toxic and deadly HIV drugs. At least since 1996 parents have been charged with child neglect for failing to vaccinate their children with all government-recommended vaccines and the CDC has used taxpayer dollars to mount assaults to counter parent-led informed consent initiatives in several states.

Children are regularly denied access to state schools if their parents have challenged the ever-expanding roster of vaccines they are required to take. For girls, with the latest push for a mandatory HPV (human papilloma virus) vaccine, the total comes to 56 shots for 22 vaccines. Government allocation

49.   The Vaccine Injury Compensation Program (VICP) is a federal project that began in 1986. It relieves vaccine manufacturers, doctors, and hospitals from liability for vaccine damage. VICP has paid over $500 million taxpayer dollars to compensate families for damage and death caused by vaccines that were also paid for by your tax dollars.

50.   Jonathan Block, "Big Medicine's Blowback on Home Births," L.A. Times, July 9, 2008.

of police powers to public health officials to enforce mandatory vaccinations have given drug companies the assurance of predictable rising profits—more of the "free market" at work.[51]

This is a prime example of how the so called free enterprise system uses the state to insure its profitability at the expense of the most vulnerable population. Forced use of drugs and vaccines on children is coercive, draconian, and patently anti-democratic and unconstitutional health policy.[52] Giving the state authority and access where it does not belong—in the most sacred of spaces, your blood stream—is a creeping encroachment on individual sovereignty. The power that the state has allocated to the pharmaceutical industry now threatens our privacy, our liberty and the biological integrity of future generations.

In 1950, approximately seventy-five hundred children in the United States were diagnosed with mental disorders. As the number of drugs directed at children for mental disorders increased, the number so diagnosed has risen concomitantly. That number is at least eight million today, and most receive some form of medication.[53]

John Taylor Gatto an experienced but currently retired New York City teacher and social commentator, noted in his book, <u>Weapons of Mass Instruction</u>, the terrible effect of a milestone that has transformed American education: The Behavioral Science Teacher Education Project or BSTEP for short. This program clearly sets down government policy for compulsory schooling and outlines intended reforms for enforcement in the US after 1967. Institutional schooling will be required to "impersonally manipulate" the future of an America in which "each individual will receive at birth a multi-purpose identification number" that will enable "employers" and other

---

51. A member of the Washington, D.C City Council, David Catania, a self professed homosexual, in spite of overwhelming evidence presented of the harm and lack of necessity for mandating the HPV vaccine to prepubescent girls, used his position to mandate this vaccine. Shortly thereafter he introduced a bill to legalize gay marriage. The irony that he should want civil rights for one community while denying them to another was simply too complex for him to comprehend.

52. The 4th Amendment asserts the right of the people to be secure in their persons, houses, papers, and effects, against unreasonable searches and seizures, shall not be violated, and no Warrants shall issue, but upon probable cause, supported by Oath or affirmation, and particularly describing the place to be searched, and the persons or things to be seized.. [Author, is this a direct quote, if so, " "?]

53. Andrew, H. Weiss, "The Wholesale Sedation of America's Youth," <u>Committee for Skeptical Inquiry</u>, Nov/Dec. 2008.

"controllers" to keep track of the common mass and to expose it to "direct or subliminal influence when necessary . . . few will be able to maintain control over their own opinions . . . chemical experimentation" on minors will become normal procedure, a pointed foreshadowing of Ritalin, Adderol and other chemical interventions.[54]

By 1988 the government began pushing parents to request to have social security numbers assigned to their children at the time of completion of the birth certificate. It is still currently claimed that the assignment of SSNs to infants is "voluntary", but like the income tax, because it was neither ratified nor an apportioned tax started out as a "voluntary" tax, this SSN business will soon have the force of law.

This covert control of the population with forced vaccinations and mandated medical treatments was the objective of Abraham Flexner's intended goal in his educational reform work for Rockefeller interests. It has been useful to dumb down and infantilize society into docile complacency for use as pawns in the service of both business and the political state. Once the "dumb" are wished into existence as was expressed in Rockefeller's General Education Board's Occasional Paper Number One, they serve valuable functions: As a danger to themselves and others, they have to be watched, classified, disciplined, trained, medicated, sterilized, ghettoized, cajoled, coerced, and jailed—all at a profit. Thus, their needs demand the creation of a new level of bureaucracy that serves no productive purpose.

The General Education Board's Occasional Paper Number One was first published in 1912 as an essay, "The Country School of Tomorrow":

> In our dream . . . people yield themselves with perfect docility to our molding hands. The present educational conventions (intellectual and character education) fade from our minds, and unhampered by tradition we work our own good will upon a grateful and responsive folk. We shall not try to make these people or any of their children into philosophers or men of learning or men of science. We have not to raise up from among them authors, educators, poets or men of letters. We shall not search for embryo great artists, painters, musicians, nor lawyers, doctors, preachers, politicians, statesmen, of whom we have ample supply. The task we set before ourselves is a very simple as well as a very beautiful one...we will organize our children...and teach

---

54.   John Taylor Gatto, Weapons of Mass Instruction (BC: Canada: New Society Publishers, 2009), 5-6.

them to do in a perfect way the things their fathers and
mothers are doing in an imperfect way.[55]

The Flexner report on medical education was another level in this planned
restructuring of society. It was based on the German model of "scientifically"
based medical training. The great façade behind this vaunted policy was
immensely more complex. It included adopting an "amalgam of ancient
religious doctrine, utopian philosophy, and European/Asiatic strong-state
politics mixed together and distilled…(however), Modern German tradition
always assigned universities the primary task of directly serving industry and
the political state, but that was a radical contradiction of American tradition
to serve the individual and the family."[56]

The medical, pharmaceutical and insurance industries were organized
early in the last century by complicit minions of Rockefeller and Carnegie
to serve the interests of the corporate state rather than individual Americans.
By now, such thinking seems mundane, but they kept their purpose well
hidden, because Americans at that time knew that these were incendiary
ideas designed to undermine civil society.

Not understanding how these systems were intentionally developed
brings consternation and grief to many whose only option in resisting the
excesses and failures of this established order is to wage long and expensive
fights through an increasingly antagonistic court system. This sets a high
barrier to imposing limitations on corporate criminal behavior that can only
be addressed in civil courts. While the system is designed to catalogue the
life and movement of the individual from birth until death with a series of
numbers and ratings, there is no reciprocal oversight of the watchers. The
idea of contracts freely executed between free men has become history.

The problem is that through political bribery, called lobbying, the
political class has long ago abdicated its responsibilities to the people. No
one is watching the watchers. According to Gary Null in Death by Medicine,
iatrogenic medicine is the number one cause of death in the United States—
outpacing both cancer and heart disease. That is a statistic that will never be
allowed to seep into the consciousness of the American psyche.

At the top of the pyramidal structures that control the banking, military
and medical industrial complexes are the interests that currently control
medical education, the pharmaceutical industry, the Public Health sector via

---

55. This statement was first publicly disclosed in an obscure book The World's
     Work, 1912. It was republished as part of a collection printed by Rockefeller's
     GEB in 1913 for its selective readership. Its original date is uncertain.
56. John Taylor Gatto, The Underground History of American Education (New
     York: Oxford Village Press, 2003), 46.

the Department of HEW(Health Education and Welfare), the FDA (Food and Drug Administration), the CDC (Centers for Disease Control), the NIH (National Institutes of Health) and the Department of Agriculture—all of which are contributing to the continuing decline of the general health of the American people.[57] Although the U.S. spends more per capita on health care than any other country on the planet, it ranks 50th of 223 countries in terms of life expectancy.[58]

Since the beginning of the last century, the dynamic of the United States has been away from representative democracy and limited capitalism to more and more centralized control in every aspect of the society. The country has been weaned away from the values of self-reliance and independent thinking to become a nation who demands experts to guide their every move.

The idea of self-selected oligarchs making decisions for the masses was spelled out by Walter Lippman in two books, Public Opinion (1922) and The Phantom Public (1925). These books called for a restriction on public debate because Lippman, speaking for the political class, concluded that it was impossible for the (dumbed down) public to know what its best interests were. The common public would have to be neutralized in the name of democracy for this expert society. In the Lippman world view, common people traded in their right to be heard on policy matters in exchange for being taken care of. Nowhere was this paternalistic philosophy instituted with more vigor than in the training of allopathic physicians.

Allopathic Medicine

Farben was Hitler and Hitler was Farben. (Senator Homer T. Bone to Senate Committee on Military Affairs, June 4, 1943).

Abraham Flexner was recruited by Rockefeller interests to specifically promote allopathic medicine and turn it into a very clever marketing vehicle to sell the overpriced patented and anti-life pharmaceuticals largely controlled today by the spawn of Rockefeller interests. The combine became globalized after they partnered with Germany's I.G. Farbin. On the eve of WWII, I.G. Farbin was the largest chemical manufacturing enterprise in the world

---

57. www.guardian.co.uk, Development: "US Fails to Measure Up on 'Human Index' by Ashley Seager, July 17, 2008. "Despite spending $230m (£115m) an hour on healthcare, Americans live shorter lives than citizens of almost every other developed country. And while it has the second-highest income per head in the world, the United States ranks 42d in terms of life expectancy."

58. CIA World Fact Book 2009

and enjoyed a monopoly on chemical products manufactured in Germany. Without the capital supplied by Wall Street, there would have been no I.G. Farben, no Hitler, and no WWII.[59] I. G. Farben is of particular interest in the formation of the Nazi state because Farben directors materially helped Hitler and the Nazis to power in 1933. Directors of the firm included not only German but also American financiers. Their assignment was to make Germany self-sufficient in rubber, gasoline, lubricating oils, magnesium, fibers, tanning agents, fats, and explosives.

German I.G. made an alliance with Rockefeller's Standard Oil in order to control important patents and to cover Standard Oil's support for Hitler's Reich. After Pearl Harbor, American I.G. decided to camouflage its German parentage and sympathies with the help of Standard Oil. After purchasing an undisclosed number of shares in the Ozalid Corporation, Schering & Company, Mission Corporation, Monsanto Chemical, Aluminum Corporation, Drug (Incorporated), Dow Chemical, Antidolar Indiana, Standard Oil of California and the Du Pont Company, it changed its name to General Aniline & Film Corporation. It took over bodily the privately-owned Hoffman LaRoche Company and multiple other smaller drug companies.[60]

Now Rockefeller interests were positioned to do what they did best, create another cartel. This time it was the dual control of allopathic medical colleges and the chemical and pharmaceutical industry. It was a masterful hegemonic stroke—the empire of allopathic medicine was created. It is the dominant medicine practiced in the United States and has been exported to most of the world. Few traditional cultures have been spared the rampage of this "civilizing" force. Ivan Illich observed thirty years ago that iatrogenic medicine is "a radical monopoly which feeds upon itself.. . .[It] reinforces a morbid society in which the social control of the population by the medical system turns into a principle economic activity."[61] Illich's observations have proved prescient because in 2008, expenditures on health care accounted for 16 percent of GDP and are expected to rise to $4.2 trillion in 2016 or 20 percent of GDP.

Like the banking cartels created at Bretton Woods need ever expanding markets and manufactured wars to keep their debt-based fiat monetary system alive, the allopathic medical cartel needs manufactured diseases to sustain the profits they have come to enjoy. It is such an imbalanced system that it disseminates false information about the nature of some pathologies under

59. Sutton, Anthony , op cit
60. Morris A Bealle,. Super Drug Story (Washington, D. C.: Columbia Publishing Company, 1962), 8-9.
61. Ivan Illich, Limits to Medicine, Medical Mimesis:The Expropriation of Health (New York: Marion Boyers, 1976), 43.

the rubric of the scientific method and uses the power of government agencies such as the FDA (Food and Drug Administration) to limit consumer access to information about the health benefits of natural products and appropriate biological compensatory therapies.

The FDA has been accused of running an extortion racket against the natural products market. Cherry products, for example, cannot link to scientific articles explaining the simple biological fact that cherries ease inflammation in humans. When cherry growers began to cite this research, the FDA came down hard on twenty-nine of them and threatened legal action if they did not remove the scientific evidence about cherries from their Web sites. Such links are considered "drug claims" by the FDA. At the same time that the FDA was harassing cherry farmers, it was approving the Merck drug Vioxx that led directly to 100,000 heart attacks and to 55,000 deaths.[62]

Congressman Ron Paul, who is also an Obstetrician-Gynecologist, introduced a bill that would curb restrictions imposed by the FDA and FTC (Federal Trade Commission) regarding health claims for dietary supplements. The Health Freedom Protection Act would prevent the FDA from censoring **truthful claims** about the curative or preventive effect of dietary supplements. Only with extreme pressure from constituents would such a bill have a hope of passing in the current climate of unregulated corporate money flowing into Congress.

The constructed medical system thrives on treating the symptoms of chronic diseases with toxic and expensive chemicals while ignoring the body's natural biochemistry, biorhythms, and electrical conductivity. The current system was created from the knowledge gained by ruling elites through the management and development of the first major global corporation, the British East India Company. Modern history cannot be understood without gaining insight into the dynamic role that this company played in the industrial development of the West, the rise of communist China, and the initiation of a global agenda espoused as inevitable by intellectual, political, and business elites. It is noteworthy that the most important commodities for capitalist growth were exotic chemicals and drugs from tobacco to opium. Without drugs and drug economies, financial capitalism, in its present state, could not have come into being.[63]

---

62. Senate testimony by the FDA's own senior drug safety researcher, Dr. David Graham.

63. Carl A. Trocki, Opium Empire and Global Economy: A Study of the Asian Opium Trade, 1750–1950 (London: Taylor and Francis, 1999), 28 [Author, is this the study?]

British East India Company and Opium

THE BEIC's premier product was opium. The British had nothing to trade that the Chinese people wanted or needed, but British avarice was boundless. Britain is an island that has been able to buy the veneer of civility. However, beneath this thin veneer pulses the heart of their barbarian ancestry. When the Romans first encountered them, they had no written language, wore trousers at a time when men in the civilized world wore tunics, were loud and ferocious, painted their bodies blue, and with their white faces and red hair were said to look as bad as they smelled. Their pretense at civilization is only outpaced by their penchant for political intrigue.

Their desire for the sophisticated Chinese products of fine tea, silks, and pottery created an enormous trade imbalance for them. They had nothing but silver with which the Chinese cared to barter. Unable to curb their appetite for Chinese material goods and seeking a way to bend the Chinese to their will, they hit upon the idea of creating a demand for the addictive drug opium. The Dutch East India Company had earlier done this "free trade" in Malaysia. Opium was a product that brought grief to the user and social disruption to targeted cultures. Heavy users of opium had an average life expectancy of five years. It is now known that opiates have an inhibitory effect on the immune system. They can decrease the production of lymphocytes and have been shown to increase cancer progression in animals. Opiates activate the hypothalamic-pituitary-adrenal (HPA) axis that causes production of noradrenalin and glucocorticoids that can cause more stress on the immune system.

While 18th century "businessmen" did not know the science of the metabolic consequence of chronic opium use, they were aware of its addictive qualities and the deleterious effects it had on the user's health. The product was chosen for commercialization for these very reasons.

The people running the opium enterprise learned two major lessons from addicting the Chinese to opiates—that narcotizing drugs can weaken an otherwise impermeable society and corrupt it internally making it ripe for control and that enormous profits can be made by creating two types of addicts: those who physically crave your product and those who financially crave perverse rewards from destroying others. These were lessons not lost on the elites of Britain and the United States who ran this dirty business and who have been in charge of one of the largest global enterprises ever since— the worldwide control and distribution of narcotics. Both drug cultures, legal and illegal, as well as the global monetary system that uses drug profits to prop itself up[64] promote poverty, war, and genocide as an economic model. Given this economic model and the physical and psychological devastation that it created for the Chinese and is now creating in the United States and around the world, it should come as no surprise to any who have bothered to observe its far-reaching consequences that creating a disease category— AIDS or Acquired Immune Deficiency Syndrome—was predictable. When the products of the global drug trade started to be marketed in a spectacular way during and after the Vietnam War to the baby-boom population and their offspring, some explanation would be needed for why so many young people in the prime of their lives would become sick and die.

The baby-boom generation was the age cohort that had first been introduced to the birth control pill and the idea of sexual freedom. This was a social revolution that altered and loosened social mores. The sexual revolution combined with the drug epidemic was bound to lead to medical consequences. There was no better way to camouflage the consequences of these social phenomenona than by hiding behind a sex and blood plague, especially one that came out of Africa. The nature and expansiveness of the drug economy and its deep penetration into American culture had to remain hidden.

AIDS is a syndrome that arose out of the confluence of global drug running and global medical, social, and economic policies created with intent and malice aforethought at the highest levels. It is the result of the Bretton Woods agreement signed in New Hampshire in 1944 that came about because of the Versailles Treaty negotiated by Bernard Flexner; the eugenics policies begun under the tutelage of Simon Flexner of the Rockefeller Institute; and the development of allopathic medicine that evolved from Abraham Flexner's Rockefeller Report on Medical Education. The policies set in motion by the Flexners continue to create more problems for the world than they have solved.

---

64. Catherine Austin Fitts, "Narco-Dollars for Beginners: How the Money Works in the Illicit Drug Trade," Narco News Bullitin, 2001.

Chapter 4

HIV/AIDS: Sloppy Science or the Art of Deception?

○ ○

Much of what folks think is conspiracy is really many people acting in concert to make or protect their money.

Catherine Austin Fitts,
former undersecretary of HUD

Unconventional warfare is waged "upstream" with the assistance of those with the means, motive and opportunity to massage consensus opinion. Where are modern day battles fought? Not on the ground nor in the air nor on the seas. The mindset is the primary theater of operations. The first battlefield is the public's shared field of consciousness. The death and destruction come later.

Jeff Gates, Vietnam veteran, attorney, investment banker
and former counsel the U.S Senate Finance Committee

Beginning in 1913, the Rockefeller backed General Education Board gave millions of dollars to medical schools that disregarded naturopathy, homeopathy, and chiropractic, or any nontoxic healing modality in favor of medicine based on the use of surgery, radiation, and especially chemical drugs. Aided by the AMA, a medical monopoly was created. One of the most cleverly diabolical educational schemes was the ingenious marketing technique of training a cadre of unsuspecting physicians as a sales force for the drugs manufactured by the Rockefeller Trust. The system allows the doctor to remain aloof from the dirty business of selling while giving him the special privilege of writing prescriptions for nostrums he has been trained by the very drug companies who manufacture them to prescribe. Many of these drugs are used for the relief of chronic symptoms. They are not meant to cure, and they must by chemical composition and electron rotation patterns counter the body's basic biorhythms, internal bio-electric conductivity and biochemical systems. As a result, they have multiple deleterious effects, including death. The effects lead to thousands of deaths a year and untold disabilities. The culture has become anesthetized to this level of human waste and accepts it as "the cost of doing business." As a result of this utilitarian mind set the metrics for measuring the value of a life become no more than an actuarial notation in a drug company ledger. In the case of vaccine damage, the cost is passed indirectly onto the taxpayer and directly onto the parents, who bear the brunt and the cost of each damaged child. The National Childhood Vaccine Injury Act (PL99-660) was signed into law by President Ronald Reagan in 1986. In essence the law tacitly acknowledged that vaccines can injure and kill individuals by creating a federal vaccine injury compensation system. However, federal health officials at the HHS have moved to systematically gut the law by using tax supported lawyers from the Department of Justice to fight these claims. The taxpayers are paying government lawyers to protect the profits of the drug industry rather than the lives and health of American children. Three out of four vaccine injured children are turned away, and more than $1 billion sits idle in the vaccine injury trust.[65]

The impression is created by the medical establishment that diseases such as adult onset diabetes, hypertension and even cancer cannot be cured and must be managed with lifelong drug intervention. Not fully understanding that many chronic diseases can be reduced or reversed with lifestyle and diet modifications as well as biological compensatory therapy, many people accept the irreversibility of their disease diagnosis. This creates a practically limitless repeat customer base for both physicians and the drug companies.

For profitability, diseases are managed, they are not cured. Just as the British East India Company learned from selling opium to the Chinese— creating a market with repeat customers who demand and need your product is immensely profitable. It is the essence of "free trade." Medical myths are then created with aggressive enthusiasm, while denying the public accurate information about less expensive, but more valuable compensatory therapies.

---

65. Barbara Loe Fisher, "The National Electronic Vaccine Tracking Registry, How the Plan to Fore Vaccination Gave Birth to the National ID, a Government Health Records Database, and the End of Medical Privacy.

Disintegration of Public Health and the Rise in Modern Diseases

This philosophical framework has had profound consequences on the cost and quality of medical care, including its current inflated price and diminishing quality of care. In contrast with environmental improvements and modern nonprofessional health measures, the medical treatment of people is never significantly related to a decline in the compound disease burden or rise in life expectancy.[66] Adequate food, shelter, clothing and a stable society are far more essential to good health than the best medical care. These are public health measures that can no longer be controlled domestically by local governments because of their indebtedness to central banks and the new zero–sum religion of globalization and privatization of public assets that has gripped elites like an intractable fever.

The logical consequence of the limited philosophical worldview of allopathic medicine as a subset of the drive for global dominance is the scourge of chronic diseases that are plaguing Western societies: autism, developmental and learning disabilities, auto-immune diseases, asthma and obesity in our children; and cancer, obesity, heart disease, and diabetes in adults; and drug addiction to both legal and illegal drugs in both populations. This medical model subsumed under the domination of the military structure has led to the outbreak of laboratory created super diseases, such as Marburg and Ebola, which kill horribly and are being used as offensive weapons, most often in Africa. It has also lead to the creation of an <u>idea</u>, without scientific merit, that a single retrovirus that has never been adequately isolated, the Human Immunodeficiency Virus, is sexually transmitted, conclusively lethal, and the cause of 29 different diseases. This idea is so preposterous that if there were truly an independent scientific intellectual elite, free from the burden of the church of money, this idea would have been laughed out of existence when it was first proposed by Robert Gallo and Margaret Heckler, Secretary of Health Education and Welfare under the presidency of Ronald Reagan in 1984.

HIV/AIDS—Sloppy Science

It has been twenty-five long years since medical and political interests in this country promoted an unproven theory as fact—that a tiny retrovirus, which has never been adequately isolated, that has come to be known as <u>HIV</u> and is the cause of a collection of 29 disparate well-known diseases now recognized

---

66.   Illich, 21.

in a certain targeted subset only as the Acquired Immunodeficiency Syndrome or AIDS. One of the diagnostic criteria for stating that someone has AIDS is by being associated with or part of a "high-risk group." High-risk groups are men who have sex with men, IV drug users, hemophiliacs, heterosexual Africans, and now African American women. Although AIDS is sold as a sexually transmitted disease, long-term prospective studies of discordant partners have shown that HIV is not sexually transmitted. Further, what is called <u>HIV</u> is only found 15 to 20 percent of the time in the semen of HIV-positive patients.[67] If there is no trace of "HIV" 80 to 85 percent of the time, there is little possibility for sexual transmission.

The high-risk groups do share a common factor, which is being exposed to excessive amounts of particular oxidative or nitrosative stressors. In the West, it is poly-drug use, repeated infections and indiscriminate antibiotic use, and rectally deposited semen from multiple anonymous donors. In Africa, it is poverty, malnutrition, social disruption, and a host of long-known endemic diseases, as well as environmental toxins and vaccines. Many of the exogenous stressors are genotoxins, the exposure to which can appear as novel "RNAs" and have been misinterpreted as HIV protein templates. When a cell is critically threatened by oxidative/nitrosative stressors, genetic recombination (which may include virus proliferation) is one set of events that occurs as an emergency response.[68] Finding endogenous viruses in cells that are undergoing oxidative stress is an expected cellular repair mechanism not the cause for inventing a new viral plague.

The theory advanced by the AIDS religionists is that a tiny HIV retrovirus causes an infection that leads to immune deficiency characterized by a depletion of CD+ T lymphocytes, and then the immune deficiency leads to one of multiple old well-known diseases. This was the old equation: Tuberculosis – HIV = Tuberculosis. This is the new equation: Tuberculosis + HIV = AIDS, or in Africa Tb – HIV=AIDS. Everything is different in Africa. Just having tuberculosis is enough for a diagnosis of AIDS if the patient has the requisite weight loss, fever, and diarrhea of one month's duration. Additionally in Africa, a man or woman is said to have acquired HIV/AIDS by heterosexual contact even if the partner is HIV negative or if he/she has never had sexual intercourse. The skewed definition makes the correlation with HIV inevitable, regardless of the facts. Further complicating this lymphocyte destruction theory is the fact that many people who have

---

67.   Eleni Papadopulos-Eleopulos et al., "Mother to Child Transmission of HIV and Its Prevention with AZT and Nevirapine: A Critical Analysis of the Evidence," [Author: Journal?] , 15–16.

68.   Mark Ptashne, <u>A Genetic Switch</u> (Cambridge, MA: Cell Press and Blackwell Scientific Publications, 1992).

AIDS do not show a decreased lymphocyte count until after the onset of one of the defining diseases.

After the Gallo-Heckler announcement, an AIDS industry was created overnight that has given employment to thousands. For starters, Reagan released about a billion dollars to give the AIDS private sector industry more government money for the development of their "free enterprise" anti-retroviral drug products. Suddenly, old cancer virus hunters from the National Cancer Institute whose work was dwindling as a result of the failed cancer/virus theory became AIDS researchers. Years and billions of dollars have been spent trying to find this virus in the immune cells that the virus is claimed to be killing. Big problem—among the HIV positive, less than one in 1,000 of their CD4 immune cells normally show any "signs" of possible infection.[69] This is much too low of an infection rate to explain any decrease in circulating CD4+T cells. However, as will be shown, the theory of oxidative/nitrosative stress leading to a Th1/Th2 counterbalance of the immune system does.

In the positive people, the T cells are predominantly maturing into Th2 cells that do not live in the blood stream. The Th2 helper cells migrate to the bone marrow where the B cells live so that they can stimulate the production of antibodies. There is a concomitant decrease in the production of Th1 cells and the function of cell mediated immunity. This accounts for the increase in antibody levels in AIDS patients, the simultaneous reduction in cellular mediated immunity, and the rise of opportunistic infections. This evolutionary biologically programmed counterbalance of the immune system offers a coherent scientific explanation. It is simple and elegant because it adequately explains the pathophysiology of the problem and offers rational treatment methods. However, it is not profitable.

In the meantime, by creating the illusion of hunting for a cure, the AIDS industry becomes a shield for the deteriorating health of disparate populations who bear the brunt of global drug running and/or economic hit men—the viral invaders from global corporations and banking structures—who leave behind a trail of graves.

When researching the literature on HIV, what I found was absolutely startling. When HIV/AIDS proponents were speaking about HIV, they were not speaking about a virus because they never isolated a virus. What they were calling <u>HIV</u> was nothing more than certain cellular characteristics and activities of cells in a laboratory setting produced under very special conditions. In other words, HIV is a chimera, an imaginary monster

---

69.   Bard Rosak, et al., "Correlates of Latent and Productive HIV Type 1 Infection in Tonsillar CD4+ Cells" 19 Aurgust 1997 <u>PNAS,</u> v.94(17):9332-9336

compounded of incongruous parts. As will be discussed in a later chapter, the proteins claimed to be specific to HIV can be found at some level in everybody.[70] This is not because everyone has been exposed to HIV, but because what they identify as HIV proteins are unlikely to be retroviral but cellular in origin.

Numerous scientists and researchers have written countless articles and a plethora of books, all politely civil in assuming that a great mistake has been made. AIDS is not a mistake, and there is nothing civil about its creation and promotion as an idea. It is no less than an act of war. HIV/AIDS is a false construct patched together with sloppy science used by former Nixon's War on Cancer virus hunters to transition from one failed medical venture to a new money pit. Overnight, a virus type that was said to cause cell proliferation (cancer) was now claimed to cause cell death (AIDS). It was a lazy and profitable way of explaining the body's response to physiological pro-oxidative stressors that overwhelm the function of the intracellular energy factories, or mitochondria. It is a politically useful tool employed by the recurrent destructive energy predictably arising from an underground cesspool of utilitarian eugenics misfits. It is at best an **idea** promoted to cloud the consequences of elite high crimes and economic exploitation as they constantly create new and enlarging markets to stay ahead of their expanding empire of debt. Sooner or later every imperial structure becomes too big and too expensive for its own creators to maintain. European empires have depended on the super profits of monopolizing long- distance trade. Illegal drugs are one of the monopoly profit centers, and their long-term use leads to more than individual destruction.

Reverse Transcriptase Enzyme and Retroviruses

HIV/AIDS experts claimed to have made identification of the new sex and blood plague virus by finding an enzyme known as reverse transcriptase (RT) in the culture medium of cells taken from some of the first identifiable patients. However, Gallo combined the cells of multiple patients and mixed these cells with strong oxidizing agents and a leukemia cell line in his culture medium. The strong oxidizing agents damage DNA and would naturally lead to the increase of the enzyme RT because RT is necessary to make DNA repairs. He also neglected to mention in his original papers that he added hydrocortisone to the cell culture as well. Hydrocortisone inhibits nitric oxide (NO) gas produced by Th1 cells and promotes the formation of regenerative

---

70.   Giraldo, Robert, "Everybody reacts positive on the ELISA test for HIV, *Continuum,* Midwinter 1998/9

proteins. Regenerative proteins, also known as <u>virus-like particles</u>, are what Gallo called <u>HIV.</u>

The occurrence of cellular damage and the response of genetically programmed cellular repair mechanisms should have been anticipated. Since 1970, it had been known that the reverse transcription enzyme was capable of transcribing a molecule of RNA into DNA. The researchers who discovered this won a Nobel Prize for the importance of this finding. Before the discovery of this enzyme it was thought that the flow of cellular information was one way from nuclear DNA to cellular RNA and was never reversed. Whenever and wherever reverse transcriptase activity was detected, it was assumed that retroviruses were at work. It was soon discovered that this enzyme was ubiquitous and was in no way unique to what was called a <u>retrovirus</u>. About fifty percent of the human genome is now known to consist of virus like sequences.[71] Evidence has accumulated showing that RTs are involved in a surprisingly large number of RNA mediated transcriptional events.[72] These endogenous so-called nonsense genes exist in the thousands, and some can replicate independently and jump within and between chromosomes. For this reason, they were called by a variety of names and are vitally important in intercellular communication. In the laboratory they can be made to migrate, and when this happens, reverse transcriptase is invariably detected—which underscores that reverse transcriptase is not unique to retroviruses per se.

All of this was well known to Gallo's group in 1983 when he used the finding of reverse transcriptase to claim he had isolated a new virus. The world forgot that he had already tried to pull the same scam two previous times with HTLV-I and HTLV-II.[73] He claimed that these were leukemia viruses, or cellular proliferation viruses. When that charade fell apart, he simply found a new disease pattern to blame on one of his elusive retroviruses, this time it was HTLV-III, which eventually came to be known as <u>HIV</u>—the human immunodeficiency virus. This time the virus was said to have an exactly opposite effect.

The challenge is for the HIV causes AIDS proponents to prove in fact that HIV is an infectious virus and not a laboratory artifact. People who are HIV positive do have elevated antibodies, but these antibodies are consistent with a Th2 shift in the immune response. In fact, they are an anticipated internal physiological response to persistent external physiological challenges—such as narcotics, steroids, prescription drugs, nutritional deprivation, and other

---

71.   Mae-Wan Ho, <u>Living with the Fluid Genome,</u>(Institute of Science in Society, Penang, Malaysia 2003) 49

72   <u>Transcription</u> is the synthesis of RNA under the direction of DNA.

73   Peter H. Duesberg, <u>Inventing the AIDS Virus </u>(Washington, DC: Regnery Publishing 1996), 127.

biological stressors. And with all environmental stressors, some people are more predisposed than others to express such conditions. In the population of African descent, it is related to the expression of a human lymphocyte antigen—HLA DR5—and the fact that blacks make more IgG and IgA antibodies to the same stimulus than whites.[74] Both of these genetic factors were exploited in the development of the "HIV" antibody test, which has made it appear that blacks who take the test are more than five times as likely as whites from the same risk groups to test positive. (See the chapter, on the HIV antibody test)

There are now thousands of people who have refused anti-retroviral drugs, have changed their lifestyles and their state of mind and spirit, have altered their nutrition and are alive and well today—many are HIV free as well. The science that is calling HIV an exogenous or infectious deadly virus has yet to prove that (a) it is infectious and (b) that it is the cause of AIDS. This may seem surprising, but much of science is based on a theory that works until it reaches the limits of its theoretical possibilities. When the theory reaches its limits of explanation and a new understanding of observed phenomenon is ardently resisted, great damage ensues. People who do not have a terminal illness are told they are going to die, and sometimes they do from fright and cell damaging drug therapy. Today, most of the people dying of AIDS die from the complications of misguided, anti-retroviral therapy and the failure of medical practitioners to institute appropriate and timely compensational therapy. The phenomenon of HIV believers shouting down an alternative hypothesis and of labeling prominent and thoughtful scientists and physicians <u>denialists</u> is the antithesis of open scientific discourse. HIV/ AIDS is a theory that needs open and rational discussion rather than the strident hysteria that has been called medical discourse.

Theories are simply attempts to explain how observed phenomena may work, but the HIV/AIDS theory has devolved into religious dogma. It has to because the science is so weak it cannot and will not bear the light of public scrutiny. As a disease being exploited for profit and political purposes, its exposure must be addressed. Numerous authors have addressed the scientific questions and the fraud of Gallo and his original papers published in <u>Science</u> that started this terrible mess. None has looked at the context that has created this disaster—until now.

---

74.   D.R. Lucey et al., "Comparison by race of total serum IgG, IgA, and IgM with CD4+T-cell counts in North American persons infected with the human immunodeficiency virus type 1," <u>J Acquir Immune Defic Synd</u> 5 (1992): 325–32.

False Constructs and Evolutionary Biology

The human genome and extra-genomic cellular processes **are** absolutely brilliant. Each tiny cell in the body is alive with activity and has developed over the course of evolutionary eons the most marvelous method of communication. X-ray crystallography has demonstrated that living cells pulsate with energy color and movement.[75] Cells communicate by means of viral-like particles, electric currents, chemical emission, photons, and magnetic fields. There are about 100,000 reactions per second in all of our cells. Each cell is constantly making hollow particles or vesicles. The tiny particles are sent out carrying cargo along intricate microtubule roads.[76] The microtubule roads are linked to a finer network of actin threads. Both networks carry thousands of moving particles. Cells also make particles that travel through extra-cellular space to other cells, not to attack them, but to pass on information. The little particles have become known as <u>retroviruses</u>. The observation of the work and function of retroviruses is very important because it is relevant to classical mechanistic genetic theory, namely, that nuclear DNA is the master controller of the cell and works in a unidirectional manner by giving orders to RNA to make protein. The idea that RNA could be responding to DNA and giving it orders never occurred to the early genetic theoreticians. However, the nature of living organisms is radically anti-mechanistic.

Pyramidal and mechanistic systems work by a hierarchy of controllers and the controlled that returns the systems to set points. One can recognize such mechanistic systems in the predominant institutions of our society. They are undemocratic and non-participatory. Bosses make decisions and workers work, and in between the top and the bottom are "line managers" relaying the unidirectional chain of command. Organic systems, by contrast, are truly democratic. They work by intercommunication and total participation.[77] This is the new paradigm and understanding coming out of the laboratories of some of the most forward thinking scientists. This is the idea of intercommunication and total participation at the micro-gaian environment of the cell structure that those schooled in and wedded to the notion of hierarchical systems are struggling to come to terms with. Some may never make the transition into 21st century medicine because these new ideas challenge the very world view that is wedded to the notion of pyramidal

75. Mae-Wan Ho, "Bioenergetics and the Coherence of Organisms," <u>Neuronetwork World 5</u> (1995): 733–50.

76. LabNotes: <u>http://www.mbl.edu/publications/archive/labnote/2.3/Langford.html</u>

77. Mae Wan Ho,

social structures and the need for controllers and gatekeepers to keep the masses dependent and complacent.

Finding the reverse transcriptase enzyme was a major blow to the hierarchical theory of DNA dominance because it showed that the total activity of the cell controls the action of DNA and that communication is constant and <u>bidirectional.</u> Recent experiments with cloning confirm this observation. When genetic material was transferred to a new egg, information from changes in the cytoplasm initiated the functional capabilities of the DNA rather than the DNA initiating the functions in the cytoplasm as had been previously thought to occur. But it was the interaction of the DNA and the cytoplasm that created the energy flows in the living organism.

In 1970, the discovery of the reverse transcriptase enzyme was a revolutionary idea. This discovery was made when the Nixon's War on Cancer effort was spending mountains of money to find a cancer causing virus. The virus cancer theory never made much headway, but Gallo and the virus hunters did not let all of that research money go to waste. Instead of acknowledging that the RT enzyme was a DNA repair mechanism, they instead postulated that it belonged to a new category of viruses which were then called <u>retroviruses</u>. Today it is recognized that retroviruses are a normal part of the cell's repair and communication mechanism.

A whole body of literature supporting the evidence on the reverse transcription enzyme and the bidirectional communication of cellular DNA and RNA (mainly from Europe) was suppressed by researchers engaged in the Nixon's War on Cancer virus hunt.[78] Bidirectional synthesis requires reverse transcriptase. The enzyme, therefore, is not unique to infectious retroviruses but is common in all forms of life. This very basic science renders Robert Gallo's claim in the original papers of having discovered a new retrovirus because he found reverse transcriptase suspect at the very least.

World-renowned virologist Peter Duesberg has raised another very important issue concerning retroviruses. Retroviruses were never known to be killer viruses in man. They had been classified as benign passenger viruses. According to Duesberg, "Even very few oncogenic retroviruses—those endowed with cancer genes—hardly play a role as carcinogens for two reasons. First, viral cancer genes accidentally acquired are never kept by retroviruses after they are generated because they are entirely useless to the virus. . . .Second, even if a rare oncogenic retrovirus infects an immuno-competent animal, a small tumor will appear within days after the infection, only to disappear again as the animal develops antiviral immunity. Anti-

---

78.   Stefan Lanka,. "HIV: Reality or Artifact?" <u>Continuum</u>, April/May 1995.

viral immunity kills both the virus and all virus-infected cells."[79] In other words, retroviruses do not kill the cells in which they reside as HIV/AIDS proponents claim that HIV does to T cells.

By now you are probably asking, "So what exactly did Gallo find in his lab?" Very simply, in the old phrase from the early days of computers, GIGO—garbage in, garbage out. What Gallo was calling a new unique retrovirus or HIV was no more than a laboratory artifact. He created the conditions for the cells in his experiment to mount a heightened biochemical response (elevated cellular breakdown "viral like" products) by adding strong oxidizing agents as well as hydrocortisone to the mixture. The oxidizing agents cause cellular damage that led to the need for DNA repair, which is accomplished with the enzyme reverse transcriptase. The break down products from the damage caused by the added oxidizing agents that created the tiny non-specific vesicles of various sizes seen extruded from cells under electron microscopy, he called HIV. There is no picture of a distinct isolated "HIV" to this day. Even a high school student would know that this is bogus science. But Gallo did something even more evil. He patented a test for the "HIV antibodies" (which in effect was cellular debris) before he isolated and identified HIV as a unique virus.[80] From the beginning, it was unconscionable. For Gallo it was the glory, and for the boys at the top of the pyramid it was about social control and money.

By 1988, an Australian researcher, Eleni Papadopalos-Eleopulos, unveiled an explanation of AIDS based on the process of oxidative stress. According to Papadopulos, the stimulants used to induce "HIV" phenomena (retrovirus-looking objects plus certain proteins that may or may not be affiliated with those objects) in cultures are oxidizing agents, as are the factors uniting American AIDS patients, including street drugs, hemophilia treatments, and rectally deposited semen. Papadopulos proposed that both "HIV" phenomena and AIDS conditions are consequences of these and other stressors she would introduce in later papers (such as blood transfusions, anti-AIDS pharmaceuticals, including AZT, and antibiotics).[81]

---

79. Peter, Duesberg, <u>Inventing the AIDS Virus</u>. (Washington, DC: Regnery Publishing, 1996), 119.

80. Press Release, Gary Null 30 September 2008: *A LEADING AMERICAN SCIENTIST—HONORED AS "THE DISCOVERER OF AIDS" and "THE FATHER OF AIDS RESEARCH—IS SHOWN TO HAVE FALSELY CLAIMED THAT HE HAD DETECTED AND ISOLATED AN AIDS-CAUSING RETROVIRUS.*

81   Eleni Papadopoulis-Eleopulos, "Reappraisal of AIDS: Is the Oxidation Induced by the Risk Factors the Primary Cause?" <u>Medical Hypotheses</u> (1988) 25: 151–62

Non-specific Antibodies Not a Virus

Even more important, when independent researchers were finally able to get access to Gallo's original research, they discovered that no virus was found in any of Gallo's patients—only antibodies against something he was calling <u>HIV</u>. Antibodies are traditionally a sign that the immune system has rejected the virus. Gallo turned the function of the immune system upside down, and the medical community let him get away with that nonsense for three years before they began to speak out. He made the world believe that having immunity to a virus would lead to a disease. From the beginning, HIV science was a giant mind game designed to pacify a desperate and irresponsible homosexual community and to frighten the rest of the world into submission to the tyranny of the medical establishment. Even the selling of AZT, a failed cancer drug developed from a herring sperm extract, was a stroke of mass marketing genius.

Simple minds like simple solutions. When the "anti-retroviral" drug AZT was presented to the public, this simply reinforced that HIV was a virus, and the "experts" in government and medicine had done their work and quickly and brilliantly solved the problem with this new medicine—another magic bullet. We could all go back to sleep. There could have been nothing further from the truth.

Nixon's War on Cancer and the Wild Virus Chase

Nixon's 1971 declared War on Cancer was not only effective in suppressing pre-WWII cytogenetics research but was also equally successful at suppressing the work of Otto Warburg, a German scientist and winner of two Nobel Prizes and nominee for a third for his research. Warburg demonstrated that cancer was not an infectious disease but a metabolic problem that arose as a result of chronic oxygen deficiency. At the cellular level, chronic oxygen deficiency causes the replacement of the oxygen respiratory cycle of energy metabolism that takes place in cellular organelles called <u>mitochondria</u> with a less efficient energy production mechanism called <u>aerobic gycolysis</u> that occurs in the cells cytoplasm. Such energy transformation can lead to apoptosis of cells (a die off) and the development of chronic diseases including AIDS; if it happens acutely, it leads to necrosis—dead tissue as occurs in an acute myocardial infarction. If it occurs chronically over a long period of time, the mature cell has the evolutionary programmed option of reverting to a self-preserving embryonic state which is called cancer. More will be discussed on this in the chapter that considers the impairment of biological mechanisms underlying immune deficiency and the brilliant strategy cells have devised over billions of years of evolution to function in both optimal and hostile environments. Cancer is a mechanism of cellular self-preservation when chronically faced with a sub-optimal redox state.

The uptake of an electron (as well as a positively charged hydrogen ion aka proton) by a receiving molecule is called <u>reduction</u>. Conversely, the donation of an electron (as well as a hydrogen ion) is called <u>oxidation</u>. In living cells, the effective proportion of reduced substances to oxidized substances is called the <u>redox balance</u>. The redox potential is measured in millivolts. A distinguishing feature of living cells is the dynamic maintenance of energy flows away from thermodynamic equilibrium. This is accomplished by constant electron transfer, which, at the same time, produces proton gradients to decrease or increase the electromotive force. The movement of these electrons and protons creates energy in the form of light emissions (photons) that are reabsorbed in the healthy cell. While normal cells emit less light, cancer cells are decoupled from this photon field and show an exponential increase in light emission (energy loss) with increasing cell density. This correlates with the observation that cancer cells have a diminished capacity for intercommunication.

A fundamental principle of evolutionary biology states that the more complex an organism's evolution, the more reduced it must be. In the reduced state, there are more electrons available for energy production. In order to insure the necessary predominance of the reduction status, any oxidation of a molecule or atom must be quickly reduced again. In living cells this takes place particularly by means of sulfur containing amino acids, sulfurous peptides with low molecular weights and other sulfurous molecules.[82]

Mounting evidence from recent research has confirmed Warburg's findings and has further shown that chronic deficits in the more efficient mitochrondrial oxidative metabolism are factors in the development of many chronic diseases. One area of research has evaluated an autosomal recessive inherited condition known as Friedreich ataxia. This disease is an inherited neurogenerative disorder caused by a deficiency of a mitochondrial protein known as <u>frataxin</u>. Because of the inherited defect, people with Friedreich ataxia are subject to premature death due to cardiac failure, diabetes mellitus and insulin resistance, all due to the impaired synthesis of the energy molecule ATP. The life expectancy of those with this inherited disease is only 38 years on average, and the genetic defect leads to an increase of oxidative stress demonstrated by reduced levels of free glutathione. [83] Just as a diminished

---

82. Kremer, Heinrich, <u>The Silent Revolution in Cancer and AIDS Medicine, new fundamental insights into the real causes of illness and death confirm the effectiveness of biological compensation therapy,</u> (Xlibris 2008)

83. Schulz, T.J, et. al, "Induction of Oxidative metabolism by mitochondrial frataxin inhibits cancer growth, Otto Warburg revisted, *J of Biol Chem* 281

level of this important antioxidant leads to premature death in Freidrich's ataxia, reduced glutathione levels are similarly found to be abnormally low in AIDS patients who experience the most serious complications.

Otto Warburg's work suggests that malignant growth might be caused by a decrease in mitochondrial energy metabolism paralleled by an increased gylocolytic flux. The new research suggests that it is not so much the increase in glycolysis that may be the primary cause of malignant growth, but the reduced efficiency of mitochondrial energy conversion as the result of oxidative/ nitrosative stress. Numerous cancer specimens exhibit mitochondrial DNA deletions, reduced mitochondrial content, altered mitochondrial morphology, and impaired oxidative capacity as well as an increase in glycolytic rate and lactate production.[84] What is becoming imminently more difficult to suppress is the evidence that impaired mitochondrial metabolism, and specifically the Krebs cycle[85] activity, may promote malignant growth, and that oxidative stress is also responsible for the CD4 imbalance in the Th1/Th2 cell population in favor of the Th2 profile and increased antibody production found in AIDS patients. Th2 shift is the consistent metabolic finding in AIDS patients. No virus need apply.

Understanding these metabolic pathways is vitally important in understanding AIDS. People diagnosed with AIDS are in a hypercatabolic low oxygen state where the body becomes exhausted in attempting to repair itself. Instead of being given the appropriate antimicrobials along with compensatory nutrients and antioxidants to help the repair process, people who are HIV positive are treated with drugs that bring about the slow asphyxiation of cells that are already oxygen deprived—thus creating a self-fulfilling prophecy. People are dying from iatrogenic AIDS. Anti-retroviral drugs cause AIDS.

Antibodies and Immunity

The HIV antibody tests are another scientific conundrum never fully explained. An elevated antibody count has been historically used to identify those who have developed immunity to a disease. For example, after you receive a measles vaccine your anti-measles antibody count rises. This elevated count is claimed to indicate that you have developed immunity from being

---

(2) 977-981

84.   Ramanathan, A., Wang, C. and Schreiber, S.L. (2005) *Proc. Natl. Acad. Sci. U.S.A. 102, 5992-5997*

85.   Also known as the tricarboxylic cycle or the citric acid cyle which is envolved through a series of enzyme catalyzed reactions in the use of oxygen for cellular respiration and energy production.

exposed to that particular virus. This is the underlying theory of vaccines. If your antibody count drops, you are to said to need a booster shot for the specific purpose of raising your antibody levels called titers. It is claimed that the vaccine will raise your immunity to the disease by increasing your antibodies against this pathogen. The immune system is imminently more complex, but this is the theory that has been rolled over from the 19th century to justify the every expanding roster of mandated vaccines.

Yet in the case of HIV, when your antibody titers are already **elevated,** indicating that your body is working normally and has developed immunity to HIV, you are said **not** to be immune and are subject to the development of AIDS—a scientific wonder never explained by those promoting this theory. Yet the AIDS promoters are promising a vaccine against AIDS although they know that any vaccine would produce the exact antibodies, in which case people would be said to be immune from AIDS. Needless to say, the vaccine trials have all been gigantic failures. If you are already confused, that seems to be the point of HIV "science." Thus far, there has been no viable vaccine produced, and it will be interesting to see just how long that charade continues. (Note: It will continue as long as the money flows to this misguided research)

Epidemic Intelligence Service and AIDS

The Epidemic Intelligence Service was founded in 1951 by Alexander Langmuir, a professor of public health. It is referred to as the "medical CIA" and was first designed to act as an elite biological warfare counter-measures unit of the CDC. Langmuir also served as an advisor to the Defense Department's chemical and biological warfare programs, was part of the eugenics movement that supported the work of Planned Parenthood founder Margaret Sanger, and involved the EIS in the population control movement of the 1960s.

Since 1951, graduates of the two-year program have returned to society in various positions in state and local health departments, hospitals, government positions, the World Health Organization, universities, pharmaceutical companies, tax exempt foundations, and in the media as staff writers, editors and TV anchor men and women. EIS alumni are not disinterested parties on the look out for potential biological threats. Their job is to promote CDC policies. They remain as secretive about their membership in this agency as are members of other clandestine agencies, and because of their frontline positions have promoted fear of impending disaster to boost drug sales when no peril is imminent. Recently they have promoted SARS, smallpox, swine flu and the bird flu. The promotion of AIDS as a sex and blood plague has been one of their long-term projects.

The scientific facts about HIV and AIDS have not gotten in the way of the disease purveyors of the EIS and the marketing mavens of the pharmaceutical industry selling drugs to the medically hexed that in fact ultimately contribute to their demise. One must ponder why millions of dollars of government and private money have poured into AIDS research so out of proportion to the number of people who die from this disease in comparison with heart disease or cancer. Since 1980, more people have died each year in car accidents, and four times more Americans have been killed by prescription drugs than from AIDS. According to a 1998 ranking of U.S. fatalities, AIDS was number seventeen with 16,685 deaths compared with heart disease (725,790 deaths), diabetes (62,332) or Alzheimer's disease (22,527). Despite the small number of cases and deaths, federal funding for AIDS has been disproportionately excessive compared with other ailments that kill more Americans. For example, the National Institutes of Health (NIH) allocates $2,400 per patient in research money to AIDS compared with $230 for breast cancer, $108 for heart disease, and $28 for diabetes. Moreover, under the pretext of a growing pandemic, those with AIDS receive special emergency funds through the Ryan White CARE Act and ADAP that people with other diseases do not.[86] I am not implying that people with a positive HIV test should be ignored, but one must consider that there is always more than one agenda being served. There are political reasons for keeping HIV/AIDS on the public's mind. There are political and economic reasons that are being promoted as a Herculean problem in Africa. There are political reasons why it has become a problem among black American women, who have likely as a result of its eugenics origin always been one of the ultimate targets. Drug use among young black women has been rapidly rising consonant with their rising risk for testing HIV positive.

As an allopathic physician, when the AIDS story broke, I believed it. I lived in New York, and I had friends who had supposedly died of the dreaded disease. I was busy finishing my residency and starting my practice, and I trusted what the "experts" were telling me at medical conferences. It was not until I faced my own health challenge, unrelated to HIV, that I began to look for alternative ways to heal myself. I began to examine the history and dynamics of the profession I had chosen. My studies brought me to the realization that the allopathic medical profession is controlled from the top by the same interests that control banking, oil, precious metals, the military and associated intelligence agencies, the World Health Organization, the

---

86. "Disease Politics," ABC News 20/20, 10/11/99.

World Bank, the International Monetary Fund, and the various foundations and think tanks that frame and limit all level of intellectual inquiry in the United States and throughout their empire.

I found a 1989 report by the National Research Council that more explicitly revealed the hidden agenda behind AIDS. Originally sponsored by the Rockefeller and Russell Sage Foundations and then funded by the Public Health Service, AIDS: Sexual and Intravenous Drug Use laid out a plan for yet another social engineering scheme on a massive scale—using AIDS as the excuse. "The devastating effect of an epidemic on a community can evoke strong political and social responses," the committee noted. "An epidemic necessitates the rapid mobilization of the community to counter the spread of illness and death." The power of such a method to force cultural values is an extension of the shock doctrine based on manipulation and fear. "Ideally, health promotion messages should heighten an individual's perceptions of threat and his or her capacity to respond to that threat, thus modulating the level of fear...What is not yet known is how to introduce fear in the right way in a particular message intended for a particular audience. Acquiring that knowledge will require planned variations of AIDS education programs that are carefully executed and then carefully evaluated." The report went on to express how to attack societal moral values related to speaking and writing about sexuality in explicit terms. Again they were advocating a direct attack on our children when they stated: "Despite recent indications of greatly increased tolerance for sexual explicitness in the media and literature, that reluctance remains strong in much of the population; it is particularly strong in instances that involve the education of children and adolescents." The fear of this created AIDS epidemic would be used to fix this problem. The report continued: "The committee believes that during an epidemic, politeness is a social virtue that must take second place to the protection of life." Just as Harry Hopkins used tuberculosis as a public boondoggle, Donald Francis, an Epidemic Intelligence officer and officer of the Centers for Disease Control in Atlanta (CDC), saw the possibilities in harnessing other epidemics to advance similar agendas. He shamelessly declared, "If we establish new mechanisms to handle the HIV epidemic [these] can serve as models for other diseases."

This is why the rational voices of Peter Duesberg, the Perth Group, Stefan Lanka, Henreich Kremer and countless other researchers calling for reasoned scientific discussion about AIDS were silenced. AIDS was intended to be used as another mass social engineering program. It was never designed to answer the obvious medical questions. The Rockefeller sponsored National Research Council's report AIDS: Sexual and Intravenous Drug Use makes it clear that this crisis would be used to undermine the sexual mores of the culture. Just as opium was used to destroy China, the drug culture is being used to destroy the social fabric of the United States.

I am now old enough to remember a time when as a child I felt perfectly safe going alone to the corner store to buy a Popsicle. On a scale of one to ten, my safety factor was 10. Today, what Catherine Austin Fitts, former undersecretary of the Housing and Urban Development (HUD) Department, calls the Popsicle index has been completely reversed. The Popsicle Index is the percentage of people in a community who believe that a child can leave the home, go to the nearest place to buy a Popsicle, and come home alone safely. The influx of drugs leading to the AIDS crisis combined with the deindustrialization of the economic core and the religion of globalization are the continuum of the same process that has been driving down this index of community safety and quality of life factors over the last forty years. We now have two generations of Americans who think that drug-infested communities and gun violence are a normal way of life.

The history of the families and their extended business relationships that seek profit by unhinging cultures through flooding them with drugs and shocking people into submission with contrived events runs back at least to the horrible savagery of the British East India Company and its drive for global resource domination. The BEIC was responsible for millions of deaths in India, Africa, China, and the United States. Their "free trade" policies constricted the life blood of the fledgling colonies and ultimately led to an uprising—the American Revolution.

In order to understand the development of the AIDS crisis, one must look back to the importance of the BEIC, their drug running in the development of Western capitalism, and the transition of the United States into the United States Empire.

Chapter 5

The Deindustrialization of the Economic Core, More Immune Toxins, How China Fits into the Big Picture and the Death Knell for Dollar Hegemony

○ ○

Cul-de-sac neighborhoods once filled with the sound of backyard barbecues and playing children are falling silent. Communities like Elk Grove, Calif., and Windy Ridge, N.C., are slowly turning into ghost towns with overgrown lawns, vacant strip malls and squatters camping in empty homes.

> *The Final Stage in the De-industrialization of America 5 April 2009, "The Economic Populist"*

In a graphic illustration of the new world order, Arab states have launched secret moves with China, Russia and France to stop using the US currency for oil trading

> *Robert Fisk, The Demise of the Dollar 6 October 2009*

Isn't the only hope for the planet that the industrialized civilizations collapse? Isn't it our responsibility to bring that about?"

> *– Maurice Strong, globalist 1992*

Human beings evolved an immune protective bio-energetic system over millions of years. The system was designed to cope with bacteria, parasites, viruses, solar radiation, and the waste products of our own daily turnover of 10^{12} cells. We have survived plagues, famines, wars, and bad governments. The question remains about our survival from the central bankers and their globalized technological corporate state unfettered from local controls of the democratic process. It is a sinister force that is bent on the total defilement of the mother, Earth. Of the 100 largest economic units, 49 are countries, and 50 are corporations. The parasite is in control of the host.

Industrial, medical, and military pollution began to increase rapidly with the onset of the industrial revolution, but chemical, biological and electric pollution has been increasing exponentially over the last sixty years. The cumulative effect of toxic waste, electrical and chemical products has created a whole new set of biological stressors not experienced before in such a massive and concentrated form. Unfortunately, the human organism has had little time to adapt to this burden, which has resulted in a significant rise in modern chronic disease states. Corporations in league with the government have used the mighty megaphone of the public relations Wurlitzer to spin us into believing that the nuclear fallout and toxic sludge they produce are actually good for us and have successfully dumped the waste of civilization in our rivers, lakes, oceans, our drinking water supply, on our agricultural products, and in the air we breathe. At the same time, they are destroying the earth's lungs—the tropical rain forests. Amazingly, half of the forests have been destroyed in the last fifty years.

Many humans have maladapted to the mounting and cumulative external environmental stressors by developing skyrocketing numbers of cancers and chronic autoimmune diseases in which the body begins to attack itself. Studies on the cumulative effects to human health of the myriad pollutants dumped into the environment on a daily basis as waste from manufacturing, military weapons development, medical intervention, and now genetically modified food have been blocked by the active intervention of corporate lobbyists and their public relations firms.

During the atomic bomb testing period in the 1950s, most of the baby boomers were fed on a diet of radioactive milk and milk products.[87] Many of the manufacturing waste compounds are also endocrine disruptors that polarize the evolutionary biologically programmed immune balance to Th2 predominance as well as mimic natural hormones. Because of this property, such chemicals are able to displace our naturally produced hormones in

---

87.   Pat Ortmeyer, and Arjun Makhijani, "Let Them Drink Milk," <u>The Bulletin of Atomic Scientists</u>, Nov./ Dec. 1997.

our endocrine system and to disrupt normal physiological functions. This can lead to the premature development of secondary sexual characteristics, reproductive difficulties, immune system problems, and cancer.

A 326 page report published by he environment protection agency in Denmark discovered that ubiquitous chemical contamination is driving sperm counts down and feminizing male children in all of the developing world. The report noted that sperm counts are falling so fast that young men are less fertile than their fathers and produce only a third as much sperm, proportionately as hamsters. The birth ratio for boys is also falling.[88]

The toxins used to create plastic, pesticides, cleansers; dyes; flame retardants, and white paper, among other products are the most troublesome. These compounds have become ubiquitous over the last sixty years. As environmental stressors, these chemicals are relevant to the AIDS story because the cohort of affected men who were first diagnosed were born after WWII and were exposed to a level of oxidative stressors that was an entirely new physiological phenomenon. Because the allopathic medical system was still operating under the 19th century paradigm of the infectious disease model, doctors were accustomed to looking for isolated pathogens and a magic bullet solution to eradicate the problem. As a result, the rise in diseases resulting from environmental toxins including vaccines and antibiotics has been downplayed or ignored.

Large campaign contributions from corporate donors to national politicians that make this massive public poisoning possible has been well chronicled. Some campaign contributions can be viewed at www.opensecrets.org and other public interest web sites. But even this minimal transparency of formalized bribery to compliant legislators goes largely unchecked. Because there is so little significant scrutiny of the serious consequences of unregulated money funneled into the political system, corruption has become an endemic and intractable problem. What is puzzling is the tepid response that has been mounted to this corruption by the public. It may be reasonable to consider that the radioactive fallout from the development of the nuclear bomb project, including the fluoridation experiment of the water supply has worked to diminish the IQ of enough people so thoroughly that the country has become immobilized and confused while becoming enveloped by the dark forces of history.

During the eight years of the George W. Bush presidency, mounting and troubling medical warning signs of a country in economic decline began to breakthrough in the headlines. Although the process was accelerated under

---

88. Geoffrey Lean, "Why Boys are Turning into Girls", 23 October 2009, www.telegraph.co.uk

this particular kleptocracy, it did not start with his regime. Like any cancer, the disease process of social disruption had been ongoing for many years before it erupted as a metastatic transformation on 9/11.

One way to evaluate the well being of a society is to look at some overall health trends. Whether the health of a people is improving or declining is evidence of the general well being of that society. Unfortunately, America's health has been on a downward trend. In 2008, America's Health Rankings report, issued at the American Public Health Association's annual meeting, indicated that the life expectancy for Americans reached 78.1 years but ranked 50th behind Japan and most of Europe. A 2008 study published by the Harvard School of Public Health found that life expectancy for American women is declining for the first time since the Spanish Flu epidemic of 1918. Life expectancy for 1 in 5 American women is either going down or remaining stagnant. Most of the excess deaths are related to smoking. The CDC reported that type 2 diabetes is up 90 percent since 1997, which may be an underestimate because the numbers come from self-reported surveys conducted by the CDC in 1995–97 and in 2005–07. At least 20 percent of adults are obese in every state except Colorado. A 2008 report from the Organization for Economic Cooperation and Development (OECD) on the per capita expenditure of pharmaceuticals revealed that while France and Spain consumed the highest number of pharmaceuticals per person, the U.S. spends more than any other industrialized nation—nearly twice the amount of the thirty countries considered in the assessment,[89] yet has comparatively poorer healthcare outcomes that do not justify the expenditure.

Twenty-eight countries that spend far less per capita on healthcare and pharmaceuticals, including Britain, France, Germany, and Japan are ahead of the United States in life expectancy. The United States ranks last among industrialized countries in preventable mortality. Although U.S. researchers considered the rising rates of obesity and lack of health insurance, they made no mention of increased consumption of processed foods containing multiple chemical additives, some of which are neurotoxic as well as high fructose corn syrup[90], artificial sweeteners and processed vegetable oils. The level of obesity has risen to epidemic proportions. According to the U.S. Department of Health and Human Services, 2/3 of adults are overweight, and 1/3 are obese. The variety and quality of food Americans eat have been altered substantially

89.   "Healthy Economy," OECD Observer, October 2008.

90.   High fructose corn syrup has been linked to an increase in obesity, diabetes, cancer, and heart disease. Half of the samples tested have been shown to contain another serious toxin—mercury.

over the last forty years, and they are having a major negative impact on overall health. Portions have become gigantic.

At the other end of life's spectrum, it was noted in 2006 that the United States as a whole, ranked 27th among industrialized countries in its infant mortality rate, well behind Israel and several countries that have only recently emerged from behind the Iron Curtain. This is in spite of the fact that the United States spends 16 percent of its GDP (Gross Domestic Product) on health care—more than any other country. The next closet country is Germany with 10.5 percent.

Infant mortality is a critical indicator of social progress. As the CDC report explains, "Infant mortality is one of the most important indicators of the health of a nation, as it is associated with a variety of factors such as maternal health, quality and access to medical care, socioeconomic conditions, and public health practices." Infant mortality rate in the U.S. is now worse than twenty-eight other countries.

Diseases of poverty that were unheard of, or practically extinct, are on the ascendancy. Tuberculosis and hepatitis are rising, and leprosy, virtually unknown to Americans over the last century, exceeded 7,000 new cases brought in on the backs of newcomers since 2001.[91] The Washington Post reported that the use of antidepressants is soaring, with 1 in 10 American women using an antidepressant drug, such as Zoloft, Paxil, or Prozac. The use of these drugs has tripled in just a decade. Antidepressants have been linked to hundreds of cases of suicide and violence, including many recent school shootings.

The number of children using psychiatric drugs has soared. In 2002, about 6 percent of all boys and girls were taking antidepressants, triple the rate in the period 1994–96. About 14 percent of boys—nearly one in seven—were on stimulant drugs in 2002, double the number in 1994–96, the report found. Stimulant drugs are usually used to treat attention deficit disorder.[92]

With America's general overall health declining, their options for access to care are rapidly diminishing as well. There are reports from New Jersey to California of hospitals and emergency rooms closing and providers shutting their doors to the poor whether uninsured or covered by Medicaid or Medicare. Reimbursement levels for these programs are no longer keeping pace with the inflationary costs of either office or hospital care or pharmaceuticals, especially very expensive cancer therapy drugs. Private insurers consistently

---

91.   Frosty Wooldridge, , "Leprosy, Tuberculosis, Hepatitis Rising Fast in the U.S." American Chronicle, 31 May 2007.

92.   Shankar Vedantam, , "Anti-depressant Use by U.S. Adults Soars," Washington Post, 3 December 2004.

deny payment for standard of care as a method of wealth transfer from communities into the coffers of HMOs' CEOs—who take little risk and add a net negative value to the overall quality of living standards by rewarding themselves so generously by denying their clients care that they are paying to receive.

In Las Vegas, cancer patients who were receiving outpatient treatment at the University Medical Center have to seek treatment elsewhere as Medicaid cuts no longer cover the cost of expensive cancer drugs. Low-income children with bone and spine problems may even need to leave Las Vegas altogether for treatment because pediatric orthopedists are no longer accepting payment from Medicaid because reimbursements no longer cover the rising cost of care.[93] Senior citizens in Illinois are facing the traumatic prospect of being moved from nursing homes teetering on the edge of bankruptcy as the homes wait for months to be paid by the floundering state government. South Carolina has cut treatment for low-income women under 40 with breast or cervical cancer and stopped providing nutritional supplements for people with kidney failure.[94]

One can begin to understand the process of this devolution by examining formerly secret government documents. The unearthing of classified government records and of other documents in the public domain has shown that there were decisions made intentionally at the highest levels of government in response to the call to protect the profits and hegemonic aspirations of certain corporate and military interests. It was known at the time that such decisions were made that there would be adverse effects on the public's health. An audio tape was unearthed in the National Archives in which John Erlichman who was counsel and assistant to the president on domestic affairs, explains to Nixon how by passing HMO legislation, HMOs will make money by denying care.[95] It has been well documented that this is how they have become so very profitable. Some HMO CEOs are worth billions because they are the most efficient at harvesting their profits from the fields of misery of people who are denied necessary care. This is called rationing and it has been going on for some time.

As an example of only one of the many decisions, it is helpful to discuss why and how it was resolved to dump fluoride, one of the most toxic chemical waste products from the manufacture of atomic weapons, aluminum and

---

93. Allen Marshall, "Providers Close Doors To Poor, Medicaid Cuts Leave No Choice, Says Doctors, Hospitals" Las Vegas Sun, 16 November 2008.
94. Noam,Levey, "Struggling States Cut Healthcare Costs for Poor before Obama Can Bolster Coverage," Los Angeles Times, 14 January 2009..
95. The Miller Center of Public Affairs has this audio recording (conversation number 450-23. "Richard Nixon—Oval Office Recordings.

other industrial products into the public water supply. The government and private industry colluded by falsely claiming that fluoride was beneficial because it protected children from getting cavities.

The water fluoridation decision can be traced to Harold Hodges, a toxicologist by training, who worked on the Manhattan Project. Harold Hodges was also named by John Marks in his 1975 book The Search for the Manchurian Candidate as one of the CIA's leading research pioneers on the mind-altering drug LSD, which was also surreptitiously given to many unsuspecting victims, some of whom were psychologically damaged permanently and some of whom committed suicide.

President Eisenhower, in his farewell address to the nation, warned the people of the rising power of the military-industrial complex. It was indeed WWII and the development of the atomic bomb that unleashed a new more potent variation of a killing machine on the world. While most were terrorized by the possibility of mass annihilation from the power of the bomb, thanks to Harold Hodges and our protectors in the Pentagon, not only was the toxic residue from aerial fallout allowed to rain down on an unsuspecting population, the toxic residue from its manufacturing process was released into the water supply as one of the first experiments in mass public poisoning.

The Manhattan Project was a top secret government program responsible for constructing the ultimate horror weapon, the atomic bomb. During the project, Hodges was chief of fluoride toxicology. His laboratory was located at the University of Rochester in upstate New York. Declassified documents of the U.S. atomic bomb program indicate that both the scientists and the military knew that fluoride caused central nervous system damage yet they intentionally colluded with industry to hide this danger from the public. Public exposure of this harm became a very real possibility after they were confronted with the possibility of damning lawsuits from New Jersey farmers who themselves, their crops, and their live stock had been damaged by a fluoride spill into their water supply.

The information that the military had obtained from the number and types of illnesses to their civilian employees about the severe damage that fluoride causes to the central nervous system remained so well hidden that a generation of trained scientists were unaware of the original government research until the 1980s when Phyllis Mullenix was asked to evaluate if this chemical was harmful to children.

Phyllis J. Mullenix, is a pharmacologist and toxicologist by training. In 1987, while on the staff in the Department of Psychiatry of Boston Children's Hospital, she and her colleagues were given the task of investigating the neurotoxic effects of fluoride. She and her team were not particularly excited about the prospect of studying the effects of this chemical because they, like so many others, were under the impression from their training and the U.S. scientific literature that there would be nothing untoward to find. After all, it had been in the ·U.S water supply for years, and she trusted the experts who put it there. She was in for a bitter surprise. All the more so, because a now elderly senior scientist by the name of Harold Hodges worked in her laboratory and was aware of her research and never admitted that the government already knew that fluoride was damaging to the Central Nervous System (CNS) of humans. Unbeknownst to Mullenix, Hodges was the scientist from the Manhattan Project charged with deliberately hiding the damages that this substance caused from public perception. Although most industrialized countries have banned fluoride from their water supplies, it is found in 67 percent of U.S. water systems.

The Mullenix research was very disquieting. She found that fluoride contributed to motor dysfunction, decreased IQ, and learning disabilities, including attention deficit disorder.[96] Her group soon found that two epidemiological studies from China showed IQ deficits in children overexposed to fluoride via drinking water or soot from burning coal. Although they could find no case controlled studies, a literature review of central nervous system individual case reports in humans revealed that numerous neurological effects had been reported to be caused by fluoride: impaired memory and concentration, lethargy, headache, depression, and confusion. The same theme was echoed in once classified reports about workers from the atomic bomb Manhattan Project. These reports had been willfully suppressed from the public domain by none other than the elderly Harold Hodges who worked in her lab and remained silent to the horror he had created.

However, like so many silent weapons, mass fluoridation of the water was never about children's teeth. If this were indeed the case, why not give it only to children in children's toothpaste or another delivery system? The true purpose of the water fluoridation program is spelled out in a now declassified 1948 report. The military, knowing the true physiological problems caused by this product, was worried about litigation coming from farmers in New Jersey who had been harmed by a fluoride spill from a Du Pont plant. It reads: "To supply evidence useful in the litigation arising from an alleged loss of a fruit crop several years ago, a number of problems have been opened. Since excessive blood fluoride levels were reported in human residents of the same area, our principal effort has been devoted to describing the relationship of blood fluorides to toxic effects."

---

96.   Statement from Phyllis Mullenix on the Neurotoxicity of Fluoride, www.
    HolisticMed.com/add 14 Sept. 1998.

In order to enhance the government's position in claiming that low levels of fluoride were safe, studies were conducted on two New York Hudson River towns and Grand Rapids, Michigan. The two New York communities chosen for the original studies of water fluoridation were Newburg and Kingston, both along the west bank of the Hudson River north of West Point. Newburg's water was fluoridated while Kingston's water, as the matched control, was not. In a statewide survey conducted in 1954, J. A. Forst, M.D., a New York public health official, reported observing one-third more dental defects, including malposition of teeth, in fluoridated Newburgh, New York, than in the non-fluoridated control city of Kingston. In spite of these very damning results disproving any dental improvement in children, the decision had been made to dump this poison into the nation's water supply and the people would be programmed to accept this decision.

Because Edward Bernays, the master propagandist and Sigmund Freud's nephew, had been so successful at selling WWI to the justifiably resistant American people and cigarette smoking to women; he was conscripted to sell the idea that putting rat poison in the public water supply was good for developing healthy teeth. This became a fairly easy task once dentists were persuaded that fluoride had dental benefits. The research showing the harmful effects of fluoride was strenuously suppressed (for national security reasons, of course) and the corporate data showing any benefit was promoted as the earnest effort of honest scientists. Dentists were targeted to become the unwitting proponents of feeding this toxic waste to the American public in the name of reducing dental caries.

Capsule News, a now defunct weekly newspaper, noted in its 4 February 1956 edition, "The claim is that only 1 part of sodium fluoride to 1,000,000 parts of water will "not hurt a fly." So—if it isn't strong enough to damage the delicate membranes of the stomach and intestines (of a fly), only a nitwit would believe it would have any effect on the hard enamel of teeth." The article further stated, "The only use for sodium fluoride heretofore has been (a) as a rat poison; (b) by cattlemen to partially de-sex their bulls so they will be more tractable; (c) by the Russian secret police to make their prisoners stupid so they can be more easily brainwashed." Fluoride was being dumped into the water just as television was becoming a consumer product found in almost every home. The combination of fluoride and television has been truly successful in mind numbing an entire country.

In addition to being harmful to the central nervous system, fluoride has numerous other deleterious side effects in humans. According to Dr. John Yiamouyiannis, a biochemist and member of the Consumer Health Organization of Canada, fluoride is used as an insecticide and roach killer. As little as one tenth of an ounce of fluoride can cause death in humans. It is more poisonous than lead and slightly less poisonous than arsenic. Fluoride weakens the immune system and may cause allergic type reactions, including dermatitis, eczema, and hives. It causes birth defects and genetic damage, and because it can leach lead out of pipes, it can lead to lead toxicity which is characterized by anemia and mental retardation. Fluoride is likely to aggravate kidney disease, diabetes, and hypothyroidism. Fluoride crosses the placenta and Chinese studies indicate that the influence of a high fluoride environment on intelligence may occur early in development during embryonic life or infancy. Ultramicroscopic study of embryonic brain tissue obtained from termination of pregnancy operations in endemic fluorosis areas showed "differentiation of brain nerve cells were poor and brain development was delayed".[97] In numerous animal studies, fluoride has been shown to decrease fertility.

Fluoride is a known endocrine disrupter, and fluoride preparations were used in the 1930s to treat overactive thyroid illnesses. Patients either drank fluoridated water, swallowed fluoride pills, or were bathed in fluoridated bath water; and their thyroid function was, as a result, greatly depressed. Fluoride is an enzyme poison. Enzymes are complex protein compounds that vastly speed up biological chemical reactions. Their optimal function is what maintains our health at the cellular level. More than 75 million Americans use some form of thyroid medication.[98]

Fluoride also causes the breakdown of collagen which results in wrinkling of the skin and the weakening of ligaments, tendons, and muscles. When fluoride was left in the phosphate that was sold to farmers, it killed their crops and livestock.[99]

Fluoride was removed from livestock feed after the New Jersey farmer's sued the government for loss of crops and livestock from a fluoride gas spill during the Manhattan Project development. The farmers' animals received more consideration than people because the lawsuit won by the farmers did not stop industry from giving fluoride to humans—only livestock.

Fluoride actually causes gum damage at the concentrations used in fluoridated toothpaste at 1,000 ppm. At the cellular level, fluoride has been shown to release superoxide radicals that poison enzyme activity and slows down the ability of the gums to heal. In the 1970s fluoride was linked to an

---

97.   X.S. Li, G.H. Lang, et al., "Effect of a High Fluoride Water Supply on Children's Intelligence", Fluoride: 29(4), 190-192

98.   Thyroid medications can have harmful interactions with other drugs, 3 September 2008. www.publiccitizen.org

99.   J.Yiamouyiannis, D. Burk, "Cancer from our drinking water?" Congressional Record, Proceedings and debates of the 94th Congress, 1st session, 1975.

increase in cancer. Taylor and Taylor from the University of Texas published a study in 1965 that was based on millions of subjects and showed a 5 to 10 percent increase in cancer death rate within 3 to 5 years after fluoridation was put into the water after correcting for various demographic factors, such as age, race, and sex.[100] Fluoride has also been associated with an increased risk for the development of osteosarcoma, a rare bone cancer that occurs mostly in children and young adults.

These harmful effects will continue because fluoride is also produced as a toxic waste byproduct of many types of heavy industry, such as aluminum, steel, fertilizer, glass, cement, and other industries and must be disposed of somewhere. If it's not used as an additive to water, manufacturers would have to pay millions of dollars to dispose of it properly, so the pressure to keep fluoride listed as a healthy additive to water, and not as an environmental toxin that requires costly disposal, is great, and political pressures to keep fluoride in the drinking water is strong. The bureaucracies of various U.S. government agencies remain a key supporter of water fluoridation.

The importance of the fluoride incident illustrates how the private sector will use the apparatus of the government to close ranks to protect their economic and political interests at all costs and against the general welfare of the American people. Suppressing evidence of medical and environmental crimes under the banner of state secrets is simply pro forma. The development of the atomic bomb was considered vitally important to a small group of elites because it meant U.S. hegemony during the cold war. But the truth was that it was as much about profits as power because the Cold War was used as an excuse to siphon plane loads of public money into private hands through massive and wasteful Pentagon projects. The Pentagon has been a sinkhole ever since.

During the 1980s, they were caught paying $435 for a claw hammer, $640 for a toilet seat, and $7,600 for coffee makers. By 2001, on the eve of 9/11, Donald Rumsfeld, then Secretary of Defense, made an announcement that the Pentagon could not account for $2.3 trillion.[101] However, this shocking news was upstaged by a bigger shock the next day, and this report of a $2.3 trillion heist of taxpayer money all but disappeared from the media and down the rabbit hole as if it had never happened.

Fluoride is just one toxin, but thousands of chemicals have been dumped in our water supply, released into the atmosphere, and plowed into our soil. Antibiotics, anti-convulsants, mood stabilizers, sex hormones, pesticides,

---

100. A.Taylor and N.C Taylor. "Effect of Sodium Fluoride on Tumor Growth," Proc. Soc. Exp. Biol. Med. 119 (1965):252.

101. "War on Waste," 29 January 2002, www.cbsnews.com.

fertilizers, and over-the-counter drugs, such as acetaminophen and ibuprofen, are all turning up in drinking water in cities from California to New Jersey. Contamination is not confined to the United States. More than a hundred different pharmaceuticals have been detected in lakes, rivers, reservoirs, and streams throughout the world. Studies have detected pharmaceuticals in waters throughout Asia, Australia, Canada, and Europe—even in Swiss lakes and the North Sea.

In 2005, the Environmental Working Group (EWG) released a study that found American babies are born with an average of 287 chemical contaminants in their bloodstreams. The findings were based on tests of 10 samples of umbilical-cord blood taken by the American Red Cross from across the country. The most prevalent chemicals found in the 10 newborns were mercury, fire retardants, pesticides and the Teflon chemical PFOA, perflourooctonoic acid. One hundred eighty of these chemicals are known to cause cancer, 217 are toxic to the brain and nervous system, and 208 cause birth defects or abnormal development in animal tests. A study of the cumulative effect of multiple pollutants on human health has never been undertaken.

People of the late 20th and early 21st century have literally been bathed in a sea of toxic soup from conception until death, and so it is understandable that a toxic factor, for political and economic reasons, was quickly dismissed in favor of a viral hypothesis in the 1980s when young men began to show up with damaged immune systems. Examining toxic stressors causing immune system breakdown would inevitably lead to questions about the corporate takeover of the American state and the consequences of policies that allowed long-term pollution, vaccines, and drugs, both legal and illegal, to be dumped into the bodies of our already stressed-out children. Promotion of the general welfare is not a notion the corporate state is prone to support. It also might raise profound ethical questions about the way in which the society pays lip service to the sanctity of human life while continually creating systems and programs that are decidedly anti-life.

As the American manufacturing core began to unravel as the result of policies favoring economic trade agreements that shunted factories to cheap labor markets with even worse environmental records, so did the bodies of the most affected. It was as if we were watching the slow disintegration of our country by way of the deteriorating health of our children. Anyone paying close attention would not have been surprised that dumping a plethora of drugs and an attendant stressful lifestyle into the bloodstreams of a fragile population would produce an environmental epidemic that needed an explanation. The <u>epidemic</u> cohort of AIDS patients were largely born after WWII. It was more comforting to claim that there was an attack on the immune system by a viral invader rather than by an internal fifth column. A viral cause was chosen as the culprit for both political and economic reasons.

Classical AIDS as described in the literature was beginning to decline rapidly and was making the earnest pronouncements of a worldwide pandemic overwrought and premature when, surprisingly, the definition was expanded in 1992. The CDC published a new expanded surveillance definition of AIDS that included all HIV positive adults and adolescents who had less than 200 CD4+T lymphocyte/microliter , a total CD4+T lymphocyte percent of less than 14, or who had been diagnosed with pulmonary tuberculosis, invasive cervical cancer, or recurrent pneumonia. The expanded litany of diseases made it seem that the <u>epidemic</u> was expanding, rather than rapidly contracting.

The first definition of AIDS appeared in the 24 September 1982, issue of <u>Morbidity and Mortality Weekly Report</u> published by the Centers for Disease Control. From the beginning, the CDC admitted that there was a defect in cell mediated immunity, but instead of considering the cellular mechanisms that led to this defect, CDC pinned the blame for all of these diseases on a single virus. The idea of assigning a grab bag of unrelated diseases to one virus was preposterously lazy science that had about as much validity as the <u>evil humors</u> theory of disease.

CDC defined a case of AIDS as a disease, at least moderately predictive of a defect in cell mediated immunity, occurring in a person <u>with no known cause for diminished resistance to that disease.</u> Such diseases include KS [Kaposi's sarcoma], PCP [Pneumocystis carinii pneumonia], and serious OOI [other opportunistic infections], which include pneumonia, meningitis, or encephalitis due to one or more of the following: <u>aspergillosis</u>, <u>candidiasis</u>, <u>cryptococcosis</u>, <u>cytomegalovirus</u>, <u>norcardiosis</u>, <u>strongyloidosis</u>, <u>toxoplasmosis</u>, or atypical <u>mycobacteriosis</u> (species other than tuberculosis or <u>leprosy</u>); <u>esophagitis</u> due to <u>candidiasis</u>, <u>cytomegalovirus</u>, or <u>herpes</u> <u>simplex virus</u>; progressive multifocal <u>leukoencephalopathy</u>, chronic <u>enterocolitis</u> (more than 4 weeks) due to <u>cryptosporidiosis</u>; or unusually extensive <u>mucocutaneous herpes</u> <u>simplex</u> of more than 5 weeks duration. Diagnoses are considered to fit the case definition only if based on sufficiently reliable methods (generally histology or culture). However, this case definition may not include the full spectrum of AIDS manifestations, which may range from absence of symptoms (despite laboratory evidence of immune deficiency) to nonspecific symptoms (e.g. , fever, weight loss, generalized, persistent lymphadenopathy) to specific diseases that are insufficiently predictive of cellular immunodeficiency to be included in incidence monitoring (e.g., tuberculosis, oral <u>candidiasis</u>, <u>herpes zoster</u>) to malignant neoplasms <u>that cause, as well as result from,</u>

immunodeficiency.[102] This catchall was including in the AIDS definition the diseases that caused immunodeficiency? Were they not claiming that HIV was the cause of these diseases?

The defining phrase that allowed the entire AIDS system to be set up as it has been was the claim that the men who presented with these illnesses had no known cause for diminished resistance to these diseases. Were they kidding? A reading of these early cases reveal that most of the men had, for almost ten years or more, been using massive amounts of drugs, including poppers, the antibiotic T/S, cocaine, and heroin; had been chronically ingesting a range of prophylactic antibiotics to ward off the numerous sexually transmitted diseases they were prone to; had had recurrent sexually transmitted diseases, including viral hepatitis; had had multiple partners in a single night; had engaged in sexual activity fit for the Marquis de Sade; and had often been exhausted, stressed out, and malnourished. The CDC then stated that they had no known cause for a defect in their cell mediated immunity. What planet were the people at the CDC living on?

Finally, vaccines and the adjuvents[103] added to them and the ever rising numbers of vaccines that are mandated for children and people whose immune systems are already compromised create immuno-suppression and a rising tide of autoimmune diseases and allergies. All of this was known to physicians trained to take this type of history in the 1980s and to put it into the context of the physical presentation of the disease process. The idea that they could only come up with one theory of the disease and spend twenty-five years in blind pursuit of a phantom virus when the answer was in front of them is illogical, irrational, and inexcusable.

Unfortunately, this is the end result of the reductionist training of allopathic medicine that looks for one problem to be solved with one solution—usually the magic bullet of a pharmaceutical drug. It is also the persistence of an outmoded 19th century paradigm of disease causation. In the world of Louis Pasteur and Robert Koch, two well known 19th century scientists, the infecting organism takes center stage, and the host is the bit player. Yet, it is well known that the healthier the person, the less likely to become infected in community outbreaks of infections diseases. The narrow focus on disease causation rather than on host resistance has backed modern medicine into an inescapable corner as bacteria mutate faster than the human thought process. Unfortunately, the medical system as developed under the auspices of Rockefeller and Carnegie money established the educational

---

102. Centers for Disease Control. "Update on Acquired Immune Deficiency Syndrome (AIDS)-United States." MMWR 31 (1982): 507–08.
103. Additives to the vaccine said to boost the immune response.

principles that manipulate physicians into unquestioning handmaidens. However, the response to the AIDS outbreak rises not just to the level of negligence, but to criminal negligence. The idea that doctors spend four years studying various sciences and mathematics in undergraduate school, two more years of science in medical school, and then promptly forget the processes that are so important to the functioning of a living organism by the assignment of a name—AIDS, diabetes, hypertension—is simply lazy and unconscionable. Every patient with AIDS, diabetes, and hypertension has a history that is unique. When that history confronts the doctor, the trust or expectation is that the physician will see the history, the human person, and not the person's AIDS, diabetes, or hypertension. By not doing so, physicians fail both themselves and the patient. When the organizing powers of the medical establishment proclaimed that AIDS was caused by a virus, the programmed automatons stopped looking for the processes. They not only put themselves in a very deep hole, they dragged their patients into the bottom of the pit with them.

The common factor linking the diverse stressors that were overpowering the immune and energy systems of these AIDS patients was that they are all strong oxidizing agents or had that effect at the cellular level. Oxidizing agents are substances that have a deficit of electrons and because of their reactivity are known as <u>free radicals</u>. Free radicals alter the redox status of the cellular milieu and have been shown over time to create tissue damage that results in disease. Such damage, if caught early, can be neutralized and reversed by the introduction of appropriate reducing agents, such as vitamins and other nutritional compounds: polyphenols, trace minerals, various amino acids, and peptides, such as N-acetyl-cysteine or the master antioxidant, glutathione. In other words, many of the diseases classified as <u>AIDS</u> can be either halted or reversed by appropriate chemotherapy along with <u>detoxification and appropriate biological compensatory therapy</u>. These natural therapeutic modalities are not part of the modalities employed by traditionally trained physicians who matriculate into the Rockefeller allopathic system. It is not that they do not want to help, it is because by their training, they don't know how and many are unwilling to learn.

Sadly, many Americans are toxic, overstuffed, and undernourished. They have become accustomed to eating hollow food from which spirit, essence, and life have been extracted. After a lifetime devoid of sufficient clean water and air, vitamins and nutrients, the ability to neutralize the demands of ever-increasing toxic loads from the waste of civilization, diminishes—sometimes reaching a breaking point. This is when diseases begin to be expressed. Where and how they are expressed depends on the disposition of the individual.

AIDS has never been a widespread problem among male homosexuals. It has been limited to a small subset who engaged in a particular lifestyle. The young people who were in the original AIDS cohort were fast-track homosexuals who used multiple drugs, engaged in indiscriminate bathhouse sex, and often had multiple sexual encounters in a single night. Others in this high risk group were IV drug users who were poorly nourished, under constant stress looking for the next fix, and subject to multiple infections from needles that were not sterile. The last group, identified as high risk, were hemophiliacs who had received massive amounts of foreign proteins from repeated transfusions of blood products that were culled from multiple donors, many not in the best of health. All of these factors, cumulatively and chronically, led to the breakdown that Gallo claimed was caused by a virus attacking the immune cells.

This AIDS catastrophe is the forward projection of Simon Flexner's (the first director of the Rockefeller Institute for Medical Research a hotbed of eugenicists) contribution to the eugenics movement into the 21st century. One can no longer directly call people unnecessary; one can simply make them so by using the media to give them the image of having a deadly and contagious plague. As Zbigniew Brzezinski stated in his musings about the new technotronic society, media will be used "to manipulate emotions and control reason . . . language . . . is replaced by imagery . . . "[104] He further posits that with "persisting social crisis, the emergence of a charismatic personality, and the exploitation of mass media to obtain public confidence would be the steppingstones in the piecemeal transformation of the United States into a highly controlled society . . . and its humane and individualistic qualities would thereby be lost."

A United States that placidly accepts torture as necessary to extract information, not from the convicted, but from the accused; that accepts the bombing of women and children and the guests of wedding parties; that accepts the tasering of children and of the elderly and wheel chair bound; that accepts stripping American citizens of their rights by accusing them of being terrorists—before they have been tried in a court of law before a jury of their peers; and that accepts a return to medieval savagery, is an America that has lost its way. Its humane characteristics cannot be repaired. Such actions are the precursors that turn into shouts for the rise of a fascist/ socialist state. This is the absolute best that the visionaries and arbiters of globalization have to offer. Brzezinski and his group think-tank cousins have nothing to contribute to lifting mankind to a higher plane of existence. They

---

104.   Zbigniew Brzezinski, <u>Between Two Ages: America's Role in the Technetronic Era</u> (Middlesex, U.K.: Penguin Books, 1970), 13.

offer nothing to make the spirit soar and the mind expand. Their putrescent ideas simply foment war, disruption, and social chaos in pursuit of their control of a utopian nightmare. The media will never evaluate how people like Brzezinski and Henry Kissinger have sought to destroy intentionally what they call the <u>fiction of sovereignty</u> and have been active and up front in undermining U.S. national sovereignty in pursuit of a one-world economic order. With the intentional worldwide economic meltdown of 2007–2009, their plans are on schedule.

The United States has become a rusting shell of its former industrial self. Its economic growth, which at one time was created by the land and its people, has been stunted and drained of vitality by the concocted illusions of Wall Street hedge funds and ephemeral derivative products based on the Black–Scholes equation. This mathematical model made the absurd assumption that it is possible to borrow and lend cash at a known, constant, and risk-free interest rate. This entire high-level, unbalanced mathematical exercise in high stakes derivatives and hedge funds has turned out to be nothing more than a Vegas bet that has shorted the real wealth of the nation. Wild Wall Street betting based on computer generated assumptions of this model was a free ride for Wall Street insiders, win or lose. Wall Street insiders knew that guessing correctly would net great wealth and that making the wrong guess would net great wealth. It was a rigged system in which it appeared that Goldman Sachs was the manipulator and AIG was the underwriter of last resort—but, in fact, it was, as always, the taxpayers of the United States who once again have been sucker punched into the position of becoming the underwriters of last resort.

The United States lost 2 million jobs the first three years of the Bush presidency and a total of 2.7 million manufacturing jobs after Bush allowed the 2001 entry of China into the WTO. Michigan lost 400,000 jobs, most in the automotive sector. By the year 2008, the stream of job losses had turned into a raging torrent of 2.6 million. As of November 2008, the unemployment rate rose to 6.5 percent, [105] and by 2009, the rate reported was 9.5 percent and rising with wide regional variations. The phony derivatives bird of Wall Street had come home to roost on Main Street. Wall Street put a gun to the head of the American people and threatened to collapse the economy if the people did not bail them out. Congress obliged and gave them $700 billion of taxpayer dollars with little oversight and no strings attached. That was such a successful heist they came back to the same bank. After the heist, the economy remained on the brink.

---

105. David Goldman, "Jobs loss in 2008: 1.2 million," <u>www.cnnmoney.com</u> 7 November 2008.

Exactly two people in Congress, libertarian Republican Ron Paul and progressive Democrat Dennis Kucinich had the strength to stand up and tell the American people the truth about the Federal Reserve and the monetary system. Paul and Kucinich were both presidential candidates for their respective parties in the 2008 election. Both were denied air time, denied access to the debates, and generally were not allowed a public platform. Paul's people mounted a strong Internet campaign, but his voice was never given a fair hearing by the controlled media.

The largest group of organized terrorists operates with government sanction on Wall Street and in the City of London. Make no mistake. Financial instruments that have been devised to extract wealth and drain nations of their creativity and resources are acts of terror. The profits made from stolen equity from unregulated derivative products, fractional reserve banking and usury, with no oversight have brought more destruction to the planet than some disgruntled peasant with a homemade bomb. Wall Street's weapons of mass destruction of derivatives and usury are wealth creating for a chosen few and wealth draining not just for this country but for the entire global economy. Hedge funds drain corporations and labor of their productive wealth for short- term gain with consequent great harm to the nation's long-term interests. The financial investors do not waste thought on the people and lives they destroy, nor on the stability of the country that has allowed them to prosper. They are now globalists who have overcome the "fiction of national sovereignty" and use the specter of brown people blowing things up and newly identified diseases as a smoke screen for their fraud. The only allegiance these monetary terrorists have is to profit. Profit leads to temporal power, and power is their god.[106] They intend to get it by any means necessary. This concept seems to be very difficult for ordinary people to comprehend. It is a financial war without mercy and ordinary people are the targets.

In Fat and Mean: The Corporate Squeeze of Working Americans and the Myth of Managerial Downsizing, David Gordon reports that while the American economy had grown massively through the 1960s, real working-class wages had not grown at all for thirty years. During the boom of the 1980s and 1990s, purchasing power had risen steeply for 20 percent of the population but had actually declined for all the rest by 13 percent. After inflation was factored in, purchasing power of a working couple in 1995 was only 8 percent greater than for a single working man in 1905! How did this transition occur with so few, until the recent economic crisis, even having a clue as to how this massive wealth transfer was taking place?

---

106. As I write this, Lehman Brothers, the fourth largest investment bank in the country, has filed for bankruptcy, and the United States Congress is about to give the thieves another trillion in taxpayer dollars.

The WWII Bretton Woods Agreement led to the development of super bank IMF. The IMF not only strangles the economies of developing nations but their policies also directly leads to unfavorable trade agreements that shift strategically necessary manufacturing jobs out of the United States and puts downward pressure on the wages of jobs that remain. According to Corporate Predators: The Hunt for Mega Profits and the Attack on Democracy: "Big business has made IMF expansion a priority because, for them, the IMF is a multi-pronged welfare machine. First, the IMF bails out big banks and foreign investors when they make bad loans in developing countries—investments that are understood to be risky at the time they were made, and earn more as a result."[107]   In other words, the profits of globalization are privatized and flow upward, but the risks are socialized and flow downward. What Mokhiber and Weissman do not tell the reader is that taxpayers' taxes go directly to the Federal Reserve, a private bank, to support interest payments on unnecessarily created national debt and any loss on the risky loans made by private banking corporations.[108] It is one of the longest running boondoggles in history. As a sovereign nation, the United States has the power to print debt-free money that is not borrowed from a private bank, which would be less inflationary and would make capital available at a reasonable cost to farmers and entrepreneurs.

In addition, trade agreements, such as the North American Free Trade Agreement (NAFTA) and the World Trade Organization (WTO), have served to destroy the barriers that protect domestic commerce and agriculture—the lifeblood and true wealth of the nation. America's rise to post-WWII power was fueled not by free trade but by the logical protection of domestic strategic industry, mining, and agriculture. Congress and the various U.S. Presidents gave Wall Street the power to fritter away domestic wealth on "sophisticated financial instruments" that were no more than wild bets with taxpayers left holding the empty bag and foreigners holding our assets.

This is why the levees are breaking, the bridges are falling, the roads are full of potholes, the schools are falling apart, and the electric grids are in disrepair. The bankers will not stop until they turn the entire country into New Orleans, post-Katrina. The most productive country on the planet is feeding a tapeworm. According to Catherine Austin Fitts, former undersecretary of HUD, "In a tapeworm economy a small group of insiders

---

107. Russell Mokhiber, and Robert Weissman, Corporate Predators: The Hunt for Mega-Profits and the Attack on Democracy (Monroe, ME: Common Courage Press, 1999), 75.

108. 1984 Grace Commission Report completed by Ronald Reagan and never released. Most Federal tax receipts go not to infrastructure but to pay the debt to the private bank, the Federal Reserve.

centralize political and economic power at the expense of people, living things and the environment, in a manner that destroys real wealth. A tapeworm economy is one in which it is considered acceptable to make money from our [safe living standards] going down. In investment terms, it is an economy with a negative return on investment. It is parasitic in nature."

The way an actual tapeworm operates is to inject its host with a chemical that makes the host crave what is good for the tapeworm and bad for the host. So the Tapeworm Economy is adept at using media and education and numerous financial incentives to get us acting against our own strategic interests and instead supporting and depending on the tapeworm.

The symptoms of the Tapeworm Economy are many—narcotics trafficking that targets our children, runaway exploitive and predatory corporate practices, such as the patenting of life, terminator seeds, and the destruction of our topsoil and food supply, fraudulent inducement of debt to homeowners, students, and consumers, suppression of renewable energy technology, suppression of knowledge of cancer cures, criminal mismanagement of government credit and resources, black budget operations, and the manipulation of currency, financial and precious metal prices and markets. All of such practices introduce organized crime in all aspects of our lives, and the various transactions drain our families and neighborhoods on a daily basis, much like a tapeworm drains its host.[109]

The United States has been systematically de-industrialized and mired in a sea of red ink. The dismantling of the manufacturing base has proceeded apace. The seeds of the industrial destruction were sown by the perpetrators of the Kennedy assassination and the failure of the rule of law to bring the perpetrators to justice in that high crime. The weeds took root with the ascendancy of Richard Nixon and his controller, Henry Kissinger, and their plan to promote the expansion of China at the expense of the United States.

Nixon and Kissinger Turn the U.S. over to Communist China for the Central Bankers

Kissinger and Nixon, the self-professed "Red hater," traveled to the Far East in 1972, to prepare the opening of relations with the totalitarian Chinese state. This was happening against the backdrop of Cold War tensions with the then communist enemies in Russia, China, and in the hot Vietnam War that encompassed Laos and Cambodia as well. Nixon's China visit was a

---

109. Catherine Austin Fitts, "The Tapeworm Economy, Understanding the Drain: Case Study of Dillon, Reed and Company and the Aristocracy of Stock Profits," www.narconews.com/Issue40/article1644.html

major exercise in perception management. Just five short years before the president's visit to China, <u>Time Magazine</u> reported that China was supplying 80 percent of the weapons used against American forces to the Vietcong. The Vietnam War was still raging when Nixon was on this China visit. As expected, this treachery was portrayed in glowing terms by the compliant media as they beamed back photo ops of Nixon shaking hands with Chairman Mao and Chou En Lai. Communist China and its one billion people would be marketed in the U.S. as a nation waiting to be democratized through the mechanisms of "free trade." Chairman Mao's Red Brigades would be forgotten. The Cultural Revolution that brought death, imprisonment, and social disruption to millions was just a memory. Tiananmen Square, when it occurred, would be smoothed over by the vision of a democratized China opening her markets to Mickey Mouse and McDonald's. The overthrow of Tibet was just a blip on the radar screen. Russia had been a diversion all along. It was not the crumbling Berlin Wall that symbolized the end of Communism; it was the treacherous Nixon handshake with Chairman Mao that symbolized the end of the American Republic.

The way had been prepared for the United States Republic to bring Communist China into her fold years before when Philip Jessup, a member of the Council on Foreign Relations, a World Court Justice, and communist, wrote <u>The International Problem of Governing Mankind,</u> in which he stated: "I agree that national sovereignty is the root of the EVIL. The question of procedure remains. Can the root be pulled up by digging around it and cutting the rootless one by one?"[110] The events of 2008 and the further centralization and consolidation of the banking empire answered this question.

Jessup was a member of the Institute of Pacific Relations, which was cited as follows in Senate Report 2050, 82nd Congress, second session: "[T] he Institute of Pacific Relations was a vehicle used by the communists to orientate American far eastern policy toward communist objectives." Carroll Quigley, of course, understated their intent when he wrote, "Many of these experts which were favored by the Far East 'establishment' in the Institute of Pacific Relations were captured by communist ideology. Under its influence they propagandized, as experts, erroneous ideas and sought to influence policy in mistaken directions. For example, they sought to establish, in 1943–1950, that the Chinese communists were simple agrarian reformers rather like the third party groups of the American Midwest."[111] It certainly must be argued that the support of the China lobby was not a "mistake," but a deliberate

---

110. Philip Jessup, <u>The International Problem of Governing Mankind</u> (Claremont CA: Claremont College, 1947).
111. Carroll Quigley, Short title?, 936.

attempt to bring the United States to the position it is in today with respect to its indebtedness to China. The results speak for themselves. Those who create these policies and then get caught with their words, actions, and results can no longer scream conspiracy theory when they have been engaged in intrigue of this kind as a way of life.

Jessup also helped prepare the State Department's infamous White Paper on China. This report lavishly praised the Communists and condemned the then current U.S. ally Nationalist China under Chiang Kai-shek. Later, Jessup became one of the early advocates for the admission of Communist China to the United Nations.[112]   It is clear as Richard Gardner wrote in his 1974 Current Affairs article "The Hard Road to World Order," that these transitional processes are planned well in advance of execution.

I harbor no animosity to China per se. China did not ask to enter the stream of European history. Europe knocked at her door and hooked her on opium. While she was smoking opium, she forgot Confucius and her leaders became corrupt as was inevitable. China, in losing what was sacred to her past and because of her own internal corruption, lost the power to resist the violence and materialism of the West.

The idea that Jessup, Quigley, Brzezinski, Kissinger, and others seek to suppress from the people is that there can be no sovereign state that cannot control its own destiny, and a people can only control their own destiny if they retain control of the state's right to create money and control its value. Once the banking system was given over to a central private authority, namely, the Federal Reserve, it was only a matter of time before that authority had control of the levers of power. As predicted, the people are alienated from their government and stripped of their wealth. Over the eight years of the Bush presidency, the United States witnessed the acceleration of the concentration of wealth and power into the hands of a plutocracy with no accountability. The Obama administration is filled with a new set of members from the same Council on Foreign Relations and the Trilateral Commission that controlled the Bush presidency. The style, but unfortunately, not the substance is the only change this man brings to Washington. This is the true EVIL that Jessup was working for—the process of wealth concentration that destroys the prospect of social justice and a passive government that supports the destruction of its own state. This is why public officials are no longer held to account for crimes against the state. Unfortunately, without social justice, a society is on the path to self-destruction. It does not matter who controls the government; it is who controls the money.

---

112. **Hearings, Institute of Pacific, Relations, SISS, 4938.**

Carroll Quigley identified the perpetrators of this great conspiracy whom he admired when he wrote, "The influence of financial capitalism and of the international bankers who created it was exercised both on business and on governments, but could have done neither if it had not been able to persuade both these to accept two 'axioms' of its own ideology. Both of these were based on the assumption that politicians were too weak and too subject to temporary popular pressures to be trusted with control of the money system; accordingly, the sanctity of all values and the soundness of money must be protected in two ways: by basing the value of money on gold and by allowing bankers to control the supply of money. To do this it was necessary to conceal, or even mislead, both governments and people about the nature of money and its methods of operation."[113] (Emphasis added) The concealment of how the monetary system works so that few, even Wall Street players and certainly not Congressmen or Senators (with the exception of Ron Paul and Dennis Kucinich), have a clue how the fractional reserve system functions and how it parasitizes the wealth of the state by creating inflation. One Congressman, Keith Ellison, when asked by a caller on C-SPAN, a public events viewer call in show, about the parasitism of the Federal Reserve and why the U.S. Congress does not exercise its constitutional prerogative to control the value of money, he responded that he considered the topic so unimportant that it could be discussed over coffee but had no relevance to the current financial crisis. Congressmen like Ellison have succeeded in making themselves irrelevant.

After WWII, Communist China began moving into the global monetary system. In so doing, the American people were being programmed in a step-wise manner to accept this reality even before China was established as a state in 1949. In 1947, Congressman Richard Milhouse Nixon first introduced a motion and later introduced House Concurrent Resolution 68 stating the Congress and the President should take the initiative to call for a general conference of the United Nations "for the purpose of making the United Nations capable of enacting, interpreting, and enforcing world law to prevent war." It seems that Nixon was knee deep in the Communism and globalization business from the very beginning of his career—preparing the way to integrate the economy of the United States with the world economy and the economy of Communist China. Nixon's anti-Communist stance was a mask for public consumption. Kissinger would make sure he played ball.

The coda to this China symphony was played shortly after the 9/11 tragedy on 11 November 2001, when President George W. Bush, quietly and without great fanfare, allowed the entry of Communist China into

---

113. Carroll Quigley, Short title?, 53.

the WTO (World Trade Organization). By 2007, China outpaced the United States in exports and, according to the WTO, at the current rate of growth, will outpace Germany by 2008. Communist China has become so economically powerful that the country has threatened a <u>nuclear option</u> of dollar sales against the U.S. if its trade demands are threatened. China and Japan combined control 40 percent of U.S. debt. If China carries out its threat to liquidate their vast holdings of treasury bonds, it could plunge the United States into more prolonged recession or worse. China has signaled to the world that it wants a new global currency, the translation of which is that she will likely begin limiting her purchase of American debt.

But one must not think about this because the obvious inference is that the United States has lost its autonomy and has become a debtor nation that uses the Federal Reserve to print money for the armies and navies necessary to ensure profitable markets, dollar hegemony and cheap resources. The United States must use force to finance more economic waste. As the U.S. steals from the healthy to finance the unhealthy, there is more death—of people, healthy enterprises, animal species and the environment. The model is working for the international bankers, but the U.S. is reaching its limit of useful primacy to the empire system.

As financial investment bankers promoted the economic rise of China, they simultaneously limited capital availability to onshore productive American business. Limiting capital for productive ventures has encouraged corporations to export their factories to low-wage countries. Available money is then used by the bankers for speculation rather than for investment in productive enterprises. Corporate executives blame the high cost of American labor, and labor blames corporate executives for being short-sighted and unimaginative. Neither of them stops to consider that their lives have been controlled all along by conditions set by banks in making sure that almost every company listed on an exchange is saddled with enormous debt.

Thanks to junk bond king Michael Milkin and the corporate raiders of the high flying '80s, there is barely a concern in the United States that is still standing that can use its own profits to plough back into the company free of bank debt. This is a zero-sum game in which the object of winning is stealing the most without productive activity, and those who actually produce are the losers. It is an upside down world!

Tapeworm bankers are draining the host of its health and energy. As a result of the philosophy and the implementation of globalist policies, the United States is in economic decline. Real wages continue to fall even as productivity gains rise. In 2004, the median income for a man in his 30s, a good predictor of his lifetime earnings, was $35,010, 12 percent less than for men in their 30s in 1974—their fathers' generation—adjusted for inflation.

A decade ago, median income for men in their 30s was $32,901, 5 percent higher than 30 years earlier. The working class has long seen their jobs off-shored. The phenomenon has now moved to highly-trained, highly-skilled workers as well. Income gaps between to top 1 percent and all others are rapidly widening.

State of Black America

A report from the State of Black America 2007 is even more disheartening. Black men are more than twice as likely to be unemployed as white men and make only 74 percent as much a year. Black men are more than six times as likely as white men to be incarcerated, and their average jail sentences tend to be 10 months longer than those of white men.

At the end of 2001, 16.5 percent of the black male population had been to prison compared to 7.7 percent of Hispanic, and 2.7 percent of white men. Young black males between the ages of 15 and 34 years are nine times more likely to be killed by firearms and nearly eight times as likely to have a positive HIV test.

Of single parent black households in 2005, only 12 percent were led by men. More than two-thirds of black children lived in one-parent households in 2005, the majority headed by women.

More than 42 percent of female-headed black households with children were poor, compared with slightly more than 9 percent of married black households. The pressure on the black community is unremitting. A 2008 report on the sub-prime mortgage crisis discovered that African Americans were intentionally targeted by lending institutions for fraudulent and inflationary products, and they have experienced the greatest loss of wealth in American history. A daily radio and television program, <u>Democracy Now</u>, reported that the mortgage crisis will cause people of color to lose as much as $213 billion in assets.

Effect of Globalization on Middle America

Another study from Duke University and Booz Allen, a well-connected consulting firm, noted that companies are increasingly moving sophisticated, mission-critical functions, such as product design and research and development to China, India, and other offshore locations primarily because these countries can provide highly skilled scientific and engineering workers said to be in short supply in the U.S. and Europe. Economic disparities continue to accelerate as the global agenda advances.

Consider this from the June 2007 edition of <u>Foreign Affairs</u>, the journal of the Council on Foreign Relations (CFR) in which global plutocrats speak to each other:

> Between 2000 and 2003 alone, foreign firms built 60,000 manufacturing plants in China. European chemical companies, Japanese carmakers, and U.S. industrial conglomerates are all building factories in China to supply export markets around the world. Similarly, banks, insurance companies, professional-service firms, and IT companies are building R&D and service centers in India to support employees, customers, and production worldwide.[114]

Jessup was not mistaken. The plans he made in the 20th century to root out the EVIL of state sovereignty are bearing fruit as we cyclone into the 21st century. The result is that states like Michigan and Ohio, two of the heartland states important to the industrial age, are in an economic depression and will remain so for the foreseeable future because of the China and NAFTA (North American Free Trade Agreement) trade policies.[115] Most of the factories that created the mid-century American dream are now shuttered—permanently. The promise of an American economic dynamo based on a service economy model hyped by supply-side zealots and protégés of Milton Friedman from the University of Chicago school of thought has morphed into what the elite knew was coming all along: a lower wage, lowered expectations, and debt-filled nightmare for millions of working Americans. Middle-class dreams are being deferred. Americans who sought to limit global trade for more favorable terms were shouted down with the <u>isolationist</u> epithet. At the World Economic Forum held in Davos, Switzerland, in the spring of 2007, corporate executives were heard talking enthusiastically about outsourcing 40 million high-skilled American jobs to other countries. In 2008, a year of presidential politics, neither candidate expressed a vision for a sound economic future for the United States. President Bush, a so-called economic <u>conservative</u>, spent public money like a drunken sailor. President Obama is continuing the trend.

---

114. Samuel Palmisano, "The Globally Integrated Enterprise," <u>Foreign Affairs 130</u>, June 2007.

115. During the first year of NAFTA, wages in Mexico declined 40 to 50 percent, but the cost of living rose 80 percent. Over 20,000 small and medium businesses failed, and more than a thousand state-owned enterprises were privatized. As one scholar observed, "Neoliberalism means the neo-colonization of Latin America."

The people of the United States have been so mired in a sea of conflicting interests that while they quibble and harp at each other about being on the right or on the left, the country's wealth is being shifted away from them to the top 1 percent of the population by tax schemes, legal loopholes, and outright fraud that is endorsed by both major political parties. They seethe in frustration as cities drown, bridges crumble, electricity grids fail, as drugs and illegal immigrants, refugees from the economic policies implemented by their government, flood their communities, as their jobs get shipped offshore, and their children die in foreign lands while the oil revenue that was promised to pay for this grand folly is siphoned off un-metered and unpaid for by oil cartels with soaring profits. Former head of the Federal Reserve, Alan Greenspan, stated unequivocally that the Iraq War was waged for oil, and it barely created a whisper among the chattering class.[116] A country without a vision is a country without a future!

Coda: Infant Mortality and Illegal Drugs: The Canary in the Coal Mine

Some medical outcomes are powerful indicators of the economic and social well being of a people. One such indicator is the infant mortality rate. The rate is calculated in deaths per 1000. By 2007, infant mortality rates, declining or stagnant for many years, began to climb. The infant mortality rate in the Mississippi Delta for African American babies is 17 per 1000, as high as Sri Lanka or Russia. Smaller rises were also seen in Alabama, North Carolina, Tennessee, Louisiana, and South Carolina. In 2003, the national average for blacks (14) was more than twice the rate for whites (5.7). These increases can be directly tied to the deteriorating economic conditions in the region and to cutbacks in Medicaid and welfare reform.

The betrayal of American people and their potential is a bipartisan agenda. NAFTA, the trade agreement that hastened the demise of the industrial base was overwhelmingly passed by a Republican Congress headed by Newt Gingrich and signed into law by Democratic President Bill Clinton. This trade agreement was supported and promoted by the Business Roundtable made up of about two hundred corporate executives who disavow commitment to national interests (just as advocated by Communist Phillip Jessup) and are largely white, male, and over fifty. Under this ongoing treaty arrangement, they have proposed a superstate structure, the North American Union that would legally supersede the U.S. Constitution and would be leap years removed from the bothersome rabble. Democracy would remain in

---

116. Graham Paterson, <u>Timesonline</u>, 16 September 2007.

form but not in function. The criminal element posing as businessmen and bankers that have historically functioned in the shadows or under the cover of law have become emboldened by their successes.

The "giant sucking sound" (alluded to by Ross Perot during his 1992 presidential bid) of jobs whirling down the drain of free trade and across borders as a result of multiple business friendly trade agreements has come to pass. Mexico has become a narco-state with an estimated 12 percent of its GDP accruing from the illegal drug trade. The Mexican–US border is porous to narcotics trafficking. The NewYorkTimes reported that up to 70 percent of the cocaine consumed in this country is slipped across the U.S.–Mexican border by smugglers working with Colombia's drug cartels. Today, it is claimed that much of this drug movement is executed by illegal immigrants carrying contraband across the border. Drugs are also smuggled under the border through tunnels. However, illegal immigrants do not own planes, ships, and trucks, nor do they control the various alphabet agencies that are trained to look the other way when a drug bust leads to a big fish. They also do not control the military bases and supply terminals where these drugs are held for transfer to the street and they certainly to not control the banks and businesses through with drug money is laundered.

In February 2007, Daniel Hopsiker reported in The Mad Cow News, according to documents filed in U.S. District Court for the Southern District of Florida, that "four more American planes were seized from the 50-plane fleet of drug running aircraft amassed by Mexico's Sinaloa Cartel. Coincidentally or not, the American owners of the four planes (like the two busted earlier) were largely people and companies with special relationships with U.S. political movers and shakers, including the CIA and the U.S. Department of Homeland Security. Court filings indicated that the money to purchase the planes was laundered through a bank, whose Chairman, Dennis Nixon, is the South Texas Co-chair of John McCain's campaign. Nixon was a Bush Pioneer and Ranger in George W. Bush's two presidential campaigns. He raised $300,000 in one night for Bush's re-election bid in the Texas border town of Laredo."[117] This story will never make the nightly news. The paper of record, The New York Times, will never find this major news story "fit" to print.

There is historical precedence for this silence, especially since during the Reagan years it is now known that the then vice-president, George H.W. Bush, was working with Oliver North who was arranging drug deals to pay for Iran-Contra, an illegal operation run out of President Reagan's White

---

117. www.madcowprod.com/02072008.html.

House. Unlike people who live in lower-income public housing, he did not get evicted for that crime, he got promoted to President.[118]

The beauty of NAFTA for drug smugglers is that there is now less constraint on them to import their product. They can simply carry their illegal goods across the border in trucks and on ships and planes, and can do so with little fear of being caught. U.S. customs officials are already so overworked that they often have less than five minutes to inspect cargo in trucks crossing the border from Mexico. The shipping ports and private airports are free-for-all, with little oversight inspection. The 9/11 hijackers were linked to a narco-airport in Venice, Florida.[119]

The Department of Homeland Security should be renamed the Department of Drug Running Security. Lax border security is an open invitation to smuggle. American, Colombian, and Mexican drug traffickers all accept the invitation. Dealers with lucrative profits have bought planes, factories, and trucking companies that they can use as fronts for smuggling operations. However, their most important acquisitions are politicians, members of enforcement agencies, judges, and the media. When government officials claim that stopping this traffic is nearly impossible, it must be remembered that during WWII there was a moral will to stop contraband and spies from entering the country. The borders and ports were tightly controlled. Drug running declined precipitously.

Free trade and drug smuggling are not new phenomena supported by the economic and political structure of the United States. It is an old story that harks back to the British East India Company. To understand what is going on today, it is necessary to consider the long history of narco-trafficking and the central roll it has played in the economic development of Europe and the United States.

The history of drug smuggling as a standard business practice is a history some would like to keep well hidden. A review of this hidden history gives a deeper insight into the thinking and strategy of a small number of elites who have managed to engage most of the world in their maniacal financial and opium/cocaine-filled schemes. The ultimate goal is to control the world's destiny by controlling its finances through central banking structures and with scarlet money they leach tax free by bringing the misery of drug addiction as part of their globalized free-trade deals.

---

118. Gary Webb, Dark Alliance: The CIA, the Contras, and the Crack Cocaine Explosion. (Seven Stories Press, New York 1998).
119. Daniel Hopsicker, Welcome to Terrorland: Mohamed Atta & the 9-11 Cover-up in Florida (Eugene, Oregon: The Mad Cow Press, 2004).

The American people are under attack, and their country is in decline. They know something is wrong. They can see the changes. Their education system has robbed them of their analytical ability, and mass media have phased their brain waves into a permanently hypnotized alpha state. It seems unlikely that they will awaken from their hypnotic trance in time to save themselves. When the ultimate collapse comes, perhaps they will rouse from their slumber and take to the streets like the Argentineans in 2000–01 when their economy collapsed. They forced out a procession of four presidents in three weeks. Their uprising was not directed at a particular party but at corruption in the abstract and the current economic model of deregulated capitalism. In the streets, they used pots and pans to create a cacophonous noise while they shouted: "¡Que se vayan todos!" All of them must go!

Chapter 6

The British East India Company, Opium is King

○ ○

It seems that despite the advantages Europeans gained in "discovering" the New World and in developing a global trading system, that nothing much changed until global productive forces were significantly rearranged, and that did not take place until Europeans began to develop the global drug trade that gave them the clear edge. Even then, with their dominance over sugar, alcohol, tobacco, coffee and tea, it was still not enough to crack Asian resistance. Asia had to be brought down by something else, and that was opium

The decision by a state to sell opium to its subjects always took place in situations of political decline or at least weakness

> *Carl A. Trocki, <u>Opium, Empire</u>*
> *<u>and the Global Political Economy</u>.*

According to the United Nations, total worldwide revenues of the "transnational criminal organizations" (TCOs) are of the order of one trillion dollars, representing an amount equivalent to the combined GDP of the group of low income countries (with a population of 3 billion people).

> *Michel Chossudovsky, <u>The Globalization of Poverty</u>*
> *<u>and the New World Order</u>*

Free trade is an interesting concept and a perfect example of Orwellian double-speak. At best, it means letting the state apparatus allow business to make its own rules free of state intervention, but it is more insidious than that. It is a philosophy that considers protection of domestic manufacturers by prohibitions, discriminating duties, and commercial regulations as has been historically practiced by every successful nation adverse to business interests. Free trade is an aggressive policy of foreign traders whose arrogant and grasping spirit of monopoly determines business practices by elevation of one national interest to the detriment of other nations' interests and ultimately the elevation of banking and financial interests to the exclusion of all others.

In today's world, free trade is exemplified by the machinations of financial institutions using creative financial instruments and corporations using the taxpayer funded state apparatus including the military and taxpayer supported mercenaries to capture global markets to create monopolies by contract or the barrel of a gun. It has even been referred to rather tongue in cheek as "gun-boat diplomacy." Free trade encompasses piracy, dope pushing, human organ trafficking, slavery, and mass murder in pursuit of economic goals supported by a state structure. Britain's economic strangulation of its colonies in accordance with this philosophy ultimately led to the American Revolution, but British polices were hardly a new phenomenon.

The Dutch East India Company was one such successful crime syndicate until it was outmaneuvered by the more powerful British East India Company. The Dutch had pacified Indonesia with opium. The British would do the same thing on a much larger scale to China—and eventually to the United States. The China trade, like slavery, had nothing to do with morality, but with economic interests. It had nothing to do with vice or virtue, but with profit.

To reverse the exodus of silver from the China trade, which threatened the financial underpinnings of the British state, King George III mandated the East India Company to ship large quantities of opium from Bengal in the British Crown Colony of India to China. The dual objective was to alter the balance of payments deficit in Britain's favor and to foster drug addiction among China's mandarin class. By the time of the American Revolution, East India Company opium trafficking into China was officially reported to be twenty times the absolute limit of opium required for medical and related use.[120]

---

120. The U.S. Labor Party Investigating Team, Dope, Inc.: Britain's Opium War Against the U.S. (New York: Benjamin Franklin House New York, 1978), 12–13.

In a very direct sense, the Founding Fathers of the United States fought against the British Crown's opium policy during the American Revolution. Adam Smith, so venerated by today's global peddlers, argued in his book Wealth of Nations that opium, like corn and tobacco, was a legitimate product, the same as these other commodities, and that the objective laws of the "invisible hand" must be allowed to determine all economic activity. Anything which stood in the way, such as other national governments, was an obstacle which must be removed.[121] Smith advocated a massive increase of East India Company opium exports to China. The money from opium trading made up a sizable portion of the war chest that financed Britain's deployment of Hessian mercenaries into North America to crush the rebellion.[122] The rebellion was caused in part by the 1773 passage of the Tea Act, a tax from which the British East India Company (BEIC) was exempted. What is remarkable is that drug money is still used by clandestine international agencies to crush democratic aspirations around the globe.

The British East India Company ascended to power through bribery, corruption, and murder, all sanctioned by the state. It trafficked in both drugs and humans. In 1661, King Charles (Stuart) II granted the East India Company power to add to its charter the right to make peace or war with sovereign nations. This was an extraordinary, without parallel concession. Here was a private company given the power to make war with a sovereign nation![123] The BEIC never employed more than 150,000 mercenaries, but the power of the company was so great that they had at their disposal the British Army to fight two opium wars. They were successful in forcing opium into China, and their free trade policy, sustained by the barrel of a gun, successfully destroyed the economies of both India and China. Under British rule, just one state in India, Bengal, recorded at least 10 million deaths from starvation in 1769–70. Before the British demanded expanded cultivation of poppies for export, this area of rich delta river soil had supplied much of India with agricultural products.

The spread of opium use among the Chinese was facilitated by the China Inland Mission, protestant missionaries, who taught the Chinese "coolies" how to smoke opium for recreational purposes. In true Adam Smith style, by first creating an economic demand and then filling it, a vast opium market

---

121. Robert,Trout, "The Chinese Opium Wars," Adam Smith, Critical Assessments, edited by John Cunningham Wood (New York: Routledge, 2004).

122. Ibid., 13.

123. John Coleman The Conspirators' Hierarchy: The Committee of 300 (Las Vegas, NE: Global Review Publications 2006), 51.

was created and met by the BEIC, which brought enormous fortunes to its shareholders.[124]

By forcing opium on China, the British altered the centuries old social dynamic of culturally acceptable drug use. Since human life evolved, most cultures have made use of naturally occurring chemical substances for mind- or mood-altering properties. Almost every human culture made use of some drug, including opium. Its use was most often within the context of a highly ritualized religious, social, or medical practice. Whether it was opium, cannabis, coca, tobacco, alcohol, coffee, tea, betel, or one of the many other vegetable products, humans have regularly had recourse to some selection of them as use to soothe their bodies and spirits. Drugs, used in this social context, were controlled by the cultural dynamics of each society. All of this changed dramatically with the British importation of opium into China.

Before British commercialization of opiates, populations and nations were not habituated to the use of drugs, nor were they used as a product of commerce requiring vast production and distribution channels. The introduction and promotion of an addictive substance for use outside its cultural context as a commercial product is perhaps one of the most pervasive evils introduced by Western civilization to the world. The destructive nature of opium was well known at the time of the opium wars. Opium is highly addictive and induces passivity into the smoker. Addicts seldom lived past age fifty; heavy smokers had a life expectancy of only five years after becoming addicted.

The most famous and lasting of the opium trading houses was the firm of Jardine and Matheson. By the 1830s, they reportedly handled 6,000 chests per year for an annual profit of $100,000.[125] Jardine's main competition was from David Sasson, who belonged to a Jewish trading family that had long been established in Persia and was recorded to have shipped opium to Canton on his own account as early as 1834.[126] After the second Opium War, once opium was legalized, locally based traders, among whom were Parsi, Armenians, Jews, and Muslims, also played an important role in the trade.

What the British did was to commercialize drug production, trade, and marketing, which links these drugs to the development of capitalism. Addicting large populations to drugs has been associated with a number of fundamental transformations in human life, one of which was the appearance of large plantations worked by slave labor where a drug is produced for sale at some distant location. The trade in drugs usually results in a monopoly,

---

124. Ibid., 257.
125. Trocki, 101.
126. Trocki, 113

which not only centralizes drug trafficking but also restructures the social and economic terrain in the process. Two major effects are the creation of mass markets and the generation of enormous cash flows. The accumulation of wealth created by this historic and successive drug trading was among the primary foundations of global capitalism and the modern nation-state. However, Henry Carey, an American economist who believed in appropriate trade barriers to protect the development of national industries, observed that the system was essentially unstable and contained an inherent tendency toward bankruptcy, which required it to constantly find new sources to loot. It may be argued that the entire rise of the West, from 1500 to 1900 depended on a series of drug trades.[127] The drug trade has never ceased being an important part of global capital flows.

The cash flow out of China from this product into the hands of British and American merchants provided the financial capital to bankroll their own transition to modern industrial and corporate capitalism. The money from drugs has also financed the transition of the U.S. economy to the current phase—financial capitalism and the parasitic tapeworm economic model. The parasitic model has been so effective in destroying the energy and vitality of other nations; it is now being employed successfully in the United States to bring her ultimately into a global centralized banking structure.

The BEIC initiated and mastered the concepts of the free trade movement, just as their global counterparts are implementing them currently. To accrue large capital assets, an investor must depend on cheap labor. Current prices are kept low by the use of cheap labor pools in South East Asia, Africa, and Latin America as the result of trade agreements, such as NAFTA (North American Free Trade Agreement), GATT (General Agreements on Tariffs and Trade) and the WTO (World Trade Organization). When BEIC ruled world trade, the slave labor of India and the American South and the underpaid workers of industrial cities in major European urban areas provided low labor costs. Forcing people to work for nothing naturally pushed wages to rock bottom for those workers with the illusion that they were free. The slave and cotton trade in the South was run to a significant degree by the same families that also operated the opium traffic in the Orient. It was just business. One such family was the Dulles family, who produced the first director of the CIA and a secretary of state.

According to Anton Chaiken, "The Dulles family's upper class-status in America began when ancestor William Dulles arrived in South Carolina from India. With a fortune made in India by providing financial and

---

127. Carl A. Trocki, Opium, Empire and the Global Political Economy: A Study of the Asian Opium Trade 1750–1950 (New York: Routledge, 1999), xii.

security services for the British East India Company army, he bought a slave plantation which the family held through the American Civil War. The family's mental life was always that of the British Empire and its American colonial subordinates.

Allen Dulles's main corporate activity was as a director of the J. Henry Schroder banking company in London, a prime instrument in Montagu Norman's nazification of Germany. As partners in the Sullivan and Cromwell firm, Allen Dulles and his brother John Foster Dulles represented the Rockefeller-Harriman-Warburg combination, I.G. Farben, and virtully every other Nazi corporate organization that danced on London's marionette strings."[128]

The East India Company flooded the Indian market with inexpensive cotton goods from the slave plantations of the American South. This effectively killed the Indian cotton industry and put thousands of Indian farmers out of business. In 1810, India was exporting more textiles to England than England was exporting to India. By 1830, the trade flow was reversed. The British had put up prohibitive tariff barriers to shut out Indian finished goods and were dumping their commodities in India, a practice backed by British gunboats and military force. Within a matter of years, the great textile centers of Dacca and Madras were turned into ghost towns. By 1850, India's debt had grown to 53 million pounds. Between 1850 and 1900, the per capita income dropped by almost two thirds.[129] Does any of this seem eerily similar to China dumping cheap goods in the United States while keeping their tariffs high to U.S goods, with the result that major economic centers, such as Detroit and Youngstown, are turning into ghost towns? Recent trends show that Michigan and Ohio have been battered by both escalating job and population losses as automobile manufacturing is shipped abroad. The steel mills have been gone for more than twenty years, and Akron has long since stopped making rubber. The textile mills in the Carolinas are shuttered.

BEIC chose to expand opium production to offset the decline in tax revenues.[130] They expanded the opium business out of Bengal and surrounding States and fought two wars with China so that they could dump this poison onto their markets. Thus, four main workforces bent to their will—the laborers in Britain, the laborers and the enslaved in the United States, the

128. "British Psychiatry: From Eugenics to Assassination," Executive Intelligence Review 21 (30 July 2002),, 40.

129. Carolyn Baker, U.S. History Uncensored: What Your High School Textbook Didn't Tell You (Lincoln, NB: iUniverse, 2006), 41.

130. Today's headline might read, "The U.S. Expands Mission in Afghanistan to Increase Poppy Production to offset the decline in Tax Revenues."

peasant farmers of India, and the laborers in China. Opium was the tool the merchant classes used in transforming landless peasantry into proletarians and in monetizing their subsistence lifestyle. Opium created pools of capital and fed the institutions that accumulated it—the banking and financial systems, the insurance system, and transportation and information infrastructures. Those structures and that economy have, in large part, been inherited by successor nations of the region today.

Selling opium was highly profitable and reversed the trade imbalance between China and England, with England (and New England) growing wealthy from the violent projection of their one competitive advantage— unbridled savagery.

The enormous profits generated by opium exports had disastrous social and political effects on China and India, but British and American manufacturers came to depend on this profitability. The opium trade created profound dislocations throughout Asia. In 1770, at least 10 million people, one third of the population of Bengal, perished from starvation under British rule as a result of drought, food exports, and land cultivation in poppies for maximum profit.

In Java and the Malay Peninsula opium created a class of consumers, elite and subaltern, whose dependency on the drug boded ill for the stability of existing structures of civic and political authority. Opium consumption subverted the social fabric of indigenous society in Southeast Asia, much as its conditions of production under British East India Company rule wrought a violent transformation to the life and labor of peasants in Bengal and Bihar. The use of force by the British, through two opium wars, to push this product into China simply underscores that social values are malleable against powerful instruments of the market system. Nevertheless, a drug epidemic took hold, and it was profitable.

It is clear that many drugs, legal and illegal, are poisons when used chronically or inappropriately, and they can kill or seriously impair the user's health. Opium possessed the additional quality of being addictive. Thus addicts require a regular and often continually increasing supply of the substance. At some point, where the use of the drug becomes habitual, the user suffers not only loss of wealth, but ill health, apparent loss of "free will," and death may shortly follow. Heavy opium smokers had a much shortened life span.

By the mid-19th and early 20th centuries, physicians had begun to make note of infectious complications among opiate addicts. The involvement of the immune system in various aspects associated with the chronic use of opioids was suggested as early as 1844. The cells of the immune system possess opiate receptors that, when activated, induce a variety of functional modifications, such as the establishment of profound immune suppression.[131]

By 1916, the use of the term infectious diseases as a common cause of opiate addiction was doctrine. Physicians were also beginning to note the effect of morphine on the immune system.[132] Cloetta, in a study done in 1902, showed that chronic morphine injections resulted in leucopenia (decrease in white blood cells) in rabbits, and leucopenia in morphine addicts was described as early as 1901 by Archard and Loeper. In 1898, Cantacuzene showed that morphine modulated the expression of chemotactic and phagocytic activity both in vitro and in vivo experimental systems. He also showed that morphine-treated guinea pigs had a greater mortality rate than controls after peritoneal (intra-abdominal) injection of cholera bacilli.[133] Thus, it is clear that the immune-suppressive effects of opiates and the associated infections were well known for almost a hundred years and were well described in the literature.

Opium prepared the ground for the rise of capitalism by creating mass markets and proletarian consumers while undermining the morale and morality of political elites throughout Asia. Drug trading destabilizes existing societies not merely because they destroy individual human beings but also, and perhaps more importantly, because they have the power to undercut the existing political economy of any state.

By the early 20th century, Chinese warlords had adapted the pattern pioneered by the East India Company. They dragooned communities of peasants or tribal peoples into the cultivation of opium so they could market it to soldiers and bureaucrats at a profit in order to supply themselves with weapons. After 1927, Chiang Kai-shek, in his drive to unify China, embraced the warlords of Sichuan and Yunnan but did little to alter the economic base. In fact, when he took over Shanghai in 1927 he joined forces with gangster Du Yuesheng. Not only did Du aid Chiang in his massacre of the Communists and the Guomindang left wing but he also helped finance the fledgling Nationalist regime with his control of the area's opium revenues.[134]

The alliance between Chiang and Du's Green Gang was a very profitable one. In the very first year after the success of the Northern Expedition, the

131. N.P. Plotnikoff et al., Cytokines: Stress and Immunity (New York: CRC Press, 2006), 258.

132. Herman Freedman, Thomas Kline, Steven Specter, Drugs of Abuse, Immunity and Infection (New York: CRC Press, 1996), 5.

133. Freedman et al., 5.

134. Martin, Brian G., "The Green Gang and the Guomindang State: Du Yuesheng and the Politics of Shanghai, 1927-1927" Journal of Asian Studies 54 (1) February,1995, 82-3.

new Nationalist government gained $40 million in opium revenue, and by 1933, the income had jumped to $30 million monthly. [135] At that time, China was producing seven-eights of the global opium supply and both Du's Da Kongsi [The Big Company] and the Japanese in Tianjin had set up laboratories producing both morphine and heroin. In fact, the production levels of opiates now gave China a surplus that made it possible for China to turn the tables on the Western powers and begin exporting drugs to the United States and Europe.

American gangsters, beginning with Arnold Rothstein and going on to Meyer Lansky, Charles "Lucky" Luciano, Louis "Lepke" Buchalter, and Jasha Katsenberg, forged links with Chinese drug lords, both in Shanghai and California, to obtain supplies for the growing American narcotics market.[136] The association with these gangsters makes sense when one considers where the money comes from to support a drug habit. It is not through street muggings or well-paying jobs but substantially from organized crime activity: the numbers racket, bookmaking, protection rackets, auto theft, stolen auto parts distribution, prostitution, pornography, arson-for-hire, and similar illegal activities. Drug addiction could not exist without organized crime to provide the means of financing it.

The CIA's alliance with drug lords in the late 1940s came at a time when the global opium trade was at a two-hundred years' nadir as a result of WWII, which had disrupted international shipping and imposed tight waterfront security that blocked the smuggling of heroin into the United States. As America's narcotics use fell to its lowest level in half a century, the purity of imported heroin packets dropped from 28 percent in 1938 to only 3 percent three years later. America's addict population plummeted from 200,000 in 1924 to a tenth of that figure in 1944–45.[137] As a result of this decline, the possibility existed that heroin addiction might eventually disappear as a major social problem in the United States. Heroin supplies were small, international criminal syndicates were in disarray, and the American addict population was at a level where treatment was finally possible.

Within a decade, with the help of the aforementioned gangsters and the clandestine agencies of Britain and the United States, including a CIA headed

---

135. Marshall, J., "Opium and the Politics of Gangsterism in Nationalist China, 1927-1945" Bulletin of Concerned Asian Scholars 8 (3), July-Sept. 1976, 20-2

136. Ibid 29-30

137. U.S. Bureau of Narcotics and Dangerous Drugs, "The World Opium Situation" (Washington, DC, Oct. 1970), 10; U. S. State Department Bureau of International Narcotics Matters, <u>International Narcotics Control Strategy Report</u> (March 1990, No. 9749): 19–20.

by Allen Dulles whose family had a historical tie to the drug trade, the heroin industry had revived. By the early 1950s the global drug syndicates were again in operation. The Southeast Asian poppy fields were expanding, and heroin refineries were multiplying in both Marseille and Hong Kong. Many of the reasons for the revival of the illicit narcotics trade lie with the conduct of U.S. foreign policy and its covert action arm.[138]

During the post-WWII years, which have come to be known as the Cold War, Communism was used as the foil against which the U.S made alignments with international gangsters. From 1948 to 1950, the CIA allied itself with the Corsican underworld in its power grab against the French Communist Party for control over the strategic Mediterranean port of Marseille. With the help of the CIA, the Corsicans gained control over the Marseille waterfront, and for the next quarter of a century used that control to export heroin to the U.S. market.

Meanwhile, the CIA was also busy running covert operations in Southeast Asia along the China border in an area that has become known as the golden triangle. This is one of the most productive poppy-growing regions in the world. In 1951, the agency supported the formation of the Nationalist Chinese army for a covert invasion of southwestern China. When the invasion attempts failed in 1951–1952, the CIA installed Nationalist troops along the Burma–China border as a tripwire for an anticipated Communist Chinese invasion of Southeast Asia. Over the ensuing years, the Nationalist Army transformed Burma's Shan states into the world's largest opium producer.[139] The same tactics were applied to Laos. The CIA worked with Hmong tribesmen and used the CIA airline Air America to transport opium from Hmong villages to laboratories in the golden triangle. In their first years of operation, the laboratories exported high-grade heroin to U.S. troops fighting in Vietnam. After the U.S. withdrawal from Vietnam, the laboratories in the golden triangle exported heroin directly to the United States and captured one-third of the American heroin market.[140]

The Vietnam War compounded the drug epidemic in the United States that had begun with the CIA's exploration of LSD and other psychotropic drugs in the 1950s and 1960s. After the Vietnam War, the drug epidemic exploded from the urban centers and college campuses to small cities and towns throughout the entire nation. Only since Henry Kissinger's 1972 trip to China during the Vietnam conflict has the Chinese Communist role in

---

138. Alfred W. McCoy, The Politics of Heroin: CIA Complicity in the Global Drug Trade (Chicago: Lawrence Hill Books, 1972), 18.
139. Alfred W McCoy. 18–19.
140. Ibid.

the world opium trade been out of the headlines. The American, European, Japanese, and Soviet authorities had long insisted that Peking was a major primary producer and exporter of opium and its derivatives. According to Dope, Inc., Peking makes its real profits not from exports, but from wholesaling, retailing, and financing the opium traffic, mainly through Hong Kong where the big money is made, and Peking is a 40 to 60 percent partner with the British oligarchy in the far Eastern narcotics trade.[141] Just as in Southeast Asia, the flood of drugs, both legal and illegal, into America has not been without severe medical and social consequence. AIDS is just one of those consequences.

In 1981, six years after the end of the Vietnam War and four years before the Iran-Contra drug running, illegal weapons sales, and money-laundering scandal erupted, the CDC reported about five cases in Los Angeles of patients who suffered from the known fungus pneumocystis carinii pneumonia. Pneumocystis carinii lives quietly in 20 percent of the population without causing disease. A fungal overgrowth is characteristic of a metabolic system that is oxidized and acidic and may also arise from an overuse of antibiotics. Instead of focusing on these reversible metabolic anomalies, the CDC used this opportunity to raise an epidemic alarm to terrorize the entire world into believing that there was a new virus that was sexually transmitted, incurable, and could possibly kill off a substantial number of the world's population.

The CDC and the mainstream media began to claim that this new virus was transmitted by homosexual activity and through blood products in the West, but that the disease originated in Africa where it was transmitted by heterosexual sex. This new "sex plague" terror was the perfect opportunity to transfer the funds from Nixon's dying, wasteful and illusory war on cancer to the new war on AIDS. Fighting AIDS would be the pretext and cover story for the consequences of dumping drugs, both legal and illegal, onto the Western market. The only problem was that there was no AIDS epidemic; it was a drug epidemic. The medical consequences of two epidemics, drugs and poverty, would be turned into another profit center. The same people who could not find a viral cause of cancer would now proclaim that the same type of benign passenger RNA virus that they could not prove caused cancer could cause a selective immune deficiency that eventually expanded to cover twenty-nine different diseases. It was a rebranding stroke of genius, but it was a BIG LIE from the very beginning.

---

141. Dope, Inc., The U.S. Labor Party Investigating Team (

Just Who Is in Charge? — New England Opium Lords

There were families in New England who participated in the China trade. Many historians have asserted that the economic fortunes of this nation were built on the backs of imported Africans. Court historians have removed the story from the American narrative about many of the same slave-trading families involvement in another sordid history, that of narcotics smuggling. Many of the families have been able to buy respectability. They have become some of the most prominent and revered American icons for their ability to accumulate enormous capital and their participation in public life. The methods used to accumulate the capital through the free trade sale of humans and drugs have been conveniently removed from "responsible" historical records.

The beautiful clipper ships out of New England were racing on the high seas not only with cargoes of tea, silks, and porcelain but also and mainly with opium. The clipper ships changed the China opium trade completely. They could make three voyages per year from either side of India, and they did not have to stop along the way to buy or sell miscellaneous cargo as did the local country ships. Their loads of opium and specie were so valuable that they could afford to be dedicated to them alone.[142] Jardine Matheson, Dent & Company, David Sassoon and the American firm Russell & Co., quickly emerged as the dominant houses in the China opium trade.

Opium was the premier cash crop that fueled the British Empire to supremacy, brought fortunes to New England and endowments to the great eastern universities: Yale, Princeton, Harvard, and Columbia. It was opium rather than cotton that was truly king of the international commodities trade. From this money born of misery descended the masters of global business interests and intrigue that ultimately morphed into the clandestine intelligence agencies typified by the CIA and the British MI6. Wall Street lawyer and banker Clark Clifford formulated the National Security Act of 1947 that created the CIA. Clark Clifford is the man who brought the CIA-backed drug bank BCCI into the United States. Allen Dulles, who virtually designed the CIA and served as its director, and his brother John Foster Dulles, who served as Eisenhower's secretary of state, were Wall Street lawyers from the firm Sullivan and Cromwell. Dwight Eisenhower's personal liaison with the CIA was none other than Nelson Rockefeller. William Casey was chairman of the Securities and Exchange Commission under Richard Nixon. Former CIA Directors from William Raborn, Jr. to William Webster

---

142. Trocki, 105.

to Robert Gates to James Woolsey to John Deutch all sit or have sat on the Boards of the largest, richest, and most powerful companies in America.[143] General Walter Bedell Smith served as ambassador to the Soviet Union from 1946 to 1948. He was director of Central Intelligence from 1950 to 1953. All seven persons who are known to have served as deputy directors of the CIA under Truman and Smith came from New York legal and financial circles. Frank G. Wisner (OSS) came to the government in 1948 from the Wall Street legal firm of Carter, Ledyard, and Milburn, which represented various Rockefeller, Whitney, and Standard Oil interests. As director of the Office of Policy Coordination, which became the CIA's Plans and Division, on 4 January 1951, Wisner was in charge of the CIA's covert operations.

William Harding Jackson was Smith's deputy director in 1950–51. He had been with Carter, Ledyard and Milburn from 1934 to 1947 and was at the time of his service an investment partner of John Hay Whitney on the board of Banker's Trust.

Allen Welsh Dulles was a wartime director of J. Henry Schroder Banking Corporation whose funding of I.G. Farben and of steel magnate Fritz Thyssen helped finance Hitler's rise to power. As noted, he was a longtime partner of Sullivan and Cromwell.

Murry McConnell was president of the Manufacturers Capital Corporation on Wall Street and CIA deputy director for administration in 1950 and 1951.

Walter Reid Wolf was a vice president of the National City Bank of New York and its investment affiliate City Bank Farmers Trust. He was CIA deputy director (presumably McConnel's successor) from 1951 to 1953.

Robert Amory Jr. (son of a New York manufacturer who was a co-director of at least three Boston firms with directors of United Fruit) came to the CIA as deputy director for intelligence in 1952 (according to Who's Who).

Loftus E. Becker was with the Wall Street law firm Cahill, Gordon, Reindel, and Ohl (representing the investment firms of Dillon Read and Stone and Webster). He went on leave to the CIA in April 1951 and was named deputy director for intelligence (according to the Martindale-Hubbard Law Directory, 1965, 4707) for a year beginning 21 January 1952.

All of these men except Becker were listed in the select New York Social Register. Thus, they were members not only of New York's financial and legal elite but also its hereditary upper class. The importance of this is the known links between CIA and Civil Air transport-Air America planes flying drugs

---

143. Michael Ruppert, "CIA,Drugs and Wall Street,", www.fromthewilderness. com.

in Southeast Asia that date from this period when New York finance enjoyed a monopoly over the CIA's top civilian appointments.[144]

As times changed, the family trade went from clipper ships on the high seas to cargo ships, and then transport planes that could cover much more territory and allowed the drug trade to explode world wide and for profits to amass and to be laundered through Wall Street Banks and corporations traded on the stock exchanges.

Americans have been taught that the various U.S. intelligence agencies are ostensibly public enterprises designed to protect the public good. The sad fact is that their primary mission has always been to protect private business interests at public expense. These agencies have demonstrated a natural affinity for working with criminal syndicates. Both are practitioners of "clandestine arts"—the basic skill of operating outside the normal channels of civil society. In some instances, the CIA undermines the activities of other government agencies: ". . . CIA covert operations have often overwhelmed the interdiction efforts of the weaker U.S. drug enforcement agencies. In Southeast Asia, for example, the U.S. Bureau of Narcotics opened its first office in Bangkok with just three agents in the late 1960s, more than a decade after a major CIA covert operation—backed by several hundred agents and a fleet of aircraft—had installed a 12,000-man opium army in the mountains of northern Burma. While a handful of drug agents worked out of lowland offices trying to intercept drug shipments or discover the names of smugglers, the CIA's massive covert apparatus had been operating in the opium highlands allied with the very drug lords that the U.S. drug agents were trying to arrest.[145]

The drug running families that were the impetus for establishing the clandestine services have had a long history in this underhanded business and have long known the social, economic, and physiological damage that opium did to China and the Chinese people. For two centuries, they were unable to create a major market for their product in the United States. There was an effort to bring opium into the United States when Chinese laborers, so-called coolies, were used to build the intercontinental railways. The first large-scale importation of opium into the United States was referred to as the coolie trade by its British, Hong Kong, and Shanghai sponsors. Even before the Civil War, the same British trading companies behind the slave trade into the South were running a huge market in Chinese indentured servants

---

144. Peter Dale Scott, Drugs, Oil, and War: The United States in Afghanistan, Columbia, and Indochina (Lanham, MD: Rowman Littlefield, 2003), 200-201.

145. Alfred W. McCoy, The Politics of Heroin: CIA Complicity in the Global Drug Trade (Chicago: Lawrence Hill Books, 1991), 15–16.

into the West Coast. In 1846 alone, 117,000 Chinese were brought into the country to feed an opium trade estimated at nearly 230,000 pounds of gum opium and over 53,000 pounds of prepared (smoking) opium. Although Lincoln outlawed the "coolie" trade in 1862, the black marketeering of Chinese continued at an escalating rate to the end of the century.[146]

American labor was very cheap at the time. The reasons the Chinese were brought to the U.S. was to quell the anxiety of those who saw the rising number of Africans as an internal threat that needed to be dampened and, secondly, to create a demand for opium in the United States. Opium use became widespread by the middle of the nineteenth century, but by the 1890s the United States still had the political will to successfully reduce opiate consumption and place legal restrictions on the trade and on drug use in general, and the laws were actually enforced.

World War II disrupted international shipping and, unlike the current Homeland Security Department, America still had the moral will to have tight waterfront security that blocked, with the aid of organized mobsters, the smuggling of heroin into the United States. The U.S. addict population dropped from 200,000 in 1924 to about 20,000 in 1944-45.[147]

Opium and cocaine were used in patent medicines at the beginning of the 20th century, and some heroin was imported into the inner cities of the North. However, illicit drugs were never as widely and systematically imported into the United States until Kissinger prolonged the Vietnam War and began to trade openly with China.

By the early1950s, the global drug syndicates were again operating, but the flourishing of this trade was linked to the covert arm of United States foreign policy. Chinese opium production levels increased, and it was possible for China to turn the tables on Western powers. China began exporting drugs into the United States and Europe with the help of the CIA and home-grown mobsters. As noted, American gangsters, including Arnold Rothstein, Meyer Lansky, Charles "Lucky" Luciano, Louis "Lepke" Buchalter, and Jasha Katsenberg, forged links with Chinese drug lords, both in Shanghai and California, to obtain supplies for the growing American narcotics market.[148]

The trade exploded after the Vietnam War and the initiation by Nixon and Kissinger of a more open policy with China. Both the Chinese Communists and the Chinese Nationalists used opium to finance their movements. From

---

146. U.S. Labor Party Investigating Team, Dope, Inc.: Britain's Opium War Against the U.S. (New York New Benjamin Franklin House,1978), 37.

147. McCoy,18

148. Jonathan Marshall, "Opium and the Politics of Gangsterism in Nationalist China, 1927–1945,",Bulletin of Concerned Asian Scholars 8 (July–September 1976): 29-30.

the time of the BEIC, the Chinese never discontinued the profitable drug business with their Western partners. The upshot of the Vietnam War was the U.S. intelligence community taking charge of the golden triangle by controlling installed proxy drug lords. Hollywood even made a movie about this called Air America that starred Mel Gibson. The real Air America was no Hollywood story. It was at the eye of the storm of contrived wars for control of the opium trade in the golden triangle, which is an overlapping area of five countries: Vietnam, Laos, Burma (Myanmar), Thailand, and Yunnan Province, in China. This is one of the main regions, along with the golden crescent (Afghanistan, Pakistan, and Iran), where opium poppies are harvested on a large scale.

During and after the Vietnam War, the United States became flooded with drugs. Many soldiers returned from Vietnam addicted to heroin. It has been suggested that the war was kept going longer than necessary for this reason. In the Arrogance of Power, Anthony Summers reports on a conspiratorial and possibly illegal diplomatic intervention in 1968 by Henry Kissinger on behalf of presidential candidate Richard Nixon to extend the Vietnam War.[149] Just before the election, with General Chennault's[150] widow, Anna, as an intermediary, Nixon (Kissinger) persuaded the head of the Saigon regime to refuse to participate in the Paris peace talks arranged by President Johnson. Nixon's (Kissinger's) intrigue helped secure his election and also fruitlessly increased the loss of both American and Vietnamese lives.

However, extending the war had another purpose. Each year more and more addicted veterans were returning all across America to almost every, city, town, and hamlet. They had a disease that would spread like a cancer into every social institution and structure and break down society and undermine the rule of law. They provided the base for the retail trade—the addicted selling drugs to support their habit. Addicted veterans returned to small towns and hamlets where people had no idea of the drug- fueled nightmare the war in Vietnam would unleash on them.

---

149. In the opinion of future U.S. Ambassador Richard Holbrooke, who researched the incident as coauthor of Clark Clifford's memoirs: "What the Nixon people did (was) perhaps even a violation of law. They massively, directly and covertly, interfered in a major diplomatic negotiation . . . probably one of the most important negotiations in American diplomatic history" (BBC interview, 2000; quoted in Anthony Summers (with Robbyn Swan), The Arrogance of Power (New York: Viking, 2000), 306.

150. Chennault, hailing from a slave-owning family had been an aviator in WWII. He was responsible for the creation of Civil Air Transport, which later became Air America—the drug running air fleet in S.E. Asia.

Conveniently timed in 1970, just before the return of the heroin-addicted, strung- out Vietnam veterans and about the time that the CIA was running MK-ULTRA—a mind control and chemical/torture interrogation "research" program that was pumping mind altering drugs such as LSD into America's youth scene—Nixon declared another war, this time on drugs. The soldiers who had just defended corporate interests half way around the world would now begin to fuel another burgeoning enterprise—the prison industrial system. The following year, Nixon declared the war on cancer. Both the war on drugs and the war on cancer, as will be shown, have been sterling successes for financial interests and relate directly to the development of the HIV/AIDS crisis. The drugs and environmental toxins helped to create an oxidative stress crisis, and the war on cancer created the cover story with the virus myth.

It was at this time, during and after the Vietnam War, that a profusion of illegal drugs, experimental drugs such as LSD, and legal drugs used in an irresponsible manner, such as amyl nitrite, valium, Quaaludes, steroids, and antibiotics were targeted at the explosive baby boomer population subset that was experimenting with alternative life styles: the hippie, women's lib, and sexual revolution movements. The drugs and alternative life styles were used to induce a generation to freely take these poisons into their bodies. It was a generation that was being taught the hedonist principles of free trade: nothing was sacred; all values were relative; and if it felt good, just do it. Thus, physical and psychological poisoning and social dislocation created the crisis of immune destruction, especially at first in the sexually promiscuous gay community who seemed the most prone to excessive poly drug use. As CDC records indicate, the doctors who saw the first cases of AIDS recognized it as a problem of toxicology, of system poisoning. Their good medical judgment and sane scientific observations were soon brushed aside for a more lucrative market strategy.

The virus hunters, ego-deprived of the glory that eluded them from the failed war on cancer, were ready to bask in the accolades that they felt they deserved. Focusing on drugs that elites were supplying to America's children and youth was not going to happen. It was easier to blame the problem on a viral terrorist. The bug was easy to understand; it could be attacked with new drugs, and it was going to be very profitable. The virus hunters failed effort at finding a bug that caused cancer would be vindicated; they would simply make a collection of stress proteins, find an enzyme, reverse transcriptase, and identify some "viral like particles" in their laboratory witches' brew and call it the "isolation" of a new virus—HIV. It was alchemy that had nothing to do with the rules of the natural world, but it was a perfect match—made in hell!

It is now well accepted and understood that the illicit drug trade is a $400 to $600 billion a year international business and is protected at the highest levels by Western governments. Trade in illegal drugs is estimated at from 5 to 8 percent of overall world trade, which is slightly larger than the combined global trade in agricultural products and cars.[151]

Craig Murray, a former British Ambassador to Uzbekistan from 2002–04, has stated that he personally witnessed Jeeps with darkened windows bringing heroin through from Afghanistan, en route to Europe, while tankers of chemicals went roaring into Afghanistan. His pleas to Great Britain to intercede fell on deaf ears.[152] He clearly did not know the history of his own empire.

The only good thing to be said about the Taliban is that by 2001 they had stamped out the opium trade. Taliban leader Mullah Mohammad Omar drastically reduced opium production in Afghanistan during his last year in power, issued a religious edict banning the crop, and threatened harsh punishments in areas the movement held under its strict control. This was an affront to British and U.S. covert drug policy. As Jane's Intelligence Review (22 October 2001) noted, "[T]he ban imposed by Taliban supreme leader Mullah Mohammad Omar in July 2000 . . . resulted in some 70% of the world's illicit opium production being wiped out virtually at a stroke." The U.S. drug proxies would now become the Northern Alliance who responded to the Taliban's ban on opium cultivation in 2000 by trebling output in their sector of northeastern Afghanistan. According the United Nations Office on Drugs and Crime, by 2007, Afghanistan was back to producing 93 percent of the world's opium.

From 1979 to 1991, the United States supplied direct support for the Afghan mujahedin. By providing funds for Gulbuddin Hekmatyar, a drug trafficker selected for support by Pakistani intelligence (the ISI), the CIA helped propel Hekmatyar into becoming, for a while, the largest heroin trafficker in Afghanistan and perhaps the world.[153] During this period when U.S. interest in Afghanistan surged, Afghanistan became the world's major heroin source.

The British and American invasion in October 2001 supported the drug lords who have turned Afghanistan into a narco-state. General Dostrum (a known narco-terrorist) who began as a communist boss in the 1970s became head of the Afghan armed forces and deputy minister of defense.

151. Branko Milanovic, "Globalization and Corrupt States," YaleGlobal, 2 November 2007.
152. Ambassador Craig Murray, "," Times on Line 21 July 2007.
153. John K. Cooley, Unholy Wars: Afghanistan, America, and International Terrorism (London: Pluto, 2000), 17.

Ambassador Craig states that Dostrum is known for tying opponents to tank tracks and running over them. He crammed prisoners into metal containers in the searing sun and caused scores of them to die of heat and dehydration. He cooked them alive! Dostrum is Uzbek, and his heroin passes over the Friendship Bridge from Afghanistan to Uzbekistan where it is taken over by President Islam Karimov's people. According to the U.N. Drug Control Program, the biggest heroin and cocaine trading institutions in the world are the Burmese, Pakistani, Mexican, Peruvian and Colombian militaries (and now Afghanistan's), all armed and trained by U.S. military intelligence, in the name of the anti-drug effort, which is simply make work for a multitude of alphabet agencies as they look the other way when big shipments are encountered.

The United States has lost the political will to deter this plague. How did this happen? The top four states for drug importation are New York, Florida, California, and Texas. The top four money-laundering states are New York, Florida, California, and Texas. Eighty percent of all presidential campaign funds come from New York, Florida, California, and Texas.[154]

The U.S. military with all its high-tech gizmos and bunker busters cannot find Osama (who has been reported by many sources including the assassinated Benazir Bhutto, as dead), but the poppy fields are blooming. In January 2009, the Toronto Star reported that "there is a 'high probability' some Canadian troops serving in Afghanistan—one of the world's biggest sources of illegal drugs—will get involved in the drug trade…"[155]

Clipper Ships and University Endowments

Certain families from around the Boston area made fortunes trading not only in slaves but also in opium. Possibly the best sea-faring families of New England, including but not limited to the Peabodys, Russells, Lows, Delanos, Forbes, Cabots and Perkins, and John Jacob Astor of New York were involved in the trade. There were huge profits to be made, and it was not ethics but supply that kept them from doing even better. The British owned their own poppy fields in India, while their American competitors had to purchase Turkish opium or sell drugs on consignment for British or Indian firms.

Linda Minor, in her three-part series Why the Harvard Corporation Protects the Drug Trade, found that . . . "the successors of the opium

---

154. Michael Ruppert, "CIA, Drugs and Wall Street,' www.fromthewilderness. com.

155. Bruce Campion-Smith, "Troops Lured by Drug Trade, Report Warns," www. thestar.com 2 January 2009

smuggling companies in America quickly established a system to use their dirty profits as "venture capital" for direct investment in strategic industries and, secondly, that they funneled "charitable" donations into educational institutions to control both the huge tax-exempt endowments and to create a mask of respectability and generosity to hide the true nature of their character." It has also been well established as noted above that such clandestine business alliances led directly to the establishment of the OSS and the CIA and that the knowledge of the drug trade, its profits, trade routes, and distribution channels became part of what has become known as <u>black ops funding</u>—it has been a way of getting around the democratic process of congressional oversight for the perpetuation of clandestine wars, in country coup d'états, and assassinations in furtherance of a global economic agenda of free trade and centralized banking control—drug money funds the secret government that commits high crimes and treason against the state and remains well hidden and outside the rule of law.

Allen Dulles, the first CIA director, was the direct descendant of a family that obtained its start with the British East India Company. He was schooled by the British Intelligence Services during WWII as a member of the OSS. This was fitting, as one of the end products of WWII was the transference of the costs of running the British colonial empire to the clueless American taxpayer—who was happy to take on these expenses because they had been brilliantly programmed to think that they had won a hard fought and just war.

Profits from the opium trade helped to establish AT&T and The United Fruit Company, the Texas Mexican Railway Company, and The Chicago Burlington and Quincy Railroad. During 1873 these venture capitalists, formerly known as the <u>Boston</u> <u>Concern</u>, including John Murray Forbes and Thomas Jefferson Coolidge, started expansion of the Atchison, Topeka, and Santa Fe Railroad, which expanded across Kansas to Colorado. Their securities were marketed by the Baring Brothers bank in England, sponsor of the world's narcotics traffic throughout the 19th century.

To gain respectability, many of these well-heeled drug dealers donated large sums to various East Coast universities. John Cleve Green gave a fortune in opium profits to Princeton in the financing of three buildings, four professorships, and the Princeton Theological Seminary for a twenty-five year endowment. Abiel Abbott Low's fortune financed the construction of the Columbia University New York Campus. The Russell money went to Yale and to the establishment of the Skull and Bones society from which has come many members of the banking and clandestine services as well as politicians including both Presidents Bush and Senator John Forbes Kerry, whose ancestor was drug dealer John Murray Forbes. Warren Delano who was a partner in the opium trading house of Russell and Company was the grandfather of Franklin Delano Roosevelt, 32nd President of the United States.

The Drugging of America

By controlling the history departments of the major universities through their endowments and selection of 'appropriately inclined' department chairs, elite families have managed to keep this rather ignominious history from general discussion. By controlling the mainstream media and showing a steady stream of young African American and Hispanic males arrested for street-level drug dealing, they have been able to maintain their mask of respectability. Many street-level drug pushers can hardly read a newspaper. To think that they would be in charge of a worldwide business, establish protection and distribution networks, pay off police departments, politicians, and judges, run international covert operations with coordinated logistical support from the Pentagon and the FAA as well as assorted foreign clandestine services operating front businesses, including airlines and insurance firms, as well as launder the proceeds of at least 6 percent of the global economy is ludicrous. Yet this or some hapless Latin American peasant rather than the dapper Clark Clifford or the urbane George H.W. Bush is the vision of the average American when he/she thinks about the drug trade.

As will be shown in the chapter on Jackie-O and her paramours, the public slaying of her first husband, President John Fitzgerald Kennedy, paved the way for the ascendancy of the old crime families to total control of the state apparatus. There has been a steady decline in the social fabric of the country since that fateful event. Having been subjected to a steady barrage of crimes in high places, plus the trauma of the Vietnam War, the attack on Panama, Grenada, Nicaragua, Serbia, Iraq, and Afghanistan, the nation seems to no longer want the truth. We seem to want the government to shield us from the sad truth as we continue to look to the same people who have been complicit in creating the problems to solve them.

Prior to Vietnam there was Korea and, as the Korean War drew to a close, the French began to lose their grip on Southeast Asia. The transfer of colonial domination of the region from France to the United States arose from U.S. counterinsurgency measures that were ongoing well before the Kennedy era. The development of the chaos in Southeast Asia both Korea and Vietnam had been decided before the conclusion of WWII. The Vietnam War was instigated behind the scenes and erupted as a subterfuge, among other things, to gain control of the opium trade in the golden triangle. American was slated to be de-industrialized and America's youth were targeted as the next big market for these odious products.

The explosion of the drug culture and the failure of the war on cancer gave rise to what has become HIV/AIDS. AIDS is another long-standing, low intensity battle of psychological warfare against the American people. Subjected to a steady stream of trauma-based, mind-control techniques through the visual medium of television, they have been conditioned by this shock and awe program of chronic violence and human degradation to be confused and immobilized. Predictably, they are shell shocked. The Tavistock Institute calls such a psychological state <u>the maladaptive response</u>.

The technique of psychologically demoralizing and neutralizing the collective energy of the population began in earnest and accelerated with the public assassination of John Fitzgerald Kennedy.

Chapter 7

Jackie-O's Men, Drugs, Diamonds, and Oil for Empire, the AIDS Crucible

○ ○

It's just a handful of people that run everything...No matter what promises you make on the campaign trail—blah, blah, blah—when you win, you go into this smoky room with the twelve industrialists, capitalists scum f...ks that got you in there, and this little screen comes down . . . and it's a shot of the Kennedy assassination from an angle you've never seen before, which looks suspiciously off the grassy knoll. . . .And then the screen comes up, the lights come on, and they say to the new President, 'Any questions?'

Comedian Bill Hicks

Assassination is the business of business.

Col. J. Fletcher Prouty

An underreported factor in the political corruption of U.S. Asian policy has been the input of money, including drug money, from foreign governments through their lobbyists and PR firms . . . at the origins of this insidious influence one finds the undoubted drug involvement of the CIA's airline CAT (later Air America).

Peter Dale Scott[156]

---

156. Peter Dale Scott, <u>Drugs Oil and War</u> (Oxford, UK: Rowman & Littlefield, 2003), 4.

Although John Fitzgerald Kennedy was indeed President of the United States, a position some claim the most powerful position in the world, his brutal and public execution and his wife's refuge in the arms of men with more power than he suggests otherwise.

The center of the cyclones of shock of mid-20th century history that led to the current AIDS medical crisis was not so much John F. Kennedy as it was his wife, Jacqueline Bouvier Kennedy Onassis. This siren drew a trio of men into her life, each of whom played a starring role in the high drama, criminal activity and international intrigues that led to the development of the theory of HIV/AIDS. To understand the rearrangement of power alignments that occurred as a result of the Kennedy assassination, it is necessary to examine the lives and roles the men Jackie chose and their family, business and political relationships that played publicly and privately on the international scene.

The Sport of Social Climbing

Gore Vidal gives a rather different version of Jacqueline Bouvier Kennedy Onassis than the world has come to know. He writes that, "She had lost her virginity to a friend of mine in a lift that he had installed in a *pension* on Paris's Left Bank. They had discussed marriage. He came from a better family than hers...but he had no money. [157] She is said to have loved money more than publicity, and her life was dedicated to acquiring it through marriage, just as her social climbing mother, Janet Lee (née Levy) had groomed her.[158]

Her ambitions took her into the beds of three international power brokers whose lives and ambitions shaped the world of mid-20th century America and postcolonial Africa. The story that links these men is one of high crimes, greed, corruption, and intrigue—the world of "deep politics" and what Nietzsche calls historia abscondita, or concealed history.

Understanding Jackie's ambition for money allows for deeper insight into the greed and corruption that pervades the power elite and the women that are attracted to the men for that very reason. When fellow Roman Catholic Jack Kennedy, also on the make for glory, if not money, came her way, her desire to marry well was realized. Jack had income from a $10 million trust fund. Adequate income at the time, but, according to Gore Vidal in his memoir Palimpsest, hardly the amount that she would later need to live like her role model, Bunny Mellon. Vidal goes on to explain that, "When she told her lift lover that she was going to marry Jack, he was appalled and said,

---

157.   Gore Vidal, Palimpsest: A Memoir (New York: Penguin Books, 1995), 309.
158.   Gore Vidal, Ibid, 309-310

'You can't marry that…that *mick*.' She, coolly to the point: 'He has money and you don't."

Jackie's men were her two husbands, John Fitzgerald Kennedy, 35th President of the United States, Aristotle Onassis, a Greek shipping tycoon and possibly a capo de tuti capi,[159] and her lover until her death from non-Hodgkin's lymphoma at age 64, Maurice Tempelsman, a diamond merchant, major Democratic Party fundraiser, and economic hit man for the very powerful Oppenheimers of South Africa who, unlike the African National Congress, actually control the destiny of that country.

The African National Congress (ANC) is the African face of the new South Africa, but the Oppenheimer family is still the power that controls the economics of the South African state. In Oppenheimer-controlled South Africa, 96 percent of South Africa's arable farmland is still owned by whites, and 61 percent of people live below the poverty line, with more than a third subsisting on less than $2 a day.[160] Unfortunately for the people of South Africa, and perhaps because of Maurice Tempelsman, the ANC demanded neither reparations nor justice for the theft of their land, its rich resources, and the murder of their people. Instead of reparations, they got "truth and reconciliation."

Examining the lives and events of these three power brokers introduces the currents and countercurrents, the deep politics and international intrigues that created the history of the Cold War period and the history that leads directly to contemporary headline news.

Jackie's first husband, Senator Jack Kennedy who later became President Kennedy had a father, Joseph who had long and deep ties to the mob, including transport king Aristotle Onassis who would later become Jackie's second husband. Onassis was a shipping magnate who wielded enormous power, but had a murky business background that entwined surprisingly with the gangster pedigree of her father-in law, Joseph Kennedy. According to Vidal, "the marriage to Onassis was cold blooded but necessary." He states that, "…actually Ari was more charming and witty than she, and in the glittering European circus where, to her credit, she did not particularly want to shine, the word was, "What does he see in her?"[161]

The mob had enormous cash flows from the illegal drug business. The CIA protected and used illegal cash flows for clandestine operations. However, in the end, it was diamond merchant Maurice Tempelsman who

159. Gerald A. Carroll, Project Seek: Onassis, Kennedy, and the Gemstone Thesis (Carson City, NV: Bridger House Publishers, 1994).

160. William Reed, "South Africa: Worse Now Than Under Apartheid?" Black Press International, 5 October 2007.

161. Gore Vidal, op.cit. 310

may have had access to even greater hidden cash flows who won the Jackie prize. Her choices in succession speak volumes about her understanding and knowledge of deep power politics. Each of her men was more powerful than the former.

From the actions of these men, their families, business associates and surrounding politicians came the intrigues, power politics, and resource wars, the drug running, and the high crimes against the state, postcolonial African coups, and the consequent degradation of the human psyche, energy, and immune system that erupted like a pustule in the 1980s. Another MK-Ultra mind game unfolded that was given a title and frozen in place: AIDS.

Who Was Jackie Kennedy?

Jackie Kennedy portrayed herself as a staunch Catholic, and so her last alliance with Maurice Tempelsman, a Jewish diamond merchant and power broker for the Zionist cause, seemed more perplexing until one unearths the shadowy part of her history and the shadowy part of the history of the very powerful Maurice. According to another astonishing revelation made by Gore Vidal: Janet, Jackie's mother, was Jewish. She divorced Jackie's father, "Black Jack" Bouvier—a known affable womanizer and alcoholic—and eventually married Hugh Auchincloss. Auchincloss was also at one time married to Vidal's mother, Nina. Vidal writes, "One should note that the first of Hughdie's (Hugh Dudley Auchincloss) three high-powered wives was Russian, the second my mother, the third Jackie's mother, Janet, born Lee or, as my mother used to observe thoughtfully, Levy." Vidal continues, "Apparently, Janet's father had changed his name in order to become the first Jew to be a vice president of the Morgan Bank. My mother wondered how Hughdie, a quiet but sincere anti-Semite, would respond when he found out." As for Janet Lee, he writes. She used to say she was "of the Virginia Lees . . . until the real Lees ordered her to shut up."[162]

Maurice Tempelsman, Jackie's last liaison, is a major fund raiser and one of the most formidable behind the scenes movers in Democratic power politics. He has had a profoundly retrograde influence on recent African history and uses his gravitas for the promotion of HIV/AIDS as a politically useful tool and a cover for the industrial degradation caused by the South African Oppenheimers. The Oppenheimers control the world's supply of diamonds and much of its gold and have been represented by Tempelsman in the United States since he was in his twenties. One of the ways in which he fulfills this roll is in his capacity as a board chairman of the Harvard School of

---

162. Gore Vidal, <u>Palimpsest</u>.

Public Health AIDS Initiative. It is in the interests of his business association with the Oppenheimer DeBeers Industries and the parent company, the Anglo-American Corporation, that face massive liability from thousands of injured mine workers to keep this AIDS myth going for as long as possible.

DeBeers Consolidated Mines were founded in South Africa by Cecil Rhodes to fund the extension of the British Empire where they were neither wanted nor belonged. DeBeers has been to Africa what the British East India Company was to China. Just as the BEIC used their enormous profits to pay for their military to expand their reach into South East Asia, Rhodes created an artificial scarcity in diamonds to drive up the price of this commodity. This monopoly expression of free trade was another tool to pay for the bureaucracy and the troops needed for the expansion of the British Empire in Africa and abroad.

Deep Politics and the Death of JFK

Peter Dale Scott is a soft spoken former Canadian diplomat and poet who teaches English at the University of California, at Berkeley. Scott has written extensively on the interplay of crime networks, covert operations, and drugs. He is the author of a rather far- reaching exposé on the control of international narcotics smuggling and its relationship to the cancer of destruction that is the heart and soul of Western economic life. Understanding the relationships that he outlines in his work <u>Drugs, Oil and War</u> provides the foundation for understanding the events of the last sixty years. To ignore the significance of the China Lobby and of drug smuggling and all of its attendant corruption is to ignore the history of the rise and fall of the British and American Empires and the consolidation of power by extra-state banking and corporate structures ruled by a mere handful of men from a shadowy world of pure evil.

Scott distinguishes between what he terms <u>parapolitics</u> and <u>deep politics</u>. According to Scott, <u>parapolitics</u> is the work of covert agencies and similar organizations where secrecy is adapted as a matter of deliberate policy whereby accountability is consciously diminished. The U.S. parapolitical use of Mafia figures like Vito Genovese in postwar Italy is one example. This was a conscious operation that led to the political dominance of Italian party politics by a Mafia out of control.[163] <u>Deep politics</u>, as opposed to conspiracy theory, happens when there is habitual resorting "to collusive secrecy and law-breaking . . . these deep processes are not brought to the public eye: for

---

163. Peter Dale Scott, <u>Drugs, Oil, and War</u> (Lanham, MD: Rowman and Littlefield, 2003), xiii.

example, the way in which major drug traffickers are recurrently protected by the U. S. Justice Department, or the way in which some of the top traffickers have been recurrently named in connection with the systematic sexual corruption of members of Congress. Such arrangements are in fact, widely known, but rarely written about." [164]

Deep politics led to the assassination of JFK, and Scott gives ample evidence of this entrenched pattern of criminal activity by the ruling elite, for which they are seldom held accountable. Assassinating relatives for political and economic control had been practiced by the European aristocracy for centuries. However, assassination of political leaders became increasingly more frequent in public life since the 1960s. Scott also makes it patently clear that these patterns are rooted in the core of society and are neither aberrant nor unexpected. Criminal activity in fact is the usual way in which global business is done. It is why the United States has continually supported a series of strong men with disastrous consequences for countries but great profit for the global corporate structures: Somoza, Diem, Ne Win, Chiang, the Shah, Marcos, Salazar, Papadopoulos, Stroessner, Mobutu, Amin, Videla, Noriega, Cedras, Samper, Salinas, Suharto, Fujimori, Pinochet, Osama, Saddam, and Dostrum. Every one of these dictators and misfits had their rise to power as the result of Western intervention in local affairs for the "strategic interests" of U.S. corporate and banking businesses and their allies. Ongoing support for identifiable sociopathic personalities who are more than willing to suppress their own populations to implement and promote global business and banking interests is an endemic cultural problem that is deeply predatory, pathological and antisocial, yet it is the accepted and expected behavioral norm. Naomi Klein calls the phenomenon disaster capitalism—the rapid-fire corporate reengineering of societies that are reeling from shock—which she contends owes its intellectual origins to the University Of Chicago Department Of Economics under Nobel Prize-winning economist Milton Friedman. She is mistaken. The origins go back to Adam Smith who wrote Wealth of Nations and was a strong proponent of the free market system and Thomas Malthus, economist for the British East India Company.

Seymour Hersh, a leading investigative journalist, made an assertion, at a lecture given at the University of Minnesota that during the Bush II administration there was a Joint Special Operations Command with no congressional oversight. It was an executive assassination ring that reported

---

164. Peter Dale Scott, Deep Politics and the Death of JFK (Berkeley and Los Angeles CA: University of California Press 1996), xi.

directly to Dick Cheney.[165] The idea that the Vice President of the United States was allegedly running an assassination squad out of the White House received a really big yawn from the mainstream media who were, at the time of this incredible announcement, more bent on shocking people into preparing for compulsory vaccinations to withstand claims of a swine flu "epidemic."

There are enormous consequences from business crimes supported by laissez- faire politics. Domestically, white collar crimes account for nearly 30 percent of case filings in U.S. District Courts—more than any other category of crime. The combined burglary, mugging, and other property crime losses engendered by the country's street thugs pale in comparison with the losses from thugs masquerading as upstanding citizens. Street crime losses reach about $4 billion a year; whereas corporate losses bilk us of $40 to $200 billion a year—and that is not counting the number of lives lost by defective products and instigated resource wars. The most recent crime wave has culminated in 2008-2009, with the bail out of Wall Street banks at over $1.4 trillion and counting

After several deregulation laws were passed, including the repeal of the Glass-Steagall Act of 1933 designed to control speculation, Wall Street was a disaster waiting to happen. George W. Bush added fuel to the fire after 9-11 when he used "terrorism" to transfer more than 500 FBI agents away from bank terrorism to brown-skinned people terrorism. This diversion of resources away from the massive put options that were placed on the airlines before the event of 9/11[166] allowed the controlling financial terrorists to continue their planned economic warfare without disruption.[167]

The most egregious consequence of elite crimes is the erosion of democracy and incremental enhancement of police powers, with the people who commit the greatest crimes in positions of authority. With the exceptions of Jack Abramoff and Bernie Madoff, who seem to have been the designated fall guys, not one high-level banker or bureaucrat has been charged with fraud

165. Erick Black, "Investigative Reporter Seymour Hersh Describes Executive Assassination Ring," 11 March 2009, www.minnpost.com.

166. 9/11 was forshadowed by unprecedented put options placed on United and American Airlines. The Security and Exchange Commission refused to identify who placed the options. They were however traced back to he Deutsche Bank Banker's Trust, which was formerly headed by then Director of the CIA, Buzzy Krongard.

167. Michael Ruppert, "Suppressed Details of Criminal Insider Trading Lead Directly into the CIAs Highest Ranks—CIA Director "Buzzy" Krongard Managed Firm that handled 'put' options on UAL. http://www.fromthewilderness.com/free/ww3/10_09_01_krongard.html

or conspiracy to commit fraud—and it is doubtful that they ever will be. In fact, several of the people who were directly connected to the banking crisis (e.g., Timothy Geithner and Larry Summers) have prominent positions in the Barack Obama administration.

The most productive crimes are those in which the state structure is called to arms in support of a desired objective. Crimes created by this class bubble up through history often as cataclysmic events which are designed to alter the social, economic, political, spiritual, and medical status of large populations. Such events are proposed in position papers and developed in think tanks. They are articulated in books, such as Carroll Quigley's <u>Tragedy and Hope</u> and or Zbigniew Brzezinski's <u>The Grand Chessboard.</u> They are discussed in the classrooms of major institutions and they are printed in <u>Vital Speeches of the Day</u>; yet, when such an event materializes, it is always through some miracle of coincidence and feigned bureaucratic incompetence. Yet few, except whistleblowers, are ever fired.

The Project for the New American Century's document "Rebuilding America's Defenses," written by a group of aggressive, former Trotskyite neocons seeking to position the United States as the world's dominant military power, states that "the process of transformation even if it brings revolutionary change, is likely to be a long one, absent some catastrophic and catalyzing event—like a new Pearl Harbor."[168] Exactly one year after this document was widely distributed; the World Trade Center and the Pentagon were attacked by jets and building number 7 in New York collapsed by controlled demolition. Coincidence? In spite of another multimillion dollar <u>investigation</u>, there is ample evidence to question the findings of the official 9/11 report. Hundreds of well-qualified, independent researchers have done so besides the self-selected Washington Beltway mandarins. In a peer-reviewed journal, nine physicists concluded that active thermitic material was present in dust from the 9/11 World Trade Center catastrophe. This strongly indicates the presence of pre-planted explosives was responsible for both the towers and building 7, which was not hit by a plane, collapsing in a controlled fall in 6.5 seconds.[169]

Contrary to the contrived consensus of the court historians, such shocks or political upheavals (the assassination of JFK or the 9/11 scenario) are never spontaneous events that happen by coincidence or are the product of a lone patsy. They are planned with an uncanny degree of sophisticated knowledge

168. <u>Rebuilding America's Defenses, Strategy, Forces and Resources for a New Century</u>": A Report of the Project for the New American Century, September 2000, 51.

169. N. H. Harrit et al., "Active Thermitic Material Discovered in Dust from the 9/11 World Trade Center Catastrophe," <u>Open Chem Physics J, 2</u>: 7–31.

of the workings of highly classified internal systems along with the power to alter or to shut those systems down as needed. Such shocks have the intent and outcome of rapidly altering the social order in a desired direction. The assassination of President Kennedy was one such event. His death unleashed a torrent of demons from dark hiding places and set the world on a trajectory in which each subsequent event has become more spectacularly absurd and has led to ever more economic denial, human sacrifice, expansion of state-corporate powers, and diminishment of civil and human rights.

The deep political connections of JFK's father, Joseph P. Kennedy Sr., and his son's attempt to change the course of history led directly to his assassination and almost total control by a power center bent on world economic and military domination through the creation of global monopolies.

Current history cannot be contextualized without understanding the role in this drama played by an economist who has had much more influence than Milton Friedman, a prominent economist who worked out of the University of Chicago. Thomas Malthus, was the economist for the drug-pushing British East India Company. His philosophical ideas have been refined, but they remain the current thinking of the group who run and profit from man-made catastrophic events.

Malthus and the Economics of Scarcity

Thomas Malthus studied Latin, Greek, and mathematics at Cambridge and became an Anglican country parson before joining the British East India Company. The East India Company, one of the first global corporations to promote <u>free trade</u>, employed Malthus as their resident political economist. He taught at their employee training center, the British East India College.

The British East India Company, which started as a trading venture, was granted a charter in 1600 by Elizabeth I. By 1750, the company controlled the Bengal and Bihar opium-growing regions of India, and British ships dominated the opium trade out of Calcutta to China. By 1767, BEIC was importing two thousand chests of opium to China, and by 1793 they had established a monopoly in the opium trade.

While Malthus was the economist of the British East India Company, he developed a theory of supply which eminently appealed to the rather unsavory characteristics of the organization. Malthus postulated that the Earth, being round and finite, was not big enough to sustain a growing population. Malthus, a rather avaricious and unimaginative sort, theorized that world population would increase logarithmically against a projected limited food supply, which he thought would only grow arithmetically. He concluded that the only way to reduce an unnecessary population was by creating the conditions for vice and misery by actively inducing wars, famine, and disease. This incipient eugenics theory on the necessity of population reduction was more of an apologia in support of the perversions and plundering of the British East India Company. The theory has been proven to be eminently wrong, yet population reduction has been incorporated into the conventional wisdom of Western culture and is still a significant factor in U.S. domestic and foreign policy.

The overt and gross expression of these policies has gone underground since WWII, along with the ethnic cleansing excesses that took place in Germany under the direction of Ernst Rudin, a psychiatrist and president of the Rockefeller sponsored International Federation of Eugenics Organizations. It has become more subtle, sophisticated, and lethal. It is couched in the language of social science and such benign sounding phrases as "family planning." It is hidden by the introduction of new diseases that seem to target selected populations. Currently and domestically, the Rand Institute has been one of the military think tanks that develop policies for quiet wars directed at the mostly civilian minority poor in urban areas. They are masters of silent terrorism. The eugenics movement never died. It simply took another form.

The Rand Institute Echoes Malthus The ideas of Malthus are still very much operational and are often expressed and refined in various policy papers that spew from many of the nation's think tanks. Like the British East India College, these think tanks funded by wealthy elite as part of the tax shelter boondoggle and are used as public relations propaganda organs where hired intellectuals are paid to give a providential spin to the social and economic policies that this class seeks to implement. These planned schemes are often intentionally designed to disrupt the social fabric of the nation's urban poor. In fact, they have been structured to undermine the entire social fabric of the nation. The urban poor have been used as beta testers for social engineering programs that are eventually directed outward from urban centers into middle class neighborhoods.

In 1966, for example, a Malthusian idea was articulated by Roger Starr who headed a bogus citizens' group funded by the real estate industry when he used the Rand Institute's theory of "planned shrinkage" to justify the denial of public services to poor, largely minority communities. The stated objectives of this policy were to disrupt the neighborhoods, the economic base, and the cultural ties that had made these areas viable community neighborhoods and a potential political threat to the established order. The long-standing community support organizations and residents were to be decentralized and displaced so as to weaken their burgeoning political power.

This policy was set in motion so that the valuable property that they sat on could be reincorporated into high rent districts.[170] This was accomplished by destroying and eliminating housing in poor neighborhoods. This had the effect of increased crowding and homelessness, which became quite visible during the Reagan administration when many homeless people started sleeping on the streets of metropolitan areas. Many of the homeless were psychiatric patients who had been dumped into these communities from expensive institutional settings. From 1955 to 1992, the state mental hospital census declined 82 percent.

Industrial production was relocated farther and farther from urban centers leaving those without access to transportation, jobless. Finally, as a result of the MK-Ultra and Vietnam experience, the communities were flooded with drugs at the same time that the supportive police and fire services were drastically diminished. Crime rates predictably soared. The media ran a fear campaign about the rise of the new urban criminal class, and politicians who had contributed to the creation of the problem began to run on the promise of restoring "law and order". Wall Street responded with investments in a new profit center—private prisons built at taxpayers' expense.

Former Undersecretary of HUD Catherine Austin Fitts encountered the same social pattern in 1996 in the development of her Community Wizard Program. The Community Wizard computer software program developed by Fitts was able to track high-home foreclosure rates in neighborhoods targeted with crack cocaine distribution during the Iran-Contra era. This resulted in HUD's securitizing the defaulted mortgages and selling them to selected insiders at pennies on the dollar. The mortgage products then went into financial portfolios where they rose in value when community renewal programs began. Insiders who were connected to HUD had the information from government sources that made the securitization process a sure bet.

Communities, such as the South Bronx in New York, began to burn down after fire stations were intentionally closed based on a policy of "benign neglect" set forth by the Rand think tank. This policy was also advocated by so-called liberal Senator Daniel Patrick Moynihan from New York State. The policy took root during the Nixon administration and, as the planned shrinkage took hold, communities were disrupted by deliberate denial of services. The controlled media took the opportunity to blame the people who lived in the communities for the results of the destruction. This was the beginning of a policy of deliberately disrupting social networks that led to

---

170. Deborah Wallace and Roderick Wallace, <u>A Plague on Your Houses: How New York Was Burned Down and National Public Health Crumbled</u> (London, UK: Verso, 1998).

widespread urban displacement and homelessness, as well as an increase in drug use, disease, and mortality among the dispossessed. This was the era when Nixon, the "Red Hater," and Kissinger, his controller, opened China to trade; when the Vietnam vets were returning strung out on smack, or their dead bodies were returned, hollowed out, and desecrated a second time with the filth of heroin packets. This was the time when illicit drugs began to flood these neighborhoods, and the factories that provided jobs began to close, and be shipped wholesale, first to the union-free American South, and then to Latin America that had been purged of its grassroots leaders by successively sponsored American coups, and again later, to desperately impoverished or Communist-controlled Southeast Asia.

Contrary to popular thought, these were not isolated events. The public destruction of Kennedy as an impediment opened the door for these events to happen. After his assassination, the empire hastened its expansion and power consolidation.

Jackie's Men: John, Aristotle, Maurice

Aristotle Onassis was Jackie's second husband. He was born in Turkey of Greek parentage and is said to have arrived penniless in Argentina as a young man. In a very short period of time he is recorded to have made a fortune in the tobacco business. The story floated of making a fortune in a business in which he had no particular competitive advantage and in which there was already an established supply is not very plausible. However, if the notion that he was actually selling oriental tobacco, better known as opium, is considered, it does begin to make sense.[171]

According to the Associated Press Biographical Service:

> The Onassis story began January 15, 1906 when he was born in Smyrna, Turkey, the son of Homer Socrates and Penelope (Dologlou) Onassis. His father was a wealthy and influential Greek tobacco merchant whose family had lived in the city for generations. Because of social upheavals, the family's fortunes were reversed, and they returned to Athens in drastically reduced circumstances.
>
> In 1923 the 17 year old youth sailed for Argentina, arriving in Buenos Aires with $60 in his pocket. . . .His first job was as a telephone operator, working nights. . . He used

---

171. L.J. Davis, Onassis: Aristotle and Christina (London, UK: Grafton, 1988), 13.

his daytime hours to set up a modest tobacco importing industry. From money saved he expanded trading to grains, hides and whale oil. By the time he was 25 he had made his first million.[172]

This is a good story, but the numbers are improbable. "Onassis only had menial jobs on the surface—telephone operator, tobacco salesman making only five percent commissions, electrician at $25 per week, and cigarette vendor. Parlaying those occupations, and on his own initiative, he is supposed to have transformed $60 into over a million in a mere eight years."[173] In the 1920s, this was highly unlikely, unless the tobacco business involved the opium trade. It was legal at this time in many nations and the Onassis' family had been based for many years in Smyrna, a major port for the export of Turkey's major cash commodity—opium. At one time, the Turkish government encouraged the development of the industry by remitting the tithes on opium and poppy-seed for one year on lands sown for the first time, and by distributing printed instructions for cultivating the poppy and preparing the opium. In these directions it was pointed out that the opium crop is ten times as profitable as that of wheat. Until the Limitation Law of 1933, opium could be exported from Turkey virtually without restriction.[174]

With opium going for about $100 per pound, compared with $0.25 per pound for tobacco, it is easy to comprehend how he could have made his first million selling "Turkish tobacco."

The <u>Gemstone File</u> links Onassis to John Kennedy's father, Joseph P. Kennedy, and to the deep politics which led to Kennedy's election as the first Irish Catholic President of the United States and his demise in Daley Plaza. According to the <u>File</u>, in 1932, Aristotle Onassis struck a deal with Meyer Lansky, Eugene Meyer, and Joseph Kennedy to ship illegal liquor into Boston during prohibition.[175] In 1973, mob boss Frank Costello confirmed that he and Joseph P. Kennedy had been boot-legging partners.

These early relationships would continue to be intertwined.[176] These relationships are critical in illuminating the theory of deep politics Peter Dale Scott advocates in his book <u>Deep Politics and the Death of JFK</u>,

---

172. Sketch 4364, Associated Press Biographical Service, 1 February 1969.
173. Gerald A. Carroll, <u>Project Seek: Onassis, Kennedy, and the Gemstone Thesis</u> (Carson City, NV: Bridger House Publishers, 1994).
174. C Lamour and , M.R. Lamberti, <u>The International Connection: Opium from Growers to Pushers</u> (New York:Pantheon Books, 1974), 201.
175. Stephanie Caruana, <u>The Gemstone File: A memoir</u>(Victoria,BC: Trafford Publishing, 2006), 61.
176. Caruana, <u>Gemstone File</u>, 68..

where he observes:"Dishonesty, manipulation, and even self-deception are widespread in our nominal political democracy. So little of what really goes on is acknowledged that the notion of deep politics as earlier defined, 'political practices and arrangements that are usually repressed rather than acknowledged . . . [to be understood one must] . . . look beneath public formulations of policy issues to the bureaucratic, economic, and ultimately covert and criminal activities which underlie them."

Meyer Lansky ran the casinos in Cuba where he established Havana's dominant role in the gambling, prostitution, money laundering, and international narcotics smuggling traffic. "During the 1930s . . . with the repeal of prohibition, activities such as prostitution, hijacking, gambling, narcotics and extortion became more important to the mob. Lansky, Siegal, Luciano and Lepke set up a factory to process drugs."[177] Lansky had a direct link to the CIA and who by the 60s enjoyed protection and virtual immunity from prosecution by both the FBI and the CIA.[178] Paul Heliwell who was an OSS veteran and eventual CIA officer was counsel to Meyer Lansky's Miami bank.[179]

No drug trade however could survive long without an extensive distribution network, and Onassis could not have been in a better position. His ships were already plying waters around the globe, the Caribbean and southern U.S. . . . ."[180]

Eugene Meyer came from a prominent banking family. His father was a partner in Lazard Freres and unless the theory of "deep politics" is applied, his connections to the mob seem tenuous at best, but in 1933, he bought a struggling newspaper called the Washington Post and in 1944 the Post bought WINN, a minor radio station which had been used by numbers racketeers to calculate daily winning numbers.[181] Meyer became head of the Federal Reserve in 1930. The banking system is the laundry for drug and crime money, and drug money is used to prop up the price to earnings ratio of publicly traded corporations. Eustace Mullins stated that "Bernard Baruch, Eugene Meyer, Jr., and Paul Warburg . . . exercised more direct power over the American people than any president, because back of these men was the strength of the financial oligarchy which had maintained undisputed

177. Gage, Nicholas, "How One Gang Leader Thrives While Others Fall by the Wayside," Wall Street Journal, 19 November 1969.

178. Curt Gentry, J. Edgar Hoover: The Man and His Secrets (New York: Penguin, 1991), 531-32

179. Peter Dale Scott Deep Politics and the Death of JFK 7.

180. Carroll, Project Seek, 61.

181. Caroll, Project Seek, 59.

sway in this country since 1863."[182] Meyer has been blamed for being one of the architects of prolonging the Great Depression. Under his direction, the Federal Reserve contracted the money supply by 30 percent at a time when the money supply needed to be expanded.

Meyer turned the <u>Washington Post</u> into one of the leading propaganda arms for the global elite. Meyer's daughter was Katharine Graham. For many years her husband, Phil Graham, ran <u>the Washington Post</u> and is credited with putting together the Kennedy–Johnson ticket.

Meyer was also accused of being a war profiteer by members of the Senate and House of Representatives. A Senate subcommittee in the mid 1920s investigated charges that Meyer got a "rake off" on bond stabilization operations of the War Finance Corporation and that he had taken an active roll in undermining the Federal Farm Loan system during and just after WWI. In the late 1930s he was pushing the United States into WWII long before the general population accepted the idea. William Randolph Hearst's <u>San Francisco Examiner</u> pointed this out in a 14 April 1939 editorial: "Mr. Meyer's newspaper, the <u>Washington Post</u>, usually represents the attitudes of big business and the banks, and usually attacks President Roosevelt. Tuesday morning, however, Mr. Meyer's newspaper printed an editorial asserting that American involvement in the impending war was inevitable, and even desirable."[183] Promoting WWII was a successful strategy for Meyer because as a result of this horrendous war President Truman appointed him the first director of the World Bank, one of the institutions established by the post-war Bretton Woods Agreement. The loan policies of the World Bank altered the overt form of colonial domination and instituted a more pernicious form of tribute and extraction. Their policies have produced a net negative growth rate in nine of ten borrower nations and have contributed to stagnation and slide into deeper poverty of many less developed countries (LCDs), especially on the African continent. One of the World Bank's former Nobel Prize-winning chief economists, Joseph Stiglitz, criticized the World Bank's one size fits all four-step strategy to economic damnation and stated that the World Bank "has condemned people to death." Stiglitz says without a hint of irony, "They don't care if people live or die."[184]

Step one is privatization. This is where national leaders are convinced with the prospect of receiving a 10 percent commission (kickback) to sell national assets to private concerns. In Russia, U.S.-backed oligarchs stripped

---

182. Eustace Mullins, <u>The Federal Reserve Conspiracy</u> (Melrose, FL: Common Sense Press, 1954), 56.

183. "Keep America Out of War," <u>San Francisco Examiner</u>, <u>14</u> April 1939.

184. Greg Palast, "The Globalizer Who Came In From the Cold," <u>Observe-Guardian</u>, 10 October 2001.

the country of its industrial assets. This led to nearly a 50 percent cut in national output and caused a depression and widespread starvation.

Step two is capital market liberalization. In theory this allows investment capital to flow in and out. Mostly the money ends up flowing out. This allows currency speculaors like George Soros to attack any nation's currency.

Step three is market-based pricing, a fancy way of saying that prices on basic necessities like food, water, and cooking gas, rise precipitously, which leads to step three- and-a-half. Step three-and-a-half is what Stiglitz calls the IMF riot. This is when people become so destitute by imposed austerity that they explode into riots. IMF documents have revealed that unrest is expected, and the IMF assistance plan calls for facing down civil strife and suffering with political resolve and still higher prices.

This leads to step four, which is what the IMF and World Bank call their poverty reduction strategy: free trade. This is free trade by the rules of the World Trade Organization and the World Bank, which Stiglitz likens to the Opium Wars: "That too was about 'opening markets,'" he said. As in the nineteenth century, Europeans and Americans today are kicking down barriers to sales in Asia, Latin American, and Africa while barricading our own markets against the Third World's agriculture—except opium and cocaine.[185]

This is simply a logical extension of the Malthusian worldview projected onto current political and social realities. Information travels much faster, and the great masses, imbued with the democratic ideal, might take offense at this consolidation of financial capital and corruption unless they can be brought into the corruption as a belief that they are part of the great fight against Communism, or drugs, or cancer, or terrorism. There is always some contrived calamity, each besting the last in scope and horror that is a consequence of intended shock therapy. HIV/AIDS is more of the shock doctrine of social control. Not only is it a cover story, it is a means to an end. As social conditions deteriorate, adverse medical conditions are going to rise and are going to be exploited. But for the masters of the universe, disease is just another business opportunity.

Joseph P. Kennedy, Sr.

During the 1930s, while Eugene Meyer was running the Federal Reserve Bank and the Washington Post and pushing for U.S. entry into WWII, President Kennedy's father, Joseph, who had been a big Wall Street speculator in the

---

185. Gregory Palast, "Stiglitz vs. the Bloodsuckers, IMF's Four Steps to Damnation, The Observer, 29 April 2001.

1920s was parlaying his wins into political influence. By 1937, he headed the U.S. Maritime Commission. Collaboration between Kennedy and Aristotle Onassis is likely to have occurred when Kennedy was head of the commission. On 21 October 1937, the Maritime Commission announced the acceptance of bids totaling $991,111.93 for the purchase of 22 of 25 "obsolete vessels in the commissions laid up fleet . . . Four of the old ships were bid in by a New York concern for a Greek customer who will use them with the pledge that they will not be operated in competition with American shipping."[186] There was only one Greek customer doing that at the time in this county— Aristotle Onassis.[187] During the Truman administration, through a series of dummy companies and the help of former Representative Joseph E Casey, one of Kennedy's longtime associates, Onassis was able to buy American Liberty ships, many at scrap-metal cost. These less than ethical and perhaps illegal deals (Onassis was <u>not</u> an American citizen, which was a requirement) helped Onassis to expand his shipping empire, in which he was aligned with the Rockefeller seven sisters oil cartel.

Joseph Kennedy went on to become U.S. Ambassador to Britain, and two of his sons, with the help of his mobster ties and support of the <u>Washington Post</u>, went on to become the President (and Jackie's first husband) and Attorney General respectively of the United States. The ties that Joseph P. Kennedy had to mob and banking elite friends led first to the White House but would ultimately lead to the shot that rang out in Dealey Plaza, on 22 November 1963.

After his father's disabling stroke in 1961, John F. Kennedy began making moves that his father's banker and mobster ties would regard as double-crossing actions. Joseph P. Kennedy knew the rules of the game of deep politics. John F. Kennedy and his brother Robert began to violate the rules that govern this serious informal alliance. As will be discussed below, in their attempt to save the American Republic, they were killed and the dream died.

It was not news that Joseph P. Kennedy had ties to the mob, and the mob had ties to the various intelligence agencies. The public execution of his son made it clear where the real power centers, supported by drug money, were and how they collaborated at the highest levels to hold politicians, even the President of the United States, under their control—especially when he was interfering with business as usual. These power relationships more than anything else were at the core of the deep politics and macro-social evil that led to the death of JFK and the death of the myth of the American Republic.

---

186. "U.S. Sells Old Ships," <u>San Francisco Examiner</u>, 22 October 1937.
187. Carroll, <u>Project Seek</u>, 57.

It opened the floodgate for heroin, cocaine, gambling, pornography, repeal of banking usury laws, integration of the economic system into the world system, and the disintegration of stabilizing social structures and of the economic core.

John Kennedy Double-Crosses Father's Mob and Fed Buddies

> Washington is a place of intricate deals, shadowy alliances and quiet understandings, a place from which the millions of dollars flow forth in a never-ending stream—and a place where even law itself has been suspended and none of the usual requirements of accountability or performance or competition seem to hold sway. . . . all of this takes place against a shadowy backdrop of occurrences that include: secret political contributions, business dealings punctuated by suicides, stated campaigns to buy and control politicians, sharply inflated markups on government contracts . . . [188]

There were several moves that Jack Kennedy was making that angered real management and have been well described by Col. Fletcher Prouty and many others. Prouty spent nine of his twenty-three-year military career in the Pentagon (1955–64): two years with the Secretary of Defense, two years with the Joint Chiefs of Staff, and five years with Headquarters, U.S. Air Force. In 1955, he was appointed the first "Focal Point" officer between the CIA and the Air Force for Clandestine Operations per National Security Council Directive 5412. He was Briefing Officer for the Secretary of Defense (1960–1961), and for the Chairman of the Joint Chiefs of Staff. Prouty's book The Secret Team is an insider's view of how clandestine operations are arranged and executed. His book begins by observing: "The most remarkable development in the management of America's relations with other countries during the quarter-century since the end of World War II has been the assumption of more and more control over military, financial and diplomatic operations at home and abroad by men whose activities are secret, whose budget is secret, whose very identities as often as not are secret—in short, by a Secret Team whose actions only those implicated in them are in a position to monitor and to understand." From his vantage point as an ultimate insider, Prouty had access to the behind the scenes decision making

---

188. Donald J Barlett and James B. Steele, "The Silent Partner of Howard Hughes," Philadelphia Inquirer, 14–20 December 1975.

of some of the most momentous events in the nation's history. He understood that assassinating a president took enormous planning, flawless execution, enormous resources, access to classified information and the authority to override system protocols—none of which support the lone-nut theory.

According to Col. Prouty, The secret team had reason to want Kennedy neutralized—he was acting outside of his pay-grade. Kennedy was attempting to make major changes that would have impacted the incomes and power base of some very influential people, people who are able to mobilize with the greatest secrecy any team necessary to carry out their agenda.

"Financially the CIA was conceived in sin. Before there was a CIA, there was an OSS, the Office of Strategic Services. The OSS was the evil spawn of British Intelligence. The OSS's parent, the Coordinator of Intelligence, was authorized by Franklin D. Roosevelt in 1941, in good part to permit the Roosevelt administration to support its friends around the world no matter what the laggard and frequently isolationist Congress might prefer."[189] It must be remembered that the CIA was founded by Wall Street bankers and lawyers who were in league not only with the mob, but with foreign intelligence services who could supply assassination teams and who were not averse to doing what they felt was necessary to protect their business interests and power dynamics. These long and significant ties to the mob gave them great leverage in their ability to conduct combined worldwide clandestine and narcotics businesses.

Kennedy was trouble for them. He had vowed to break the CIA into a thousand pieces. This would threaten the power base of Allen Dulles and the Wall Street lawyers and bankers whose interests Dulles was protecting. He was changing the way large military contracts involving billions of dollars were being handled, and he was considering de-escalating the Cold War by beginning disarmament of the nuclear weapons arsenal—removing some insiders from this lucrative loop. One such insider was Col. D. Harry Byrd, a leading defense contractor, a Dallas/Houston oil and gas man, an adherent of radical right policies, and the owner of the Dallas Book Depository. After the assassination, he had the window from which Oswald supposedly took the shots at Kennedy framed and hung on his wall as a trophy.

Kennedy was determined to draw down rather than escalate U.S. involvement in Vietnam. This was spelled out in his last National Security Action Memorandum 263,[190] dated 11 October 1963. This would have

---

189. Burton Hersh, The Old Boys: The American Elite and the Origins of the CIA (St. Petersburg, FL: Tree Farm Books, 1992.).

190. Kennedy was killed on 22 November. NSAM 273 replaced 263, but it was prepared on 21 November, the day before Kennedy's death by McGeorge Bundy, who was at a conference in Honolulu on the 20th and was flying back

undermined the plan to introduce massive narcotics into the United States and would have threatened Wall Street portfolios that use drug money to beef up their price to earnings ratios, and therefore CEO pay. He was committed through executive order 11110 to return the power to the United States Treasury to create debt-free money and to determine its value back from the private banking institution called the <u>Federal Reserve</u>. This would eliminate numerous banking frauds and frequent devaluation of the currency. This sound money policy would have allowed the rational growth of the United States economy without becoming indentured to central banks, and it would eliminate the type of financial meltdown that occurred in 2008. But more than anything, it would have hindered the now occurring consolidation of global financial power that was begun at Bretton Woods. These actions infuriated the military, parasitic military contractors, the CIA, and the international bankers.

Kennedy was blamed for withdrawing air cover for the disastrous Bay of Pigs incident that had been planned during the latter days of the Eisenhower administration by Allen Dulles, by which the CIA would make another attempt to overthrow Castro. The mob hated Castro, not because he was Communist—after all it was the CIA who had helped him gain power,[191] but because he had put the kibosh on (Onassis?) Lansky's Cuban Mafia-dominated gambling and drug-running enterprise. This was a huge money laundering business for Wall Street and their mob friends. According to Sam Giancana, "In exchange for his underworld services, Mooney (Sam Giancana) said the CIA looked the other way—allowing over $100 million a year in illicit drugs to flow through Havana into the United States. It was an arrangement similar to all the rest they'd made, he said. The CIA received 10 percent of the take on the sale of the narcotics, which they utilized 'for their undercover slush fund.' Such illegally earned monies were stashed away by the CIA in Swiss, Italian, Bahamian, and Panamanian accounts."[192] Because Castro did not play by Wall Street rules, companies, such as Standard Oil of N.J., Domino Sugar, the American and Foreign Power Company, the

---

on the 21st! It became official policy on 26 November, only four days after the assassination.

191. "We put Castro in power," flatly stated former U.S. Ambassador to Cuba Earl T. Smith during congressional testimony in 1960. He was referring to the U.S. State Department and CIA's role in aiding the Castro rebels, also to the U.S. arms embargo on Batista, also to the official U.S. order that Batista vacate Cuba. Ambassador Smith knew something about these events because he had personally delivered the messages to Batista.

192.   Chuck Giancana, <u>Double Cross: The Explosive, Inside Story of the Mobster Who Controlled America</u> (New York: Grand Central Publishing, 1993).

Freeport Sulphur Company, and ITT met with Allen Dulles days before Christmas in 1960 suggesting that it was time for the U.S. to take direct action against Castro.[193] Castro was getting in the way of business as usual.

The anti-Communists were infuriated with Kennedy for his lack of enthusiasm for taking out Castro. This was the height of the Cold War, and many were fearful of having a Communist country ninety miles from U.S. shores. Kennedy publicly supported,[194] after the Eisenhower–Dulles orchestrated murder of Congolese President Patrice Lumumba (which occurred three days before Kennedy was inaugurated as President),[195] the nationalist ambitions of the Congolese people as they struggled to free themselves from the chains of Belgium and mining concerns, such as Union Miniere that had a vested interest in splitting that nation apart. And finally, the Israelis were not happy because Kennedy was also putting pressure on Prime Minister Eshkol about commencing inspections at their illegal top-secret nuclear installation at Dimona. In other words, Kennedy made a lot of very powerful enemies of suit-wearing psychopaths who operate in the shadows of the deep politics of world events and who wield the power and the means and the ability to shape these events in their favor.

A decision was made at the highest levels to neutralize him. The assassination occurred in a very public venue as a warning to any future president who might step out of line with the economic and political goals of this powerful global elite. It was a very public statement of power relationships. Lyndon Johnson got the message. The Vietnam War was expanded, and the direction of the country was returned to the status quo ante. As the war continued for a total of twenty years, the drugs increased slowly at first and then exponentially with the returning veterans. The bankers were happy. They retained control of the U.S. money supply and the U.S. Congress. The CIA was happy because they could continue their clandestine work in service to financial capital without interruption, and the military-industrial complex was happy because taxpayer money was funnelled into their expensive cost overrun projects and endless wars.

After John Kennedy's death came the public executions of Martin Luther King, Jr., and Robert Kennedy. A decade of social protests involving dogs, cannons of sprayed water, lynchings, bombed churches and dead children,

---

193. David Barrett, "The Two Stories About the Bay of Pigs You Never Heard," History News Network, George Mason University.

194. How he operated privately on matters involving Africa conformed to the dictates of Tempelsman.

195. Although he was murdered on 17th January, the news of his death did not reach Washington until 13 February 1961. Jim DiEugenio, "Dodd and Dulles vs. Kennedy in Africa," Probe 6 (January–February 1991).

and murdered civil rights workers, murdered college students from Jackson State in Mississippi to Kent State in Ohio, murdered Black Panthers in their homes in their beds, urban riots, and a paroxysm of violence culminated in the beating of demonstrators at the 1968 Chicago Democratic convention. The baby boom generation was traumatized by the onslaught of recurring "future shock" so that when the heroin-filled body bags returned from Vietnam and the CIA/Mob dumped LSD and other psychotropic mind-altering drugs amid college students and social outcasts, they were programmed to "turn on, tune in, and drop out." The Tavistock inspired MK-Ultra mass mind control program was entirely successful.

A further note on Jackie: She was a visitor on Onassis' ship the <u>Christina</u> a month before her husband's slaying and was consoled by him immediately after her husband's murder.[196] Because of the deep connections to the Kennedy family through Joseph P. Kennedy, some found this rather odd. Others did not.

The opium trade was built around the functions of banking, shipping, and insurance. With profits amassed from the sale of <u>tobacco</u> during the 1920s, Onassis built a fleet of cargo ships and an international empire. His shipping business was expedited with the help of Joseph P. Kennedy when he was head of the U.S. Maritime Commission. Onassis was soon shipping seven sisters' oil around the globe

In the <u>Gemstone File</u>, Stephanie Caruana alleges that during WWII Onassis was "selling oil, arms and dope to both sides . . . and went through the war without losing a single ship or man."[197] He was either protected or had an enormous streak of luck for four years because in that period there were almost four hundred other Greek ships that were sunk at sea.

The <u>tobacco</u> salesman and shipping magnet had relationships with some of the most powerful people of the time. Many were seen boarding his floating office on his yacht <u>Christina</u>. One of his alliances was with Hjalmar Schacht, president of Hitler's Reichbank, whom Onassis hired after WWII. Schacht helped Onassis build tankers in Germany after the war. Onassis was reportedly very close to Winston Churchill as well.

Maurice Tempelsman

Maurice Tempelsman has had such a profoundly negative influence on the recent history of many African nation states that he warrants his own chapter. To summarize here, he was Jackie's last liaison prior to her death.

---

196. Gerald A. Carroll, <u>Project Seek</u> 21.
197. Stephanie Caruana, <u>Gemstone File</u>, 61.

Tempelsman is less well known generally than Kennedy and Onassis but has nonetheless been a significant force on the Washington, D. C. scene for almost six decades. He has been the wizard behind the curtain orchestrating much of the sad and terrible drama that has played out in Africa in favor of the South African Anglo-American Corporation, the De Beers Diamond cartel, and related industries and interests. He is a diamond merchant and economic hit man for the Oppenheimers, owners of DeBeers Diamonds and world class manipulators. Why was he uniquely important to De Beers?

In the 1940s, De Beers was indicted by the U.S. Justice Department for price fixing under the Sherman Act. The U.S. also believed De Beers had rationed the supply of tool diamonds to the U.S. during the Second World War and had severely damaged the war effort. In attempting to prohibit this from happening again, the United States passed legislation to set up a national diamond stockpile. De Beers, despite its despicable behavior and indictment during the war, needed a way to ensure it was the source of this stockpile. The company sought a middleman to manage its business deals with the U.S. government. Early in the 1950s, Tempelsman met with the Oppenheimers who rule De Beers and became its middleman.[198] He was uniquely supplied with millions of diamonds to sell to the U.S. as its strategic reserve. Most of these diamonds came from the Congo and South Africa, two of the countries claimed to be hardest hit by HIV/AIDS.

Jackie's men were a study in contrasting, opposing, and interwoven powers that have driven major events over the last fifty years. Each man was more powerful than the last. The death of her first husband lifted the veil on the demonic energy vying for global control. Kennedy's public execution was the opening gambit in a series of unfortunate incidents that led to an expansion of the Vietnam War. The consequence of this war was a burgeoning drug trade and the development of new oil fields off the Vietnamese coast. These developments would be of great benefit to the expansion of Onassis' shipping empire. Tempelsman emerged as a power player in the Democratic Party and became a back-door ambassador for protecting the economic interests of foreign businesses ruled by the Oppenheimers and like-minded resource thieves largely centered in Israel and the U.S. These banking and mining interests have caused enormous economic destruction in many of the emerging African nations as a result of strategies orchestrated by Tempelsman on behalf of the Oppenheimer family businesses. The coups against and assassinations of the brightest of Africa's leaders have allowed Tempelsman to enrich himself and his patrons, the Oppenheimers, while

---

198. Janine Roberts, Glitter & Greed: The Secret World of the Diamond Cartel (New York Disinformation Company, 2003), 161.

he pours blood-tainted funds into the coffers of the Democratic Party. The funds assure that politicians like Bill Clinton and Madeline Albright look the other way when genocide, such as occurred on their watch in Rwanda, takes place. Tempelsman has made it easier for global corporations to plunder the African continent.

The men who were drawn to Jackie created the Malthusian world that needs explanation in a time of instant communication. The explanation for their carnage must naturally lead away from the power players who create it and point in the direction of the "present preference," oversexed victims of anomie and a nonexistent virus. HIV/AIDS would take the blame. All of this misery needs a coherent cover story, why not a bio-weapon "idea" as a politically useful tool? It was as good a cover story as any, and it certainly made impeccable business sense.

Chapter 8

Maurice Tempelsman, HIV/ AIDS and the U.S.–Israeli African Geopolitical Strategy

○ ○

President 'Ordered Murder' of Congo Leader

Forty years after the murder of the Congolese independence leader Patrice Lumumba, evidence has emerged in Washington that President Dwight Eisenhower directly ordered the CIA to "eliminate" him. The evidence comes in a previously unpublished 1975 interview with the minute-taker at an August 1960 White House meeting of Eisenhower and his national security advisers on the Congo crisis. The minute-taker, Robert Johnson, said in the interview that he vividly recalled the president turning to Allen Dulles, director of the CIA, "in the full hearing of all those in attendance, and saying something to the effect that Lumumba should be eliminated." Mr. Johnson recalled: "There was stunned silence for about 15 seconds and the meeting continued."

Martin Kettle, Washington Guardian, 10 August 2000

The South African <u>Mail and Guardian</u> reported that there is an international scramble for the wealth of the Congo and that "billions of dollars will be made." There is a vast contrast between the billions to be made and the estimated $1 billion that left Katanga province in 2005 and the unending suffering of the average Congolese. One Congolese miner interviewed by

Global Witness says, "We know that the Congo is rich. But despite this—we do not even have enough to eat. Only one category of people profits." Congolese live on an average of $100 a year, and 80 percent of the population lives on 30 cents a day. The Congo is a classic case of modern day serfdom and the depravity of those seeking to benefit at the expense of others even if millions more Congolese must die. Surely, King Leopold II would have a wry smile on his face knowing that over a hundred years later the plunder and pillage that he began continue uninterrupted with impunity.

Drugs, Diamonds, Gold, and Deep Politics

All diamonds currently on the market are blood diamonds—all of them. There are few if any exceptions. Like opium and cocaine commodities, they are used to purchase arms and finance civil wars, extralegal covert activities, land theft, and genocide. Like opium, the profits are laundered through international banks. There is no such thing as conflict-free stones, in spite of the whitewashing of the World Diamond Congresses' <u>Kimberly Process</u>. After Janine Roberts published her exposé of the diamond industry, <u>Glitter and Greed</u>, and made the explosive documentary <u>The Diamond Empire</u>, depicting atrocities as routine business practice committed by the international diamond business, the industry was nervous to protect its image, profits, and monopoly control. In 2003, the U.S. Congress, which easily bends to the will of Maurice Tempelsman money and Israeli pressure, passed the Clean Diamond Act, which was intended to sweep the idea of conflict diamonds into the mineshafts of history. The General Accounting Office noted in 2006 that the law was weak and deeply flawed. Since at least 1996, Russ Feingold (D-WI) who co-sponsored the Senate version has been heavily funded by Leon Tempelsman & Son.

The Kimberly process was partially instituted through the work of Robert Rotberg at Harvard University where Maurice Tempelsman chairs the International Advisory Council at the Harvard AIDS Institute of the School of Public Health. Rotberg and Tempelsman shared a panel at the Council on Foreign Relations with people like Walter Kansteiner, National Security Director under Bill Clinton and director of a gold company involved in Congo's bloody eastern zone. With the help of Oprah publicizing the Kimberly process and the Hollywood propaganda film "Blood Diamonds," diamond sales in the U.S. actually improved. The clueless hip-hop cultural icons epitomized by the vapid Kimora Lee Simons consider these blood diamonds a necessary statement to announce their total cooptation by the most degenerate elements of society.

Diamonds are common and cheap. Their value is created by market control, well- placed propaganda and market manipulation. Since the time of Cecil Rhodes, there have been millions of these worthless stones locked in the vaults of diamond bourses to insure the artificially high, monopoly-fixed prices of such "demon worthless rocks of desire." This is a commodity that is tightly controlled by a small group of individuals who form a spider web of misery and intrigue that leads from South Africa to Tel Aviv to Brussels and New York. These sparkling gems are not a girl's best friend, but a warmonger's best asset of untraceable funds to pay for guns, corrupt politicians, assassins, and chaos in the pursuit of an agenda run out of Israel.[199]

When Jackie's second husband died, she fell into the bed of Maurice Tempelsman, a man with deep links to the CIA, whose path was lined with blood diamonds, the apartheid system, and a holocaust of dead Africans. Maurice Tempelsman, Jackie's last lover until her death, is one of the men in the shadows who play the game of deep power politics.

Tempelsman is a diamond trader and an economic hit man for the Oppenheimers who control most of the diamond and many of the gold concessions in Southern Africa. Although he was born in Belgium, he is part of a small group of individuals largely originating out of Israel and the United States who have ushered in an unimaginable reign of terror and genocide in Africa that goes largely unreported or is grossly distorted by the Western media. The Tempelsman empire remains rock solid behind Leon Tempelsman & Sons, De Beers, and Lazare Kaplan International—supplier of Tiffany's and Cartier's diamonds.

An economic hit man is a highly paid professional who cheats countries around the globe out of trillions of dollars. They funnel money from the World Bank, the U.S. Agency for International Development (USAID) and other foreign aid organizations into the coffers of huge corporations and the pockets of a few wealthy families who control the planet's natural resources. Their tools include fraudulent financial reports, rigged elections, payoffs, extortion, sex, and murder. They play a game as old as empire, but one that since 9/11, has taken on new and terrifying dimensions for people in the first world.[200] These (mostly) men, such as Tempelsman, are the true face of terrorism. They are highly paid middlemen, agents of business interests that choose to use terrorism and repression to shock populations into submission for the purpose of hijacking their natural assets.

---

199. "Israel's Dynamic Diamond Industry," www.diamondworld.net, 23 August 2006.

200. John Perkins, Confessions of an Economic Hit Man (San Francisco: Berrett-Kohler, 2004).

It was noted during the truth and reconciliation commission in South Africa that "Captains of Industry, particularly those associated with diamond and gold mining (such as those represented by Tempelsman) pioneered many of the core features of what later came to be known as apartheid." These entrenched racist practices allowed firms to earn excess income by paying low wages and transferring the costs of ill-health, old age, and work related injuries to the workers themselves and to the women caregivers in the distant "Bantustans.".

The problem of worker ill-health stems from the hazardous and dirty businesses that diamond and gold mining are. These commodities are often embedded in asbestos or silica, two substances that form fine particles during the mining process and are damaging to lung tissue. Both of these substances can form inflammatory scar tissue in the lung that can lead to cancer, respiratory diseases, and tuberculosis. Respiratory problems have been somewhat reduced in the U.S. mining industry because of Department of Labor's Occupational Safety and Health Division (OSHA). The apartheid system deliberately supported hazardous mining conditions. It has taken a serious toll on the overall public health of Southern African countries and directly relates to what is called AIDS in this area.

Oppenheimer Anglo-American Corporation

Sir Ernest Oppenheimer and Lincoln William Honnold established the Anglo-American Corporation in 1917 with J. P. Morgan Finance. Morgan was the American agent for the English Rothschilds. In 1929, the company bought DeBeers from successors of Cecil Rhodes. Through Anglo, the Oppenheimers own shares in all of South Africa's mining houses. The Oppenheimers also own the nation's largest steel works, travel agency, brick factory, discount house, automobile dealership, and computer software firm. Anglo-American has become South Africa's largest banking concern.[201]

Anglo-American and DeBeers control all of the diamond and gold mines in South Africa as well as copper and coal. As of 2000, they controlled 80 percent of the world diamond market and almost half of the capitalization of the Johannesburg Stock Exchange.[202] Even in post-apartheid South Africa, they reportedly run their mines like slave plantations and have doggedly refused to institute even minimal mine safety standards. Wherever DeBeers, Anglo American, and their partners such as Dan Gertler and his partner

---

201. John Summa, "Anglo American Corporation: A Pillar of Apartheid," Multinational Monitor, September 1998.
202. "Diamonds, Gold and South Africa," Univ. of California, Davis, Geology Dept., March 2000.

Beny Steinmetz and their company DGI—do business these substandard conditions are reported to occur.

In 1995 the Leon Commission on occupational health published its report. The commission found that dust levels in the mines have not changed in half a century. The implication is that many thousands and perhaps millions of miners have died uncompensated of silicosis, asbestosis, tuberculosis and cancer. The mining company knew that the risk of silicosis could be reduced by preventing the release of dust during mining or by providing miners with respirators. It should have provided clean overalls and adequate washing and laundry facilities. Finally, Anglo American should have removed all dust from the miner's hostels,[203] but protected by the apartheid system they helped introduce, the company did nothing. There are mining engineering companies that provide a variety of methods to control dust particles: wet dust suppression systems, dry dust suppression systems, foam or fog suppression systems, dust residual systems, and water cannon systems. Reportedly, these systems have seldom been effectively used in South African mining. In 1983, the chief safety engineer of an unnamed South African mining corporation told the *Economist* that "production is more important than safety."

Société Minière de Bakwanga (MIBA), an Oppenheimer offshoot business, has been cited for shooting "illegal" diamond workers on its concessions in Mbuju Mayi, the diamond capitol of the Congo. "Every day, hundreds of unemployed Congolese take similar risks in the diamond fields of Mbuji-Mayi," wrote Amnesty International in 2002. "And every day, dozens of gunshots ring out as guards employed by MIBA seek to deter 'illegal' miners."[204] The BBC reported in August 2006 that MIBA security guards were sniping unemployed diamond miners.[205]

The average life expectancy of Congolese miners is about 42 years. In Angola the people are literally mining for their lives: Miners in Angola are forced into "illegal" mining because Angola's mining security companies push people off their own land. While agriculture and commerce in the region require the direct authorization of the Provincial Governor, not one miner has been granted a license for diamond exploration or subsistence agriculture. The "legitimate" government of Angola forces desperate people to resort to "illegal" activities to survive.[206]

203. Jock McCulloch, "Counting the Cost: Gold Mining and Occupational Disease in Contemporary South Africa," African Affairs 108 (431):221–40.
204. Amnesty International, "Diamonds Cost Lives," October 2001.
205. "Diamond miners killed in DR Congo," BBC News, 7 August 2006.
206. Marques, Rafael, Operation Kissonde: The Diamonds of Humiliation and Misery, 2006. www.cuango.net/kissonde/texto/KisondeING.pdf.

Three private military companies (PMCs) have been targeting miners in Angola. The mercenary firms Alfa-5, Teleservices, and K&P Mineira defend Angola's big diamond firms like Sociedade de Desenvolvimento Mineiro (Sodiam), Sociedade Mineira de Cuango, and Sociedade Mineira Luminas. Human rights researcher Rafael Marques documented case after case of PMCs arresting, beating, and torturing local people. They stop locals from fishing in their rivers, growing their own food, or living traditional lives; they have forced sexual relations on family members, including same-sex rape and sodomy.[207] The PMCs operate behind Angola's public diamond company, Endiama, and have exclusive rights to Angola's diamonds. Endiama owns 99 percent of the shares in Sodiam, which has a joint venture with Lazare Kaplan International (LKI), a Tempelsman family company.

In South Africa, DeBeers diamonds are embedded in asbestos, and hundreds of thousands of miners have suffered miserably or died of asbestos related diseases—cancer and leukemia, with development of secondary tuberculosis. Diamond dust is extremely toxic and, as noted by the Leon Commission, Anglo-American and DeBeers took no action to protect their workers. As long as the system of apartheid was in place, they did not have to worry about black workers rights—they had none. It was not until 1994, when the African National Congress gained political traction that the mining companies began to contemplate their possible legal liabilities. This is when pulmonary tuberculosis suddenly became an AIDS-defining disease.

DeBeers claims that toxic dust in their mines is harmless and has refused to improve worker safety. Tony Davies, Professor Emeritus of Occupational Health, reported that "when 200 retired miners from the Premier Diamond Mine were tested, every single one was found to have asbestosis. Yet very few know the danger. It has been hidden for decades."[208] The company obtained legal exemptions from this dangerous feature of their mine operations on the basis that the dust in their mines is uniquely safe! It thus conducts what is called "dry mining"[209]

A CDC report from the Division of Respiratory Disease Studies estimated that the rate of pulmonary tuberculosis in South Africa rose from less than 40 per 1000 in 1975 to 150 per1000 in 1998—an increase of 375 percent

---

207. Rafael,Marques, "Operation Kissonde:.The Diamonds of Humiliation and Misery," www.cuango.net/kissonsde/texto/indice Lhtm, 8 July 2006.-

208. Janine Roberts, Glitter and Greed: The Secret World of the Diamond Cartel (St. Paul, MN: Consortium Book Sales and Distribution, 2003), 2003.

209. Roberts, Janine Fear of the Invisible: How Scared Should We Be of Viruses and Vaccines, HIV and AIDS? (Bristol, UK: Impact Investigative Media Productions, 2008), 159, 204.

in twenty-three years.[210] It is not surprising, according to reports, that the company has since blamed this rapid rise in the incidence of tuberculosis on AIDS, inferring that working conditions are irrelevant. The cynical use of AIDS as a method to neutralize potential legal action against Premier Diamond's sub-standard mining practices is rather typical of the "impeccable business decisions" of this organization. What possible liability could accrue to a company that has a graveyard full of dead workers and cities full of injured workers who have a disease that was "sexually acquired"?

Exposure to silica dust is a risk factor for the development of pulmonary tuberculosis in the absence of silicosis, even after exposure to silica dust ends.[211] It is not a coincidence that mycobacterium tuberculosis is the biggest killer in South Africa and that the HIV antibody tests cross reacts with mycobacteria to make it appear that HIV is running rampant in South Africa. In Africa, all the rules of medical diagnosis have been changed. In the U.S., a test known as ELISA is considered very inaccurate, and no diagnosis of HIV infection is made without performing another antibody test known as the Western Blot for confirmation. However, for the most part, Africans are not even tested. It is too expensive. When they are tested, the least accurate ELISA is used. HIV ELISAs are not accurate enough to diagnose an American, yet it is deemed accurate enough for Africans who are much more likely to test positive because of the cross reactivity of the test to diseases like Tb, malaria, leshmeniasis and measles—diseases that have been common in Africa for generations. More on the cross reactivity of HIV tests will be presented in the chapter on HIV Testing.

To compound the problem, in Africa, AIDS is usually not diagnosed with an antibody test at all, the diagnosis is instead based on nonspecific clinical symptoms. This is called a "clinical case definition," and was originally developed by the WHO in 1985. It consists mainly of persistent fever, cough, and diarrhea and weight loss. It is nearly impossible to distinguish these symptoms attributable to AIDS from those of malaria, tuberculosis, or malnutrition. Diarrhea and weight loss are common problems in areas where there are both poor sanitation and lack of adequate running water. In the townships, where the miners live, there are miserable squalid conditions, poor infrastructure including open sewers, squatters, high unemployment, and hardly any home-grown vegetables. Enteropathogens contracted as a result of such environmental conditions are directly associated with increased

---

210. Health Effects of Occupational Exposure to Respirable Crystalline Silica, DHHS (NIOSH) Publication No. 2002-129, April 2002.

211. E. Hnizdo and J. Murry, "Risk of Pulmonary Tuberculosis Relative to Silicosis and Exposure to Silica Dust in South African Gold Miners," Occup Environ Med. 55 (July1998): 496–502.

permeability of the small intestine, which leads to diarrhea and severe wasting and what has become known as <u>slim disease.</u>

So, in Africa, the bar has been set extremely low to make an AIDS diagnosis. Contrast this with Europe and the United States where AIDS is defined by a series of specific diseases or laboratory findings and a positive HIV test, often more than one. Contrary to all of the rules of medical observation and diagnosis, the WHO "Bangui" rules exist conveniently only in Africa. This has led to an era of medical abstraction and blunder, unprecedented in scope. The lack of any requirement for such a test in Africa means that, in practice, many traditional African diseases can be and are reclassified as AIDS. Even Myron Essex of Harvard, whose work speculated on the African origin of HIV, states that "malnutrition and general lack of medical services contributed to diarrhea, tuberculosis, and other common African diseases that signify AIDS."[212]

Old disease dressed up as AIDS lead people to be stigmatized and isolated by their social group in such a way that the overwhelming nature of the diagnosis itself can lead to death. The rules are so arbitrary that if African patients left Africa, very few would remain AIDS cases. Postmortems are seldom performed in Africa to determine the actual cause of death. According to the Global Burden of Disease Study, Africa maintains the lowest levels of reliable vital statistics of any continent—a microscopic 1.1 percent. When AIDS experts are asked to prove actual cases of AIDS, terrifying numbers dissolve into vague estimates of HIV infection.

This politicization of medical diagnosis has been a great economic benefit to the DeBeers Anglo American enterprise. Instead of their workers having plain old work-related Tb they are now cursed with an AIDS diagnosis. It is not a coincidence that Templesman chairs the International Advisory Council at the Harvard AIDS Institute of the School of Public Health. It makes good business sense. It is a way of protecting his profits by way of protecting the profits of the Oppenheimer companies. If the company had to pay living wages, correct its mine hazards, improve the living quarters of its workers, and pay restitution for the number of injured and dead workers that result from their standard business practices, the cost would certainly limit their obscene profits. In this respect, HIV/AIDS is as stated in the PNAC document, a "politically useful tool."

The scientific literature on HIV antibody testing produced references to seventy diseases or conditions that could possibly cause false-positive reactions on HIV ELISA and/or Western Blots. Many of the conditions are quite prevalent in Africa, including tuberculosis, malaria, leprosy, Q-fever,

---

212. <u>New Scientist</u>, 18 February 18 1988.

tapeworms or other parasites, as well as leishmaniasis.[213] What was very interesting and worrisome to me as an obstetrician is that when the HIV tests are done in Africa at all, they are often done in prenatal clinics with the ELISA test, which is known to give frequent "false positive" results. One of the conditions that can trigger a false positive result is pregnancy! Even the packet insert in the ELISA test kit from Abbott Labs contains the disclaimer: "There is no recognized standard for establishing the presence or absence of HIV-1 antibody in human blood." Furthermore, the placenta is full of what are called <u>retroviruses</u>—not to cause problems, but likely as messenger molecules involved in DNA replication and repair.

In 1999, of 10 countries with the highest incidence rate (per 100,000) of tuberculosis, 7 were in Africa: Zimbabwe 584; South Africa 526; Kenya 484; Mozambique 433; Ethiopia 397; Uganda 351; and the Democratic Republic of Congo 320.[214] This is in comparison with U.S. rates reported in the <u>Journal of the American Medical Association</u>, in 2006, as 4.6.[215] Tuberculosis began to decline in Western countries as a result of improved socioeconomic conditions that led, in turn, to better nutrition and living and working standards; application of primitive public health measures; and the dawning realization that tuberculosis was probably an infectious disease and beginning sequestration of (contagious) consumptives in hospitals and sanatoriums. Rising rates of tuberculosis, like infant mortality, are indications of economic deterioration within a given society.

All of the defined Bangui symptoms and <u>African AIDS</u> diseases have been endemic in Africa for generations. Kaposi's sarcoma, an AIDS indicator disease, was described by physicians of Kemet about 1600 B.C. and described in the Ebers Papyrus stored in the library at the University of Leipzig, Germany. According to Professor P.A.K. Addy, head of Clinical Microbiology, University of Science and Technology in Kumsi, Ghana: "Europeans and Americans came to Africa with prejudiced minds, so they are seeing what they wanted to see. . . .I've known for a long time that AIDS is not a crisis in Africa as the world is being made to understand. But in Africa it is very difficult to stick your neck out and say certain things. The West came out with those frightening statistics on AIDS in Africa because it was unaware of certain social and clinical conditions. In most of Africa,

---

213. Christine Johnson, "Why the "AIDS Test" doesn't work in Africa," <u>Rethinking AIDS,</u> January 2001.

214. Paul D. Van Helden, "The Economic Divide and Tuberculosis," <u>European Molecular Biology Organization Reports 4</u> (September 24-28, 2003).

215. "Trends in Tuberculosis Incidence—United States, 2006," <u>JAMA</u> <u>297</u> (April 25, 2007).

infectious diseases, particularly parasitic infections, are common. And there are other conditions that can easily compromise or affect one's system."

Dr. Konotey-Ahulu from the Cromwell Hospital in London expresses a similar view: "Today, because of AIDS, it seems that Africans are not allowed to die from these conditions (from which they used to die before the AIDS era) any longer. If tens of thousands are dying from AIDS (and Africans do not cremate their dead) where are the graves?" According to him, the uppermost question in the minds of intelligent Africans and Europeans in that continent is: "Why do the world's media appear to have conspired with some scientists to become so gratuitously extravagant with the untruth?"[216]

The answer is fairly straightforward. AIDS is part of the business model being used by the West to explain away the numerous atrocities committed by extractive corporations as a part of their routine business practices on this continent. Maurice Tempelsman, an icon of such business interests, has invested his entire life in supporting this business model whereby workers' lives are ended abruptly by deliberate business decisions that privilege profits over human life. The accumulating corpses of the dead become part of the mounds of human detritus left behind with the toxic sludge from the mines. It's just business.

Templesman has played a key role over the course of the last six decades in the destabilization and economic ruin of several African countries. He has moved for years in the most powerful political circles and has counted the Roosevelts, Kennedys, and Clintons as friends.[217] He arranged a meeting for Harry Oppenheimer with President-elect John Kennedy. He has helped to shape U.S. foreign policy in Africa in De Beer's favor for a long time. According to letters found in Justice and State Department files, "Maurice had become Mr. Oppenheimer's unofficial U.S. representative in the 1950s, when he (sic) was still in his twenties. He still visits Congress and the White House and has long been a powerful advocate for diamond cartel interests."[218]

By sitting on the board of the Harvard School of Public Health's AIDS Initiative, Templesman has made sure that the atrocities he instigates in Africa as a staunch advocate for mining interests are misconstrued as the HIV/AIDS crises. They list him as follows:

> MAURICE TEMPELSMAN, Chairman of the Board of Directors of Lazare Kaplan International Inc., the largest cutter and

216. Eleni Papadopulos-Eleopulos and Valender Turner, "Aids in Africa," Rethinking AIDS (January 1995).

217. Janine Roberts, Glitter & Greed: the Secret World of the Diamond Cartel (St. Paul, MN: Consortium Book Sales and Distribution, 2003), 174.

218. Ibid., 170.

polisher of "ideal cut" diamonds in the United States. He also is senior partner in the firm of Leon Tempelsman & Son, a company active in mining, investments and business development and minerals trading in Europe, Russia, Africa, Latin America, Canada *and* Asia. Mr. Tempelsman serves on the International Advisory Council of the American Stock Exchange.

Mr. Tempelsman served as Chairman of the Corporate Council on Africa until 2002 and is now Chairman Emeritus.

A member of the Board of Trustees of the Africa-America Institute (and a past Chairman), Mr. Tempelsman is also a Director of the National Democratic Institute of International Affairs, the Center for National Policy and the Business Council for International Understanding.

This résumé omits that Tempelsman is chairman of the American Jewish Congress, a Zionist pressure group that claims it works closely with the Israeli military. SEC filings show that Lazare Kaplan International (LKI) directors are high-rolling lawyers and investment bankers. One director belongs to the law firm that once represented President Kennedy. LKI is also connected to the euphemistically named United States Agency for International Development (USAID), a front group used to control food politics. [219]

Tempelsman's participation in the National Endowment for Democracy is even more problematic. NED and its partners facilitate political interventions in foreign countries. The NED's core affiliate, the Center for International Private Enterprise, works, for example, with USAID in Afghanistan (opium, oil), and is linked to Bechtel. NED's core affiliate the National Democratic Institute counts Maurice Tempelsman and Madeleine Albright as directors. Richard Gephardt has served on the boards of NDI and NED, both of which funded Congo's "historic national elections" from 2004 to 2006 and have been funding the opposition MDC Party in Zimbabwe for years. This has led to continuing destabilization and stalled land reforms.

NED directors tied to Tempelsman include: Howard Wolpe; Richard Holbrooke; and Morton Abromowitz. Wolpe was Clinton's Special Envoy to Africa's Great Lakes Region and director of the "Africa and U.S. National Interests" Project of the Ninetieth American Assembly, where some sixty-

---

219. Keith Harmon Snow, "Chloe's Blood Diamond, Angola Rock sold for $16 million to GUESS jeans founder," <u>Global Research</u>, 24 November 2007.

nine representatives from elite military, intelligence, and corporate interests attended closed door think-tank proceedings: Maruice Tempelsman funded it.[220] Holbrooke, Wolpe, Abramowitz, John Deutch[221] are "experts" for the intelligence consulting firm, Intellibridge, founded by Tempelsman's confidante Anthony Lake.[222] Wolpe was on the board of Africare, as well as Joseph Kennedy and former Senator Bill Frist. Holbrooke is president/CEO of the Global Business Council on AIDS, whose director Mark Moody Stuart is a director of Anglo-American mining and former director of Royal Dutch Shell (ret. 2005). Holbrooke and Tempelsman are on the board of the Africa-America Institute, along with former USAID official Gayle Smith, Clinton's National Security negotiator for Rwanda and Uganda, member of the Council on Foreign Relations and the Corporate Council on Africa whose chair is Maurice Tempelsman.[223]

This is the rest of the Maurice Tempelsman story. Belgian-born Maurice has a long history of association with the turmoil in the Congo (and Central and Southern Africa) that goes back to their initial independence from Belgium and the assassination of their nationalist first Prime Minister, Patrice Lumumba, and subsequent instillation of the chosen strongman—Mobutu. Tempelsman became a key supporter of this dictator before the murder of Patrice Lumumba by arranging the funding that flowed to Mobutu. When the newly independent Congo's first premier Lumumba pledged to return diamond wealth back to the Congo in the early 1960s, Tempelsman, helped engineer the coup d'état that consolidated the dictatorship of 29-year-old Colonel Mobutu. He also was involved in facilitating another coup, this one against Ghana's Kwame Nkrumah. Diamonds were at stake in each.

The Congo is the second largest country in Africa. For decades, under Belgium rule, it was ruthlessly stripped of its natural resources: copper, tin, rubber, zinc, ivory, and agricultural products such as cacao, coffee, and palm oil. King Leopold claimed that everything in the Congo belonged to him. This was certainly true, as the Belgium government ran the country's railroads, mines, smelters, cacao and palm oil plantations, factories, and hotels

220. Rick Hines and Keith Harmon Snow, "Blood Diamonds, Doublethink, and Deception over Those Worthless Little Rocks," Z Magazine, 1 June 2007, 22.

221. After Gary Webb publish his exposé of George H. W. Bush running drugs from the White House during Iran Contra, Deutch, director of the CIA, made an unusual trip to Watts to speak with neighborhood residents.

222. Lake was Clinton's National Security Advisor who, somehow, happened not to call any high-level cabinet meetings to discuss the ongoing genocide between the Tutsis and Hutus.

223. Hines and Snow, "Blood Diamonds," 22.

through front corporations. The corporations answered to King Leopold, [224] and Leopold answered to the Rothschilds who became the court bankers in 1853. All of that was threatened by an aspiring political leader by the name of Patrice Lumumba who, in 1959, announced the formation of a national political party to oppose Belgium rule of his country.

The Congo suffered years of unspeakable brutality under Belgium rule, especially the savagery experienced under Leopold II. Leopold's people committed gruesome horrors and turned the whole of the Congo into a massive slave-labor camp. Leopold's people brutalized millions and slaughtered at least 15 million people. In just twenty-three years, Leopold's agents managed to kill half of the population. There was no Nuremberg for his crimes against humanity! There is no holocaust museum for the people of the Congo for this disaster! At the famous colonial Tervuren museum in Brussels, there is no mention of Leopold's crimes. Perhaps the Congo was the laboratory and prelude to what Europeans did to other Europeans during WWII. .

Indeed, hands and other limbs were routinely hacked off the living, smoked, and brought forth in baskets at the feet of officers to extract more bullets or prove that native 'sloth' had been duly punished. Many units on patrol had a designated "keeper of the hands."

Lumumba made the naïve mistake of announcing to the world that he intended to nationalize the Congo's rich natural resources for the benefit of the embattled Congolese people. He was well aware how wealthy in natural resources his country was and how this wealth had been stolen to enrich the

---

224. John, Coleman, <u>Diplomacy by Deception</u> (Carson City, NV: Bridger House Publishers, 1993), 218.

Belgium crown and their investors. His idea of using the resources of the Congo for the Congolese people was anathema to the global economic power and especially to the Oppenheimers. Within seven months of Lumumba's election, he was liquidated. His body was hacked to pieces and stuffed in a vat of acid. To this day, he was the only truly democratically elected leader of the Congo.

Tempelsman was also behind the coup to overthrow another popular African leader, Kwame Nkrumah of Ghana. Nkrumah made several strategic moves that irritated the DeBeers diamond cartel. The first was the marketing of Ghanaian diamonds outside the control of apartheid South Africa and DeBeers. The second and probably the most frightening to European/Israeli interests was his pan-African vision of forming a defensive union of African states.

On 8 August 1960, Nkrumah made a secret formal agreement with Lumumba to form a joint federal state of Ghana and the Congo. It was to have a common currency and joint foreign affairs and defense departments. It was going to be called the African Union Government. Other African states were to be invited to join "with a view to liberate the whole continent of Africa from colonialism and imperialism."[225] This pact was made during the Cold War when Communism was the convenient foil. Nkrumah sought development aid from both camps. The CIA made their usual move; hand picked former Ghanaian finance minister Gbedemah and laid plans for a coup.

Letters found in the State Department from George Ball castigated Tempelsman for the careless leak of the coup plans. The CIAs hand-picked Ghanaian successor, the finance minister Gbedemah, used Tempelsman's office in Accra rather than the U.S. Embassy to communicate covertly with the U.S. government. Even though the coup was mismanaged and evidence pointed directly to Tempelsman, U.S. President Kennedy, while publicly supporting the drive for Ghanaian independence, remained "more appreciative" of Tempelsman's role than Undersecretary of State for Economic Affairs Ball, and he recommended that Tempelsman not be "downgraded."

Shortly afterwards, Kennedy approved legislation to allow diamond barter deals to be done for reasons of political advantage rather than U.S. stockpile requirements. This was effectively a permit for Tempelsman to arrange deals intended to support covertly pro-American-Israeli African politicians, such as Mobutu.[226] This was the private, behind the scenes, deep

225. Kwame, Nkrumah, <u>Challenge of the Congo: A Case Study of Foreign Pressures in an Independent State,</u> (London: Panaf Books, 1967), 30-21
226. Janine Roberts, <u>Glitter & Greed</u>, 218.

political machinations characteristic of every U.S. president toward the African continent. Kennedy was no different from the rest. Templesman paid his way in blood diamonds for the Democratic Party to look the other way as the diamond industry commits genocide and land theft as routine business practices.

Nkrumah was eventually overthrown in a CIA-backed coup in 1964. The new government predictably gave back to DeBeers the exclusive marketing contract for their diamond production.[227]

Occasionally, Tempelsman is a big donor to the Republican Party, but he has predominantly been a deep pockets contributor to the Democratic Party. He has been a regular supporter of the campaigns of John Kerry (D), Ed Royce (R), Tom Daschle (D), Barack Obama (D), Maxine Waters (D), John Rockefeller (D), Richard Gephardt (D), Howard Wolpe (D), Patrick and Edward Kennedy (Ds), Hilary Clinton (D) and the 1988 win of George H. W. Bush.

Tempelsman also exploited ties with Anthony Lake, Clinton's national security advisor, who intervened at the U.S. Export-Import Bank on Tempelsman's behalf.[228],[229] Lake's influence allowed Tempelsman to gain U.S. Ex-Im Bank and U.S. overseas Private Investment Corporation backing for multimillion dollar diamond projects in war-torn Angola and Congo. Templesman's interests in Zaire (now the Democratic Republic of the Congo—DRC) were negotiated through Lawrence Devlin, longtime former station chief in Zaire, who helped to arrange the assassination of Patrice Lumumba and the coup by a junior U.S. trained officer, Mobutu Sese Seko. Develin retired in 1974 but intervened with Mobutu's gang to insure the prosperity of Templesman's diamond syndicate.[230]

Lake was a former Peace Corps volunteer to Ethiopia and once served on the national security staff of Henry Kissinger during the Nixon administration. He wrote his Ph.D. dissertation at Princeton on Nixon's Africa policy, with the title: "The Tar Baby Option." Lake returned to government in the Carter administration where he helped shape Africa policy. Lake recycled again as a

227. Seymour Hersh, "CIA Said to Have Aided Plotters Who Overthrew Nkrumah in Ghana," Dirty Work 2: The CIA in Africa, edited by Ellen Ray et al. (Secaucus, NJ: Lyle Stuart,1980)..

228. Keith Harmon Snow, and Rick Hines, "Blood Diamond, Doublethink & Deceptions over Those Worthless Little Rocks of Desire, 20 July 2007. http://www.globalresearch.ca/index.php?context=va&aid=6441

229. Madsen, Wayne, 92–93.

230. Keith Harmon Snow, "The Matrix: Depopulation and Perception Management, part 2: Central Africa," VOICE (Pioneer Valley, MA), March/April 2001.

national security advisor in the Clinton administration during the Rwandan genocide when, according to Samantha Power, "During the entire three months of the genocide Clinton never assembled his top policy advisers to discuss the killings. Anthony Lake likewise never gathered the "principals"— the Cabinet-level members of the foreign-policy team. Rwanda was never thought to warrant its own top-level meeting. When the subject came up, it did so along with, and subordinate to, discussions of Somalia, Haiti, and Bosnia. Whereas these crises involved U.S. personnel and stirred some public interest, Rwanda generated no sense of urgency and could safely be avoided by Clinton at no political cost. The editorial boards of the major American newspapers discouraged U.S. intervention during the genocide. They, like the Administration, lamented the killings but believed, in the words of an April 17 <u>Washington Post</u> editorial, "The United States has no recognizable national interest in taking a role, certainly not a leading role."[231] However, this was less than the truth. There were U.S. footprints all over this orchestrated slaughter.

From the beginning of the Rwandan civil war in 1990, Washington's hidden agenda consisted in establishing an American sphere of influence in a region historically dominated by France and Belgium. The U.S. planned to displace France by supporting the Rwandan Patriotic Front and by arming and equipping its military arm, the Rwandan Patriotic Army.[232]

The genocide was sparked by the terrorist downing of a plane carrying two African heads of State, the presidents of Rwanda and Burundi, both Hutus, as well as many French officials. Wayne Madsen revealed that a French investigation in 2004 discovered a connection to an organization that goes by the name of the <u>International Strategic and Tactical Organization</u> (ISTO), which represents political and corporate interests, including Armitage Associates, founded by George W. Bush's first Deputy Secretary of Defense Richard Armitage and Kellogg Brown & Root, then a subsidiary of Halliburton.[233]

Paul Kagame, who headed the Rwandan Patriotic Front (RPF), a militant organization formed in Uganda, had been trained at the U.S. Army Command and Staff College in Leavenworth, Kansas. The College focuses on fighting war and military strategy. Kagame returned from Leavenworth

---

231. Samantha Powers, "Bystanders to Genocide," <u>www.theatlantic.com</u>, September 2001.
232. Michael Chossudovsky, <u>The Globalization of Poverty and the New World Order</u> (Quebec, Canada: Center for Global Research, 2003), 111.
233. Wayne Madsen, <u>Jaded Tasks: Brass Plates, Black Ops and Big Oil</u> (City?:Trine Day, 2006).

to lead the RPF shortly after the 1990 invasion.[234] The Africa Direct submission to the UN Tribunal on Rwanda reported: "From 1989 onwards, America supported joint RPF [Rwandan Patriotic Front]–Ugandan attacks upon Rwanda. . . .There were at least 56 'situation reports' in [U.S.] State Department files in 1991. As American and British relations with Uganda and the RPF strengthened, so hostilities between Uganda and Rwanda escalated . . . By August 1990 the RPF had begun preparing an invasion with full knowledge and approval of British Intelligence."

After the slaughter, among the ninety-nine person entourage who accompanied Clinton to Africa in 1998 was Maurice Tempelsman. Clinton reportedly came to review his diamond investments in Africa. This was exactly so. The blood diamonds had paid many to shut their eyes and hearts to the people of central Africa, and slaughter was orchestrated to advantage American and Israeli business interests. The U.S. did nothing to interfere, because they had three actors in the game: Laurent Kabila who replaced Mobutu in the DRC, Yoweri Museveni in Uganda and Paul Kagame in Rwanda. Tutsi Rwandan exiles, headed by Paul Kagame, were an integral part of Museveni's army. As the genocide began, Kagame's forces launched an offensive from Uganda into Rwanda. It did not halt the massacre of Tutsis, but it succeeded in driving the disorganized Hutus into neighboring Congo. This was an excuse to invade the eastern Congo. The whole exercise was to destabilize and take control of the eastern Congo border contiguous with Uganda and Rwanda that is resource rich. The Americans were assured of their player in this contrived tragedy, the new head of the Rwandan Tutsi-dominated state, Paul Kagame. His forces then invaded eastern Congo, chasing the fleeing Hutus.[235] Uganda and Rwanda are two of the largest recipients of U.S. and British military aid in Africa.[236]

Behind the local African warlords are the real players: Exxon Unilever, Branch Energy, and Bechtel and the diamond cartels among others. These are secretive corporations that, with the support of the U.S., U.K., and French Governments, fund, arm, and train private mercenary armies. Players like Hans Van Lujik and Bernard Legrand of Royal Dutch Shell; General Ed Soyster of Military Professional Resources; and even covert U.S. forces are deployed. With their secret backers and alliances, African <u>leaders</u> like Paul Kagame and Yoweri Museveni, and their many jungle warlords, have waged

234. Michael Chossudovsky, "Rwanda: Installing U.S. Protectorate in Central Africa,"<u>www.globalresearch.ca</u>.

235. Ford, Glen, "A Tale of Two Genocides, Congo and Darfur: The Blatantly Inconsistent U.S. Position," 18 July 2007, <u>www.blackagendareport.com</u>.

236. Blair, David, UK Telegraph, April 29, 2006: "British Ally behind world's bloodiest conflict", <u>http://www.telegraph.co.uk</u>:

war-as-cover for private profit. These proxy armies are depopulating parts of Africa.[237]

In 2003, UN Chief Prosecutor del Ponte described how she was told that she must drop all investigations of Kagame's crimes, or risk being removed from office. When Judge Del Ponte insisted that the evidence *required* that he be prosecuted for war crimes and genocide, she was removed from her office at the Rwanda Tribunal within 90 days, at the insistence of the U.S. and Britain.[238] The ICTR (International Criminal Tribunal for Rwanda) has evidence, military-I exhibit DNT 365 that specifically implicates the direct involvement of President Paul Kagame and his military in the 1994 fatal rocket attack the killed two presidents and French nationals.[239] To show how selectively the United States pursues the so called war on terrorism, Kagame who seems to be Africa's version of Pol Pot lectured and was honored in 2008 at MIT and he was 1 of 100 Time finalists for 2009 of the most influential people in the world.

According to the CIA Factbook, the Democratic Republic of the Congo (DRC) abounds with "cobalt, copper, niobium, tantalum, petroleum, industrial and gem diamonds, gold, silver, zinc, manganese, tin, uranium, coal, hydropower, timber." All of these resources are exploited by European, Israeli and American corporations that maintain their own mercenary armies to guard the extraction fields. For generations they have run their patches of Congolese land like governments, with the support of France, Belgium, the United States, Israel, and other powers. The so-called civil war effectively gave them full autonomy in the wake of Mobutu's corrupt demise, as the power of the central government in Kinshasa, crumbled. Mass carnage raged around them, but did not interrupt the extraction process. As the Washington Post concurs, the Congolese genocide has not become part of the American political discussion. It is just business and a lucrative one at that.

Since the initial coups to topple Africa's postcolonial pan-African leaders, diamonds have been extensively used to discreetly fund wars, coups, repression, worldwide terrorism, and dictatorships in Africa and abroad. In a Green Paper on "Private Military Companies," 30 August 2002, the U.K. government accused De Beers of employing such military companies for

---

237. Snow, op cit
238. Hartmann, Paix et chatiment les gueres de la politique (Flamarion, Paris 2007) and Del Ponte, War Criminals and Me (2008).
239. ICTR defence evidence in Military-I, Exhibit DNT 365. March 8.2007 Affidavit of QC Michael Hourigan (and supporting affidavit of Amadou Deme)

"covert reconnaissance" in Botswana, Namibia, and Angola. De Beers was listed five times. No other company was listed more than once.[240]

Fouad "Fred" Kamil, a Lebanese mercenary, was hired by Percy Stilltoe a former British MI5 agent who established a security service for the Oppenheimers. Kamil, in turn, recruited and organized more armed agents. When interviewed for the documentary The Diamond Empire, Kamil alleged that he and his recruits set up ambushes in Sierra Leone to kill diamond traders not authorized by De Beers and the local government. He also said he laid minefields to kill smugglers and independent traders—and thus, in practice, indiscriminately killed many innocent people.[241]

Diamonds can pay for a lot of private military contractors (PMC). Such private armies are popping up all over Africa. The use of PMCs enables governments and corporations who use these contractors to cover their tracks and avoid accountability. These groups seem to be operating at will and outside local or international law. Evidence that may otherwise be made available to the public under freedom of information legislation is impossible to obtain from private contractors. The Vinnell Corporation was the groundbreaking PMC directly involved in military and intelligence operations in South East Asia from 1965 to 1975. At the height of the Vietnam War, it had more than five thousand employees in Vietnam. A Pentagon official described the force as "our own little mercenary army in Vietnam. . . .We used them to do things we either didn't have the manpower to do ourselves, or because of the legal problems."[242]

Africa is plagued by poverty as a consequence of assault from the slave trade; years of colonial rule, World Bank and IMF loan policies, and now these PMCs. The PMCs bring more war, a chief cause of poverty. War completely undermines a country's development prospects by destroying schools, hospitals, and vital infrastructure. The poisons used to kill in war take fertile agricultural land out of use for years to come. Eighty percent of the world's poorest countries have suffered a major war in the last fifteen years, and nine of the ten countries with the highest child mortality rates have suffered from conflict in recent years. [243] Nine of the ten countries are

---

240. Roberts, Glitter and Greed, 216.
241. Ibid., 216.
242. I. J. Cilliers Douglas,, "The Military As Business" Military Professional Resources, Inc., edited by J. Cilliers, and P. Mason, Peace, Profit or Plunder? The Privatization of Security in War-Torn African Societies (Institute for Security Studies, 1998).
243. "International Cooperation at a Crossroads: Aid, Trade and Security in an Unequal World," UNDP Human Development Report (New York, 2005), chapter 5.

in Africa: Angola (187.5), Sierra Leone (140), Mozambique (137.2), Liberia (125.7), Guinea (123.l), Niger (119.5), Somalia (118.5), Malawi (117.5) and Mali (115.9). [244] A white paper produced by a U.K. group, "War on Want" noted that there were private military contractors who have worked recently or are currently working in the Congo (where between 5 to 10 million people have been killed), and in Zimbabwe, Equatorial Guinea, Angola, Liberia, the diamond rich Kono District of Sierra Leone, and Nigeria.

The mercenary companies provide a wide variety of services previously carried out by national military forces. However, they remain outside the law and because they have no national allegiance constitute a threat not only to the countries in which they operate but also to every country on the planet. The services they provide include direct combat, intelligence, training, security in conflict zones, consulting and planning, maintenance and technical assistance, operational and logistical support, and post-conflict reconstruction.

To the people who come in contact with these landlocked privateers, there is little to distinguish between such soldiers and the country of origin soldiers where their headquarters are located. This has been a very big problem in the Iraqi conflict.

Cynthia McKinney Uncovers Foreknowledge of Genocide in Congo

According to a Congressional hearing chaired by former Rep. Cynthia McKinney (D-Ga.) on "Covert Action in Africa: A Smoking Gun in Washington, D.C." evidence was presented that implicated the U.S. Government, the UN, private militias, and Western economic interests of having complete foreknowledge of pending civil unrest in Africa, and they all refrained from action prior to the Rwandan genocide. An estimated 800,000 or more people were killed in this paroxysm of insanity. The goals in letting this slaughter happen were to use war, disease, hunger, and poverty to cover up the centuries-old exploitation of the African continent. As a SAIC (Science Application International Corporation) report stated, "Displacing people has become a goal of war, not just a consequence." This is the definition of terrorism.

In his role as middleman for the DeBeers cartel, Maurice Tempelsman, according to submitted evidence, helped shape practically every major covert action in Africa since the early 1950s. Declassified memos and cables between former U.S. presidents and State Department officials over

244. www.mapsoftheworld.com 2006.

the last four decades implicate Tempelsman as having direct input in the destabilization of the Congo, Sierra Leone, Angola, Zimbabwe, Namibia, Rwanda, and Ghana. The hearings confirmed that he was directly involved in the overthrow of Ghana's first elected President, Kwame Nkruma, and the CIA-backed assassination of Congo's first elected President, Patrice Lumumba.

The Western countries now have practically unrestricted access to diamonds, gold, cobalt, manganese, petroleum, natural gas, timber, uranium and columbium tantalite, a strategic and scarce mineral found almost exclusively in Eastern Congo and used by Western nations in computer chips.

Project Censored 2007 reports that an estimated six to seven million Congolese have perished in the West's accelerated pursuit of the Congo's wealth since 1996—and the world remains silent because the media that is controlled by the same interests who profit by plunder has led the world to believe that Africa is dying from the ravages of AIDS. AIDS is the subterfuge for the economic destruction of a continent and psychological warfare against the African people of the Diaspora. Tempelsman as chairman of the Harvard School of Public Health's AIDS Initiative intends to keep it that way. It's just business!

Chapter 9

Kissinger and Nixon: China, Vietnam, Drugs, Cancer, and the HIV Connection

○ ○

Of all the enemies to public liberty war is, perhaps, the most to be dreaded because it comprises and develops the germ of every other. War is the parent of armies; from these proceed debts and taxes . . . known instruments for bringing the many under the domination of the few. . . . No nation could preserve its freedom in the midst of continual warfare.

James Madison Political Observations, 1795

Some of them (U.S. troops in Vietnam) are trying opium. And we are helping them . . . Do you remember when the West imposed opium on us? They fought us with opium. And we are going to fight them with their own weapons. . . .The effect this demoralization is going to have on the United States will be far greater than anyone realizes.

Chinese Prime Minister Chou En-lai, in conversation with Egyptian President Gamal Abed Al Nasser, June 1965

We know now that limelight and a brass band do more to persuade than can be done by the most elegant train of syllogisms. It may be hoped that in time anybody will be able to persuade anybody of anything if he can catch the patient young enough and is provided by the State with money and equipment.

Bertrand Russell, The Impact of Science on Society

"U.S. policy toward the third world should be one of depopulation."

Henry Kissinger, 1978

When honest historians begin to ruminate about how the constitutional structure and the economic dynamism of America were undermined by a parasitic element that maneuvered themselves to the center of political and economic power, the starring roll will go the 20th century version of the David Copperfield character Uriah Heep-- Henry Kissinger, one of the most odious cold-blooded creatures on the planet.

The question I always had about Henry Kissinger was where did he come from? He clearly had no pedigree. He was certainly a nobody. However, he is smart, amoral, and ruthless—all of the characteristics that would have been nurtured by his mentors for his role on the world stage. Unless his tutelage at Tavistock, the major British mind control think tank (psychological warfare unit) and the influence of Sir John Rawlings-Reese who pioneered research on psychological warfare against civilians are examined, his meteoric rise is inexplicable.

Before he was unleashed on America, Kissinger received training under John Wheeler Bennett, top intelligence director of the British Round Table and chief of MI6 field operations—a very high powered world player. He then moved on to Harvard University where he and fellow student Zbigniew Brzezinski were schooled in monetarist policies under British-educated William Yandell Elliott, a great defender of the British Empire and the Southern Confederacy. Finally, he rounded out his education in being groomed as a front man for the ruling elite by serving under George Franklin[245] and Hamilton Fish Armstrong[246] at the Council on Foreign Relations.

Clearly, since he has yet to go prison, he is still being protected at the highest levels from the consequences of his numerous crimes against the people of this planet from Vietnam, Cambodia, and Laos to East Timor and Chile.[247] Kissinger was the central figure in opening trade negations with China at the height of the Vietnam War when China was supplying weapons to the Vietcong for use against U.S. soldiers. Documents released by the CIA indicate that China was supplying most of the infantry weapons, mortars, and rockets used in South Vietnam as well as Antiaircraft artillery, ammunition for Howitzers field guns, and light tanks.[248]

According to the documentary "The Trials of Henry Kissinger," Kissinger was directly involved in deliberately prolonging the Vietnam War. The film's producer asserts that Kissinger conspired to sabotage the developing Vietnam peace accord in 1968 brokered by Lyndon Johnson and his chosen successor, Hubert Humphrey.

While Kissinger worked unofficially as an advisor to the American negotiators, he secretly funneled sensitive information to the Nixon campaign that served to discredit the peace talks and helped to get Nixon elected president. This treachery allowed the war to continue for five more years and for tons of heroin to be imported into the United States.[249] Ironically, Kissinger was awarded the Nobel Peace Prize in 1973 for hammering out a deal almost exactly like the one he scuttled at the LBJ-initiated Paris peace talks in 1968.

Understanding Kissinger's role in the prolongation of the Vietnam War and his simultaneous push to open trade with China is central to understanding both the steps put in place to de-industrialize the United States and how massive amounts of heroin began to flow into the country. Kissinger's actions did not start the flow of illegal narcotics into the country;

---

245. Executive director of the CFR from 1953–71.
246. Editor of Foreign Affairs who was bent on the destruction of U..S. sovereignty by articulating a globalist vision.
247. Christopher Hitchens, "The Case Against Henry Kissinger," Harper's Magazine , March 2001.
248. CIA released documents, "Sources of Military Equipment to the Vietcong and North Vietnamese Military Forces," November 1, 1968.
249 Robin and Laura Clifford, "The Trials of Henry Kissinger." This is a review of a documentary by filmmakers Alex Gibney and Eugene Jarecki based on Christopher Hitchens' book The Trial of Henry Kissinger.

they simply accelerated and amplified a trend that had taken shape with a CIA/Tavistock program under code name *MK-ULTRA*.[250]

MK-ULTRA was organized mass psychological warfare directed against civilians. Psychological warfare is done to foster disruption in such a way that makes it difficult for any individual to understand just how he or she is under attack. These tactics were developed to an art form by the British Tavistock Institute. Ultimately, the MK-ULTRA program was attempting to do to the U.S. in a more scientific way what the British East India Company had done to China in an effective but less scientific way. It involved the use of drugs, torture, and "psychic driving"[251] in an attempt to control human behavior as predictably as a rat in a maze. It also involved the introduction to white youth the use of drugs and of unrestrained sexual mores.

The Tavistock Institute had been long interested in the psychological control of civilian populations for military purposes. In 1948, Montagu Norman, one of the British bankers who financed Hitler's rise in Germany, sponsored a gathering for the National Association for Mental Health in the U.K. At this International Congress on Mental Health, the World Federation of Mental Health was formed to determine the direction of world psychological services. Norman picked chief of the British military's psychological warfare department and Tavistock Institute chief Brig. Gen. Dr. John Rawlings-Rees as president of the World Federation.[252] Rawlings-Rees was one of Henry's mentors, and he was responsible for ushering in a new era of the eugenics movement by using the cover of psychology and psychiatry as social and medical disciplines. This new strategy, disguised as scientific medicine allowed the eugenicists to distance themselves from the atrocities that one of their disciples, Rockefeller-supported Ernst Rudin, had so successfully orchestrated in the death camp slaughters for Nazi Germany.

Rawlings-Rees was the perfect man for the job. He had outlined his broad objectives at a speech he delivered to the Annual Meeting of the National Council for Mental Hygiene in June 1940:

---

250. MK-ULTRA was a mind control and chemical interrogation research program that was responsible for introducing drugs such as LSD on a massive scale to the civilian population

251. Victims would have loudspeakers hidden under their pillows or through unremovable earphones. Tapes would be played over and over again to burn phrases into what was left of their memory—many had had numerous electric shocks, been sleep deprived, and sometimes had partial lobectomies.

252. Anton Chaitkin, "British Psychiatry: From Eugenics to Assassination," Executive Intelligence Review 21 (30 July 2002).

Especially since the last world war we have done much to infiltrate the various social organizations throughout the country, and in their work and in their point of view one can see clearly how the principles for which this society and others stood in the past have become accepted as part of the ordinary working plan of these various bodies. That is as it should be, and while we can take heart from this we must be healthily discontented and realize that there is still more work to be done along this line. Similarly we have made a useful attack upon a number of professions. The two easiest of them naturally are the teaching profession and the Church: the two most difficult are law and medicine. . . .If we are to infiltrate the professional and social activities of other people, I think we must imitate the Totalitarians and organize some kind of fifth column activity!

Rawlings-Reese and the roster of <u>mental health</u> professionals from these organizations have been some of the most exotic collection of enemies of humanity on the planet. Understanding the motivation and objectives of Rawlings-Rees gives a glimpse of what Kissinger was sent to the United States to do. It helps to explain the development of U.S. foreign policy under his direction and the people who have followed in his footsteps. Rawlings-Rees did not shrink from this public admission of the infiltration of fifth column activity into democratic societies. Kissinger was his point man in America.

Another psychiatrist from the Tavistock Institute was German Kurt Lewin, who became director in 1932. Lewin developed a social engineering strategy that has become known as <u>the shock doctrine.</u> Lewin is credited with much of the original Tavistock research into mass brainwashing and applying the results of repeated trauma and torture (of individuals) in mind control to the society at large.[253] Of course such work was couched in more benign language. Lewin is credited with the model of the change process of human systems. The key to Lewin's theory was to see that human change, whether at the individual or group level, was a profound psychological dynamic process that involved painful unlearning without loss of ego identity and difficult relearning as an individual cognitively attempted to restructure his or her thoughts, perceptions, feelings, and attitudes.

In short, Lewin was postulating that if terror was used on a widespread basis then control could easily be exercised from an external point. Another way of stating this is that through controlled chaos, the populace can be

---

253. Jim Kieth, <u>Mind Control, World Control</u> (Kempton IL: Adventures Unlimited Press, 1998).

brought to the point where it willingly submits to greater control. Lewin contends that society must be driven into a state equivalent to an "early childhood situation." He calls such societal chaos fluidity.[254] Individuals would then willingly give up more of their freedoms for what they consider greater security and submit themselves willingly to greater controls. Nothing illustrates this point better than the augmented state powers that were swiftly instituted following 9/11: surveillance systems, a stampede to war, enactment of prepared legislation (the Patriot Act) that altered the tenants of the Bill of Rights, internal domestic spying, elevation of the presidential role to the status of monarch by the issuance of a multitude of executive orders, and the ever diminishing rights of the individual. .

The Tavistock Institute is linked into many high-powered elitist groups and think tanks—Bilderberg group, the Stanford Institute, the Institute for Social Relations, the Hudson Institute, the Heritage Foundation, the Hoover Institution, the Center for Strategic and International Studies and the Rand Corporation, of which Zbigniew Brzezinski is a member.

Lewin's work in the development of rapid change strategies is now the standard way governments do business. Political strategists and business people have recognized that by exposing a whole nation to unexpected massive trauma, a society can be sufficiently overwhelmed to give up willingly more and more of their freedoms for what they perceive as greater safety. In the United States, such mass psychological traumas began in earnest with the assassinations of John F. Kennedy, Malcolm X, Martin Luther King, Jr., Robert Kennedy, and the wholesale slaughter, even in their beds while sleeping, of members of the Black Panther Party. These traumas were heightened and seared into the minds of ordinary Americans by television, which had become a standard appliance in most homes. The public executions of notable people who were bothersome to the elite agenda occurred against the backdrop of daily horrors in the Vietnam War shown on nightly news— the war that was needlessly prolonged by Kissinger's machinations. Because these public assassinations were real world exercises in mass mind control, the real perpetrators, for political reasons, were never brought to justice. Using shock and awe strategies to coerce populations into whimpering submission has become standard operating procedure. And of course, there can be no better way to disrupt societal norms than to concoct a war on terror and then proceed to blow things up.

It should be no surprise that the HIV/AIDS travesty has been used as another exercise in traumatic mass mind control. Those hexed by the HIV antibody test, to their detriment, run willingly into the arms of the very

---

254. Ibid., 44.

people who created the problem. The fear generated from the diagnosis keeps rational thought at bay. People are victims of incessant propaganda campaigns by drug companies that profit mightily from human misery. Through constant use of fear and disinformation people become alienated from their own spirit. They become like those in the T. S. Elliot's poem <u>The Hollow Men:</u>

We are the hollow men
We are the stuffed men
Leaning together
Headpiece filled with straw. Alas!
Our dried voices, when
We whisper together
Are quiet and meaningless
As wind in dry grass
Or rats' feet over broken glass
In our dry cellar.

Shape without form, shade without colour,
Paralyzed force, gesture without motion;

Those who have crossed
With direct eyes, to death's other Kingdom
Remember us-if at all-not as lost
Violent souls, but only
As the hollow men
The stuffed men.

No better control of the disembodied mob has been devised than to delude them into accomplishing their own subjugation and enslavement.

During the Vietnam era, Timothy Leary, with the help of the CIA's Cord Meyer, worked out of Harvard and vigorously promoted the use of the drug LSD. These "teachers" preyed on their vulnerable and impressionable students. One of Leary's grad- school classmates, CIA contractor Frank Barron, in 1960 with government funding, founded the Harvard Psychedelic Drug Research Institute. Another of Leary's Harvard associates included OSS psychologist Harry Murray. One of Dr. Murray's many test subjects was a Harvard undergraduate math major, <u>Theodore Kaczynski who became known as the Unabomber.</u>[255] The media never told Kaczynski's side of the story. Kaczynski was an experimental subject in the investigation of how to

---

255. Michael E., Kreca, "How the U.S. Government Created the 'Drug Problem' in the USA," <u>www.lewrockwell.com.</u>

dissociate people from themselves in such a way that they would become unquestioning automatons in service to the state. Kaczynski was portrayed as a madman. Perhaps he developed a psychiatric illness as a result of such unethical experiments, but his observations on technological society proved he had not lost his powers of intelligent observation. He actually agreed with the conclusions reached by Bzrezinski in Between Two Ages: America's Role in the Technetronic Era, namely, that freedom and technological progress are incompatible.

According to Bzrezinski, "The technotronic era involves the gradual appearance of a more controlled society. Such a society would be dominated by an elite, unrestrained by traditional values. Soon it will be possible to assert almost continuous surveillance over every citizen and maintain up-to-date complete files containing even the most personal information about the citizen. These files will be subject to instantaneous retrieval by the authorities."[256] This data retrieval system was immediately implemented by the change president, Barak Obama. It must be remembered that Bzrzinski has been an advisor to President Obama and one of Obama's first acts as president was to push for a second bank stimulus bill which was approved for $787 billion in February 2009. There was an earmark in that bill for $36.5 billion to create a nationwide network of electronic health records—which will be subject to instantaneous retrieval by the authorities.[257] This coincides with the push by the drug companies Novartis, Proteus Biomedical and VeriChip to have patients implanted with microchips ostensibly so that they can be monitored for compliance with their drug regimes. But VeriChip announced at a presentation to investors that they are designing their implanted chip to link to online databases containing all your medical records, credit history and your social security ID.[258] Welcome to the world of Big Brother.

The Harvard-inspired human experiment continued for almost twenty-five years under the CIA's MK-ULTRA program. Columbia University also had a unit run by Harold Abramson who first "turned on" Frank Fremont-Smith. Abramson also gave LSD for the first time to British anthropologist Gregory Bateson, sometime husband of Margaret Mead. Then in 1959,

256. Zbigniew Bzrezinski, Between Two Ages: America's Role in the Technetronic Era (New York: Viking Press, 1970).

257. Robert O'Harrow, Jr., "The Machinery behind Healthcare Reform", http://www.washingtonpost.com/wp-dyn/content/article/2009/05/15/AR2009051503667.html

258. Jim Edwards, "Microchip Implant to Link Your Health Records, Credit History, Social Security", 5 October 2009, http://industry.bnet.com/pharma/10004616/microchip-implant-to-link-your-health-records-credit-history-social-security/

Bateson gave LSD under controlled experimental conditions to Beat poet Alan Ginsburg at Stanford University. Subsequently, Dr. Leo Hollister at Stanford gave LSD to mental patient turned author Ken Kesey and others, and thus it was said to have spread "out of the CIA's realm."[259] These human experiments resulted in several deaths, many psychiatric problems and the conditioning of a generation to the casual use of drugs, both legal and illegal. The millions in payout for damages in tort costs naturally were born by the U.S. taxpayer. Sidney Gottlieb, a main researcher and poisoner- in- chief for this project conveniently died in March 1999 just as several new cases involving victims of his experiments were being pursued.[260] Gottlieb presided over the CIA's technical services division and supervised preparation of lethal poisons, experiments in mind control, and administration of LSD and other psycho-active drugs to unwitting subjects.

CIA perpetrators of the MK-ULTRA civilian project, as usual, walked, including the Swiss drug company Sandoz AG that was responsible for the development and distribution of lysergic acid (LSD). Sandoz was owned by S.G. Warburg, of London. This drug company was part of the wide-ranging Warburg banking family assets. During WWII, one arm of the family, James Paul Warburg, was an advisor to President Franklin Roosevelt while another Warburg, Max, was one of Hitler's financial backers. James's father, Paul Warburg, was sent to the United States to write the Federal Reserve Act of 1913. James Paul Warburg also financed and co-founded, with Marcus Raskin, the Institute for Policy Studies that promoted the new left counter-culture and the use of LSD,[261] a drug his family's company manufactured.

The introduction of LSD was a new social phenomenon with two obvious impacts: the drug counter-culture of the 1960s and the student revolution, both of which were associated with widespread use of mind-altering substances. Both of these projects that targeted American youth were financed with $25 million by the CIA.[262] During the British East India era, the Christian China Inland Mission introduced opium to the Chinese on a large scale. Two centuries later, rock musicians (Beatles, Rolling Stones, etc.), and the music industry in Western countries brought the rapture of drug use and sexual promiscuity and made it socially acceptable to the young fans of this genre.

---

259. Anton Chaitkin, "British Psychiatry: From Eugenics to Assassination."

260. Alexander Cockburn and Jeffrey St. Clair, "CIA's Sidney Gottleib: Pusher, Assassin, Pimp, U.S. Official Poisoner Dies," Counter Punch

261. John Coleman, Conspirator's Hierarchy: The Story of the Committee of 300 (Las Vegas: Global Review Publications, 1997).

262. Bryon T. Weeks, "Tavistock, The Best Kept Secret in America," July 31, 2001

This cultural revolution of the 1960s, the brain child of the CIA's MK-ULTRA program, paved the way for the widespread introduction of hard drugs—heroin and cocaine—into the United States. The introduction of these drugs had been planned to happen as a result of the Vietnam War and the re-emergence of China as a world power. Chinese Premier Chou En-Lai made very clear the intentions of the Chinese when he stated, "Do you remember when the West imposed opium on us? They fought us with opium. And we are going to fight them with their own weapons. . . .The effect this demoralization is going to have on the United States will be far greater than anyone realizes."[263] In this goal, he was facilitated by the work of Henry Kissinger.

Wherever Henry Kissinger has gone, the stench of death and destruction soon follows. This has been his mission, his life's work. This vile mass of spiritless form has served his elite masters well. Kissinger has been a skillful manipulator at upholding the delusional utopian vision of creating a world with a unitary government and economic system—the new high-tech feudal society. He describes the process by which this macabre nihilist vision is being brought to fruition, as "the birth pains" that of necessity must be experienced to lead to the development of this new world order. This man's background and connection to much of the social chaos and war that have characterized the last fifty years and his status as an elder statesman whose wise council is sought in times of crisis simply underscore the moral decay of the controlling financial interests that have seized the reigns of the United States government.

Edward Bernays, a nephew of Sigmund Freud, was the chief theoretician of the Tavistock Institute of Human Relations. His job was to define methodologies to shape and form public opinion. Bernays devised a method whereby agents, such as Kissinger, would be brought into the scheme of things to promote the New World Order secretly as the actual agenda of the United States. Kissinger's role in planning wars in the Middle East, Korea, and in Vietnam is well known; as is his role in fomenting the first Gulf War.[264] Kissinger's "Energy Security" plan was adopted by Bush I and applied to Iraq. Kissinger reasoned that seizing Middle East oil as a preventive measure would be acceptable to the people of the United States, and an idea that could easily be sold to the Congress.[265] He was right on both counts.

263. Salvador Astucia, <u>Opium Lords, Israel, the Golden Triangle and the Kennedy Assassination.</u>

264. John Coleman, <u>Conspirators' Hierarchy: Committee of 300</u> (Las Vegas: Global Review Publications, 1997), 25.

265. John Coleman, <u>Diplomacy by Deception</u> (New York: Bridger House Publishers, 1993), 155.

During May 1973, the Bilderberg Group held its meeting at Saltsjoeban, Sweden under the chairmanship of Nazi Prince Bernhard of the Netherlands. Its purpose was to impose the "oil shock" of 1973, which was blamed on OPEC. That too was crafted by Henry Kissinger.[266] In 1973, the price of crude oil was about $1.70 a barrel. The oil companies were making from $15 to $18 billion a year in profit. Those were enormous profits. However, by 1980, without increasing output or the cost of production, the same oil companies were making $300 billion in profit. The oil embargo was a tactical maneuver in the art of worldwide economic warfare with the end goal of massive wealth transfer to a chosen few. The embargo was blamed on the Arabs, but this was nonsense. Oil was their only source of income. Testimony recorded in the <u>Congressional Record</u> at the time indicated that the storage tanks in the oil-producing nations were full. They were waiting for tankers to take the oil. Simply put, the oil industry was creating its own shortage to raise the price drastically and was making the Arabs and OPEC the designated patsies. The ultimate goal was to raise the price of oil that the consumer paid, get the Arabs to deposit their increased earnings in thirty year certificates in U.S. Banks, then use those certificates to lend money to third world countries knowing that they would default on their loans. Because the banks put the certificates in subsidiary holding companies, when the loans defaulted the holding companies could declare bankruptcy and the Arabs were bilked out of their principle. In the meantime, the defaulting countries were made to turn over their hard assets (arable land, old growth forests, water rights, minerals, oil etc.) to the lending institutions in perpetuity.

The Bilderberg Group, with Kissinger as their middleman, was simply declaring economic warfare on the entire planet. Clearly, it was a highly profitable war. Sheikh Ahmed Zaki Yamani, who was Saudi Arabia's OPEC minister at the time, corroborated this account a few years ago: "I am 100 percent sure that the Americans were behind the increase in the price of oil. The oil companies were in real trouble at that time, they had borrowed a lot of money and they needed a high oil price to save them." Yamani says he was convinced of this by the attitude of the Shah of Iran, who in one crucial day in 1974 moved from the Saudi view, that a hike would be dangerous to OPEC because it would alienate the U.S., to advocating higher prices.

"King Faisal sent me to the Shah of Iran, who said, 'Why are you against the increase in the price of oil? That is what they want? Ask Henry Kissinger—he is the one who wants a higher price'."

---

266. F. William Engdahl, <u>A Century of War: Anglo-American Oil Policits and the New World Order</u> (London: Pluto Press, 2004).

Yamani contends that proof of his long-held belief has recently emerged in the minutes of a secret meeting held on a Swedish island, where U.K. and U.S. officials determined to orchestrate a 400 percent increase in the oil price.[267]

Kissinger was the central player orchestrating world events during the Nixon administration. It was unlikely that Nixon had either the sophistication or the contacts of a world politician to control Kissinger. It is much more likely that it was Kissinger who controlled Nixon.

Nixon started his career as a pawn of the banking cartel when they sponsored him to defeat the troublesome California Congressman Jerry Voorhis. Voorhis was one of the few congressmen who had a clue about the scam known as the <u>Federal Reserve</u>. He wrote an insightful little book, <u>Out of Debt, Out of Danger</u>, in which he advocated issuance of non-interest bearing national bills. He was one of the few that understood the irony of the notion that <u>sound</u> money was created through the government or the individual going into debt. However, money that was debt and interest free as the result of the government itself was not <u>sound money</u> and a very dangerous thing. Voorhis, an independent thinker, was anathema to the banking industry. Nixon was not.

Edward Mandell House, an unelected advisor to President Woodrow Wilson encouraged Wilson to use the American military to enter into a strictly European conflict, WWI. This was done after Wilson won his election by pledging in his campaign to keep the country out of war. To make sure the bankers could make their profit on the backs of American people from this little venture, the Federal Reserve Act was passed in 1913 and the Income Tax law was passed (but never ratified),[268] essentially making the entire U.S. work force and their progeny collateral for government borrowing from these banking privateers.

Nixon had his Kissinger, who kept the Vietnam War going beyond any reason except the known outcome —the addiction to narcotics of thousands of U.S. GIs, the embrace of Communist China, the offshore oil wells, and the bankrupting and the planned deindustrialization of the U.S. economy by members of the Council on Foreign Relations.

It is not widely known that President Nixon was a casualty in the war against the drug invasion of the United States. Had Nixon not taken up the most basic interests of the nation in launching a wholesale effort to shut down

---

267. F. William Engdahl, Ibid.

268. The <u>only</u> record of the 16th Amendment having been confirmed was a proclamation made by Secretary of State Philander Knox on 25 February 1913, wherein he simply declared it to be "in effect," but never stated it was lawfully ratified.

drug trafficking—from the top down—it is likely that he would not have been unceremoniously forced out of office by Henry Kissinger. Documents are available in the public domain from the Drug Enforcement Administration and other executive agencies showing that Nixon's "War on Drugs" was directed at the top—at the banking institutions, the transportation grids, and only then at the distribution channels delivering the volumes of drugs onto the streets and country.[269] But Nixon was not entirely innocent. He used the specter of widespread drug use in the "lawless" African American community to run a strong "law and order" campaign that pushed the race button of many white voters. Nixon, like so many politicians who fail to read and learn from history was an easy mark to take down. His hubris and his need to record his deeds for posterity was his own undoing. Ironically, Kissinger went on to win a Nobel Peace Prize whereas Nixon barely escaped going to jail. That in itself speaks volumes about who had the real power in that relationship.

In April 1968, a group of financiers, economists, politicians, scientists and industrialists met at the Rockefeller estate in Bellagio, Italy to promote the aims of the one world economic order. Out of that conference developed another organization, the Club of Rome. In line with their Malthusian roots, the Club of Rome published a series of papers advocating a new world economic order and a deliberate shrinking of world population. In one of their landmark studies, "The Goals of Mankind," they attacked the idea of further industrial expansion and urban growth in Western nations, particularly the United States. It was a plan to end both industrial and agricultural expansion in the country. According to Stanford Professor Paul Erlich, "A massive campaign must be launched to de-develop the U.S. De-development means bringing our economic system into line with the realities of ecology and the world resource situation." Erlich simply updated the Malthusian theme of population overload he first proposed in a 1968 book, The Population Bomb. His book predicted that hundreds of millions would die from famine and starvation in the 1970s and 1980s. His wishful thinking proved wrong. However, the theme of population reduction (and U.S. deindustrialization) continues to be promoted as policy initiatives toward less-developed countries. The current Obama White House Science Czar John Holdren co-authored a book with Erlich in the 1970s, Ecoscience: Population, Resources, and Environment that advocates forced population reduction.

---

269. U.S. Labor Party Investigating Team, Dope, Inc.: Britain's Opium War Against the U.S. (New York: The New Benjamin Franklin House Publishing Company, 1978), 51.

By 1974, after the Club of Rome made population reduction part of the global agenda, the United States National Security Council under the direction of Henry Kissinger developed its own version of the Club of Rome documents, <u>National Security Study Memorandum 200 (NSSM 200)</u>. This memorandum explicitly discusses a strategy by which the United States would aggressively promote population control in developing nations to have access to natural resources thought necessary to protect the U.S. and Western corporate strategic interests. Kissinger claimed that burgeoning populations in the Less Developed Countries (LDCs), especially those that had natural resources coveted for U.S. strategic interests, were a national security threat. This becomes important in the understanding of how the AIDS crisis has been construed and used as a "politically useful tool" in resource rich areas of Africa.

It must be understood, however, that when these documents refer to U.S. strategic interests, they are not referring to the people of the United States, but to those Americans who dominate, control, and own the American economy. As usual, because of these goals, American people were propagandized about the extensive foreign aid sent to these poor countries. The public was led to believe that their leaders were sending massive humanitarian aid overseas. This, of course, is sheer nonsense. Most taxpayer funded foreign aid is spent on the military, the clandestine agencies, and on projects managed by Western companies. Little aid is funneled to the local economies of developing countries. <u>Foreign Aid</u> is often just another wealth transfer boondoggle and crony payoff. There was quite a scandal in 2005 when it was revealed that the United States Agency for International Development, or USAID, which distributes foreign aid, was spending 95 percent of its malaria budget on consultants and 5 percent on goods, such as nets, drugs, and insecticide.[270]

According to a 2008 Friends Committee on National Legislation Report, of the total taxes collected in 2007, 43 percent went for military expenditure and 1 percent was used for foreign aid. Israel is still the top recipient of taxpayer largesse by receiving an acknowledged $3 billion per year and possibly as much as $15 billion from beleaguered American taxpayers who cannot even get their own bridges, levees, and energy grids repaired.

Keeping the Club of Rome depopulation agenda in mind, very little foreign aid actually goes to countries in desperate need in a way that would improve infrastructure, hygiene, sanitation and nutrition. Condoms and vaccines and are not what the third world needs. The UN has reported that 40,000 people still die each day from starvation and that a million people die

---

270. Reuben Keyama and Donald McNeil, Jr., "Distribution of Nets Splits Malaria Fighters," <u>International Herald Tribune</u>, 9 October 2007.

on an annual basis from malaria—largely infants under one year of age.[271] Why promoting AIDS and allowing foreign aid to be funneled into the coffers of the politically connected continues to be policy is revealed in the infamous Kissinger National Security Memorandum 200:

> In order to assist the development of major countries and to maximize progress toward population stability, primary emphasis would be placed on the largest and fastest growing developing countries where the imbalance between growing numbers and development potential most seriously risks instability, unrest, and international tensions. These countries are: India, Bangladesh, Pakistan, Nigeria, Mexico, Indonesia, Brazil, the Philippines, Thailand, Egypt, Turkey, Ethiopia, and Colombia. Out of a total 73.3 million worldwide average increase in population from 1970–75 these countries contributed 34.3 million or 47%.

According to NSSM 200, the following elements would need to be implemented to affect this plan:

1. Legalization of abortion—which was accomplished in the U.S. in 1973;
2. Financial incentives for countries to increase abortion, sterilization, and contraception-use rates;
3. Indoctrination of children;
4. Mandatory population control and coercion of other forms, such as withholding disaster and food aid unless the LDC (less developed country) implements population control programs.

NSSM-200 indicates that the image of the United States must be maintained as a benign observer rather than the instigator of these population control policies. This was done through the auspices of the World Bank and IMF as well as NGOs (non-governmental organizations) such as the UNSAID (United States Agency for International Development), the UNDP (United Nations Development Program) and the UNFPA (United Nations Fund for Population Activities).

The foreign policy imperative of NSSM-200 was codified on 26 November 1975, when Brent Scowcroft who followed Kissinger as National Security Advisor after Gerald Ford replaced Richard Nixon. According to John Coleman, Nixon was likely out maneuvered and set up for disgrace by

---

271. www.cdc/gov/malaria/impact/index.htm

Kissinger because of his preference for going after the top drug dealers and for his reluctance in the bombing of Cambodia and Hanoi.[272]

Not only did they not get approval from Congress for bombing Cambodia but they also tried to conceal the truth from Congress and the American people that there were 3,500 bombing sorties that killed 600,000 people who still tilled the soil with water buffalos.

To bolster the argument of future population conflicts and the need for population reduction in the Less Developed Countries, Kissinger cites numerous global conflicts, most of which were confirmed to have been supported by covert intelligence agencies of the United States and/or Israel in support of global commercial interests. Nine years after this policy paper went into effect, the global AIDS scare was manufactured.

The use of fear of disease and the subsequent creation of a "philanthropic" response to gain the public's goodwill has been a long-term strategy of the Rockefeller-controlled medical cartel.

Opening Trade with China and the Globalization Scam

While thousands of Americans and millions of Vietnamese were dying to "save the world from Communism," Kissinger was making secret trips to China, the world's most populous Communist country, to meet with Premier Zhou Enlai to begin trade talks. That China was supplying the Viet Cong with weapons, including opium, to use against American soldiers was just part of the birthing pains for the new world order. Kissinger, instead of being tried for treason for this venture, was hailed as a hero who opened up trade with China. Good propaganda creates its own parallel reality. It was only after Kissinger's 1972 trip to China that the Chinese role in the world opium trade ceased to make world headlines. The spin the media gave to the American people after Kissinger's secret meetings with Chinese premiere Zhou En-lai paved the way for Nixon's visit to China was that the diplomatic exchange would normalize relations with the world's most populous country and trade would create a more "democratic" environment in China. This sounded reasonable, even enlightened, as this was spun as a strategy for nuclear deterrence in the Cold War with Russia. The spin was interesting since the policy from WWII until Nixon's China trip had been to promote fear of Communism. After the Nixon trip, in an Orwellian about face, the world was told that Chinese Communism would uniquely surrender its harsher elements to the magic of McDonalds, Coca Cola, and <u>free market</u>

---

272. John Coleman, <u>The Committee of 300</u>, 319

economics. However, there was another free market policy that was being put into place by the Vietnam War.

The sudden burgeoning of heroin addiction among GIs in 1970 was the most important development in Southeast Asia's narcotics traffic since the region attained self-sufficiency in opium production in the late 1950s. By 1968–1969, the Golden Triangle region was harvesting close to one thousand tons of raw opium annually, exporting morphine base to European heroin laboratories, and shipping substantial quantities of narcotics to Hong Kong, both for local consumption and re-export to the United States. Although large amounts of chunky, low-grade no. 3 heroin were being produced in Bangkok and the Golden Triangle for the local market, there were no laboratories anywhere in Southeast Asia capable of producing the fine-grained, 80 to 99 percent pure, no. 4 heroin. However, in late 1969 and early 1970, Golden Triangle laboratories added the final, dangerous, ether precipitation process and converted to production of no. 4 heroin. Many of the master chemists who supervised the conversion were Chinese brought in especially from Hong Kong. In a June 1971 report, the CIA said that conversion from no. 3 to no. 4 heroin production in the Golden Triangle "appears to be due to the sudden increase in demand by a large and relatively affluent market in South Vietnam."—meaning the American soldiers. By mid-April 1971, demand for no. 4 heroin, both in Vietnam and the United States, had increased so quickly that the wholesale price for a kilo jumped to $1,780 from $1,240 the previous September.[273]

Once large quantities of heroin became available to American GIs in Vietnam, heroin addiction spread like a plague. Previously nonexistent in South Vietnam, suddenly no. 4 heroin was everywhere: Fourteen-year old girls were selling heroin at roadside stands on the main highway from Saigon to the U.S. army base at Long Binh; Saigon street peddlers stuffed plastic vials of 95 percent pure heroin into the pockets of GIs as they strolled through downtown Saigon; and mama-sans, or Vietnamese barracks' maids, started carrying a few vials to work for sale to on-duty GIs. With this kind of aggressive sales campaign, the results were predictable. In September 1970, army medical officers questioned 3,103 soldiers of the Americal Division and discovered that 11.9 percent had tried heroin since they came to Vietnam, and 6.6 percent were still using it on a regular basis.[274]

---

273. New York Times, 6 June 1971, 2.
274. Capt. Gary C. Lulenski (MC), Capt. Larry E. Alessi (MC) and Sp4c Charles E. Burdick, "Drug Abuse in the 23rd Infantry Division (Americal)," September 1970, 9.

The real truth is that the opening of China by Kissinger was about business. Although it has had a profoundly net negative impact on the U.S. economy and social organization, it was very beneficial to Henry and the international peddlers. Henry heads China Ventures, a company engaged in joint ventures with China's state bank. As its brochure explains, China Ventures invests only in projects that "enjoy the unquestioned support of the People's Republic of China." In September 1989, John Fialka wrote an article "Mr. Kissinger Has Opinions on China—and Business Ties," for the Wall Street Journal, in which he explores the private business interests behind U.S. foreign policy—a very unusual step for this newspaper. What this article did not explain was that this was just more of the trade that the British East India Company had begun coming back into the open. Drug money had made Hong Kong fabulously wealthy, and all of that laundered money needed a place to invest openly. The drug money would go into China's industrial development. This was good for business. American workers cost too much, and Chinese workers, sufficiently pacified by the brutality of the Communist regime in the slaughter of laborers, students, and intellectuals from the Cultural Revolution to the protest at Tiananmen Square in 1989 would work for slave wages. It has been estimated that up to sixty five million people were killed under the direction of Chairman Mao Tse Tung. The Chinese regime had also adopted a one-child per family rule. The Club of Rome's plan was coming to fruition. Now the drugs would not only be flowing into China but also out of China and into the veins and bloodstreams of U.S. Vietnam veterans and America's soon to be out-of-work, disengaged, infantilized, mis-educated, and alienated youth.

A 2008 report from the U.S. Council General's office for Hong Kong and Macau states, "The People's Republic of China is a major drug transit country to regional drug consumers in neighboring parts of Asia as well as for international drug markets (though not the U.S.)." The denial by the Council General, for political and economic reasons, of Chinese opium entering the U.S. as heroin is highly unlikely. China has been reported to still be a major exporter of heroin to the U.S. market.[275]

In any event, addicting military men and using them as mules for the importation of heroin into the country was of no importance to Kissinger. They were simply pawns to be used and discarded after the war. Kissinger revealed his true feelings about the military when he stated that soldiers are "dumb, stupid animals to be used" as pawns in foreign policy.[276] Turning

---

275. "The Opium Kings," PBS Frontline.
276. Carl Bernstein, and Bob Woodward, The Final Days (New York: Simon and Schuster, 2005).

them into drug addicts was of no consequence to him. It did have a great impact on the social fabric of American cities and towns, and it led to the next Nixon administration brain storm, the "War on Drugs" scam.

Nixon's War on Drugs Scam

The Vietnam War was largely a turf war between two factions of Europeans, the Americans/British and the French, using Vietnamese nationals as their proxies, vying for territorial prerogative over the spoils of Vietnam and South East Asia. Colonel Edward Lansdale was the architect of this little escapade. Lansdale had mastered the CIA's repertoire of covert action techniques, including sabotage, psychological warfare, and counterinsurgency. When he arrived in Saigon in May 1954 on the orders of Allen Dulles who was reportedly working against the expressed wishes of President Eisenhower,[277] he was fresh from engineering President Ramon Magaysay's successfully executed and bloody counterinsurgency campaign against the Philippine peasantry. Now he would take on the French government and the Corsican underworld, which from the late nineteenth century onward had a thriving black market business in currency and opium smuggling.[278]He began the same counterinsurgency measures in North Vietnam that he mastered in the Philippines committing political, psychological and terrorist acts designed to drive a wedge between the local population and Ho Chi Minh's growing revolutionary movement. Ho had worked closely with the OSS during WWII against the Japanese who had invaded Vietnam. Because of his loyalty to the U.S. in support of their war efforts, he naively counted on U.S. support for his drive for an independent Vietnam. Plans had already been made after WWII to divide Vietnam into two sectors.

With an open checkbook from the U.S. taxpayer, 1.1 million frightened northern Vietnamese were resettled in the South: 660,000 were transported by U.S. Navy ships and the rest by CIA airline planes. The transported people, many of whom were Catholic, were recruited to become supporters of the U.S. backed Ngo Dinh Diem. From April 1956 the Military Assistance Advisory Group (who set up and trained Diem's army) demolished any commitment to the Geneva agreement. Protesting that free elections would be impossible in the North, Diem and his American sponsors abandoned any prospect of free elections in the South. These developments along with increasing repression of the Viet Minh and their sympathizers provoked a

---

277. Correspondence from Col. F. Prouty to Jim Garrison, www.prouty.org.
278. Alfred W. McCoy, The Politics of Heroin: CIA Complicity in the Global Drug Trade (Chicago: Lawrence Hill, 1991), 156.

communist response.[279] The plan to divide Vietnam into two sectors was made by Truman, Churchill and Stalin in 1945 at the Potsdam conference. The north was to be controlled by the Chinese and the south by British interests. Landsdale was the facilitator.

Kennedy was assassinated in 1963, for multiple reasons as discussed earlier, but largely for his orientation away from S.E. Asia. A change in U.S. policy toward Vietnam would have altered the course of history in keeping with the plans made in 1943 in Cairo and Teheran by T.V. Soong[280] and his Asian masterminds [281] and in 1945 at Potsdam by Truman, Churchill and Stalin to divide both Korea and Vietnam into two zones for the deliberate purpose of strengthening China's sphere of influence.

The CIA team led by Lansdale[282] had already been stirring up trouble in Vietnam for nine years without congressional approval or oversight. After Kennedy's murder, the Vietnam War was escalated and allowed to continue for another eleven years. History fails to teach that this was a twenty-year-war—and for what? Each year of the conflict produced another crop of heroin addicted veterans returning to the United States. By 1971, a pure kilo of No. 4 heroin increased in price by 44 percent, from $1,240 in September 1970 to $1,780 in April 1971, despite a 30 percent <u>decline</u> in the number of GIs serving in Vietnam during the same period.[283] Moreover, the rapid growth of exports to the United States spurred a dramatic leap in the price of raw opium in the Golden Triangle. One American trained anthropologist who spent several years studying hill tribes in northern Thailand reports that "between 1968 and early 1970 . . . the price of raw opium at the producing village almost doubled from $24 to $45 a kilogram.[284] Although the growing rate of addiction among remaining U.S. troops in Vietnam probably accounted for some increased demand, increased exports to the American domestic market provided the major impetus behind the price rise.

---

279. John Dumbrell, <u>Vietnam: American Involvement at Home and Abroad,</u> <u>"BAAS" phamplet, 1992.</u>

280. The Soong family were Chinese agents of the House of Sassoon. With Sassoon/ Rothschild money, they carved up China into drug regions dominated by warlords.

281. Prouty, Letter to Jim Garrison: Soong from prominent family, educated Harvard, Governor of Central Bank of China, Minister of Finance (note the Harvard, banking, opium, money laundering connection).

282. Col. Prouty identified Lansdale as one of the "tramps" in Dealey Plaza the day Kennedy was shot in Dallas.

283. <u>New York Times</u>, 6 June 1971, 2.

284. Alain Y. Dessaint, "The Poppies Are Beautiful This Year," <u>Natural History</u>, February 1972, 31.

In anticipation of the addicted soldiers returning home en masse, the Nixon administration busied itself in 1971 declaring a War on Drugs. Coincidence? The Vietnam War ended rather ignominiously four years later. The United States lost 58,000 and had over 350,000 causalities. Some have estimated that as many as 3 million Vietnamese were slaughtered as well as hundreds of thousands in Laos and Cambodia. The Vietnam War had served it purpose—the oil companies got access to drilling rights off the coast of Vietnam, the drugs flowed, and China was strengthened by giving her a greater sphere of influence in the region. The psychological character of the United States had finally been penetrated and reduced to gelatin by a steady onslaught of assassinations: Kennedy, Malcolm X, King, Kennedy and the vile imagery from a savage war beaming nightly into people's homes. A subset of the baby boomers was undoubtedly traumatized by the Tavistock Institute inspired shock and awe treatment to the point that with the aid of another Tavistock-inspired CIA program, MK-ULTRA, a home-grown underground drug culture began to permeate the society. The young people were unwittingly falling into the trap that had been set for them by Kissinger, Nixon, and the global elites who saw Vietnam as just another step in the "birth pains" of their utopian vision of a wholly integrated global state in which capital and goods would flow freely, but in which the rights of people would be significantly curtailed—the high tech technotronic state.

After Nixon's declaration of a new drug war front, drugs and Uzis, both linked back to the CIA, poured over the United States borders and into all communities. The drug strategy had the greatest impact in minority communities that were already under attack by the DOD's Rand Institute initiative of "planned shrinkage" and "benign neglect" policies. As communities of color were struggling to survive the Rand created onslaught, new drug terrors, first heroin and then cocaine from Latin America, were massively marketed to their children. This was followed by both Nixon's and Reagan's tough "law and order" politicking, the increasing militarization of the domestic police forces and the filling of private for profit jails with nonviolent American youth. The big new U.S. industries were drugs, policing, and prisons: drugs leading to crime, crime leading to increased spending on crime prevention, prevention leading to the rapid militarization of local police forces and more and larger jails as another profit center for Wall Street.

War on Drugs Spawns Prison Industry

As the plan predicted, crime escalated. The controlled media, creating other psy-ops, made it appear as if the crime wave was largely a black problem.

According to the National Institute of Drug Abuse, an estimated 12 percent of drug users are African American. Yet, predictably, they make up nearly 50 percent of all drug possession arrests in the U.S. that enter the penal system.[285] According to the National Drug Strategy Network, African Americans make up less than one-third of the population in Georgia, but their arrest rate for drugs is five times greater than the white arrest rate. In addition, since 1990, African Americans have accounted for more than 75 percent of persons incarcerated for drug offenses in Georgia and comprise 97.7 percent of the people in that state given life sentences for drug offenses. In six California counties independently surveyed in 1995, 100 percent of individuals sent to trial on drug charges were minorities, although the drug-using population in those same counties was more than 60 percent white.[286]

A CNN article in 1996 cited U.S. government figures that show more than 90 percent of all federal prosecutions for crack cocaine in 1995 were of African American defendants. In addition, unlike convictions for powdered cocaine and other drugs (which wealthier, white defendants are more likely to use), a conviction for selling crack cocaine can carry a lengthy prison term without benefit of parole.

The media hype about black men running wild with automatic weapons and drugs was another Tavistock-inspired shock treatment to instill fear in Middle America who was likewise being targeted by the same drugs. The big drug runners, including then Vice President George H. W. Bush and Oliver North were rich and free to run more drugs. That was the point. Drugs and Uzis were the perfect excuse to give rise to the national security state where citizens are now under constant surveillance, and police roll into American neighborhoods in armored vehicles with SWAT teams as if they were in Baghdad—the implementation of the law and order agenda was promoted most vociferously by the very politicians who were using drugs to support their political agenda.

Flooding working class neighborhoods with illegal drugs became the new method for urban renewal and pacification. As the jobs got shipped to Latin America and China, the workers were too dumbed down by an increasingly irrelevant secondary education system; were pacified and made docile by fluoride-laced drinking water; became obese and lethargic by the consumption of toxic and overprocessed food; were totally unaware of the history of the labor movement because of deliberate miseducation; and finally were just too stoned to mount an organized resistance. They were trapped by their own alienation as victims of this silent war.

---

285. "The Black and White of Justice," Freedom Magazine, vol. 128
286. Ibid.

As the industrial base was moved offshore, the drug war gave rise to a new private prison industry designed to control both the black and white communities. As factory jobs became scarcer, and farms had been mechanized and imported cheap illegal Mexican labor, blacks went to prison in record numbers, and whites got jobs as prison guards.

As drugs and guns flowed into neighborhoods, many homeowners abandoned their hard won working class homes for safer terrain. As drugs and guns moved in, property values began to fall. Housing and Urban Development (HUD) vultures scooped in to buy the abandoned properties for pennies on the dollar. HUD properties were then packaged as defaulted mortgage bundles and sold to corporate and university portfolios at deflated prices. Certain neighborhoods, especially in black and minority communities, were particularly targeted. The purchasers of these mortgage bundles seemed to have insider information and foreknowledge of investment appreciation as city planners made projections for development and urban renewal projects years in advance.

Historically, the Chinese Opium Trade and the African Slave Trade provided the financial foundation for the Boston "Bluebloods." It was not surprising that the Harvard Endowment Fund and the Harvard Management Corporation were involved in the insider HUD purchases.[287] The key was the relationship between (1) government guaranteed/insured mortgages, (2) asset seizure/forfeitures, and (3) private companies that derive profits from an inside track with both government programs. Besides Harvard, the other primary investors in the funds were Capricorn Investments and Herbert S. "Pug" Winokur, Jr.

Winokur, former executive vice president and director of Penn Central Corp, CEO of Capricorn Holdings, and managing partner of three Capricorn Investors Limited Partnerships, was one insider who may have benefited from the assault against open bid auctions for defaulted HUD mortgages.

Not incidentally, from 1988 to 1997, because of his large investments, Winokur was also the chairman and CEO of DynCorp, a U.S. government contractor for the Department of Defense, NASA, Department of State, EPA, Center for Disease Control, National Institute of Health, the U.S. Postal Service and other U.S. government agencies. DynCorp was involved in the buying and selling of women and children for prostitution in the Bosnia conflict and was rewarded for human trafficking by the Pentagon with contracts to provide police advisors and trainers in Baghdad!

---

287.   Uri Dowbenko, "BUSHWHACKED: HUD Fraud, Spooks and the Slumlords of Harvard," <u>Conspiracy Digest: Real News that Connects the Dots</u>, 2000.

As pertaining to HUD mortgages, according to SEC registration documents (S-1), DynCorp was the prime servicer of the Department of Justice Asset Forfeiture Fund, having procured a five-year contract with the Department of Justice worth $217 million from 1993 to 1998. The one thousand-person contract required staffing at over three hundred locations in the U.S. and involved support of DOJ's drug-related asset seizure program.[288] In other words, DynCorp, knowing beforehand that such assets would appreciate, was free to target the real estate assets it wanted to put into the portfolios of associated firms. It was a perfect insider's game.

The war on drugs had other benefits as well. It has allowed the various U.S. alphabet agencies to wage war against any constructive response by local Latin American campesinos to their feudal situation. It seems that there is a correlation between a poor human rights climate and U.S. aid. The worse the human rights climate, the more American aid increases. The worse the human rights climate, the better the business climate. According to Noam Chomsky, a plausible theory of U.S. foreign policy would contend that human rights are irrelevant but that improving the climate for foreign business operations is highly relevant.[289] The war on drugs, now replaced by the war on terror, is used to continue the pattern of extractive capitalism, drug running, money laundering, and human trafficking. This is the dark side of <u>free capital flows.</u>

It should also be noted that the American economy itself is addicted to drugs. Drug money is essential to the health of what has become, because of banking policies, a parasitic tapeworm economy. Without drug prohibition, besides limiting the private prison business, insurance companies would be smaller and less profitable. The magistrates, judges, lawyers, police, prison guards, and foreign owners would be twiddling their thumbs. Hospitals would be closing down surplus beds. The entire AIDS industry would fold. Supplies of house security paraphernalia would collapse, and drug counselors and therapists would have to find new work. Purveyors of electronic equipment would be deprived of the business that comes from replacing stolen video recorders and computers.

However, the most important issue is this: Estimates are that from $100 to $250 million in drug profits are laundered through U.S. banks every year. The multiplier effect (6x) of $250 million is $1.5 trillion per year in U.S. cash transactions. Corporations trading on Wall Street, including many implicated in money laundering schemes where products are sold with

---

288. Uri Dowbenko, "BUSHWACKED."
289. Noam Chomsky, "American Foreign Policy," delivered at Harvard University, 19 March 1985.

questionable bookkeeping throughout drug producing regions, all have stock values that are based on annual net profits. Known as price to earnings or the POP, the multiplier effect in stock values is sometimes as much as a factor of thirty. Thus, for a firm like General Electric or Piper Aircraft to have an additional $10 million in net profit based on the drug trade, the net increase in the company's stock value could be as much as $300 million. If the drug trade goes, stock values would collapse.[290]

Katherine Austin Fitts, a former HUD undersecretary, once gave a lecture to over a hundred "spiritually inclined" Americans during which she revealed that the import of drugs plaguing their communities was being done deliberately to maintain the POP of stock values. She asked the people in the audience to raise their hands to indicate whether they would like to see drugs disappear and lose their stock value or keep the drugs and their stock values. Only one hand shot up for getting rid of the drugs. America lost its moral core on the way to the bank. Chinese Premier Chou En-Lai was correct. It would seem that the whole country is addicted to drugs or drug money.

Finally, because of the war on drugs, more than 5.6 million Americans are in prison or have served time, according to a report by the Justice Department, that is, 1 in 37 adults living in the United States. In the land of the free, this is the highest incarceration level on the entire planet.

While an increasing load of toxic and highly oxidative drugs was attacking the mitochondria and energy and immune systems of America's youth, another plan was hatched just in case someone might make the connection between poly drug use and these sick young people. This time a new war would be declared—Nixon's war on cancer. As money poured into the hunt for the viral cause of cancer, science changed from making objective observations based on fact to fantasyland. It was known, for example, in the 1960s that viruses were often seen in cells undergoing mitotic division. This had no relationship to infection or cancer development. According to Etienne de Harven an electron microscopist, the 1970 to 1980 years were dominated by a series of ideas that would never have withstood scrutiny ten or twenty years before. It became acceptable to postulate that when viruses cannot be seen by electron microscope in cancer cells, biochemical or immunological methods supposedly identifying viral markers were enough to demonstrate viral infection of the cells under scrutiny. Such markers can be an enzyme (reverse transcriptase), an antigen, various proteins, or some RNA sequence. Never seeing the viral particles was conveniently explained by the integration of the viral genome into the chromosomes of the alleged

---

290. Michael Ruppert, "The CIA, Drugs and Wall Street," From the Wilderness, 29 June 1999.

infected cells. De Harven goes on to acknowledge that "to accommodate with such interpretations implied complete oblivion of all we knew from previous research on cancer in experimental animals."[291] Before then, visible steps of viral replication (for example, budding) were always observed and regarded as essential for the spreading of infection from cell to cell.

Another step in the HIV set up was put in place when another shortcut that has had disastrous consequences was proposed. It was assumed that any material banding at 1.16 gm/ml in a gel medium after centrifugation, represented retroviruses. This was sheer nonsense. True retroviruses might band around that density, but so do a lot of microvesicles and proteinaceous debris, making the isolation and identification of pure virus virtually impossible by taking shortcuts and not following standard proven protocols.

Finally, it was well known that viruses that infected cells have a marked cytolytic effect on the infected cell. By contrast, retrovirus carrying cells maintain excellent viability and released viruses can be easily recovered in the culture supernatant without the need to apply any growth factors stimulation to the cultures (as was done by Gallo).

So, first the logical rules for virus isolation were changed, and the next step in this empty cancer war was to pump money into the system and create large numbers of jobs for researchers who would hold to these false tenets. The intellectual freedom to think along other avenues of cancer research rapidly dwindled; especially when major pharmaceutical companies offered tantalizing contracts to support polarized retrovirus research. The priority was to demonstrate, at any cost, that retroviruses had something to do with human cancer, a hypothesis that did not receive the slightest support before the war on cancer. Such a misdirected research effort would have been relatively inconsequential as long as public health was not involved. Unfortunately, the emergence of immunodeficiency syndromes in 1981 gave the retrovirus establishment an opportunity to transform what could have been only an academic flop into a public health tragedy.[292]

From the empty hunt for a cancer-causing virus came the cover story that was given to the world. The cancer industry had spent fruitless years looking for a viral cause of cancer. When this boondoggle was reaching the limits of its viability, the effort was suddenly redirected to look for a virus as a rationale for widespread drug toxicity. Two scientists, Montagnier in Paris and Gallo in the United States, failures at finding the viral cause of cancer, complied. The cover story they willingly helped to contrive would

---

291. Etienne de Harven, "Retroviruses: the recollections of an electron microscopist," <u>Reappraising AIDS</u> (Nov./Dec. 1998).
292. Etienne, de Harven, "Retroviruses."

be the phantom virus HIV. HIV, described as both a type-C virus and a lentevirus, (two entirely different types of viruses) was claimed to be the cause of twenty-nine different old diseases that were conveniently re-branded as the result of a fraudulent antibody test to nonspecific ubiquitous cellular proteins. Thus, the reason for millions dying around the globe would not be a collusion of government and private enterprise policies. It would not be the drug-running of the global elite. It would not be their extensive money laundering capacity. It would not be the industrial policies of South African plutocrats. It would not be the consequence of the structural adjustment programs of the World Bank and the IMF. No, the elite would be exonerated from their crimes. People would die because of their careless debased sexual mores. Sex would no longer be an expression of shared energy between two lovers. It would become a terrifying weapon—something else to spread mass fear and hysteria.

Millions of young people would become sick, thousands would die in the West, and millions would die in Africa. It would all be blamed on AIDS. In the West, the excess deaths would be from the rampant importation of toxic drugs and an associated MK-ULTRA induced lifestyle and the widespread irresponsible use of toxic antibiotics. In Africa, deaths would come from ideas emanating from the Club of Rome advocating a reduction in population in LDCs, a policy adopted by the U.S. and made public in two documents: Kissinger's NSSM 200 and Scowcroft's NSD 314. The poor, the sick, the dying would be blamed for the creation of their own misery. It's just business.

The war on cancer had a bigger secondary reason for the virus hunt. Cancer is the most profitable disease for the big pharmaceutical cartels. One cycle of treatments with one drug can cost as much as $30,000. When you consider that one in three Americans can expect to have a cancer diagnosis at some point in life, a collapse of this paradigm would also collapse massive profits. The drugs purposely introduced for use by those unfortunate enough to fall into the HIV trap are all carcinogenic and organ toxic. People are dying from the very drugs that target the virus. Since the HIV virus has never been isolated, there is no gentle word for this—it is murder!

Cancer, like immune deficiency, is a functional disease of the respiratory enzyme systems in the mitochondria, an organelle found in the cell's cytoplasm. It is not a structural DNA disease as the cancer industry has come to believe. If cancer is functional that also means that cancer is a reversible disease. That cancer is reversible has already been shown by certain clinical phenomenon demonstrated in organ transplant patients. During the 1960s and 1970s significant clinical observations were recorded with some organ transplant patients treated with the immune suppressing drug, azothioprine.

The patients developed transplantation AIDS—Kaposi's sarcoma and opportunistic infections. The tumors disappeared spontaneously without leaving a trace when the azothoprine drug was withdrawn.[293],[294]

Corticosteroids and nitrite inhalers were two drugs widely used in the gay community, some of whose members were the first to be diagnosed with AIDS. Many developed Kaposi's sarcoma. It seems that nitrites and the aza group of azothioprine have a comparable nitrogen action profile that block oxygen dependent cellular respiration that takes place in the mitochondria. If anyone had bothered to read the literature, this was a clue. There was no need to call up the ghost of a phantom virus to explain a phenomenon that had already been observed in another immune suppressed population.

The finding validated the work of Otto Warburg, a German biochemist and another member of the infamous Warburg banking family. In 1931, Otto was awarded the Nobel Prize for elucidating the mechanism for cellular respiration and its effect on the transformation of a cell to cancer. By the 1960s, when this work was coming to fruition and was making inroads into clinical practice, the research money was abruptly stopped and transferred to the virus hunters who got the research money from Nixon's war on cancer. In 1960, the anaerobiosis of cancer cells was established as fact. This is when methods were developed to measure oxygen pressure inside tumors in the living body. Nixon's war on cancer directed research money away from this promising area to a futile hunt for elusive viruses. Curing cancer was not going to happen. Cancer is too lucrative a business for the Rockefeller pharmaceutical syndicate to tolerate cures. The research money was withdrawn from the development of Warburg's ideas of oxidative metabolism as the key to unlocking the cancer problem. Warburg's research was not taught in medical schools and several generations of physicians were steered away from this line of inquiry. The usual characters began to call Warburg's findings "quackery." It has been almost thirty-six years since Nixon's declared cancer war, and the end result has been approximately 21 million cancer deaths.

Today . . . the cancer effort is utterly fragmented—so much so that it's nearly impossible to track down where the money to pay for all this research is coming from. And what money! It is estimated that U.S. $14.4 billion is spent each year on cancer research. "When you add it all up, Americans have spent . . . close to $200 billion, in inflation-adjusted dollars, since 1971." It

---

293. Hans Jochim Ehlers, "Interview Heinrich Kremer," Raum + Zeit, Nov./Dec. 2001.

294. O. Klepp, O. Dahl, and J.T. Stenwig, "Association of Kaposi's Sarcoma and Prior Immunosuppressive Therapy: A Five-year Material of Kaposi's Sarcoma in Norway," Cancer 42 (Dec 1978): 2626-30.

is certainly justifiable to ask for an accounting of that one-fifth of a trillion dollars.[295]

Aids and the Winds of Change

The political, economic, and social changes initiated by Kissinger through Nixon have had profound consequences to the most vulnerable populations—minorities in the United States and Africans who had only recently come from under the yoke of colonial rule. Just as African Americans were demanding and gaining full constitutional rights and Africans were seeking independent governance including control of their own resources, HIV/AIDS bubbled up from the Kissinger/Nixon cauldron of evil—the cancer and drug wars.

Because of the planned de-industrialization in the U.S. and "structural adjustment" programs in Africa, both communities of Africans were becoming culturally dislocated by drugs and poverty in the U.S. and extreme poverty and land theft in Africa. The respective policy strategies of "benign neglect" in the U.S. and "planned shrinkage" in Africa were a new silent war front. Silent wars are covert and while their outcome is planned and predictable, their methods must remain obscure. The villain who would take the blame was a phantom virus grown in the squalid Petri dish of fear because fear is the preferred method of mass control and it was one more Tavistock-inspired future shock that is just business.

---

295. Ralph Moss, <u>Townsend Letter for Doctors</u>, June 2004.

Chapter 10

Iran-Contra and the Politics of Neighborhood Destruction and Cultural Disintegration, Oxidative Stressors and African AIDS

o o o o o o o o o o o o o o o o o o o o o o o o o o o o o o o o o o o

The term "acquiescence" would imply that the government simply turned a blind eye. But when one looks behind that word and what the government's actions were, as well as what is already known as a matter of public record, these are not acts of "acquiescence."

They are much more proactive, and they are tantamount to a conspiracy by the United States Government to traffic narcotics for the purpose of generating ongoing covert revenue streams.

U.S. Government sponsored criminal activities include:

1. The appointment of CIA and FBI personnel to have direct contact with narcotics traffickers
2. The manipulation of US Customs to ensure certain aircraft and ships were not inspected and
3. The maintenance of secured shipping routes and narcotics storage facilities by the United States Military.

Al Martin, <u>The Conspirators: Secrets of an Iran-Contra Insider</u>

Richard Grasso, former head of the SEC, meeting FARC guerrilla leader in Columbia—San Francisco Examiner, 6 July 1999. On retirement from the SEC, Grasso received a $140 million cash payout.

As a second year medical student, having completed the grueling work of learning anatomy, physiology, biochemistry, and related subjects, my classmates and I were now being prepped to practice our skills on real living patients. I remember the excitement, anticipation, and dread I felt at my own awkwardness in this new role as doctor-in-training. One of our first exercises in the art of medicine was an assignment to take a detailed history and to perform a physical examination of an assigned patient. To my chagrin, my very first patient was comatose, on a respirator and unresponsive to external stimuli. I believe the only reflex he demonstrated was the Babinski reflex. The Babinski reflex occurs when the great toe flexes toward the top of the foot and the other toes fan out after the sole of the foot has been firmly stroked. In a person over the age of two, this indicates damage to the nerve paths connecting the spinal cord and the brain. The prognosis is usually grim, and there is a differential diagnosis of about seventeen diseases that can present with this finding.

I remember standing dumbfounded in front of that patient, fearing that my first assignment in history taking would be a bust. I completed my physical examination and then turned to his very massive hospital chart. He had been on that ward for a long time. I reviewed the chart and made it back to rounds in time to recite my findings. Since that first patient, I have seen thousands of people and taken thousands of histories, but that first patient taught me a lesson I shall never forget. What if all of the historians who recorded in that man's chart before I arrived were wrong? What if they were as confused as I was, but were simply more authoritative in the expression of their confusion? The man in the bed could no longer speak for himself, but perhaps there were clues suggesting the resolution to his predicament that we were all missing.

This indeed has been the problem with AIDS medicine and its contextual history. The people who are said to be HIV positive do not have the power to speak for themselves and to tell their histories. Because of the planned failure of the public school systems that are more concerned with social control and indoctrination than with educating the masses, Americans are not only economically and politically illiterate, they are even more scientifically illiterate. They know more about how their cars function than their own bodies. They are more concerned with the quality of gas that goes into their engine than the food that goes into their mouths. The fear of being HIV-positive is palpable, but an HIV-positive test is like a name tag on the toe of a dead man. It is nothing more than an identifier. It does nothing to tell the story of how he ended up on that slab and how he might have avoided that fate.

There is much confusion in AIDS medicine that is expressed authoritatively and if challenged defended with haughty anger and pomposity rather than facts. Much of it is scientifically improbable and leads to a dead end. The HIV theory was first proposed to explain three phenomenona in the original cohort of patients, mainly in gay men, IV drug users, and hemophiliacs: The high frequency of Kaposi's sarcoma, a blood-vessel malignancy, a few opportunistic infections, mainly a fungus, pneumocystis pneumonia, and a decrease in serum T4 lymphocytes. It was clear that no single infection could cause this wide- ranging disease pattern so the theory proposed that the sine qua non of HIV infection was the destruction of CD4+T cells by the virus and T cell destruction created the conditions for the diseases to occur. However, it was noted from the very beginning that the virus could barely be found in T cells and many patients did not exhibit a decrease in CD4+ T cells until after the onset of one of the AIDS defining infections—thus undermining the entire premise of the theory. This impediment was of no great importance. With the Epidemic Intelligence Service and the WHO hyping the plague angle, it was only the image, the illusion that mattered, because this is what would be remembered.

There was also a whole body of evidence showing that there were many factors from infections, to sun exposure and to a diurnal variation that could lead to decreased T4 cells. Because so many people developed AIDS before their T cells decreased, T4 cell decrease is neither necessary nor sufficient for the development of AIDS.

The problem, however, is that from both a biochemical and electromagnetic level of cellular function there is a big gap of unexplained phenomenon in getting from T cell destruction to the catalogue of AIDS defining diseases. The process has to be logically congruent. Retroviruses had never been shown to kill cells, and even if they did, there still had to be a biochemical or a bio-electric mechanism that initiated the process. The most common factor uniting the AIDS risk group was their long-term exposure to exogenous immunosuppressive agents that were also oxidizing. Oxidizing agents drain cells of potential energy stored in electrons in the thiol (Sulfur-Hydrogen bond) system, altering the redox potential of the cell and thus its efficient functioning. The key to understanding living organisms is the concept of energy flow. In living organisms, energy is trapped at the electron level. It is stored not only as vibrational and electronic bond energies, but also in the structure of the system. This allows energy to be mobilized coherently and make available the entire spectrum of stored energy for work, whenever and wherever energy is called for.[296]

The redox potential is a way of measuring energy flows and storage. According to the redox theory of cellular function, potential energy is stored in electrons in the thiol protein/peptide system. For the individual cell and ultimately the organs to use this energy to perform various functions, some of the electrons must be transferred to oxygen. In the process the cell becomes oxidized (decreased energy potential). The cellular electrons are then replenished by electrons found in food (antioxidants), and the cycle can began again.[297] If there is chronic overuse of the stored electron potential because of exposure to environmental oxidizing agents or malnutrition, then, depending on the disposition of the individual, diseases will begin to manifest.

The big question is how did so many people become comatose to the clues? Peter Duesberg in America, Hassig, Kremer and Lanka in Germany, the Nobel Laureate Kerry Mullis, the Australians out of Perth headed by Elani Papadopulos-Eleopulos and Val Turner, as well as many others had been for years making similar claims about the cause of AIDS, much different from the AIDS establishment.

---

296. Mae-Wan Ho, The Rainbow and the Worm, the Physics of Organisms, (2006 World Scientific, New Jersey) 78.

297. Eleni Papadopulos-Eleopulos, "A mitotic theory," J. Theor.Biol.96 (1982):741–58.

Duesberg made the case in his book <u>Inventing AIDS</u> that the underlying cause of AIDS was the drug epidemic. The Perth group expanded this idea to the biological level and identified drugs as a category of oxidative stressors. Popadopulos, a physicist, understood the process in bio-electric terms. The Germans began to revive the ideas of evolutionary biology with the understanding that over the millennia the cell has developed predictable mechanisms for coping with external oxidative and nitrosative stressors, whatever their origin, and that the pattern of diseases called <u>AIDS</u> could be understood by exploring the predictable consequences of evolutionary biology and the nature of energy metabolism at the cellular level.

This notion of oxidative stress gave an explanation of the African AIDS problem, because illegal drugs were not a common factor on the continent. Essentially, what all of these respected researchers were considering is the roll of environmental stressors, which can be toxic, traumatic, infectious, nutritional, or psychic in the development of the new spate of immune deficiency. If there was something catastrophically happening environmentally to create this syndrome, then what was it? To identify the trends leading to AIDS, one had to leave the confines of the clinics and hospitals and delve into the murky history of international drug running, international banking, and the deep politics of espionage.

Opium and heroin were drugs imported from the East, but another drug imported from Latin America is even more damaging to the immune system, and that is the product that began to show up in a major way in the 1980s—crack cocaine.

Another important historical clue in the AIDS-drug crisis was the Iran-Contra Affair. The influx of narcotics has had significant impact through corruption of the legal system, the banking system, and legislative bodies, and the general decline in the economy and general health parameters of the country cannot be overstated. The trafficked drugs are oxidative stressors and, as such, a new theory of AIDS was proposed that could explain all of the diverse findings in the varied disease patterns.

The oxidative theory predicted that AIDS would remain in the restricted risk groups; that the only sexual risk factor would correlate with receptive anal intercourse because sperm are highly oxidizing; that both antibody positive and antibody negative drug users would develop AIDS irrespective of whether the needles are clean or not or whether the drugs are used intravenously or not; that in Africa there was neither a new disease AIDS nor a new virus HIV; that the decrease in CD4+ T4 cells is not specific and is neither necessary nor sufficient for the syndrome to appear; that the tissues of AIDS patients and those at risk would be oxidized in general and that they would have a low sulphydryl (-SH sulfur-hydrogen) group levels; that AIDS can be prevented by stopping exposure to the oxidizing risk factors by using currently available therapeutic (anti-oxidants in general and SH containing, in particular) substances.[298] The HIV/AIDS theory has predicted nothing correctly. The oxidative theory has been spot on and therefore useful as a therapeutic model.

Recent research has shown that crack users were over three times more likely than nonusers to die of AIDS-related causes, after controlling for age, race, use of HAART (antiretroviral therapy), problem drinking, income, education, duration of illness, and baseline virological and immunological indicators. Crack users had greater CD4 T cell loss and were more likely than nonusers to develop new AIDS-defining illnesses, and these results persisted when controlling for heroin use, any injection drug use, tobacco smoking, symptoms of depression, and hepatitis C virus co-infection. In other words, crack cocaine causes AIDS.[299]

Cocaine has been shown to affect immune function through the release of corticosterone. Acute administration of both cocaine and corticosterone produces an enhancement of the Th2 dependent antibody response and a rise in Th2 cytokines, a measure of humoral immunity and a propensity to shift the system toward Th2, possibly at the expense of Th1 cell-mediated responses. Cocaine is also known to produce severe damage to liver cells. This has been shown to occur because cocaine produces oxidative metabolites that inhibit mitochondrial respiration and lead to a depletion of the energy molecule ATP and to subsequent cell death.[300] Cocaine is also known to reduce B cell function, natural killer cell function, with attenuated killing capacity and monocyte-macrophage function with decreased ability to inhibit the growth of tumor cells.[301]

So it must be understood that drawing attention to the Drug/Oxidative Stress hypothesis would also draw attention to the nature of the drug problem and the relationship between drugs and the clandestine agencies, drugs and the military, drugs and the banking and insurance industries, and drugs and political campaign contributions. The people involved in this business are slimy, but they are anything but stupid. Creating the AIDS crisis was both

---

298. Eleni Papadopulos-Eleopulos, "Looking Back on the Oxidative Stress Theory of AIDS," Continuum Magazine 5 (1998/99): 30–35.

299. J.A. Cook et al., "Crack Cocaine, Disease Progression and mortality in a Multicenter Cohort of HIV-1 Positive Women," AIDS 22 (2008): 1355–63.

300. Franziska Boess et al., "Effects of Cocaine and Its Oxidative Metabolites on Mitochondrial Respiration and Generation Of Reactive Oxygen Species," Biochemical Pharmacology 60 (2000): 615–23.

301. W. Xu, et al., "Cocaine Effects on Immunocompetent Cells: An Observation of in Vitro Cocaine Exposure," Int J Immunopharm 21 (1999): 463–72.

an economic and a politically useful tool. So when Iran-Contra erupted, it was more of the same.

Iran-Contra was an illegal covert operation run from the Reagan-Bush White House that involved the CIA in illegal arms sales to Iran in exchange for hostages, supplying weapons to the Nicaraguan Contra terrorists or freedom fighters in exchange for drugs that were then sold to Americans— mostly crack cocaine to African American and Hispanic neighborhoods. It also encompassed the Savings and Loan scandal and the destruction of this segment of the banking industry that ultimately once again, got dumped in the laps of defrauded American taxpayers.

Ronald Reagan was a disaster for the human family. His administration brought permanent revolutionary changes to the U.S. system of government that have only just become obvious to the oblivious. He was contemptuous of the environmental movement and once quipped, "If you've seen one redwood you've seen them all." To the Interior Department, Reagan appointed James Watt who systematically opened millions of acres of government land to commercial exploitation. At the Environmental Protection Agency (EPA), Ann Burford, his appointee, used her position to protect corporations that were dumping and poisoning the environment.

He willfully assaulted the human services infrastructure in the United States and boasted that he had eliminated over a thousand programs that served lower-income groups. He had his "Let them eat cake" moment when he proposed that ketchup and pickle relish would suffice for vegetables in school lunches. While raising taxes on the poor and middle class, he slashed them by 60 percent for the ultra-rich.

He put Elliot Abrams, one of Leon Trotsky's[302] wandering ghosts, into the Human Rights Division of the State Department with orders to dismantle it. The administration then sent files of confidential testimonies that Pat Derian, under President Carter, had obtained from refugees from repressive countries to the police in those countries. The Immigration and Naturalization Services subsequently deported many of the refugees to countries where brutal police were waiting for them at the airports.[303]

While he was stacking the benches with far right judges who were sympathetic to corporate interests and disdainful of the rights of citizens, his administration was importing massive amounts of cocaine and using their own created drug crisis to expand the Nixon War on Drugs program that

---

302. A Marxist and one of the leaders of the communist October Revolution in Russia. He was born Leyba Bronstein.

303. John Sockwell, The Praetorian Guard: The U.S. Role in the New World Order (Cambridge, MA: Southend Press, 1981).

ballooned the incarceration rate for nonviolent drug offenders and transferred substantial property of the poor and middle class to the state and private corporate entities under <u>seizure</u> laws. While Nancy Reagan was cynically telling America's youth to just say no, her husband and his Vice President, George H.W. Bush (who had been head of the CIA and an ambassador to China), were using the created crisis of the War on Drugs as justification for the curtailment of civil liberties.

Iran Contra

Gary Webb is dead. His death was ruled a suicide even though it was reported that there were two gun shot wounds to the head. Webb will long be remembered for his book <u>Dark Alliance,</u> which was first published as a series of articles in the <u>San Jose Mercury News</u> in 1996. The story exposed what became known as the <u>Iran-Contra drug scandal</u> and the U.S. government's marketing of crack cocaine to its own citizens in South Central Los Angeles, in the 1980s. The CIA's <u>Inspector General Report Vol. II on Drug Trafficking</u> confirmed the allegations.

According to Webb, during the 1980s, there were two covert operations overseen by the National Security Council of the Reagan administration. Essentially, the NSA was managing narcotics trafficking directly from the White House under the direction of Oliver North and then Vice President George H. W. Bush—an old Skull and Bones[304] and CIA man. The operations involved the illegal sale of weapons to Iran and the provision of covert aid to the Nicaraguan Contra insurgency in contradiction to congressional authority. Fourteen people were eventually indicted or convicted of crimes. George H.W. Bush became a made man[305] and was duly rewarded with the Presidency of the United States.

The caper involved not only arms sales to Iran but also the solicitation of funds from third-party governments as well as wealthy Americans to pursue a foreign policy agenda in Central America that was clearly illegal. During the course of the independent council's investigation, persistent rumors arose that the administration had sanctioned drug trafficking as well in order to have another source of operational funding. The charges were successfully deflected until Gary Webb's <u>Dark Alliance</u> exposé confirmed beyond a

---

304. William Huntington Russell was co-founder of the Yale Skull and Bones society. He was first cousin to Samuel Russell who made his fortune dealing drugs—-opium to the Chinese.

305. A made man is a mafia term used to signify someone who has been officially accepted into the organization after committing the first contract killing referred to as "making your bones".

reasonable doubt the government's links to drug trafficking in the United States.

According to Al Martin, a retired U.S. Navy Lt. Commander and former officer in the Office of Navel Intelligence, who was intimately involved in the affair—Iran-Contra was just a "ruse." The ruse was to arm a 50,000 man army in Nicaragua by means of (government) sanctioned trafficking in cocaine, by means of trafficking weapons, and by means of the intricate and complex network of State sponsored, State organized, and State protected fraud. Martin claimed that it was a huge conspiracy to commit wide- ranging frauds:

- Fraud perpetrated upon savings and loans and commercial banks.
- Fraud perpetrated on securities firms and insurance firms.
- Fraud perpetrated on the Internal Revenue Service through a variety of illicit tax shelters.

This was a new and rather bold scheme operated at the highest levels of government . . . It was an operation, Martin claimed, that, at its peak in 1985, involved over 5,000 individuals.

The essential concept was to refinance and to replenish the coffers of what constitutes, as the then Assistant Secretary of State Elliott Abrams said publicly, "a Shadow Government in the United States," a government that the American government turns to when it wishes certain illegal covert operations to be extant pursuant to a political objective.

It's been estimated by the Kerry Commission, and re-estimated by the Hughes Commission, that U.S. institutions and individuals were defrauded out of $5 to $7 billion. Most of the money was guaranteed by the U.S. treasury—the taxpayers. It is money that the taxpayers of the United States, having been defrauded by their own elected officials and employees, will ultimately have to pay.[306]

Iran-Contra was not the first time the government's direct involvement in narcotics trafficking was so ably chronicled. Alfred McCoy, writing in the 1970s, documented the involvement of the CIA and the military in heroin and opium trafficking in Southeast Asia. McCoy discovered that narcotics had been an ongoing source of covert funding for years.

The War Conspiracy by Peter Dale Scott, Ph.D. of U.C. Berkeley is another exposé that traces the connections between drug trafficking in Southeast Asia and American Intelligence operations. Scott gives detailed references about two important players in the intelligence game, C.V. Starr

---

306. Al Martin, The Conspirators: Secrets of an Iran-Contra Insider (Pray, MN: National Liberty Press, 2002), 12

and Paul Helliwell, both of whom have been tied to the drug trade.[307] Helliwell pioneered the art of illegal financing of intelligence activity to avoid bureaucratic (congressional) oversight and accountability. He formulated techniques for creating banks and businesses to cover CIA operations. Those connections also led directly to the China lobby and firms identified as either CIA proprietaries or affiliates, such as Sea Supply, (run by Helliwell), Civil Air Transport (CAT), a CIA proprietary, Civil Air Transport Company, Ltd.,—a separate firm not owned by but affiliated with the CIA through CAT, and Air America, an evolution of Civil Air Transport.

C.V. Starr was a British insurance magnate who worked with OSS member "Wild" Bill Donovan to use his commercial and insurance connections in occupied China and Formosa to create deep cover intelligence network. He was the founder of Asia Life/C. V. Starr Companies in the 1930s that was incorporated as AIG in 1967. These relationships have a direct connection to the Wall Street banking crisis of 2008.

Unaware of heroin and opium trafficking from Asia as part of the Vietnam debacle and of the long history of global peddlers of international commerce in narcotics, many observers were taken aback by the scope of the Iran-Contra episode and of the financing operation involved. The operation reached into the American banking system (money laundering) and included various forms of financial fraud. Al Martin claimed in his book The Conspirators, that this fraud gave the operation a link to the scandals that enveloped the savings and loan industry in the late 1980s.

Before the 2008 Wall Street bail out, the Savings and Loan scandal was possibly the largest theft in the history of the United States. Essentially, the ploy was to get Congress to raise the Federal Deposit Insurance Corporation insured limit from $40,000 to $100,000 while simultaneously deregulating the industry. This two-part strategy allowed bank owners to lend themselves money knowing that they would never pay it back. This was akin to the banks suddenly opening their vaults and allowing every two- bit-swindler with a briefcase to walk through and take what they pleased—and they did!

In essence, what happened in the S&L scandal was that a gang of criminals, including the CIA, the Mafia, Washington politicians, and others all participated in raping the nation's S&L industry, eagerly sidling up to the trough while it lasted. The politicians took away the controls over the S&L industry, while increasing the bag the taxpayer would hold if it all came crashing down. Selected S&Ls were randomly chosen to be investigated, but a common pattern was found. The same people would keep appearing,

---

307. Michael Ruppert, "Hostages: A multi-part FTW report—A.I.G." www.fromthewilderness.com.

working at one S&L, looting it until it went under, then going to work for another, and repeating the same process.[308]

The same people that figured so highly in the Iran-Contra scandal, where drugs were brought into the United States and arms shipped to U.S.-controlled mercenaries in Central America, were also laundering drug money through the S&Ls that were being looted, in George Bush's backyard, by his buddies.[309] Although the official investigation concluded that probably no more than 15 percent of the losses incurred in the scandal were due to outright fraud, official investigations always downplay or ignore fraud and corruption. While there is no doubt that numerous factors played their role in the scandal, fraud and corruption may have accounted for more than half of the losses. A U.S. Comptroller of the Currency Report, 1988 stated that less than ten percent of Savings and Loan failures were strictly due to economics, and the Government Accounting Office issued a report in 1989 that identified insider abuse and fraud at 64 percent of the banks that failed in 1987.[310]

When Congress later held hearings on Iran-Contra, one of the most explosive documents revealed was a Memorandum of Understanding (MOU) covering the period from 2 March 1982 to 3 August 1995. In March 1998, the CIA Inspector General testified that there had existed a secret agreement between CIA and the Justice Department, wherein "during the years 1982 to 1995, CIA did not have to report the drug trafficking by its assets to the Justice Department." As Michael Levine, a former DEA agent commented, "[To] a trained DEA agent this literally means that the CIA had been granted a license to obstruct justice in our so-called War on Drugs; a license that lasted, so the CIA claims, from 1982 to 1995."

The actual request from Central Intelligence Agency Director William Casey to then-Attorney General William French Smith is still not in the public domain. But two letters, one from Smith thanking Casey for his request and a follow-up by Casey, are both available on the Internet. They were released as part of an internal CIA report that explored allegations of CIA involvement in drug trafficking. In the first document, Smith thanks Casey for his letter (the one that is not public) and says: ". . . in view of the fine cooperation the Drug Enforcement Administration has received from CIA, no formal requirement regarding the reporting of narcotics violations

308. Stephen Pizzo, Mary Fricker, and Paul Muolo, Inside Job: The Looting of America's Savings And Loans (New York: Harper Collins, 1991).

309. Prescott Bush, George's father, had worked for Brown, Brothers, Harriman one of the money-laundering banks used by Helliwell in the 1940s.

310. Wade Frazier, "The savings and loan scandal and public accounting," www.aheatedplanet.net/savings.htm#savings

has been included in these procedures."—William French Smith, Attorney General.

Casey in return thanked the Attorney General for his understanding:"I am pleased that these procedures, which I believe strike the proper balance between enforcement of the law and protection of intelligence sources and methods, will now be forwarded to other agencies."—William J. Casey, Director, Central Intelligence Agency

Why would the CIA ask to be exempt specifically from drug enforcement laws? According to Congresswoman Maxine Waters (D-Calif.), who at one time called for full disclosure of the facts, "The CIA knew that the Contras were dealing drugs. They made this deal with the Attorney General to protect themselves from having to report it."[311]

When this caper began to fall apart, Admiral Poindexter was the designated fall guy for the Reagan and Bush administration. Poindexter is an extremely smart but a rather unscrupulous character. He graduated in the top of his class at the Naval Academy and went on to earn a PhD in physics. He was National Security Advisor at the time. He was convicted of lying to Congress, destroying evidence and defrauding the government, behavior becoming an officer but clearly not a gentleman.

When the whole sordid Iran-Contra affair broke open, Reagan and Bush claimed to be shocked that such a thing could happen in their White House. However, Reagan had publicly extolled the virtues of the drug-running Contras as "freedom fighters." Reagan may have been in the beginning stage of Alzheimer's, but Bush was an old CIA operative, and it is highly unlikely that he did not have control over the military and intelligence departments as related to this operation. Had Poindexter not taken the stand to claim that he never informed Bush about the specifics of Iran/Contra, impeachment proceedings would have followed, which Bush with all of his powerful protection would not have been able to avoid. In this, Bush was assisted by Congressman Lee Hamilton, whose investigation of the covert action was so poorly carried out as to amount to a total whitewash of the guilty parties, including Reagan and Bush.[312] Lee Hamilton did such a bang up job covering up Iran/Contra that he was assigned the same function for 9/11 as well.

> I have put thousands of Americans away for tens of thousands
> of years for less evidence for conspiracy with less evidence
> than is available against Ollie North and CIA people. . . .
> I personally was involved in a deep-cover case that went to

311.   Martha Honey, "US, Don't Ask, Don't Tell," In These Times, May 1998.
312.   John Coleman, Diplomacy by Deception (Carson City, NV: Bridger House Publishers, 1993), 128.

the top of the drug world in three countries. The CIA killed it.—Former DEA Agent Michael Levine, CNBC-TV, 8 October 1996.

The Clinton's rise to the White House was fuelled by Iran–Contra operations in Arkansas.[313] The drugs and arms transshipments point in Mena, Arkansas had allegedly been one of the most significant operations occurring under the aegis of the National Security Council's (NSC) Oliver North. According to reports, every month of the operation millions of dollars of arms and drugs flowed through the airport at Mena. The stories of drug-running escapades and the deaths of many people who tried to stop or expose them, including two teenage boys who witnessed such drops and were found dead on the train tracks near the airport, were explored endlessly on the Internet but were effectively suppressed from the "official reality" of national TV or newspapers. There were nine different official investigations into Mena after 1987, from allegedly compromised federal grand juries to congressional inquiries suppressed by the National Security Council in 1988 under Ronald Reagan to still later U.S. Justice Department inaction under George Bush. Officials repeatedly invoked state security to quash most of the investigations.

Court documents do show clearly that the CIA and the DEA employed Barry Seal who was flying planeloads of cocaine into Mena, during 1984 and 1985, for the Reagan administration's celebrated sting attempt to implicate the Nicaraguan Sandinista regime in cocaine trafficking.[314]

When the Clintons arrived in Washington, there were numerous efforts to investigate government narcotics trafficking and fraud. Sally Denton and Roger Morris probably got the closest. Their article on Mena was pulled by the Washington Post at the very last minute, eventually to run in Penthouse in the summer of 1995. However, the journalist who finally broke through the nation's mass denial was Gary Webb, and he made it through, thanks to the Internet, a medium much harder to control than the broadcast or printed press.[315]

The year before Webb's story was released in the San Jose Mercury News, Katherine Austin Fitts, former Under Secretary at the Department of Housing and Urban Renewal (HUD) and former partner with the Wall

313. Katherine Austin Fitts, "Narco-Dollars for Beginners: How the Money Works in the Illicit Drug Trade, Part III, Drugs as Currency", www.narconews.com

314. Sally Denton and Roger Morris, "The Crimes of Mena," Penthouse, July 1995.

315. Katherine Austin Fitts, "The Myth of the Rule of Law, or How the Money Works: The Destruction of Hamilton Securities Group," 12 August 2002.

Street investment company, Dillon and Reed, launched her own business, Hamilton Securities. The company, with satellites located in inner-city neighborhoods, developed a software program called <u>Community Wizard</u>. The software was designed for use by citizens to identify how government money is spent locally. It allowed ordinary citizens access to information about government expenditures and contract opportunities that were usually assigned to Washington insiders. It was a very powerful and threatening tool for those who wanted to continue operating shadowy criminal enterprises at government expense, free from the scrutiny of Congress and citizens. It gave ordinary people the same knowledge as insiders who were making a fortune on the aggregation and low-bidding and procurement of lucrative government contracts.

The software was able to identify neighborhood patterns of defaulted HUD mortgage loans for the District of Columbia, New Orleans, and South Central Los Angeles. At the same time that the Webb story broke, Hamilton Securities discovered, with the use of the Community Wizard software, high and expensive rates of HUD mortgage defaults within areas of heavy narcotics trafficking in South Central Los Angeles. The Community Wizard program was able to produce targeted community maps that highlighted the pattern of single-family foreclosures on single-family HUD-backed mortgages. What was surprising about these maps was that they serendipitously brought some very important but obscure information into focus. On careful examination, the maps disclosed that all of the HUD foreclosures were in the center of areas where the crack cocaine epidemic had occurred. What was further revealed by looking at the HUD data was that, during the 1980s, thousands of middle-class African American wage-earning families with mortgages lost their homes. Why? There were drive-by shootings, the whole neighborhood deteriorated, crack people moved in next door, the children were being gunned down or were going to jail, and so families were forced to leave the neighborhood. A house that had a value of $100,000 was suddenly appraised at $40,000 because nobody wanted to buy it. It could not be sold, so people often just walked away from the chaos, leaving their investment behind.[316] This was more of what the Rand Institute had labeled as "planned shrinkage."

Hamilton Securities' place-based maps also showed that someone else came along and bought thousands of homes for 10 to 20 cents on the dollar

---

316. Catherine Austin Fitts, "The Myth of the Rule of Law or how the money works: the destruction of Hamilton Securities Group," <u>SRA Quarterly</u> (London), November 2001; www.scoop.co.nz/mason/stories/HL0208/S00055.htm, 12 August 2002.

in the years right after the crack cocaine epidemic. One of the large investors was the Harvard Endowment Fund, which was still beefing up a very large tax-free investment portfolio for short-term capital gains from the destruction of African American communities and asset forfeiture brought on by the drug trade.

Harvard University is governed by two boards: The Harvard Corporation comprising the president and seven Fellows of Harvard College and the Board of Overseers. The Corporation is self-perpetuating and fills its vacancies itself, with the consent of the Board of Overseers. Overseers are elected by the alumni at large. Harvard Corporation oversees Harvard Management, the company that manages the endowment, and Harvard College.

Herbert S. "Pug" Winokur, Jr., was one of the Fellows. He was also chairman of the board of directors of DynCorp. DynCorp served as the lead contractor to the Asset Forfeiture Fund of the Department of Justice. The company also had a $600 million government contract to provide knowledge management for enforcement and forfeiture operations as part of the war on drugs in the United States, Columbia, Peru, and Bolivia.

Although the CIA's Inspector General admitted to agency drug trafficking in 1998, there have been no open congressional hearings as promised. Using DynCorp services, the Reagan-Bush administration was systematically targeting homeowners and taxpayers to finance covert operations during Iran–Contra. DynCorp was scooping up real-estate assets in drug-plagued neighborhoods for packaging into bundles for HUD auction sales. This was a military operation, not just in Nicaragua but also directed against targeted inner-city neighborhoods, largely black and Hispanic communities.

As the CIA memorandum of understanding demonstrated, U.S. government- sanctioned drugs flowed into targeted neighborhoods. Neighborhoods were destroyed. Vultures like DynCorp (Pug Winokur) swooped up the real estate and land assets that were packaged and sold to investment companies, such as (Pug Winokur's) Capricorn Holdings that made large profits from ethnic cleansing and subsequent urban renewal. The extent of Harvard's investments in Capricorn and its funds, if any, are unknown. On several occasions, Harvard and Capricorn invested side by side. Pug was serving on the Harvard board and the board of Enron when Enron went bankrupt. The Harvard Endowment, before that bankruptcy, was aggressively and profitably selling Enron stock.[317]

The CIA-financing model OSS agent Helliwell developed has become a model for domestic financial terrorism. Malcolm X was castigated after

---

317. Catherine Austin Fitts, "Dillon Read & Co. Inc. and the Aristocracy of Prison Profits," http://www.dunwalke.com/non_flash.htm.

the Kennedy assassination when he linked U.S. foreign policy that had been responsible for the deaths of foreign leaders to Kennedy's death in Dealey Plaza by observing, "The chickens have come home to roost." The chickens have turned into monstrous genetically modified super droids. The financial model is the usual tapeworm economic model of free trade: Use the money of the targeted group to steal their own property. Get the poor to buy drugs by using their own money, and then take that money to bring in more drugs. The massive infusion of drugs into a neighborhood destroys property values. Private equity firms soon arrive to scoop up the properties for pennies on the dollar. The same pattern repeated itself in cities around the nation: Washington Heights in New York, in Washington D.C., and in South Central Los Angeles.

Prof. John Metzger, at the University of Michigan, documented this pattern of "urban renewal."[318] Metzger has a doctorate in urban planning. He reveals that the Kerner Commission Report produced in 1967 after the Detroit riots made it official U.S. government policy that no more than a quarter of the population of any major inner city should be minority. It was called spatial deconcentration.[319] Spatial deconcentration theory is based on a military strategy for establishing control over urban areas and was later referred to explicitly in HUD documents. It was decided during this era that the American capital structure had no intention of incorporating into the social structure the economically disfranchised in the nation's inner cities. Because poverty had become so concentrated in the inner cities, hopelessness overwhelmed the residents, and the government had resolved to dilute it. Such hopelessness had the social effect of a fire near a powder keg. The thinking was that if the ghettoes were thinned out, the chances of a cataclysmic explosion capable of destroying the American way of life would be equally diminished.

Bernard Weissbourd, another strategist from Chicago wrote a paper that was unearthed entitled "Urban Strategy," in which he proposed a "one-four-three-four" plan. He postulated that because minority populations in the inner city represent a growing political threat by their growing numbers, a strategy had to be quickly developed to thin out their numbers and prevent them from overwhelming the nation's biggest cities. He suggested that this be accomplished through a series of federal and private programs that would financially induce minorities to migrate to the suburbs until their absolute

---

318. Mike Ruppert, "Wall Street, CIA and the Global Drug Trade, Nexus Magazine 8 (October-November 2001); extract available at www.nexusmagazine.com.
319. 17 Ibid.

numbers inside the cities represented no more than one-fourth of the total population.[320]

Given the policy of HUD to reduce the number of minorities in urban neighborhoods, Fitts's disclosure of the evidence of this policy through her Community Wizard Program made her dangerous. Fitts's Hamilton Securities company was soon under attack by the Justice Department. It seems that someone was getting nervous about the possibility that HUD might be involved in securities fraud surrounding mortgage sales as well as ethnic cleansing, American style. Fitts has since lost her life's fortune of millions of dollars in defending herself against unfounded allegations designed to keep her quiet, but she speaks and writes insightfully on the nation's parasitic economy. She is developing models for average Americans to learn how to protect themselves from what she calls the tapeworm economy. Her writings can be found at www.solari.com.[321]

What Fitts has to say is fundamentally important to understanding how drugs and money work in the society that it becomes abundantly clear that the War on Drugs is meant to continue and that the consequences will continue to show up in the nation's hospitals, emergency wards, and prisons. Unfortunately, the drug epidemic is also fueling a very profitable financial holocaust that is impacting not only inner-city neighborhoods, but the entire economy. It is not just billions of dollars of wholesale capital movement, defaulted HUD mortgages, U.S. Treasury intervention in the market, Federal Reserve bailouts of hedge funds, and IMF bailouts of Wall Street investors, money laundering out of Russia, or narcotics trafficking but ordinary people and businesses are being destroyed. The currency is also becoming debased, which is another form of indirect taxation. As of November 2008, the St. Louis Federal Reserve indicated that the aggregate monetary base is growing at an annualized rate of almost 800 percent (785.7 percent).[322] The dollar may soon be worthless. As long as the people of the United States continue to act as if the credit of the United States does not belong to the people of the United States, the expansion of the money supply and debasing of the currency by the privately owned Fed will continue.

While the parents are under financial attack, the children are the targets of both legal and illegal drug trafficking. The children are being deliberately dumbed down in crumbling schools, and the parents' small business equity is being extracted from under them by the religion of free trade buttressed

---

320. Yolanda Ward, "Spatial deconcentration"
321. For anyone who wants to understand how the money works in this economy, Fitts' writings are a must read.
322. The Fed stopped reporting on the M3 money supply in 2006.

by international trade agreements, such as NAFTA and the WTO. The cruel twist is that citizens are funding the financial ruin that is killing them and their children. The silent weapons are working as planned.

How the Money Works: The Destruction of Neighborhoods

Fitts delineates in "The Myth of the Rule of Law" a six-point program on how the economic model of destruction works. The model leads to an ever increasing national debt that leads to more centralized control. She comments that the mechanisms of the model work the same both domestically and internationally. Some call it the securitization process. Some call it privatization. Some call it globalization. What this means is that the management of resources becomes ever more centralized and concentrated in fewer hands. This is done through a system of securitization based on privilege, insider information (for example, Pug Winokur), and coercion rather than through performance and the rule of law. This is how wealth is transferred to the top 1 percent. It is very similar to the World Bank's four-point plan outlined by former World Bank head, Joseph Stiglitz. It is not a mistake that the area from K Street that houses so many lobbyists to the Capital is called the "Golden Triangle".

1. First, all retail sales are consolidated into a few large corporations, including franchise operations, cutting out local small business.
2. Then all local government functions are privatized and outsourced to a few large corporations, or they are subjected to such overwhelming federal regulation that they can be controlled and managed for the benefit of a few large corporations and their investors.
3. Next, buy up all of the land and real estate, or encumber them with mortgages in a way that is as profitable as possible and allows you to get control when you want. (There are few if any small farmers left, and the 2008 mortgage crisis will cause people of color to lose up to $213 billion, leading to the greatest loss of wealth in modern U.S. history—even bigger than the S&L scandal).
4. The entire process is financed with profits from narcotics and organized crime, which you market into the neighborhood. This enables the financing of expansion in a manner that lowers the cost of capital and conveniently lowers the initial price of the investment and/or weakens the competition. (there are no taxes on drug profits and the returns are higher than the stock market). The local businesses and land are then bought with the losses of the locals' own money at

a fraction of the cost. No one sells her home faster and cheaper than a mother trying to make bail or pay a lawyer to save her family from jail or death. That is why narcotics trafficking is the ultimate form of neighborhood leveraged buyout.

5. This is all leveraged with tax shelters, private tax-exempt bonds, municipal bonds, government guarantees, and government subsidies—all protected with complex securities arrangements.

6. Finally, ensure that the only companies and mutual funds allowed meaningful access to capital are those run by syndicate-approved management teams. To raise significant campaign funds, candidates for political office appoint syndicate-approved management teams. Investment syndicates define the boundaries of managed competition that cycle all capital back through their pipelines. That means that the only local boys who can make good are those who play ball with the syndicate.

It is in this way, using drug money, that private equity in a community can be extracted at a near infinite rate of return to investors and a highly negative rate of return to taxpayers. This is why globalization is eviscerating the American economy and destroying numerous small local farms and businesses. This is why illegal drugs will continue to be an integral part of the American economy. And this is why the AIDS story will be vigorously endorsed by the medical hierarchy as long a possible. It is just business.

Fitts, a former investment banker, calculated the cash flow sales from drug profits available for reinvestment for every year from 1947 to the present. She projected growth using the compound growth rate of the Standard and Poor's 500. What she discovered was that the amount of equity owned by those who profit from the drug trade would be enormous. Crime pays. Those who profited from the drug business and other organized crime cash flows own a controlling position on just about everything on the New York Stock exchanges.

This is the very profitable legacy of the opium trade. According to John Coleman,

"The Bank of International Settlements and the International Monetary Fund are nothing more than the bully-boy clearing houses for the drug trade. The BIS makes no distinction when it comes to distinguishing between 'legitimate' flight capital and what is laundered drug money."[323]

Coleman, a former MI6 British Secret Service agent, claimed that he had been informed by IMF agents of a meeting held in Hong Kong that they

323. John Coleman, The Committee of 300 (Las Vegas, NV: Global Review Publications, 2006), 281.

could literally cause a run on any country's currency using narco-dollars to precipitate a flight of capital. The drug business is the largest single enterprise in the world today, transcending and dwarfing all others. It has allowed the rise of a criminal shadow government to take control of the legitimate government in a masterful exercise of fifth-column infiltration, with few people being any the wiser.

Drugging America also has other secondary functions besides profitability. It debilitates the segment of society most prone to resistance and rebellion—the young. During the height of the Civil Rights and Vietnam War resistance movements the CIA, in another government sanctioned program, MK-ULTRA, began to introduce a multitude of drugs into the nonconformist youth scene.[324] It was a veritable drug supermarket where large numbers of psychologically vulnerable young people were targeted for the use of cocaine, nitrite inhalants, amphetamines, heroin, LSD, marijuana, PCP and a host of other psychoactive drugs. By the 1980s and Reagan administration's sponsoring of the Iran-Contra episode, crack cocaine made its first appearance. About ten years after the beginning of this drug mania, the hospitals began to see clusters of unusual opportunistic diseases in middle-class white male homosexuals. These types of disease clusters had heretofore only been seen in IV-drug users and immune-suppressed organ transplant recipients, but they had been seen and were not new phenomena. The newness was the cluster of these old diseases in middle-class white males with whom the medical establishment could more easily empathize. This identification with the patient population by the treating physicians is what raised the alarm. The same diseases in the poor, the old, and the debilitated had never been a cause for overarching concern or the need to create a new disease paradigm to explain the phenomenon.

The early patients were mostly young men who had seemingly blown their immune systems after years of dosing themselves with poisonous toxins, so generously supplied by their own government, and with toxic thoughts and toxic behaviors as well. They were also suffering from poor nutrition, insomnia, lack of sanitation, and cellular intoxication from miscellaneous persistent drug use. Yet the medical establishment hierarchy ignored one of the fundamental principles of medical social history taking and went instead on a wild goose chase looking for a virus. The mass poisoning resulting from the drug crisis at the root of these problems that had been intentionally created was ignored in favor of virus hunters. AIDS became a new money

---

324. Michael E. Kreca, "How the U.S. Government Created the 'Drug Problem' in the USA," www.lewrockwell.com

pit. The dissident voices advocating alternate theories were obviously silenced for both political and economic reasons.

African AIDS

At about the same time that the young men were showing up in America's emergency rooms, rumors began to circulate in the Western media about a similar condition that was claimed to be devastating whole villages in Africa. Stories of abandoned orphans and ghost villages were headlined daily in the Western press. The media gave the impression that there was something new afoot in Africa that was killing off the people—some new terrible tropical infection. By repetition of the visuals they reinforced the viral meme intended to infect the universal collective mind. Africa would be accused of bringing AIDS to the world.

What the media neglected to say was the new <u>infection</u> was an economic virus spread systematically courtesy of the World Bank, the IMF, and global extractive corporations. The same neoliberal policies that were leading to the degradation and deindustrialization of America's core were also devastating many of Africa's fragile economies and leaving its people more destitute than when the European colonial powers overtly departed from the continent. A memorandum written by Lawrence Summers is a perfect demonstration of the thinking and strategies of the new economic colonialists.

Summers was chief economist for the World Bank in 1991 when he wrote a memo in which he suggested that the World Bank encourage more migration of dirty industries to the Less Developed Countries (LDC):

> The measurements of the costs of health impairing pollution depend on the foregone earnings from increased morbidity and mortality. From this point of view a given amount of health impairing pollution should be done in the country with the lowest cost, which will be the country with the lowest wages. I think the economic logic behind dumping a load of toxic waste in the lowest wage country is impeccable and we should face up to that. . . . I've always thought that the under-populated countries in Africa are vastly UNDER-polluted, their air quality is probably vastly inefficiently low compared to Los Angeles or Mexico City."[325]

---

325. Lawrence Summers, World Bank Memo for general distribution, dated 12 December 1991.

When the memo became public in February 1992, Brazil's then Secretary of the Environment, José Lutzenburger, wrote back to Summers: "Your reasoning is perfectly logical but totally insane. . . . Your thoughts [provide] a concrete example of the unbelievable alienation, reductionist thinking, social ruthlessness and arrogant ignorance of many conventional 'economists' concerning the nature of the world we live in. . . . If the World Bank keeps you as vice president it will lose all credibility. To me it would confirm what I often said . . . the best thing that could happen would be for the World Bank to disappear." Sadly, Mr. Lutzenburger was fired after writing this letter, and Summers was appointed Treasury Secretary on 2 July 1999 and served through the remainder of the Clinton Administration. He was then named president of Harvard University. In the summer of 2000, he supported the Enron attacks on the California energy grid in claiming that there was too much regulation, and he supported the Gramm-Leach-Bliley Act of 1999 (GLBA), also known as the Financial Services Modernization Act, that repealed provisions of the Glass-Steagall Act of 1933, which enabled the Wall Street crisis of 2008. He was also one of the supporters of the Russian privatization scheme, in which a handful of government insiders were able to purchase formerly state owned enterprises for pennies on the dollar. His tenure as president of Harvard University was a gigantic flop largely because of his arrogance, insensitivity and lack of leadership skills. After such sterling successes, he became an <u>economic</u> adviser to President Barack Obama—the <u>change</u> President.

One of the consequences of the World Bank attitude toward using Africa as a dumping ground for the waste of Western nations has been the dumping by European and Asian firms of toxic waste off the coast of Somalia. They have been off-loading toxic waste for twenty years, destroying the Somali coastline and fishing areas. The waste that washes ashore includes radioactive uranium waste, lead, and heavy metals like cadmium and mercury. There are also industrial, hospital, and chemical waste as well. The continued destabilization of this region with weak or nonexistent governments allows such pollution to continue. The continuing destabilization of this region of Africa will be used as the ruse to get the Africom command on African soil, which thus far every country on the continent has resisted.

The Western nations, in addition to staging multiple coups and ethnic violence and using the strategy of the World Bank and IMF, have been waging all out economic warfare on Africa for decades. The promotion by vested Western corporate interests in the ceaseless proxy wars and gun running has driven people as diverse as the Ndebele to the Bushmen of the Kalahari from their traditional lands on which minerals or oil are located. This process has created famine, massive dislocation of populations into urban slums and refugee tent cities. As a result, traditional agriculture, commerce, and social institutions have been disrupted and have led to widespread hunger and malnutrition. A strategy of the World Trade Organization has been to dump subsidized agricultural products on nations whose farmers receive no assistance. This has had the effect of destroying small farms in developing nations and the ability of many countries to keep pace with the food demands of growing urban populations. There is untold misery being inflicted once more on the African continent and the people are dying, not from viral AIDS, but from nutritional and infectious AIDS. The deficiency of just one vitamin, vitamin A, causes blindness in half a million children every year, and many of them are dead within twelve months because of a suppressed immune system and subsequent growth retardation and respiratory diseases.

Malnourished, socially disrupted, and toxic people are very susceptible to infections, including mycobacterium which the men are bringing to their communities as a result of mining lung damage, and parasitic infections from substandard sanitation and clean water supplies. They are also susceptible to extreme psychological trauma known as post-traumatic stress disorder associated with great social upheavals. Prolonged psychological stress suppresses the immune system through the hypothalamic-pituitary-adrenal axis and the unopposed chronic outpouring of corticosteroids from the adrenal gland. There are many reasons for people to be immune suppressed. Just as there is no sexual and blood transmitted pandemic in the West, there is no heterosexual infectious <u>HIV</u> viral pandemic in Africa that is killing off the population.

However, an economic virus developed from the reptilian minds of people like Larry Summers has led to increased and widespread poverty and to a rise in malaria and tuberculosis, both age-old diseases that have been long known on the continent. Africa's population is increasing at a rate of almost 3 percent a year, which is faster than any other region of the world— but the areas coveted by Western powers for their natural wealth are being systematically destabilized and depopulated. The Congo, Sudan, the Blacks of South Africa, and Zimbabwe have been particular targets.

Two stories highlighted in the Project Censored 2007 "most important news stories that didn't make the news" relate to the economic woes of both the United States and Africa. Story # 4 is that while hunger and homelessness are increasing in the United States, the Bush administration planned to make the problem go away simply by suppressing the information about the data. This was done by eliminating the production of a survey widely used by federal and state programs for low-income and retired Americans. Bush's proposal marked at least the third White House attempt in as many years to do away with federal data collection on politically prickly economic issues.

Story #5 is titled "High Tech Genocide in the Congo." It seems that while the world's attention has been directed to Darfur in the Sudan, or the alleged atrocities of Mugabe in Zimbabwe, according to the UN relief coordinator, six to seven million people have died in the Congo since 1996 as a consequence of invasions and wars sponsored by Western powers trying to gain control of the region's mineral wealth. At stake is control of natural resources that are sought by U.S. corporations—diamonds, tin, copper, gold, and more significantly, coltan and niobium, two minerals necessary for production of cell phones and other high-tech electronics; and cobalt, an element essential to nuclear, chemical, aerospace, and defense industries.

How do you get away with killing six million people—again—without the world so much as blinking an eye? It is quite simple. The public has been conditioned since the racist 18th and 19th century writings of the British invaders of Africa and the updated Hollywood productions of such masterpieces as "Birth of a Nation," "Gone With the Wind," and Tarzan movies that Africans have no history. The world, including many of African descent, has been led to believe that civilizations such as Kemet, Nubia, Kush, Zimbabwe, Ghana, Benin, and Timbuktu that developed highly complex and sophisticated social structures before Europe was Europe never existed. Since the meme that has infected the Western psyche is that Africans are wild heathens that need to be managed and are therefore unable to manage their own affairs except under the tutelage of some great white father, stealing their wealth is justified. As Larry Summers would say about stealing the wealth, "the logic is impeccable." Further, the only recent images of Africa that the Western media never tire of portraying seem to be of starving children or child soldiers. The press conveniently fails to mention that while USAID holds up food supplies, international arms dealers supported by Western governments are doing a brisk business arming the paramilitary thugs whose leaders have been trained in counterinsurgency tactics and warfare at U.S. military bases.

So when the medical propagandists started talking about a blood and sex plague from Africa by way of Haiti similar to a monkey virus, the visual image was etched into the collective consciousness of the planet. When millions of people began to be ethnically cleansed, it was not because of resource wars. It was because of their child-like indulgences and lack of self-discipline. Over and over again, pictures of sick and starving Africans, victims of IMF and World Bank monetary policies or a mercenary-supported corporate grab for their ancestral lands were plastered onto the front of newspapers and television screens, and the world was made to believe these people were dying of AIDS. The health consequence of this long-standing economic warfare was now AIDS.

Former presidents (who hire <u>men</u> like Larry Summers) pretending to have a conscience and to promote their image as great humanitarians take every opportunity to sear into the public psyche the idea that AIDS is an African crisis. This unprincipled promotion of the HIV/AIDS viral meme not only benefits the major pharmaceutical cartels but also others who paid for their rise to the Oval Office. One of such people is a rich, politically well-connected diamond merchant who chairs a committee of a major East Coast public health school that raises money and awareness to make sure that AIDS is persistently seen as an African problem. The world is lulled to sleep by another hopeless African tragedy. There will be no holocaust museums for these Africans.

The consequences of opening trade with China, the prolongation of the Vietnam War, and the Iran/Contra Affair, long-standing World Bank and IMF structural adjustment programs, and prolonged lung damage from mining injuries have been an unprecedented mass poisoning of large groups of people, an anomalous event in evolutionary history. What was knowable was the response of the evolutionary biologically programmed counterbalancing efforts of the human immune system that the larger medical community failed to recognize. By ignoring the knowable biological processes they could hypothesize in a vacuous way that it was caused by a phantom virus. But a virus, real or phantom, has never been able to account for the manifestations of the acquired immunodeficiency syndrome.

Because of the intensive exchange that takes place between the immune cell network and the neuroendocrine system, the origin of human stress whether conveyed biochemically, neurologically, electromagnetically, or through quantum dynamics has a limited biologically programmed expression at the cellular level. It makes no difference to the cell whether the disruption is caused by microbes, the body's own antigens, psychic trauma and pain, protein deficiency syndrome, or antioxidant impairment as a result of faulty nutrition, nitrites, and nitrosamines, bacterial toxins or pharmatoxic substances, serious injuries or burns, operations or organ transplants, radiation damage or environmental toxins, drug abuse or doping agents, contaminated coagulated proteins or multi-transfusions, vaccines or antibiotics, or congenital acquired factors. The immune cells and other cell systems will always react, modulate, and adapt, and will follow the same evolutionary biological laws.[326] This is a mystery only to those who have an economic and political reason for it to be so.

---

326. Heinrich Kremer, <u>The Silent Revolution in Cancer and AIDS Medicines</u> (Bloomington, IN: Xlibris Corp., 2008), 165.

Some of this cell biology was not completely known at the time that the virus hunters were making their pronouncements, but enough was known that it was clear that they had not isolated a virus; they had no proof that this virus was transmissible; there were no photographs of a viral isolate; and they certainly did not biochemically characterize this virus, according to their own viral isolation techniques. But more than anything, the viral theory has been a spectacular failure at explaining the diseases and the predicted epidemiology of a global pandemic that has never materialized.

The medical hierarchy intentionally chose not to consider the immune suppressing environmental factors confronting the young patients. This was not the first time in recent medical history that pressure was applied from higher funding levels to violate the rules of science and of nature by sublimating science to the social and political agendas of the financial elite.

The idea that the hierarchy of the medical community would suppress evidence that might be used to cure people is not a new phenomenon. The case that I am establishing is of an industry that is controlled at the top by people whose interests are very different from that of the average physician. From the time that the Rockefeller interests and the eugenics ideology took control of medical education there has been a consistent zealotry biased toward the use of patent drugs and vaccines and away from natural healing modalities. It is just business.

There has been a constant and consistent degradation of the environment, the air we breathe, the water we drink, the food we eat. Deliberate confusion is sown by those who have vested interests in the profitability of the industry even if it means the sacrifice of lives. After all, it is a silent war, and although it creates little noise, it is indeed responsible for millions of deaths.

There have been other medical calamities that have been run in similar fashion to the current AIDS disinformation wars. AIDS is simply a modern version of what will be discussed in a later chapter, the SMON and Pellagra stories.

Chapter 11

SMON, Pellagra, The Eugenics Blueprint for Creating and Sustaining a Medical Crisis

o o o o o o o o o o o o o o o o o o o o o o o o o o o o o

Deception is a state of mind and the mind of the State.

James Jesus Angleton, Head,
CIA Counter Intelligence, 1954–74

The most merciful thing that a family does to one of its infant members is to kill it.

Margaret Sanger

Moreover, they [Negroes] are quite led away by the fallacy of numbers. They want the black race to survive. They are cheered by a census return of increasing numbers and a high rate of increase. They must learn that among human races and groups, as among vegetables, quality and not mere quantity really counts.

W. E. B. Du Bois, "Black Folk and Birth Control," 1938

SMON

AIDS is not the first time that the medical community has committed grievous errors in claiming that a noninfectious disease is caused by a microbe. As recently as the 1950s Japanese physicians thought that there was a new virally-caused epidemic that, in fact, turned out to be an iatrogenic epidemic caused by the drug clioquinol and was of their own making. The condition appeared mainly in Japan and was known as <u>SMON</u> (subacute myelo-optical-neuropathy). Most of the patients were middle-aged women who exhibited an unusual combination of symptoms that included diarrhea, internal bleeding, and nerve degeneration including weakness and paralysis in the legs. The disease seemed to break out during late summer and appeared in clusters within families and around certain towns. This outbreak was occurring at about the same time that stories about viral diseases, especially polio, were being hyped in the media. The story of SMON is not only a classic case of group-think causing intellectual paralysis, but a moral tale about the lack of integrity of the pharmaceutical industry.

Suspicions that clioquinol had a more sinister side began to creep in during the 1960s when a Swiss vet reported to CIBA that several dogs which had been treated with Entero-Vioform one of the brands under which the drug was sold, had succumbed to fatal epileptic fits. Two years later the company issued a warning to veterinarians, but although the drugs were produced for human use, they not only did not take any measures to warn about the dangers of use by humans and continued to stress the safety of the drug.

The disease outbreaks in Japan never had the epidemiological characteristics of a new infectious problem as it did not strike randomly in the population but was largely confined to middle-aged women. It was much less common among men, and almost absent in children and there was no evidence of an infectious agent in blood or body fluids. The patients had no clinical signs of infection: fevers, rashes, headaches, etc.. However, because of the polio scare, the virus hunt was on, and it blinded physicians to the fundamental nature of the problem. It also created somewhat of a panic in the population about the possibility of a new infectious disease. When patients went to medical centers to inquire anxiously about their stomachache or diarrhea, many were admitted to isolation wards and treated with clioquinol, thus enlarging the SMON statistics.

Of Japan's known victims, 50 per cent returned to their normal routine within two years. Recovery for the remainder was slower. Ten to fifteen percent were left permanently disabled and there was a seven percent fatality.

The University of Tokyo estimated that as many as 30,000 people may have suffered some damage.

The problem was compounded because it was mistakenly identified as a viral syndrome. The adherents of the virus theory of the disease continued for years to prevail. As the outbreak progressed, the viral cause of SMON went unchallenged, but the viral enemy was changed from an echovirus to a coxsackie virus, a type of passenger virus known to infect the digestive tract. This new theory of a coxsackie agent soon proved to be nothing more than laboratory contamination. When the virus hunt proved futile, researchers began to look for a possible bacterial agent as the cause. That too proved to be a dead end.

More years passed. More patients became ill and more physicians continued to ignore a key element of patients' clinical histories. Finally, a team of researchers recognized that there was a historical commonality in the SMON patients. They had all been prescribed clioquinol, the same diarrhea-fighting drug that was marketed under two different brand names: Entero-Vioform or Emaform. The anamnestic evidence indicating that these patients had all been prescribed the same drug had been long ignored as insignificant and non-contributory. The drugs were prescribed for problems of the digestive tract—which was mistaken as an early symptom of SMON.

The question that one should raise at this point is how did this drug get marketed without the necessary toxicology studies? As noted, Ciba-Geigy knew from animal studies of the dangers of the product, but failed to warn physicians. One enterprising pharmacologist in Japan finally preformed toxicology studies. Hoping to see if he could recreate the nerve damage seen in humans he gave clioquinol to laboratory mice. No nerve damage occurred in the mice, but all of them died from the drug. This was of course a big clue that (a) the drug was toxic and (b) that it was absorbed into the bloodstream from the intestinal tract. This evidence was still blatantly ignored because the researchers had locked their minds onto an infectious etiology. That SMON could be iatrogenically caused and noncontagious was beyond consideration.

In 1967 the study group of the National Hospitals on SMON reported as follows: Entero-vioform (clioquinol's brand name), mesaphylin, Emaform (home producer of clioquinol), chloromycetin and llosone were often prescribed to SMON patients, but no link was found between Entero-vioform and SMON. This report referred to Entero-vioform in particular so that clioquinol must have been suspected by someone in the study group. Dr. Tsugane, who was responsible for the survey, said that the survey was not thorough enough to unearth clioquinol as a causative agent. One of the reasons could have been that clioquinol had been used as a drug for the intestinal disorders of SMON, and it was hard to believe that clioquinol was toxic rather than a remedy.[327]

Finally in 1975, almost twenty-five years after the first outbreak, another commission reviewed the disease epidemiology and the animal experiments and came to the conclusion that the cause of the problem was most likely the drug clioquinol. Although there were case reports of isolated episodes in other countries, the bulk of the cases remained in Japan. It turns out that the Japanese doctors were overprescribing the drug. The doctors, being the real virus, refused to identify themselves as the creators of this iatrogenic tragedy. The virologists continued to look for a viral cause of the disease even after it disappeared with the ban on clioquinol.[328] The epidemic's toll officially ended in 1973 after there had been thousands of fatalities—not from a virus, but from the drug.

Many patients and families were so outraged at learning that Ciba-Geigy (the pharmaceutical company that manufactured the drug) had disregarded previously reported cliquinol toxicity that they filed a lawsuit in May 1971 against the Japanese government, Ciba-Geigy of Japan, fifteen distributors of the drug, and twenty-three doctors and hospitals. Patients were awarded compensation, but the story that the virus hunters ignored the evidence of a toxic cause for many years and sacrificed thousands of human lives went quietly into the medical memory hole. The story that SMON research had ignored evidence of a toxic cause for more than two decades and had sacrificed thousands of human lives to a flawed virus hypothesis based on belief rather than observable science was too embarrassing to the virus-hunting establishment to record.

This episode did not stop Ciba Geigy from marketing and selling this drug in many less developed countries where gastro-intestinal symptoms are common and record keeping is poor. When asked at a Geneva press conference why they were not prepared to suspend the sale of the drug until its effects and side-effects were clarified, they replied with a straight face that, "We have no medical reason to be afraid of the drug. Do you think that a big multinational company would continue sales of a compound or a product if this would mean danger to human lives?"[329]

Historically, SMON, Pellagra, and HIV fit the same pattern dynamics. A group of people get sick with the same or similar symptoms. The hierarchy

---

327. T.E, Soda, <u>Drug-Induced Sufferings: Medical, Pharmaceutical, and Legal Aspects</u> (Amsterdam: <u>Excerpta Medica</u>, 1980).

328. Peter Duesberg, <u>Inventing the AIDS Virus</u> (Washington, D.C. Regnery Publishing, 1996), 11–29.

329. Dexter Tiranti, "The Devil's Alternative:, January 1981, <u>The New Internationalist.</u>

of the medical community overrides scientific evidence and clinical judgment concerning the possibility of an environmental cause of the problem, and instead claim there must be an infectious agent. They spend years and millions of research dollars looking for the elusive bug. In the end, thousands are harmed or are killed. When the medical community finally wakes up to the disaster, it quietly goes away. Some make millions treating a disease that is either iatrogenically caused or compounded by iatrogenic error. The profits gained from human suffering are enormous.

Biochemically, SMON, Pellagra, and HIV are all diseases that impact the cellular metabolism of the mitochondria—the tiny cellular organelles where energy is made in the form of a compound called ATP or adenosine triphosphate.   The mitochondrion is also the major organelle that helps to control the redox potential of the cell environment measured in millivolts. In living cells, the effective proportion of reduced substances to oxidized substances is called the redox balance.

It turns out that clioquinol uncouples the process of oxidative phosphorylation (the formation of ATP) in the mitochondria. Pellagra is a niacin deficiency. Niacin is a precursor for the $NADP^+$/NADPH (nicotinamide adenine dinucleotide phosphate), an electron transfer couplet that contributes to the production of ATP. This couplet also makes an important contribution to the redox balance as a non-thiol electron transfer couplet that serves as a source of electrons to maintain the reduction status of the glutathione system.[330]

A true hallmark of those who are HIV positive and go on to develop AIDS is a deficiency of the master antioxidant, glutathione. If glutathione is chronically depleted as the result of long-standing oxidative stress or malnutrition, the redox potential of the cell is altered and oxidative damage to mitochondrial DNA and to energy production enzymes inhibits the production of ATP. Not having enough energy to maintain its differentiated status, changes begin to occur at the cellular and organ level that eventually present, depending on the disposition of the individual, as diseases. With less energy available the cell has three options: cell death, cell degeneration as occurs in disease states, or cell transformation as occurs in cancer. This is the reduced version of complex biochemical and electromagnetic energy production, but the idea is that all three pathologies, SMON, Pellagra, and now AIDS, are the result of altered cellular electrical potentials with resulting alterations in mitochondrial metabolism. This energy flux then alters the

---

330. F.Q., Shafer, and G.R. Buettner, "Redox Environment of the Cell as Viewed Through the Redox State of the Glutathione Disulfide/Glutathione Couple," Free Radical Biology & Med.30 (2001):1191–1212.

signals for DNA and RNA synthesis, protein synthesis, enzyme activation, and regulation of the cell cycle. These electrochemical signals determine if cells live or die or degenerate or transform into cancer.

With SMON, the doctors kept giving patients more of the medicine that was destroying their ATP. With Pellagra, the medical community claimed that it was caused by an infection rather than a nutritional deficiency and kept feeding people the same diet lacking in the important nutrient niacin that is necessary for ATP production. Finally, with HIV, patients who were in a hypercatabolic metabolic state and highly oxidized were not metabolically compensated and were given the drug AZT (Azidothymadine) which, because of its nitroso chemical moiety, accelerated these deleterious metabolic processes. Fifty percent of patients who survived after being placed on AZT developed a cancer within three years.

The idea of giving a compound whose likely function was to terminate mitochondrial function to those whose main problem was already reduced energy production by the mitochondria because of long-standing oxidative stress was either a major scientific blunder or a deliberate poisoning of the mitochondria oxidative physhoylation energy system.

At the First World Congress on AIDS, Dr. Lewis Thomas, director of the Memorial Sloan Kettering Cancer Center in New York, gave a public lecture in which he stated: "What is needed, of course, is a series of human experiments, planned and executed in order to answer the sort of question which automatically raises itself: what would happen if you were to remove the putative defense mechanisms of cellular immunity in human beings? Would this affect either the incidence or clinical course of cancer?" Thomas went on to acknowledge that he was aware that the AIDS patients were presenting with similar cancers to the organ transplant patients who had been purposely immune suppressed with azothioprine, cyclosporine A, and corticosteroids so as not to reject the transplantation graft. He even recognized that there was tumor regression in both AIDS patients and organ transplant patients when AZT or the drugs given to organ transplant patients were stopped. Given that this observation of reversibility was known at that time, it is absolutely unconscionable that this man would promote the search for a viral agent as the causative factor. It is evident that the disease hypothesis of an "AIDS agent" and an "immune suppressive virus" was from the outset introduced as a speculative construct lacking any substantial proof.[331] And as Thomas stated, it was a way of doing expansive and global human experimentation ostensibly to answer a question about the role of cellular immunity in the

---

331. Heinrich Kremer, The Silent Revolution in Cancer and AIDS Medicine (Bloomington, IN: Xlibris, 2008), 68–70.

development of cancer. It has been twenty-five years. Undoubtedly, Dr. Thomas has his answer. As a matter of fact, given his comments, he had it before this worldwide human experimentation was begun.

Pellagra

Pellagra is a multisystem disease caused by a vitamin deficiency as a result of near starvation conditions of extreme poverty that occurred mainly in localized areas in the formerly slave-holding South. In the post-Civil War South until the middle of the 20th century, living conditions for poor blacks and many whites were no better than in many less developed countries today. Sanitation often consisted of open sewers and outhouses. Malaria was a common infection and was not controlled until it became a problem for the U.S. military on Southern bases during WWII. This is when the military and local communities began widespread spraying of the poison DDT in almost 5 million rural homes.[332]

Outbreaks of pellagra were common in the post-Civil War South among cotton mill workers and the formerly enslaved who found themselves newly enslaved to a post- Civil War policy that turned them into "sharecroppers." Sharecropping was an updated form of European feudalism in which tenants farm the land of absent landowners who extract profits in such a way that the tenant is seldom able to free himself from the constraints of the contract. At the end of the planting season, the tenant is often in more debt to the landowner than at the beginning. As a result of their poor circumstances, the diet adopted by many Southerners consisted mainly of white food: pork fat, corn in the form of bread or "pone" fried in pork grease, and molasses made from corn or sorghum. During the late 1920s, maize kernel constituted 32.5 percent of all the food intake of Southern blacks. The diet was not much better for poor whites. This diet barely met the caloric needs of the individual, and it was devoid of many nutritional requirements. It ultimately resulted in a disease state, known as pellagra, as well as an overall weakening of the immune system.

Pellagra is characterized by the four Ds—dermatitis—rough red skin eruptions, diarrhea, dementia, and finally, if left untreated, death. It is caused by an insufficient dietary intake of niacin, one of the B vitamins. The four Ds are some of the same symptoms described in nutritionally deficient people who are said to have AIDS—especially in Africa among people who are known to have slim disease, a muscle- wasting condition that has been associated with AIDS.

---

332. CDC, Eradication of Malaria in the United States (1947–1951). .

Pellagra was first characterized by Spanish physician Gaspar Casal in 1735 and in 1771 by an Italian physician Francesco Frapolli, who observed that it was endemic among the Italian peasants. Although pellagra had afflicted numerous people in the United States, it was not until 1906, when Dr. George H. Searcy discovered a rash of cases among the inmates of an insane asylum in Alabama, that it was recognized as a public health problem.

Over a hundred thousand people were afflicted every year throughout the poorest sections of the nation, mainly in the Southern states and in addition to the four D's exhibited other symptoms of weakness, tiredness, insomnia, loss of appetite, disorientation, and disinterest in their surroundings. Because of the climate of the South, many of these people were also afflicted with malaria and hookworm. Much of the South had all of the characteristics of an undeveloped third-world country. A few people were wealthy, there was a modest middle class, but most lived in abject poverty and suffered from clinical malnutrition.

The popular media of the day portrayed poor Southerners as racial and classist stereotypes. Hollywood could not get enough of the lazy and addled minstrel Steppen' Fetchit Negro and the poor white trash of the South epitomized by the Jukes and Kallikaks[333] made famous by eugenics scholars.

By the time pellagra became rampant in the former slave-holding states, there had already accumulated a body of literature by physicians who observed that this disease was not infectious and was caused by poor nourishment, and usually appeared under conditions of severe economic deprivation. A 19th century French doctor, Theophile Roussel produced a study in 1866 that demonstrated that European outbreaks of pellagra invariably coincided with periods of shortages of fresh meats and vegetables. Roussel accurately concluded that the underlying cause of this problem was insufficient nourishment—and was related to the corn-based diet, common among the poor in times of food shortages.

A corn-based diet was not entirely the culprit. After all, the Aztecs had built a highly complex civilization with a corn-based diet. They, however, knew a secret of which the conquistadores remained ignorant. The Aztecs used a process known as nixtamalization in which the dried corn was soaked in an alkaline solution. This soaking allowed the vitamin and protein content of the corn to be released as the pericap was removed from the grain. This process of releasing all of the corn's inherent nourishment gave the Aztecs the

---

333. The Jukes and Kallikaks were pseudonyms for two families used by the eugenics movement to argue that there is a genetic predisposition toward antisocial behavior and low intelligence.

health and strength to build a spectacular civilization—promptly destroyed by the onslaught of the rapacious and disease-carrying Spaniards. When the Europeans brought this new grain to their continent, they neglected to use this process. By ignoring fundamentals, the ignorance of the conquering conquistadores, in addition to the devastation brought by their rapine to the New World, contributed to the death of millions of European and North American poor.

Eugenics—Why Victims of Pellagra Were Allowed to Die

The Rockefellers and other East Coast elites, including Prescott Bush, the father of George H.W. Bush, funded and supported the pseudoscience known as eugenics.[334] Eugenics is simply one of the constructed paradigms used to explain the wide economic disparities between rich and poor so prevalent throughout Western industrial societies under sway of the free market economic model of social organization. They make the claim that social and cultural patterns are the result of heredity and can be controlled by selective breeding. The eugenicists consider that those who are targeted by or excluded from full participation in this particular system are simply degenerates who need to curb their breeding habits. Julian Huxley, the first director-general of the United Nations Educational, Scientific, and Cultural Organization (UNESCO) and a member of the Eugenics Society, stated their position when he observed: "We must face the fact that now, in this year of grace, the great majority of human beings are substandard: they are undernourished, or ill, or condemned to a ceaseless struggle for bare existence; they are imprisoned in ignorance or superstition."[335]

Although the breeding habits of the poor are made the overriding issue, it is, in fact, the prophets of scientific racism who help to create the conditions of poverty by defending low wages, long working hours, child labor, unsafe working conditions, consolidation of land ownership, pollution, and poor resource conservation in agriculture, mining and manufacturing. Industrial and banking giants have no problem using the full force of the police apparatus of the state supplanted by private military contractors. In the early part of the 20th century, the biggest PMC was the Pinkerton Agency. State militias were also employed to enforce these conditions. In the South, terrorist organizations, such as the White Citizens Council and the Ku Klux Klan,

---

334. Webster G. Tarpley and Anton,Chaitkin, George Bush: The Unauthorized Biography (Joshua Tree, CA: Progressive Press, 2004), chap. 4.
335. Julian Huxley, Evolution in Action (New York: Signet, 1957), 132.

made sure that black and white workers remained divided and openly hostile. There were considerable brutalization and many deaths of U.S. labor leaders who were attempting to organize for better wages and improved working conditions. The eugenicists were responsible for instituting an all-out class war on those they considered inferior.

The eugenics philosophy had a significant influence on the organization of state and corporate power for use in maintaining the stratified class structure. As an example, the power of the state in league with corporate interests was brought to full force against working men and women in a Colorado mining town on 20 April 1914 in an event known as the <u>Ludlow massacre</u>. The face-off between Rockefeller's hired guns and the miners raged for fourteen hours, during which the miners' tent colony was pelted with machine-gun fire and ultimately torched by the state militia. A number of people were killed, among them two women and eleven children who suffocated in a pit they had dug under their tent. The deaths were blamed on John D. Rockefeller, Jr. The Rockefeller family owned one of the mines attempting to unionize—the Colorado Fuel and Iron Company. Eugenics was the justification for killing the men, and their women and children who were involved in this strike. The idea that workers had equal rights under the law that the oligarchs were bound to respect was an anathema to the eugenics world view, and they felt perfectly justified in employing this type of terrorism and injustice when their interests were threatened. They still do.

Simon Flexner, the brother of Abraham, who had redesigned medical education to promote Rockefeller pharmaceutical interests, was the first director of the Rockefeller Institute for Medical Research. This became the center that translated eugenic beliefs into medical practice. From the beginning, Flexner was interested in <u>viral</u> or infectious causes of disease, including cancer. This was before the advent of electron microscopy so the viral cause of disease and the efficacy of vaccines developed to combat these viral invaders was purely theoretical and entirely inconclusive as a public health measure. But the children were going to be delivered up for ritual sacrifice. From reading early independent [not controlled by Rockefeller money] medical evaluations of the true outcomes of mass vaccination programs, one can glean the harm that has come from this project: Dr. Henry Bybee of Norfolk, Virginia stated, "My honest opinion is that vaccine is the cause of more disease and suffering than anything I could name. I believe that such diseases as cancer, syphilis, cold sores and many other disease conditions are the direct results of vaccination." Dr. Herbert Snow, senior surgeon at the Cancer Hospital of London, voiced his concern, "In recent years many men and women in the prime of life have dropped dead suddenly, often after attending a feast or banquet. I am convinced that some eighty percent of these deaths are caused by the inoculation or vaccination they have undergone. They are well known to cause grave and permanent disease to the heart. The coroner always hushes it up as 'natural causes'." Dr. W. B. Clarke of Indiana found that "cancer was practically unknown until compulsory vaccination with cowpox vaccine began to be introduced. I have had to deal with at least 200 hundred cases of cancer, and I never saw a case of cancer in an unvaccinated person." And finally, a well known medical practitioner, D. J.M. Peebles of San Francisco has written a book on vaccination in which he says, "The vaccination practice, pushed to the front on all occasions by the medical profession through political connivance made compulsory by the state, has not only become the chief menace and the greatest danger to the health of the rising generation, but likewise the crowning outrage upon the personal liberties of the American citizen, compulsory vaccination, poisoning the crimson currents of the human system with brute-extracted lymph under the strange infatuation that it would prevent smallpox, was one of the darkest blots that disfigured the last century."[336]

Eustace Mullins noted in his book, Murder by Injection that "Medical historians have finally come to the reluctant conclusion that the great flu 'epidemic' of 1918 was solely attributable to the widespread use of vaccines. It was the first war in which vaccination was compulsory for all servicemen. The *Boston Herald* reported that forty seven soldiers had been killed by the vaccination in one month. As a result, the military hospitals were filled, not with wounded combat casualties, but with casualties of the vaccine. The epidemic was called 'the Spanish Influenza', a deliberately misleading appellation, which was intended to conceal its origin. This flu epidemic claimed twenty million victims; those who survived it were the ones who refused the vaccine."[337] Patients who were treated in allopathic hospitals had a thirty percent mortality rate while those treated with homeopathic remedies has less than a 5 percent mortality.

Flexner also headed a stable of some of the most flagrantly racist scientists who used their knowledge to do harm to those they considered their inferiors. The Rockefeller money was used liberally to promote the eugenics theory and their financing of this center was the medical extension of that philosophical attitude. From 1909–39, the Rockefeller Institute, under the direction of Simon Flexner, housed a series of researchers who experimented on humans in a way that was the prelude to WWII German human experiments under

---

336. Eustace Mullins, Murder by Injection,(The National Council for Medical Research, Virginia 1995) 130-134

337. Eustace Mullins, Ibid. 138

the auspices of another Rockefeller-sponsored organization, the Kaiser Wilhelm Institute.

One of the Rockefeller researchers was French-born, Nobel Prize winner, Dr. Alexis Carrell who proposed in his 1935 best-seller Man, the Unknown that small euthanasia stations be equipped with suitable gases to "humanely and economically" dispose of the mentally ill and criminal class, described as "useless and harmful beings." He believed that mankind could better itself by submitting themselves to the restraints of an "elite" group of intellectuals who would implement and enforce a program of eugenics. To that end, he supported the Vichy government in France that was in league with the German Nazi party.

Another Rockefeller researcher, Dr. Hideyo Noguchi, published data on injecting an inactive syphilis preparation into the skin of 146 hospital patients and normal children in an attempt to develop a skin test for syphilis. Later, in 1913, several of the children's parents sued Dr. Noguchi for allegedly infecting their children with syphilis. However, the prize for the most odious behavior should be bestowed on Dr. Cornelius Rhoades.

Rhoades, a prophetic example of the ethics exhibited by the eugenics philosophy, came to fame by experimentally injecting multiple Puerto Ricans with cancer cells. When the experiment was done, a total of thirteen people were murdered. When asked about the reason for the study on Puerto Ricans, Rhoades replied, "The Porto Ricans (sic) are the dirtiest, laziest, most degenerate and thievish race of men ever to inhabit this sphere. . . . What the island needs is not public health work but a tidal wave or something to totally exterminate the population. I have done my best to further the process of extermination by killing off eight (the number who had died as of the letter) and transplanting cancer into several more." Initially written in a confidential letter to a fellow researcher, Rhoades's boast of killing Puerto Ricans appeared in Time magazine in February 1932. Instead of being tried for murder, Rhoades was fittingly rewarded by becoming head of the U.S. military's Biological Warfare Division and facilities in Maryland, Utah, and Panama. He later was named to the U.S. Atomic Energy Commission where he conducted massive radiation experiments mainly on African Americans. He was one of a group responsible for dumping toxic fluoride into the water systems of the United States.[338]

Eugenics was a term coined in the 1880s by one of Charles Darwin's cousins, Francis Galton. Galton, like Darwin's other cousin Thomas

---

338. Harriet A. Washington, Medical Apartheid: The Dark History of Medical Experimentation on Black Americans from Colonial Times to the Present (New York: Doubleday, 2006), 216–43.

Malthus—the political economist for the British East India Company—was a propagandist for the exploitative economic policies of the criminal British aristocracy in league with its merchant class, such as pushing opium in China. Eugenics was nothing more than a rationale and a utopian social philosophy masquerading as science in support of an artificial British and American class structure. In their consistently psychopathic way, they thought the world was theirs to plunder and things were just fine, as long as they had unfettered access to all of the resources that they desired, no matter the human or environmental cost. Their philosophy exonerated them from their crimes against humanity as they considered those impoverished and destitute or genetically malformed as surplus population—easily disposable and easily replaceable. This is attested to in their many writings and actions.

They had a firm belief that they used to absolve themselves from their most horrendous crimes. Their conviction was founded in the hedonistic economic philosophy of free trade that any human in a poor position in society was there not because of macro-economic conditions, but because of fate and an inherited inability to do better. It was the person's destiny to be impoverished, to use drugs, to be enslaved, to work sixteen-hour days, to sell his children into slavery or prostitution because it was genetically predetermined.

To prove their point, they have, without apology and with the highest ideals of their civilization, destroyed many cultures, languages, wildlife and wildlife habitats, rainforests, waterways, and hundreds of millions of human beings. After their theory was so successfully implemented by Stalin in Russia and in Germany during the period of WWII by another Rockefeller-sponsored organization, the Kaiser Wilhelm Institute, under the direction of Ernest Rudin, they publicly retreated from the promotion of this theory. Privately, they continued to fund research and population reduction programs to support their ideas. They have never changed their thinking about these matters; they just found that it was no longer socially acceptable to voice such opinions so publicly. However, in 2009, that did not stop Ruth Bader Ginsburg, Justice of the Supreme Court, in a New York Times interview, from commenting on the Court's ruling that upheld the Hyde Amendment, which forbids the use of Medicaid for abortions by stating, "Frankly I had thought at the time Roe was decided, there was concern about population growth and particularly growth in population that we don't want to have too many of." (Emphasis added) A justice of the United States Supreme Court in 2009 is admitting that abortion is a eugenics tool instituted to weed out the undesirable.

Under the pretense of an interest in the physical welfare of the public, they practice another form of thought control masquerading as philanthropy.

They continued to practice the same policies, but now they were couched in more subtle and sophisticated language. Organizations still imbued with this philosophy include: Planned Parenthood, the Pioneer Fund, UNESCO, the Human Genome Project, United Nations Population Fund, the Population Council, the World Bank, USAID, and the Society for the Study of Social Biology, the conservation movement and the World Wildlife Fund. There are many others, but one of their most pernicious capers at population reduction has been the vaccine agenda. Advocating mass vaccination to deter infectious outbreaks has more than anything been a deliberate attack on the planet's children. The vaccines are laced with neurotoxins and abortafactants. Millions of children have been permanently damaged, and there is still no end to the long-term consequences of such mass public poisoning.

In a most Orwellian way, the intentional destruction of concentrated black urban communities became targets of "planned shrinkage" and "benign neglect." Toxic drugs, social disruptions, and starvation leading to immune deficiency became a "sexually transmitted" virus. Committing genocide in the Congo became African economic development and structural adjustment. The merging of the economies of the democratic United States with Communist China was hailed as the inevitability of globalization. The destruction of the American manufacturing base became the happy face of Wal-Mart. Those who opposed the unbalanced trade agreements were called isolationists. Fanciful terms to describe incessant crimes against humanity are cleverly packaged and sanitized by paid propagandists that work in the nation's think tanks and well paid public relations firms.

To combat what eugenicists describe as unfavorable traits in the lesser stock of humans, they advocate certain forms of intervention—abortion and sterilization. Because the underlying premise that poverty, low IQs, and susceptibility to infectious and other diseases are inherited traits, it would be much better for this population to have few if any children. In England, it was primarily directed against the poor—who also happened to be white. In the United States, it was more virulently racist in that it was directed against the Irish, southern Europeans, working-class Jews, Native Americans, and especially the blacks.

The fit—chosen by a self-selecting process with the desire and means to use unremitting violence against the weak—were encouraged to reproduce. The unfit—defined by the self-selected fit—were encouraged and often helped to limit their reproduction. It must be noted that when unfit blacks were property and contributed to the wealth of the people who now wanted to destroy them, they were encouraged to breed indiscriminately. Each successful birth increased the wealth of the owner. Humans were traded like cattle or stock and were openly traded on Wall Street. In the 1700s, Wall

Street was one of the major slave-trading centers in the United States. In 1991, during a dig for a new skyscraper in the area, a burial ground of twenty thousand anonymous Africans was discovered—Africans who died young from the back-breaking labor of developing this new world. When Africans were slaves, fecundity produced profits. Now that they were no longer a profit center like other commodities they became excess labor to a system that was becoming increasingly more mechanized. Furthermore, they had a vitality and resiliency that frightened these keepers of European civilization. They were rebranded by the eugenicists as human waste that needed to be discarded.

One of the programs instituted by the eugenics movement was mass sterilization without consent of thousands of children and women in the United States who were classified as feeble-minded. Some may have been feeble-minded, but most were simply poor and/or malnourished. The nonconsensual sterilization programs continued unabated well into the 1970s, especially in the South where thousands of black women underwent coercive sterilization under threat of termination of welfare benefits or the denial of medical care. The practice was so common it was known as the Mississippi appendectomy.[339]

Margaret Sanger, founder of the U.S. branch of Planned Parenthood, was a staunch proponent of this theory. It was her aim to contain the inferior races through segregation, sterilization, birth control, and abortion. She wrote: "Birth control is thus the entering wedge for the eugenic educator. . . . the unbalance between the birth rate of the 'unfit' and the 'fit' is admittedly the greatest present menace to civilization. . . .The most urgent problem today is how to limit and discourage the over fertility of the mentally and physically defective."[340]

Sanger was very clever in her marketing of this theory to the black community. Just as today many prominent blacks have jumped on the HIV/AIDS abstinence/condoms bandwagon. In Sanger's time, it was called The Negro Project, and it was designed to limit the black population by promoting sterilization and birth control. Of course, it took a more high-minded tone. Sanger enlisted the support of prominent blacks who enthusiastically supported people who wanted them destroyed. W.E B. Du Bois, a preeminent scholar of his day, wrote in "Black Folk and Birth Control," about the issue of the "inevitable clash of ideals between those Negroes who were striving

---

339. Fannie Lou Hamer, a leader of the Mississippi Freedom Democratic Party, told an audience in Washington, D. C., that she too had a complete hysterectomy without her consent.
340. Margaret Sanger, Birth Control Review (October 1921), 5.

to improve their economic position and those whose religious faith made the limitation of children a sin." He criticized the "mass of ignorant Negroes" who bred "carelessly and disastrously so that the increase among [them] . . . is from that part of the population least intelligent and fit, and least able to rear their children properly." Charles S. Johnson, first black president of Fisk University, wrote that "eugenic discrimination" was necessary for blacks. He said that high maternal and infant mortality rates, along with diseases, like tuberculosis, typhoid, malaria, and venereal infection, made it difficult for large families to adequately sustain themselves. Not surprisingly, as was true of the dominant culture, as the economic and social conditions of black families improved, and as families moved from rural to more urban areas, the number of children each couple produced diminished. The economic situation changed the dynamic, not exhortations of self-righteous religious moralists, in support of racist policies.

Sanger also attracted to her cause the funds of a wealthy true believing benefactor, Clarence Gamble, a scion of the Procter and Gamble Soap Company and graduate of Harvard Medical School. Gamble was given free reign in the State of North Carolina to practice his experimental birth control methods. While Sanger was looking for "colored ministers" to support her project, she wrote a remarkable letter to Gamble stating, "We do not want word to go out that we want to exterminate the Negro population and the minister is the man who can straighten out that idea if it ever occurs to any of their more rebellious members."[341] Gamble, in turn, proposed that ministers enlist the aid of black physicians and attempt to organize a "Negro Birth Control Committee" in each community. In a private memo concerning the "Colored Steering Committee," Gamble wrote: "There is great danger that [the project] will fail because the Negroes think it a plan for extermination. Hence let's appear to let the colored run it."

Gamble expressed his sentiments when he wrote: "To date less [sic] than 2,000 insane and mentally defective North Carolinians have been sterilized under the existing law—a figure that represents less than one out of every 41 of the State's estimated mentally unfit. This means that for every one man or woman who has been sterilized, there are 40 others who can continue to

341. Margaret Sanger to Clarence Gamble, 13 October 1939, Sanger Smith Collection, quoted in Linda Gordon, Women's Body, Women's Right: Birth Control in America (New York: Penguin Books, 1990), 332–33.M Margaret Sanger to Clarence Gamble, October 19, 1939, Sanger in Linda Gordon, Woman's Body, Woman's Right:1990,] 332-33

pour defective genes into the State's blood stream to pollute and degrade future generations."[342]

Gamble used part of the fortune made by Procter & Gamble products (including soap) to finance birth-control projects for the poor in many parts of the world. He helped to push through legislation in 1937 legalizing birth control in Puerto Rico; the law specified that birth control material was to be distributed by trained eugenicists. He supported birth control distribution in Appalachia and in rural Japan. A leader in Margaret Sanger's Birth Control Federation, it was he that suggested that they set up a "Negro Project," using black clergy and physicians to promote birth control. He founded the Pathfinder Fund, another one of such philanthropic endeavors to promote population control in selected countries.

Pathfinder International, the so-called charitable organization, still exists. Its latest project is the promotion of the idea that HIV is a sexually-transmitted disease and the cause of AIDS. Their funds have been augmented by the American taxpayer through USAID (U.S. Agency for International Development). During the Bush I presidency, spending for birth control in nonwhite countries was one of the few items that headed upward in his 1992 budget. The USAID Population Account received $300 million, a 20 percent increase over the previous year. In 1972, when Bush was U.S. Ambassador to the United Nations, he prodded USAID to make contact with the old Sterilization League, which had changed its name to the Association for Voluntary Surgical Contraception.. With taxpayer dollars, the U.S. government began paying the old fascist group to sterilize nonwhites in foreign countries.

As recently as 1995, abortifacients were still being discovered in vaccines distributed by WHO and other NGOs (nongovernmental organizations) to young girls and women in Mexico, Africa, Thailand, Nicaragua, and the Philippines.[343] A right to life group, the Pro-Life Committee of Mexico was suspicious of a tetanus vaccine protocol. Usually tetanus is given as a single shot to both sexes. In Mexico the protocol excluded all males and children and was only directed at women of reproductive age. Instead of only one shot, multiple shots were recommended. WHO denied culpability when the abortefacient HCG (human chorionic gonadatropin) was discovered in some vials of the vaccine. The hormone is placed in the vaccine so that antibodies will be developed against it. This is similar to giving a vaccine against a virus. The hope is that the next time that the woman becomes pregnant, instead

342. Clarence J. Gamble, "Better Human Beings Tomorrow," *Better Health* (October 1947), 14, 15.
343. Vaccine Weekly 29 May–5 June 1995, 9–10.

of antibodies protecting the pregnancy, the HCG antibodies will attack it, causing an abortion.

The Population Council has been involved in the development of similar anti-fertility vaccines. After WWII, John D. Rockefeller, III, and John Foster Dulles campaigned against the growth of nonwhite populations and in 1952 launched the Population Council. This organization still exits and is still advocating zero population growth in the U.S., family planning in the developing world, and the expansion of the Club of Rome's zero growth population. The Population Council has a history tied to forced sterilization and eugenics. Population policies are now imposed on Less Developed Countries (LDC) by stipulations in World Bank contracts. To the multinational corporations who benefit from the policies, they make perfectly good business sense. Clearly, staff with few or no children can live on substantially less money, thereby reducing pressure on corporations to pay better wages. Moreover, the worker who takes a paid <u>holiday</u> to undergo surgical sterilization will not need or request parental leave later on. Companies may also hope to maximize employee attendance by limiting the number of children workers have to care for in the event of sickness or some other emergency situation. Above all, many large companies are likely to see the long-term goal of population control as being in their own self-interest because they feel threatened by the growth of the laboring classes—especially because their banking policies are putting downward economic pressure on this group.

Some of the more prominent members of the early eugenics movement include:

- J. P. Morgan, Jr., chairman, U. S. Steel, who handled British contracts in the United States for food and munitions during World War I;
- Mrs. Mary Duke Biddle, tobacco fortune heiress;
- Cleveland H. and Cleveland E. Dodge and their wives, who used some of the huge fortune that Phelps Dodge & Company made on copper mines and other metals to support eugenics;
- Robert Garrett, whose family had amassed a fortune through banking in Maryland and the B&O Railroad, who helped finance two international eugenics congresses;
- Ms. E. B. Scripps, whose wealth came from United Press (later UPI);
- Dorothy H. Brush, Planned Parenthood activist, whose wealth came from Charles Francis Brush (1849–1929), who invented the arc lamp for street lights and founded the Brush Electric Company;

- Margaret Sanger, who used the wealth of one of one of her husbands, Noah Slee, to promote her work. Slee made his fortune from the familiar household product, 3-in-1 Oil; [344]
- Irving "Breed out the unfit and breed in the fit" Fisher, an economist whose models of interest and capital have contributed to the current economic decline;
- Rockefeller, Carnegie, and Harriman money all went to this cause.

These wealthy individuals laid the foundation of the eugenics movement, the principles of which were later applied by Hitler in Nazi Germany and to the Nuremberg Race Laws of 1935 that led to the extermination of millions of Europeans. Clearly, the slaughter of other humans was of little concern to this crowd who wantonly developed justification for the support of these rather unsavory policies. The eugenics philosophy was developed into the military doctrine of <u>total war</u>—which considers attacks on civilians and their economic infrastructure an integral part of a victorious strategy. It was used for several centuries in the pacification of nonwhite people. It was authorized by Pope Nicholas V in his <u>Rominus Pontifex</u> bull of 1455 when he separated the world between Spain and Portugal. His edict settled the dispute as to which one of them would have the right to murder people in Africa, Asia, and the Americas—the Caribbean included—and confiscate their real and personal property. That this form of warfare was turned on other Europeans during the Second World War should have come as no surprise to any student of history.

The idea of destroying what was considered excess undesirable populations was also the mind set that comfortably suppressed for over twenty years the knowledge of the cause of pellagra and allowed thousands of people, mostly Southern blacks and poor whites, to die unnecessarily. For twenty years, high-level members of the eugenics movement knew, because they had access to the research, that thousands of people could be spared from dying this miserable death. For twenty years, they suppressed the knowledge. For twenty years, they used their money and access to the media and to the medical profession to disparage anyone who went against their presentation of pellagra as an infectious disease. They worked the pellagra angle the same way that they are working the HIV-causes-AIDS angle today: by distributing false information and disinformation, by using bought and or like-minded physicians to discredit publicly those who want to address the science, not irrational passions, by obfuscation and slander and by well-placed propaganda campaigns waged in the mainstream media and by selected celebrities and,

---

344. John Cavanaugh O'Keefe, <u>The Roots of Racism and Abortion: An Exploration of Eugenics</u>, chap. 12, <u>www.eugenics-watch.com</u>.

as always, by funneling money only to those scientists who go along with the viral theory of AIDS.

The Eugenicists Politicize Pellegra

The Eugenics movement was fostered in the United States by the scions of the opium and slave trades and East Coast liberal establishment. In 1904, the Station for Experimental Evolution was funded by grants from Andrew Carnegie, Cornelius Vanderbilt, J. P. Morgan and John D. Rockefeller. In 1950 and 1951, John Foster Dulles, then chairman of the Rockefeller Foundation who could trace his lineage back to the BEIC and the slave-holding South, led John D. Rockefeller, III, on a series of world tours focusing on the need to stop expansion of nonwhite populations. By 1952, Dulles and Rockefeller set up the Population Council with millions of dollars from the Rockefeller family. This was simply an extension of the work begun at Cold Spring Harbor in 1915. Mrs. E. H. Harriman donated 80 acres of land in Cold Spring Harbor, Long Island, and $300,000 to the project to establish the Eugenics Records Office.

The philosophic bent of the eugenics movement was not much advanced beyond European thought before the medieval period, but they were so certain of their rectitude that they openly told the press exactly what they planned. That their ideas were morally bankrupt and socially violent were lost on these self-interested reptilian zealots. The following are the actual headlines from the <u>New York World</u> newspaper on 4 September 1915:

MRS. E. H. HARRIMAN BACKS A GIGANTIC STEP IN EUGENICS WOULD CURB DEFECTIVES BY THE HUNDREDS OF THOUSANDS OVER SERIES OF YEARS. TO MAKE RACE PERFECT, AID OF ROCKEFELLER AND CARNEGIE HOPED FOR IN WORLD WIDE CAMPAIGN—Headline

By 1915, the Eugenics Office was well aware of and informed about the findings of the work of Dr. Joseph Goldberger in discovering that the cause of pellagra was a nutritional deficiency. But Harriman, Rockefeller, Carnegie, and the eugenics group were intent on inflicting suffering and death on people whom they considered inferior. Instead of spreading that information publicly, the Eugenics Office urged a diet of corn—with knowledge that this in fact was the base diet being currently used by those suffering from this disease. They were aware that the corn-based diet was deficient in a life enhancing nutrient, and even when Goldberger showed that it could be remedied for pennies a day with brewer's yeast, the Eugenics Office continued to mount a public relations campaign to attack viciously any medical researcher who claimed that a proper diet could prevent Pellagra.[345]

Mrs. Harriman ordered the Eugenics Office director, Charles Benedict Davenport, "to heap contempt on the 'nutrition theory'." Davenport was well suited for the job. He had expressed in a published article his disdain for the Irish whom he singled out as 'defectives who genetically were not able to ward off tuberculosis.' So with that moral and scientific view of humanity, he had no qualms about complying with her demand.[346]

Davenport supported the theory that pellagra was a communicable disease. He claimed that variations in reactions to the infectious agent were caused by hereditary differences in people.

Dr. Joseph Goldberger and Pellagra

In 1914, Joseph Goldberger, a young physician and epidemiologist, was dispatched by the Surgeon General to travel South to see if he could discover the cause of pellagra, a medical condition that was devastating the workers in the cotton manufacturing industry. Goldberger immediately observed the obvious—that the doctors and nurses who worked in the prisons, asylums, and old age homes where pellagra was rampant were not getting this disease. He also observed that only mill workers and sharecroppers who lived in the poorer sections of town seemed to be affected. These were immediate visible clues that mitigated against an infectious process. He made note of the different diets between the two groups—the doctors eating meat and vegetables, and the inmates, farmers, and mill workers the customary corn-based diets. The typical corn/pork diet was high in fats and carbohydrates and lacking in sufficient protein and nutrients.

Goldberger presciently worked with an economist to examine data that might indicate why people were not able to afford a balanced diet. Between 1900 and 1913 national wage rates had increased by about 25 percent compared with wage rate increases of 5 percent in the South. Concomitantly, the cost of food had increased by 60 percent. These identifiable economic factors were causing great hardship for many Southerners, black and white. The economic and scientific data were exactly contrary to the ideas that the eugenics movement wanted to portray, and they were not going to let the observations of this man intrude on their plans. Goldberger had essentially

---

345. John Coleman, <u>The Conspirator's Hierarchy: The Committee of 300</u>, 157–58.
346. Ibid., 158.

made the same observations as the French doctor, Theophile Roussel, in 1866, when he stated that European outbreaks of pellagra invariably coincided with periods of shortages of fresh meats and vegetables.

Blacks in the South, as usual, were under the most economic strain. While African Americans comprised 10 percent of the population, they suffered 50 percent of the deaths from pellagra. The eugenics mouthpiece and "pellagra expert" Davenport claimed, however, that "colored persons are less subject to the disease on the whole than white persons."

Harriet Washington, in her groundbreaking book Medical Apartheid, makes the point that after the Civil War medical services for the freedmen were sabotaged for lack of financial support. "When the freemen's camps dissolved, no public-health support replaced them. Poverty and desperation trapped southern Blacks into an insidiously indirect new form of slavery— sharecropping. The exploitative, abusive medical care of slave owners was replaced by no medical care at all for poor blacks, and disease and death ran rampant through the black population . . . scientific medicine, bolstered by census data perpetuated the belief that Blacks' inherent inferiorities, not exposure, starvation, and neglect catalyzed by . . . privation, caused their public health disaster."[347] Further, Alphonso Taft, a member of the Yale Skull and Bones Society that was founded by a family member of the Russell Crime family opium syndicate, became U.S. Attorney General in 1876– 77. He helped organize the backroom settlement of the deadlocked 1876 presidential election. The bargain gave Rutherford B Hayes the presidency (1877–81). Hayes withdrew U.S. troops from the South where they had been enforcing black rights. The betrayal of black citizens was an economic and social disaster that created an apartheid system that lasted more than a hundred years and was compounded by the racist pseudoscience promoted by the eugenics movement.

Because of pressure emanating from the eugenics movement out of Cold Spring Harbor, millions of black undesirables died of the ravages of pellagra. Washington makes the point that "fraud and abuse have often been traveling partners when it comes to research into African American health."[348] The suppression of Goldberger's findings by Harriman and her group was no exception.

Because of the weight of his collected evidence, Goldberger was inclined to conclude that pellagra was not an infectious process but somehow related

---

347. Harriet A. Washington, Medical Apartheid: The Dark History of Medical Experimentation on Black Americans from Colonial Times to the Present (New York: Doubleday, 2006), 152.

348. Ibid., 153.

to the dietary habits of the poor in the South. He next followed up with more human experiments on prisoners and his family. By dietary manipulation of white prisoners, he created, then cured pellagra in twelve prisoners, thereby dissociating pellagra from a <u>black</u> disease.

Goldberger, his wife, and several researchers even went so far as to inject themselves with the blood of pellagra patients and swallowed dough balls impregnated with the skin and excreta of the sick patients. None of these people contracted pellagra as a result of these interventions. He discounted in a rather dramatic way the widely-held assumption propagated by the Cold Spring Harbor genetic-determinism adherents. Pellagra was not a communicable disease, but a vitamin deficiency disease. It was not inherent among a particular population because of hereditary deficiencies, but was a consequence of their extreme economic stress.

Harriman recruited prominent doctors to condemn the dangerous nutrition hypothesis. One such doctor drew applause at a medical conference when he described as "pernicious" the newspaper publicity that told people that there was no danger from pellagra except from poor food and cooking.[349] Nevertheless, scientific racism coupled with media control trumped scientific facts, and it was not until thousands had died that the U.S. Public Health Service addressed the problem of nutritional deficiencies. After the Federal Reserve manipulated the stock market crash of 1929 and triggered the Great Depression, the bankers, manufacturers, merchants, office managers, white-collar hucksters, and the authors of nasty editorials about the hereditary shiftlessness of the South's poor were themselves bankrupt, penniless, and hungry by the hundreds of thousands. They ceased their Malthusian objections to federal relief programs. It was not until 1935 that evidence about niacin was so incontrovertible that the Cold Spring Harbor theory and its recommended corn diet were discredited. The director of the U.S. Public Health Service admitted that they had known for twenty years (since Goldberger's experiments) that the disease was caused by a dietary deficiency but failed to act because most of the deaths occurred in poverty-stricken black communities where the people were considered hereditary inferiors.[350]

Extreme economic conditions continue to plague half of the world's population, and just as the economic conditions of the South were directly related to health outcomes, so are the economic conditions being created today.

---

349. Elizabeth Etheridge, <u>The Butterfly Caste: A Social History of Pellagra in the South </u>(Westport, CT: Greenwood Press, 1972), 99.

350. John Coleman, <u>The Conspirator's Hierarchy</u> 158.

Globalization and Its Adherents—Neo-Malthusians

One of the unheralded practices of creating the Global Village is what Jeremy Brecher and Tim Costello call Global Pillage. Policies codified by international trade agreements and instituted by the IMF and World Bank, the international banking structures, enable international corporations to lower their costs by lowering the standards for the environment and conservation, for labor costs and health and safety measures, and, ultimately, standards for the consumer. With tax incentives for investment, corporations move freely across borders to areas of the globe where they can pay the lowest wages, lowest taxes, and have the freedom to pollute, destroy old growth forests, and avoid organized labor.[351] Over the last twenty years, the standard of living for most of the world's poor has diminished by design, especially in inner-city America and in Africa. However, the standard of living is also being lowered for middle-class American men. According to the Pew Charitable Trust's Economic Mobility Project, there has been a 12.5 percent drop in median income adjusted for inflation.[352] After inflation, purchasing power of a working couple in 1995 was only 8 percent greater than for a single working man in 1905. The gilded age and Malthusian economics have returned with a vengeance.

The Southern landowners and the cotton mill owners of the early 20th century similarly contributed to the degradation of living standards by the failure to pay wages that were at par with inflation. As the economic data indicated, the workers were underpaid and overcharged. Their maladies were brought on by poverty and starvation but were cynically blamed on hereditary inferiority.

Today, to challenge the doctrine of free trade or to propose that globalization is a zero sum game is heresy. Both policies knowingly disrupt and distress traditional communities and social structures and are globally lowering living standards in both rich and poor countries. Forty thousand people die daily from starvation[353] vs. 1.25 to 10 deaths from terrorism. Who

---

351. Jeremy Brecher and Tim Costello, Global Village or Global Pillage: Economic Reconstruction from the Bottom Up (Cambridge, MA: South End Press, 1998).

352. Gregory Acs and Seth Zimmerman, U.S. Intragenerational Economic Mobility from 1984 to 2004: Trends and Implications (Philadelphia, PA: Pew Charitable Trusts), 2008.

353. W. R. Beisel, "History of Nutritional Immunology: Introduction and Overwiew," Am Inst Nut (1992). The 1990 World Summit for Children at the UN attended by fifty Heads of State, estimated forty thousand deaths occur each day worldwide in children under the age of 5.

is really terrorizing the planet? Is it "Muslim extremists" or Wall Street and London bankers? Chose wisely, your life may depend on your choice.

Early 20th century titans as neoglobalists today never considered the health implications of their macroeconomic policies. After all, they are doing what they do to improve the race at the expense of inferiors. They were and are wedded to the insidious belief that the market is the final arbiter of human relations. A more vapid, inherently unnatural, amoral, and soulless philosophy could not possibly be imagined and orchestrated as world policy.

One Major Vitamin Deficiency

Currently, half the world's population, more than 3 billion people, is living in abject poverty. According the United Nations statistics, someone dies of starvation every 3.6 seconds. Nearly a billion people are illiterate; more than a billion people do not have access to safe water; some 840 million people go hungry or face food insecurity; and about one-third of all children under the age of five suffer from malnutrition. The estimated cost of providing universal access to basic social services and transfers to alleviate income poverty is between $50 to $80 billion, which is less than 0.5 per cent of global income.

It would be logical to conclude that the billions of people living under such conditions of chronic malnourishment and in unsanitary conditions would be prone to the development of preventable infectious diseases, diseases that are reversible in people in Western nations become deadly in this population.

The biggest disease plaguing the planet is that of Western civilization and its super Ponzi scheme of central banks and monetary inflation that have legalized organized thievery, usury, and fractional reserve banking and call it an economic system. Now that the populations of the world have had a status change from humans to persons and been assigned a computer-generated number, the returns on this investment to the control grid are simply massive.

AIDS is the new Pellagra. Pellagra was the result of a niacin deficiency that arose from malnourishment. Just as people who are told they have AIDS, the people who suffered from pellagra also had lower natural levels of resistance to all manner of infectious and parasitic diseases—from common colds to influenza, pneumonia, tuberculosis, dysentery, worms, malaria, and yellow fever. In other words, the major deficiency of this single vitamin led to a collapse in the immune systems of the people so afflicted. There was no virus involved.

This is not a far cry from the problems of nutritional deprivation being seen in drought, war-ravaged and World Bank-pillaged countries today. Children born to chronically malnourished mothers suffer from:

1. Low birth weight;
2. Intrauterine growth retardation and poor brain and neurological development;
3. High rates of often fatal infectious diseases—ordinary childhood diseases such as measles become deadly in malnourished children;
4. Poor development of the pelvic bones in girls leading to cephalo-pelvic disproportion (CPD) which can cause injury from traumatic birth to the brains and bodies of the children of the world's poor;
5. Very high incidences of infection caused by poor sanitation and often fatal dysenteries and diarrheas in the malnourished children of the poor.

These are conditions that have reached epidemic proportions in some areas of Africa and are called AIDS by the same archetypal mind set that buried Dr. Goldberger's research for well over twenty years, much as they have attempted to silence alternative AIDS theories for twenty five-years. As America's inner cities are being decimated by deindustrialization and drugs and as the African continent is being plundered by vested Western interests, millions die of curable diseases.

If anyone thinks that the focus on population reduction of the eugenics adherents has changed should pay heed to a speech given by Dr. Erick R. Pianka at the 109th meeting of the Texas Academy of Science at Lamar University in Beaumont, Texas in March 2006. According to John Ballantyne, Pianka "argued that the sharp increase in human population since the onset of industrialization was destroying the planet. He warned that the Earth would not survive unless its human population was reduced to a tenth of its present number. . . .He called for drastic solutions. . . . After praising the Ebola virus for its efficiency at killing, Pianka paused, leaned over the lectern, looked at us carefully and said, 'We've got airborne 90 percent mortality in humans. Killing humans. Think about that.'" After advocating killing off 90 percent of the world's population with a deadly and horrifying airborne virus, he received a rousing applause and the Academy presented him with a plaque in recognition of his being named 2006 Distinguished Texas Scientist.[354] Pianka also expressed support of China's forced sterilization policies and lamented that AIDS took too long to kill people off.

---

354. J. Ballantyne, "A Texas Scientist Advocates Killing Nine-Tenths of the World's Population by Airborne Ebola Virus," www.newsweekly.com.au

It has been twenty five-years since the AIDS tragedy began. There is ample scientific evidence to bury this failed theory of an inevitably fatal sex and blood plague caused by an elusive virus. Perhaps the AIDS hoax is finally running its course. News headlines from around the world have begun to proclaim that the global AIDS crisis has been overblown and that the AIDS industry is too big and out of control. AIDS has been considered a terrible humanitarian tragedy. AIDS is not a humanitarian tragedy; it is a crime against humanity. It is just business.

Chapter 12

Burroughs Wellcome, the Eye of the Storm, Why Aids Drugs Cause AIDS

○ ○

Indeed it seems the most destructive (and perhaps the most dangerous) characteristic of that species of the genus Homo we conceitedly label <u>Sapiens</u> is not his wisdom but his reluctance to admit ignorance. Rather than do so, he is prone to posit an hypothesis and, all too frequently in the absence of supporting evidence, comes to believe it. Thus are myths created.

Dr. William Roe

There is nothing else in the health care field that can do what a good prescription drug can do—on the money side. It is a business to be envied by all.

<u>New York Times</u>, *29 July 1989*

An underlying theme in the AIDS saga is the corruption of medical science as a logical outcome of setting priorities based on the business needs of financial capitalism rather than real community health needs. Indeed, because of their unbridled arrogance, financial capitalists see themselves as divine. They actually think they create reality. In their delusional creation of illusions they violate every possible natural law. The products created from an anti-life, fear-based mind set are engendering many of today's health/earth crises.

Financial capitalism, at its core is deeply predatory, parasitic, and anti-life. Its goal is the monopolization of the world's resources, production facilities, labor, technology, markets, transport, and finance backed up currently by the might of the U.S. military, industrial, and banking complexes that are controlled and supported by the clandestine services. Because it is a game of usury combined with monopoly in which the strategy is to co-opt or crush competition, it recognizes only two poles, winners and losers.

The concentration of power in the banking system has been instituted in stages. The original hope for America was that she might be able to hold fast to the tenets of the Constitution that was designed to dampen some of the more reptilian and Darwinian impulses of the free market economic philosophy. However, compromises made early on gave the devil a foothold in the door, and that was all that was needed to wage a war to control the money supply. During the presidency of Woodrow Wilson, the Congress of the United States ignorantly allowed the power to control an interest-free money supply sufficient to allow free commerce without monopoly aggregation to be forever lost. With the passage of the Federal Reserve Act, the institution of an Income Tax and the rise of tax free foundations, the power to control the money supply, to create busts and booms, to start wars, and to create inflation passed to this private bank largely controlled by foreigners.

Wilson gave the beast life and signed the Federal Reserve Act in 1913 by assigning to a private banking cartel the privilege that was mandated for the people. Wilson, by signing this bill into law, sealed the fate of the country. He had done what Jefferson warned against and what Andrew Jackson had struggled against. He had assigned the wealth of the nation to the masters of debt. When he realized what he had done it was too late. Lamenting his actions he stated, "I am a most unhappy man. I have unwittingly ruined my country. A great industrial nation is controlled by its system of credit. Our system of credit is concentrated. The growth of the nation, therefore, and all our activities are in the hands of a few men. We have come to be one of the worst ruled, one of the most completely controlled and dominated Governments in the civilized world no longer a Government by free opinion, no longer a Government by conviction and the vote of the majority, but a Government by the opinion and duress of a small group of dominant men."

As we move into a new millennium, the usury beast has won another round and America, along with much of the world, is being gobbled up into the stepwise progression of the next utopian consolidation by a band of ruthless oligarchs. The monopoly nature of financial capitalism that uses the fractional reserve and usury trick to aggregate money, being a man-made construct and outside of the realm of natural mathematical possibilities makes it unstable and characterized by cycles of boom and bust.

The principle methods it has chosen to buttress this instability is through war and war substitutes. Creating an "AIDS" crisis was a war substitute. Several government institutions in collusion with the pharmaceutical industry created the AIDS crisis. By simultaneously promoting the use of immune suppressing narcotics and immune suppressing pharmaceuticals, a predictable medical consequence of altered immunity became a reality. This manufactured crisis was then used profitably to sell products that enlarged their market further. Those who died as a result of this market strategy were collateral damage. Because financial capitalism is also the game of survival of the fittest, only the most ruthless win out in the struggle for existence. This makes exploitation both logical and natural. The free market philosophy, in fact, makes exploitation of others morally acceptable. The eugenics adherents crystallized that idea into a movement. That movement had an orgasmic flux during the Second World War when 50 to 70 million people lost their lives—so much so that the planet was actually horrified by the public specter of the rape of a continent and culture. The movement went underground, but it is far from moribund.

Pharmaceutical companies, under the control of the eugenics dynamic and the petrochemical industry, have been on the winning side of history over the last fifty years. This became a reality not so much because their products are the best for healing but because they crushed the competition and gained monopoly control of a medical discipline, allopathic medicine, as well as the lucrative patent drug market. Of course, drug companies also make products that are useful, but it should be abundantly clear that their main goal is not to make products that are meant to heal. They have chosen to concentrate on products that treat symptoms and that keep patients in a holding pattern, if they are lucky, and can cause irreparable damage or death if they are not. This casual acceptance of drug damage from "side effects" happened because this industry, dominated from early on by Rockefeller interests who were tied directly to the chemical and banking cartels, knew how to take control of the market by controlling both politicians and the flow of information. The industry is able successfully to drown out information that either shows the extreme danger of their products or is opposed to their marketing strategy. They label healers as quacks, and the quackery of drug companies is called medicine. Because drug companies have become expert at hiding adverse events associated with their products, the notion of the right to informed consent is another illusion.

One of their strategies was to gain control of medical research with tax-free financing through the foundation boondoggle.[355] Another, was to legislate into existence and then gain control of the regulatory arm of the industry—the FDA (Food and Drug Administration). The FDA was sold to the people as the protector of their health from the medical hucksters who have long made their living by preying on people's fears. John D. Rockefeller was well aware of this because his own father was one such huckster. Claiming to be a doctor, he sold unrefined Pennsylvania petroleum in bottles, at enormous profit, out of the back of his wagon as a cure and a preventive for cancer. It killed more people than it cured, but it was highly profitable.

The leadership at the CDC and the FDA has been controlled by a revolving door of people who come out of the very industry they are supposed to be policing. The CDC is also controlled by their clandestine service, the Epidemic Intelligence Agency that was the brainstorm of another eugenicist bent on population control, public health professor Alexander Langmuir. To that end, the CDC has advocated and the FDA has approved an ever increasing roster of vaccines laced with neurotoxins to infants and children. Consequently there are millions of brain damaged and neurologically impaired children that not only have the more severe damage of autism or Asberger's syndrome but have been labeled ADH or ADHD and become candidates for more pharmaceutical drug products.[356] The FDA has done a bang up job of passing inspection on pharmaceuticals for public consumption that kill (over 100,000 people a year). The CDC and the FDA have been used to suppress research, clinics, and physicians who offer alternative therapies that might in any way undercut the business and profits of big Pharma. They actively suppress information and access to care that would allow open competition with the products that get their stamp of approval. [357] It is the job of the FDA

---

355. In 1953, Congressman Carroll Reese held hearings on tax-exempt foundations and exposed how they were being used to move the United States toward a one-world state. René A. Wormser, in his book <u>Foundations: Their Power and Influence</u>, focuses not on the idea of <u>communist subversion</u>, as did the Reese Committee, but on the emergence of an elite that has control of huge financial resources that have allowed them to concentrate power in the hands of an interlocking and self-perpetuating group. This is power that operates outside the rule of law.

356. D. A. Geier, P.G King and M.R Greir, "Mitochondrial dysfunction, impaired oxidative-reduction activity, degeneration, and death in human neuronal and fetal cells induced y low level exposure to thimerosal and other metal compounds, <u>Toxicological and Environmental Chemistry; 2009</u>, 1-15, iFirst

357. On 15 January 1999, the Circuit Court of Appeals in Washington, D.C., ruled that the FDA's suppression of health claims for nutritional supplements

in particular to protect the profits of the industry while feigning concern for the health of the people. That the cost of health care in the United States is so out of line with the cost in other Western countries and the overall health of the U.S. public is declining is a testament to their success.

This method of operation derives from the Malthusian marketing strategies of the British East India Company that pushed opium into China. As previously discussed, that strategy was to amass enormous wealth by creating a mass market of addicted consumers whose very lives were controlled by the desire to acquire the product. Once the demand was assured and growing, the competition was co-opted into the enterprise or killed off. Any resistance to this method of operation was handled by using the controlled apparatus of the state up to and including the military. Millions perished as a direct result of the drug and by starvation because of the cooptation and use of arable farm land for poppy production. At the time the British East India Company operated, the system was called colonialism. Today, the operational agencies are the international banks, and it is called globalization. In this zero-sum-game, there are only winners and losers.

One of the big winners in the AIDS game has been the drug company Burroughs Wellcome. Burroughs-Wellcome was the drug company that supplied Stanley with the medical supplies that allowed him to locate Dr. David Livingston in Africa. They supplied the missionaries who often preceded the European militaries in India, Ceylon, Japan, America, and Central Africa by providing them with tablets, tinctures, first aid kits, bandages and dressings so that they could bring civilization to the natives. Burroughs-Wellcome's medicine allowed Europeans to penetrate and colonize the continent of Africa, destroying cultures, bringing diseases like syphilis, extracting humans and resources and leaving devastation in their wake.[358]

The Wellcome name has been subsumed by mergers with two other British pharmaceutical giants. The company merged with Glaxo in 1995 to form Glaxo Wellcome, and then this entity subsequently merged again in 2000 with SmithKline Beecham to become Glaxo Smith Kline. The Wellcome name was dropped, and perhaps for good reason. More than any other pharmaceutical entity, Burroughs Wellcome helped create and perpetuate the AIDS crisis by state sanctioned mass poisoning of millions of people.

---

was unlawful and unconstitutional. The FDA made its purpose known with respect to dietary supplements when it recorded in its Dietary Supplement Task Force Report that "the agency should ensure that the existence of dietary supplements on the market does not act as a disincentive for drug development."

358. M. Slotow, "The Opening Up of Africa" SA Med J 60, (1981):577.

Burroughs Wellcome pioneered the development of immune suppressing drugs for clinical practice.

The following pharmaceutical drugs, all very much related to the AIDS problem, were products that came out of the Wellcome laboratories and have a nitroso group structure as a common characteristic:

- Amyl nitrite: Initially used as a vasodilator in angina patients and then as a sexual doping agent for its ability to relax the anal sphincter. It was universally used by homosexual men who first developed illnesses as the result of the depression of cell mediated immunity.
- Azothioprine: Designed to immune suppress organ transplant patients intentionally so that they would not reject the graft.
- AZT: Promoted as an anti-retroviral, but in fact is a mitochondrial toxin.
- Trimethoprim: An antimicrobial that is a combination preparation with sulfamethoxazole, a sulfonamide derivative that, in addition to its antimicrobial action is immunosuppressive and carcinogenic and has caused degenerative DNA damage in numerous human cell systems.

It is well known that nitrites and aromatic amines cause a condition known as <u>methemoglobinemia,</u> a state in which the oxygen carrying capacity of hemoglobin is reduced. If this condition becomes chronic and the cell is not able to get sufficient oxygen, not enough energy in the form of ATP will be produced. This in turn causes alterations in the cell redox status and alters signal transduction, DNA and RNA synthesis, protein synthesis, enzyme activation, and even regulation of the cell cycle. Many of the compounds containing a primary nitroso group have been shown, either directly by animal experimentation or indirectly by tests in bacteria, to be actually or potentially carcinogenic. The chronic use of nitrite inhalants has been linked directly to the development of Kaposi's sarcoma.

Understanding how these drugs work, their potential toxicity, and how they came to be widely distributed is the piece of the puzzle that not only makes it abundantly clear how the AIDS crisis began, how it has been sustained, and how it can end.

More than fifty years ago research began with the idea of inserting analogs of purine (adenine and guanosine) and pyrimidine (thymine and cystosine) building blocks blocs of the nucleic acid of the genetic material DNA into microbes and cancer cells to inhibit their growth. This line of research has been followed because the medical industry has mistakenly theorized that cancer is the result of structural alterations in nuclear DNA, rather than a functional alteration of metabolic processes controlled by the cell redox environment.

Wellcome developed several of these compounds that contained a nitroso group. The idea was that because the microbe and cancer cells were rapidly dividing, they could be targeted with little downside to normal human cells. However, because the body normally turns over 10^{12} cells every day, this has not been the case. This <u>brilliant</u> idea discounted the fact that many normal human cells divide rapidly, especially the cells of the immune system. In effect, these substances not only produced antimicrobial effects but were also immune suppressive and carcinogenic in the host.

One of the drugs of the above group, Azothioprine, was developed for just the purpose of suppressing the immune system so that patients receiving organ transplants would not reject the foreign grafted tissue. As a result, many transplant patients using this drug developed transplantation AIDS— Kaposi's sarcoma, lymphoma, and opportunistic infections. The patients who most often developed this problem were people of Jewish (Sephardic), Italian, and African ancestry who had an HLA (human lymphocyte antigen)- DR genetic marker. This will become important in the discussion of the adverse outcome of the drug AZT on Hispanics and African Americans in Veteran Administration drug trials and in the HIV antibody test. It should also be noted that when Azothioprine was withdrawn from treatment in the transplant patients, there were occasions when the Kaposi's sarcomas and lymphomas disappeared—underscoring that cancer can be a reversible disease and was known to be so before the AIDS era.

Nitroso compounds result from reactions from other chemicals called <u>akylamines</u>. It has been known for years that these compounds can cause a variety of diseases, including immune deficiencies and cancer. So, from the very beginning of the mass marketing of these drugs, it was understood that they were Frankenstein products that could suppress microbial disease and could also create an epidemic of immune deficiency in chronic or long-term users. They were first widely marketed and used in such a way that they contributed to the development of and then exacerbated the problem of immune deficiency disease—destroying people who were looking for a reprieve.

Following the BEIC product development model, Burroughs Wellcome first created drugs that contributed to the promotion of immune deficiency, and then when people were desperate and dying, it offered them a drug that finished them off by compounding the immune deficient status. It was creating and expanding its market. It was just business.

Metabolism of nitroso compounds produces mutagens, teratogens, and potent carcinogens in thirty-nine different animal species. Volatile nitrites have been shown to produce deleterious effects on human lymphocytes in vitro and in vivo. This consequence has been known about these compounds since the 1940s. For example, in an American automobile factory where one of the nitroso compounds, dimethylnitrosamine was used as a solvent, two men were accidentally poisoned. One man recovered after signs of liver damage; the other died in a clinical accident, and autopsy revealed a cirrhotic liver with regenerating nodules. Working with the solvent over a period of ten months, two of three men in a British industrial research laboratory showed signs of liver injury. One died of bronchopneumonia, and an autopsy found liver cirrhosis. The other technician developed a hard liver with an irregular surface but recovered after exposure to the solvent ended.[359]

It was known that nitroso compounds could induce tumor growth at a wide variety of sites including, but not limited to, skin, nose, nasal sinus, esophagus, lung, bronchi, brain, thymus, lymph nodes, and blood vessels. These are the sights where the original cohort of AIDS patients often developed Kaposi's sarcomas and lymphomas after many years of volatile nitrite inhalant use. The patient anemnesis containing this information was screaming to be interpreted correctly in the context of this tragedy. Instead, the tragedy of young men in the original AIDS cohort was destined to be exploited in such a callous way that it defies all rational explanation.

These compounds were known to be highly potent carcinogens; a single administration to infant animals can result in high tumor incidences when the animals reach adulthood. Yet, as will be noted, the FDA recommended, in violation of United States law, AZT, a known carcinogen for use in pregnant women. These compounds also appear to induce neoplasms transplacentally and can result in brain and spinal cord and renal tumors in the animal model. Nitroso compounds were also found to be potent mutagens causing both fetal death and resorption or deformities in those (animal models) that reach term.[360]

In relation to the early AIDS crisis, the timing of production and sales of volatile nitrites for recreational use was the new life-style factor that brought this problem to attention. The prevalence of nitrite use among a subset of male homosexuals was very high, and almost every case of Kaposi's sarcoma in the original cohort of AIDS patients included a history of prior chronic nitrite use. The age group of patients in whom Kaposi's sarcoma and AIDS

359. Ronald C. Shank, "Toxicology of N-Nitroso Compounds," Toxicology and Applied Pharmacology 31 (1975): 361–68.
360. Ibid.

developed was consistent with the cohort initially exposed for seven to ten years before the onset of acute symptoms.[361]

Amyl Nitrite

Amyl nitrite was developed to be used as a vasodilator for people who had a heart condition known as <u>angina</u>. Until 1960, it was a controlled substance and required a physician's prescription. Quite suddenly and inexplicably, the FDA eliminated the prescription requirement.

Controlling the availability or the scarcity of a desired product to create a planned market penetration and price level was another past strategy learned from the opium trade in the Far East. By the end of the 17th century, Europeans had changed the nature of the opium trade. Opium was no longer only a medicinal drug or a buffer against stress but also had become a drug used primarily for pleasure. By releasing amyl nitrite from its prescription requirement, a huge market was created for the pleasurable aspects of this drug.

From 1961 to 1969, a subset of the homosexual community began using this drug as a sexual doping agent because of a transient high and anal sphincter relaxation. After the market was created by the abolishment of the prescription requirement, the FDA then suddenly reinstated the prescription requirement in 1969. This action by the FDA facilitated the development of a new industry that stepped into the breach, marketing brands of butyl and isobutyl nitrites. One of the most brilliant advertising campaigns of all time commenced. Within only a few years, hundreds of thousands of men were persuaded that <u>poppers</u> were an integral part of the <u>gay identity</u>. Advertisements in journals that catered to a homosexual audience conveyed the message that nothing could be more butch or sexier than to inhale noxious chemical fumes. Bulging muscles were linked to a drug that, like opium, tobacco, or cocaine, could ultimately lead to death and even faster death when all of these drugs were combined in chronic usage.

At its peak, the poppers industry was the biggest money-maker in the homosexual world, grossing upwards of $50 million per year. By 1974, the poppers craze was in full swing, and by 1977 poppers were in every corner of gay life.[362] Many of the men were concomitantly using trimethoprin/

---

361. G.R. Newell, P.W. Mansell, M.R. Spitz, J.M. Reuben, and E.M. Hersh, "Volatile nitrities, use and adverse effects related to the current epidemic of the acquired immune deficiency syndrome" <u>Am J Med 78</u> (1985): 811–16.
362. John Lauristen, "Queer Advertising, from poppers to protease inhibitors," www.virusmyth.net/aids/data/jlpoppers2k.htm.

sulfamethexasole (T/S) as an antibiotic prophylaxis against repeated bouts of sexually-transmitted diseases. By 1981, poly-drug-using young men began to show up in clinics and hospitals with opportunistic infections and Kaposi's sarcoma. Against clinical evidence, the medical hierarchy chose to ignore the drug use evidence that was well known in both the medical and scientific literature and claimed that the symptoms must be caused by a virus. This was a cruel hoax from the very beginning.

Larry Kramer used his 1978 novel Faggots to decry the alienation of the fast-track homosexual community and to describe the intensity of sexual promiscuity in bathhouses that was used to fill the existential void and psychological angst that many of the men experienced. He specifically listed many of the drugs they used:

- MDA, MDM, THC, PCP, STP, DMT, LDK, WDW, Coke, Window Pane, Blotter, Orange Sunshine, Sweet Pea, Sky Blue, Christmas Tree, Mescaline, Dust Benzedrine, Dexedrine, Dexamyl, Desoxyn, Strychnine, Ionamin, Ritalin , Desbutal, Opital, Glue, Ethyl Chloride, Nitrous Oxide, Crystal Methedrine, Clogidal, Nesperan, Tytch, Nestex, Black Beauty, Certyn, Preludin with B-12, Zayl, Quaalude, Tuinal, Nembutal, Seconal, Amytal Phenobarb, Elavil, Vallium, Librium, Darvon, Mandrax, Opium, Stidyl, Halidax, Caldfyn, Optimil, Drayl.[363]

The same company, Wellcome, which had first manufactured amyl nitrite and T/S would soon develop another product for use by patients who were showing up with damaged immune systems, another drug from its nitroso stable that would accelerate the process of immune system damage even faster. Wellcome had to be aware that nitroso compounds could suppress the immune system, because another one of their products, Azothioprine, was marketed for just that purpose for transplant patients.

Azothioprine

The main problem with transplanting organs and tissues from one person to another is that the recipient host does not recognize the new tissue as its own. Instead, it attacks it as foreign, in the same way it attacks germs—to destroy them. In order to prevent a rejection of the transplanted tissue, patients are given drugs such as cyclosporin A, steroids, and azothiorpine that are used intentionally to suppress their immune systems. Azothioprine was well

---

363. Larry Kramer, Faggots (Jackson, TN: Grove Press, 2000).

known to trigger transplantation AIDS—opportunistic infections, Kaposi's sarcoma, and lymphomas in transplant patients. The medical literature is full of case reports of patients who developed Kaposi's sarcomas and lymphomas while on this drug. The problem with opportunistic infections was also well known. But a more important observation in these transplant patients was this: Some of the patients, who developed Kaposi's sarcoma, even when it was disseminated, had complete regression on withdrawal of the drug.[364] Of course, this is also true of many people who had AIDS or a positive HIV test and are alive and well many years after the dreaded diagnosis. The common characteristics of "long-term non-progressors" are that they stopped the street drugs, did not take the pharmaceutical drugs, and claimed health as their birthright. This was made clear by a study of rehabilitated intravenous drug users who had completed treatment and remained drug free. They had half as many HIV positive tests as intravenous drug users who had just begun detoxification treatment. Among those who remained drug free for a year, the frequency of having a positive HIV test was only a quarter of that among former users who had remained drug free for less than a year,[365] demonstrating that HIV was a reversible phenomenon.

The average interval between transplantation and the use of Azothioprine and onset of KS was about eighteen months. The data sheet for Imuran, the brand name for Azothoprine states, "It has been reported that reduction or discontinuation of immunosuppression may be associated with partial or complete regression of non-Hodgkin's lymphomas and Kaposi's sarcomas. . . .IMURAN should not be given to patients who are pregnant or likely to become pregnant in the near future without careful assessment of risk versus benefit. There have been reports of premature birth and low birth weight following maternal exposure to azathioprine, particularly in combination with corticosteroids. There have also been reports of spontaneous abortion following either maternal or paternal exposure." Yet the FDA maliciously approved AZT, which has a similar action profile, for use in pregnancy.

The diagnosis and subsequent treatment of this problem, claimed to be caused by a virus rather than known environmental stressors, constituted malpractice because: the transplantation AIDS phenomenon of opportunistic infections and tumor development after the use of azothioprine was well known and well described in the medical literature; it was not caused by a virus, but a manufactured immunosuppressive drug of the nitroso group; the

---

364. L. Margoulis et al., "Kaposi's Sarcoma in Renal Transplant Recipients, Experience at Johannesburg Hospital, 1966–1989," SAMJ 84 (1994): 16–17.
365. A.R. Moss, et al., "HIV Seroconversion in Intravenous Drug Users in San Francisco, 1985–90," AIDS 8 (1994):223–31.

physicians who saw the original patients stated in their assessment that "the patients do not know each other and had no known common contacts or knowledge of sexual partners who had similar illnesses," and moreover they did not have "compatible histories of sexually transmitted diseases."

The biological consequences of this class of chemical compounds were willfully ignored by the medical hierarchy. The generation of post-WWII babies had been shocked and suckered into the use of narcotics and pharmaceuticals to support a Tavistock- inspired lifestyle. The social phenomenon of the chronic and serial use of these known immune toxins was an epidemiological catastrophe waiting to happen. By adding another deadly Wellcome drug—AZT— to the mix, the situation was simply compounded and prolonged. The medical hierarchy clearly wanted to promote a sex and blood virus plague with the benefit of selling more products and doing unthinkable human experimentation. However, more than anything, there was a desire to use sex and to promote a promiscuous lifestyle to children and adolescents as a way of undermining the moral values of the culture. This type of human experimentation could only be tolerated and excused under the phony conditions of a manufactured crisis.

AZT

Azidothymidine, or AZT, was first isolated from herring sperm cells in 1961, and in 1964 was synthesized as 3'-azido—3'-deoxythymidine by Horowitz from the Michigan Cancer Foundation. The National Cancer Institute then transferred the data and technology for the synthesis of AZT to Burroughs Wellcome. The significance of this drug originating in herring sperm will be discussed further on. Animal experiments using this drug in mice and rats with leukemia showed the development of lymphomas. As a result of its tumor-causing effects and lack of inhibition of leukemia cells, it was not released for clinical human trials for cancer treatment. Even though AZT was deemed unfit because of its toxicity to give to cancer patients, it was rushed through clinical trials in the most haphazard way and pushed onto the market in record time for this developing new market.[366] This was done by the FDA under the direction of Dr. Frank Young. Consumer advocates such as Sidney Wolfe charged that Young's reign was one of lawlessness, in terms of collusion between the industry and government. Young eventually had to resign, under the shadow of a generic drug scandal.

---

366. John Lauristen, "FDA Documents Show Fraud in AZT Trials," New York Native, 30 March 1992.

Most clinical trials can take more than ten years. The AZT drug was approved for widespread use, after the shoddiest of research, in less than five months (17 weeks to be exact). This was pure evil. It had to be known that this drug was going to do more damage to already damaged patients—and it did. People whose immune systems were already fragile were going to be given a drug that would be sure to finish them off. But a more nefarious scheme was afoot. People who were not ill, but who had a positive HIV test were going to be encouraged to take a drug that would eventually give them AIDS. This mass iatrogenic poisoning increased the death rate, making the illusion of the inevitable fatality of the disease as pronounced from on high, a reality. This created even more demand for the drug that was killing people.

English and French researchers examined over a three-year period, 1,749 HIV positive but healthy people in thirty-eight clinics in the U.K., Ireland, and France who were given AZT. This was called the <u>Concorde Study</u>, and it was conducted by the British Research Council and its French counterpart. The team concluded that AZT neither prolongs life nor staves off symptoms of AIDS in people who are HIV antibody positive but still healthy. The study found that AZT was too toxic for most people to tolerate, had no lasting effect on HIV blood levels, and left patients with fewer CD4+ cells than they started with. A Veteran's Administration study from 1991 showed the same poor results with the additional findings that blacks and Hispanics fared less well with early AZT therapy. The VA study evaluated 338 HIV positive individuals with AIDS, who were divided into two groups. Both groups were given AZT but in a different dosage—which, of course, is not a controlled trial. A controlled trial is done by giving one group the study drug and the other a placebo so that the true effects of the drug can be distinguished. Dr. John Hamilton reported that no benefit for either treatment group was detected for survival or at the combined chemical end points of AIDS and death. He said that the early AZT resulted in transitory benefits for whites, and neutral or harmful effects in black and Hispanic patients. No mention was made of the high risk of cancer (as much as 50 percent) for those taking the drug. However, Burroughs Wellcome, in collusion with the FDA, restated the findings of the study in such a way as to make it seem that AZT conferred some beneficial effects when used early, even in black and Hispanic patients. It was just business.

The effectiveness or the toxicity of the AZT was never the point. If that had been the case, it would have stayed on the dusty shelf where it had long remained after failed trials as a cancer drug that caused cancer. According to Celia Farber, two of the researchers from the Concorde Study team admitted to coming under pressure from Burroughs Wellcome concerning their findings. One researcher exclaimed, "Yes, there has been pressure, and it has been placed at the very highest level!" Even though in these two studies it was clearly shown that the drug offered no benefit and was causing cancer in 50 percent of the patients, Dr. Anthony Fauci, director of the National Institutes of Allergy and Infectious Diseases (NIAID), recommended that anyone with HIV antibodies and less than 500 CD4 cells should start taking AZT at once. At that time, that meant approximately 650,000 people in the U.S. Much of the Concorde Study data on toxicity was not allowed to be revealed.[367]

In addition to colluding with Burroughs Wellcome in the suppression of adverse events and with the projection of a market of 650,000 people, the FDA conferred <u>orphan</u> <u>drug status</u> on AZT. <u>Orphan</u> drugs are medications that are required by fewer than 200,000 patients annually in the U.S. By conferring this status, even though the projected market was three times that amount, Burroughs Wellcome would have exclusive marketing rights and tax relief for the production of AZT for seven years. With the prodigious help of the FDA, Burroughs Wellcome was about to make enormous profits by planned human experimentation of a drug known to cause AIDS and cancer. The "invisible hand of the free market" was at work. Since the drug hastened the demise of AIDS patients, the cost of the drug would be relatively cheap ($5,000 to $15,000 per patient), compared with the cost to the insurance industry of hospitalizations avoided ($150,000 to $200,000). Earlier AIDS cases had drawn hospital care from nine to eighteen months, which threatened to bankrupt some insurers.

While the FDA was conferring "orphan" status on this drug, researchers at the NIH published research data that claimed "anti-HIV inhibition" in T-helper immune cells of AIDS patients after AZT treatment. The market went wild, and the stock price of Burroughs Wellcome almost quadrupled within a year.

The fallacy that a hypothetical retrovirus caused AIDS was used as an excuse to use carcinogenic drugs in human subjects to determine whether the loss of the functions of T-helper immune cells could cause the development of tumor cells. This hypothesis allowed for the deployment of a substance group (nitroso compounds) that was already known to have immunosuppressive effects and to cause the formation of tumor cells. Using the excuse of retrovirus inhibition in order to allegedly prolong the life of the inevitably moribund HIV positive patients, it was possible to prescribe such experimental substances without ethical scruples to willing human patients.[368]

---

367. Celia Farber, "AZT is Death," <u>Spin</u>, August 1993.

368. Heinrich Kremer, The Silent Revolution in Cancer and AIDS Medicines (Bloomington, IN: Xlibris Corp., 2008), 270.

AZT is claimed to work by inserting itself into the viral DNA chain in such a way that the viral DNA cannot be completed and therefore the virus is unable to replicate itself. This is why AZT is called a DNA chain terminator. The theory is that AZT prevents retroviral replication by integrating into the DNA chain in place of the natural building block, thymidine, either by using the HIV enzyme Reverse Transcriptase (RT) or by the use of the natural nuclear enzymes of the DNA polymerases. The claim is that this false AZT building block integrated into a DNA copy of the HIV RNA via the RT enzyme of the supposed retrovirus HIV, shuts down the replication because of a wrong base pair. The provirus genome of HIV would then remain incomplete and could no longer be reproduced with the aid of the cell division apparatus of the host cell, as new infectious retrovirus HIV. The theory of how this DNA chain terminator works sounds plausible but it is pure fantasy. However, it is a theory that the invisible hand of the market sold to physicians and the public that, unfortunately, has nothing to do with reality.[369]

According to Henreich Kremer:

> AZT is a synthetic nucleotide, the precursor of a nucleoside triphosphate that merely docks one phosphate atom. In order to be integrated into DNA, regardless of whether it is "HIV provirus DNA" or nuclear DNA, the nucleoside monophosphate AZT in the nucleus must have three phosphate atoms and could only then be incorporated at the growing end of the DNA as a nucleotide by an "HIV RT" or nuclear enzyme DNA polymerase. In this case the synthetic nucleoside monophosphate AZT would become the DNA nucleotide Azidothymidine triphosphate (AZT TP) that is capable of integration. Countless studies over the last decade, however, have clearly shown that only about 1% of AZT is transformed to AZT TP—thus, at prescribed AZT doses of between 500 and 1,500 mg per day, much too little to be able to cause any kind of inhibition of "HIV provirus DNA" or nuclear DNA as a "DNA terminator" as claimed effects of AZT state.[370]

Where AZT does the most damage is not in the proviral DNA, but in the mitochondria. AZT has been shown to be maximally toxic to the energy producing intracellular organelles called mitochondria. The damage to the mitochondria makes sense when considering the various organ systems

---

369. Ibid., 274.
370. Ibid., 274.

damaged by use of AZT. AZT is reported to cause anemia, leucopenia, nausea, muscle atrophy, bone marrow suppression, dementia, hepatitis/liver failure, and death.

A study focusing on the cardiovascular toxicity of AZT reported that "AZT treatment increases superoxide (free radical) production" and "the effects of AZT on endothelium-dependent relaxation are eliminated by pretreatment with a free radical scavenger" (antioxidants) which strongly indicates that AZT toxicity is due to its free radical generating capacity. This study also provides the scientific inference that AIDS can be caused, as predicted by the Perth Group out of Australia, by superoxide free radicals and oxidative stress. In fact, AIDS is a free radical and oxidative stress induced condition that appears more easily in people with malnutrition and with low organic selenium intake.[371] Selenium is a mineral necessary for the optimal functioning of several enzymes involved in the OX/PHOS system.

AZT causes increased mitochondrial lipid peroxidation and oxidation of mitochondrial glutathione. Changes in the ratio of reduced to oxidized glutathione cause changes in the cellular redox environment and can alter signal transduction, DNA and RNA synthesis, protein synthesis, enzyme activation, and regulation of the cell cycle. AZT also works by inhibiting the enzyme cytochrome c oxidase, which is part of the electron transport chain in the mitochondria. By inhibiting this enzyme, AZT effectively shuts down the mitochondrial synthesis of ATP energy production. This underscores the point that AIDS is really not an immune deficiency, but an energy deficiency problem that, because of evolutionary biologically programmed cellular responses, manifests as a Type 2–Th2 counter-regulatory balance of the cells of the immune system. (see chapter--What is Causing Immune Deficiency?) Because of extreme oxidation caused by lifestyle factors and pharmaceutical drugs, the immune system is pushed in a particular, but anticipated, direction. It follows that therapy with appropriate reducing agents would be the biological compensation pushing it back into balance.

This brings the discussion back to Azidothymidine, which is isolated from sperm cells of herring in 1961. The obvious question that should have been raised is this: What was the natural function of Azidothymidine in the sperm cells of vertebrates? This has to do with sexual propagation in eukaryotic (cells with the nucleus in an enclosed membrane) organisms. Eukaryotic organisms that propagate sexually inherit the energy producing mitochondria DNA from the maternal side only. Therefore, the mitochondria in the sperm have

---

371. Jose Garcia de le Asuncion, et al., "AZT Induces Oxidative Damage to Cardiac Mitochondria, Protective Effect of Vitamin C and E,", Life Sciences 76 (2004): 47–56.

to be deactivated before fertilization can occur. Furthermore, the developing embryo has no way of eliminating intracellular agents because of their type 2 cytokine dominance (discussed in What is Causing Immune Deficiency?), and therefore for the survival of the embryo, the sperm cell cannot introduce intracellular agents to the egg. Mitochondria and not nuclear DNA are the cell targets of AZT. [372] Whether azidothymidine or similar substances are formed in human sperm cells has not been studied, but there are indications that this could be the case.

By inactivating cell respiration enzymes in the mitochondria, AZT not only has immunosuppressive and carcinogenic effects but also antimicrobial ones as well. The enzyme cytochrome c oxidase and other enzymes oxidized by AZT are also present in bacteria, fungi, and protozoa. The clinical apparently beneficial effects of AZT are not based on killing a phantom virus, but on the fact that there is different absorption of this substance by the body's cells versus the microbial cells. AZT has the effect of poisoning the mitochondria of the microbes and therefore does reduce microbial stress in the short run. This gives the impression that the drug is killing the virus. The patient can begin to feel better. However, because the drug is also attacking the patient's mitochondria, he will inevitably begin to deteriorate.

Clearly, AZT causes AIDS. When patients begin to deteriorate after any brief respite because of the antimicrobial effect, they are told that the HIV has developed immunity to the drug and that the HIV is killing them, when, in fact, it is the drug, AZT. But, of course, the idea that the virus is the culprit is sheer nonsense. The AZT is targeting human mitochondria as well as the mitochondria of the intracellular invaders. This is the very reason it has so many deleterious side effects. They are not side effects; they are the main effects of the AZT drug.

Before the approval of AZT by the FDA in the spring of 1987, one of their toxicologists had internally issued an urgent warning about AZT as a possible carcinogenic rat poison. The study of AZT using the toxicological standard method of "cell transformation assay" and other processes produced the following results: "This behavior is characteristic of tumor cells and suggests that AZT may be a potential carcinogen. It appears to be at least as active as the positive control material, methylcholanthrene (an extremely potent carcinogen) . . . "[373] (emphasis added).

The FDA ignored its own report and violated their guidelines in licensing this drug for distribution. Burroughs Wellcome falsified the toxicology

---

372. Maria Barile, et al., "Mitochondria As Cell Targets of AZT (Zidovudine), General Pharmacology 31 (1998): 531–38.

373. Kremer, The Silent Revolution., 280.

findings by stating on the AZT information insert: "The significance of these in vitro results is not known."

The FDA's toxicologist criticized this claim and unmistakably stated: "The sentence: 'The significance of these in vitro results is not known.' is not accurate. A test chemical which induces a positive response in the cell transformation assay is presumed to be a potential carcinogen."

In the U.S., the therapeutic use of potential carcinogens on humans is allegedly forbidden by law—except when the invisible hand of the market is at work. The FDA's internal toxicological reports about AIDS and cancer-causing effects of AZT first became public knowledge through the Freedom of Information Act (FOIA).[374] It did not matter. It had been determined at the highest levels that AZT was going to be marketed. The truth of its toxicity was irrelevant to the invisible hand of the market in alignment with the heavy hand of the FDA. Burroughs Wellcome was the winner. Those stigmatized with a positive HIV test were the losers. It was just business.

In 1990, the market for this state-sanctioned mass poisoning was expanded when the FDA approved AZT not only for use in AIDS patients but also for unlimited treatment of symptom-free "HIV positives," new born babies, children, adolescents, pregnant and non-pregnant women, and men with and without recognizable risks.

The entire architecture of the AIDS industry has been established on building blocks of lies. The initial research of Gallo claiming that HIV was the probable cause of AIDS was a lie. The use of a patented antibody test to screen for a nonexistent virus was a lie. However, the lies used to sell a drug that caused severe damage to blood and muscle tissue, caused cancer, and ultimately led to the death of people who were desperate and ill were criminal acts of premeditated bodily harm. Giving patients who were suffering from severe oxidative and nitrosative stress a drug that would compound that stress even further was sheer lunacy. Given the fact that AZT, like azothioprine, was an immune suppressor, giving it to patients who were already immune suppressed without detoxifying their already poisoned systems was willful, unconscionable, and criminal. All of this was done in spite of the fact that there was no virus and no one had been able to prove the pathogenic mechanism of the provirus DNA of the retrovirus RNA, despite the largest capital investment and the most intensive research efforts in medical history.

---

374. Ibid.

Trimethoprin/Sulfamethoxazol

From 1980, another antibiotic drug from Burroughs Wellcome, Trimethoprim/Sulfamethoxazol (T/S) was routinely used to treat AIDS patients for <u>Pneumocystis carinii</u> pneumonia (PCP). PCP was so common in the early patients it is considered one of the AIDS indicator diseases. PCP is a fungus. An overgrowth of fungi generally indicates an extreme acidification of body fluids. This acidification is a metabolic red light which is seldom addressed by allopathic medicine except in diabetics. It will be discussed further in the chapter on therapeutic interventions.

Trimethoprim bonds to the enzyme that converts the essential folic acid to the biologically active form tetrahydrofolate (THF). This enzyme is named dihydrofolate reductase (DHFR). Folate, one of the B vitamins, is necessary for the production and maintenance of new cells and for the synthesis of DNA bases (mostly thymine but also purine bases) needed for DNA replication. Folate deficiency hinders DNA synthesis and cell division by affecting co-enzyme synthesis and the metabolism of certain amino acids. Folate is also necessary for the production of the energy molecule ATP in the mitochondria.

Beginning in the 1940s, drugs were developed to block the enzyme DHFR. One of those drugs, methotrexate, was used to inhibit rapidly replicating cancer cells. It was soon recognized that DHFR blockers also blocked the enzymes in bacteria, fungi, parasites, and mammalian cells, including humans. This fact was used to design DHFR blockers that could selectively bind to microbial enzymes with more tenacity than human DHFR enzymes. This was another illusion. Trimethoprim was one of these agents designed to inhibit bacterial growth. Researchers then hit upon the idea of combining trimethoprim with sulfonamides for business rather than clinical needs. Trimethoprim had been invented by Wellcome in its United States laboratories and patented in 1957. But just five months previously, a Japanese firm, Shionogi, had registered sulphamethoxazole for exactly the same purposes, and licensed its use to the pharmaceutical super-giant Hoffman-La Roche. The headquarters of Roche were at Nutley, New Jersey, just across the Hudson River from Wellcome. Roche was concerned about the potential threat posed by the Wellcome rival, and the shotgun marriage that followed involved mixing five parts of the bigger company's drug with one part of that from the smaller.[375]

---

375. Brian Deer, "The Pill that Killed", <u>The Sunday Times (London)</u> March 20, 1994

Sulfonamides inhibit folic acid synthesis by another pathway. By combining these two substances, it was thought that this folic acid double action would increase the bactericidal effects of this compound. This drug hit the market at about the same time as the beginning of the decade of sexual liberation of homosexuals and the rising use of street drugs, including nitrite inhalants. Urban physicians and their homosexual patients had the impression that they could use this drug combination prophylacticly to safeguard against infections, especially in the climate where men were having unprotected sex, often with several partners in one night in unsanitary bathhouses. These young men, in addition to all of the other drug use, began to regularly self-medicate with T/S before a night on the town. A couple of tablets of T/S and a pocket full of amyl nitrite, a nose full of cocaine, and a bloodstream full of alcohol, uppers, downers, and the rest was like standing in front of an on rushing train and daring it to hit one. It did, with a vengeance. It was a trap, and these young homosexuals walked right into it.

The metabolism of the double folic acid inhibitor T/S is an important part of the AIDS story. Because bacteria, fungi, and parasites have the same mitochondria as humans, the consequence of using T/S should have led to the following assumptions: Sulfamethoxazole blocks the synthesis of folic acid in both human and microbial mitochondria, and therefore human cells are as vulnerable as the microbial cells; trimethoprin likewise blocks the activation of folic acid in mitochondria and in intracellular microbes, and therefore human mitochondria are just as vulnerable to trimethoprin as bacteria cells.

The metabolic product of sulfamethoxazole, especially the toxic product hydroxylamine, has to be detoxified by glutathione, the three amino acid master anti-oxidant. Toxic nitroso compounds from the chronic use of T/S combined with nitrite inhalants deplete the glutathione, thiol antioxidant pool. The lack of this powerful antioxidant leads to nitrosative and oxidative stress and to inhibition of cytochrome oxidse in the respiratory chain of the mitochondria. This decreases the production of ATP the energy molecule, leads to mtDNA damage and to disruption of protein synthesis. Some of the listed side effects include: a sometimes fatal allergic reaction-- Steven-Johnson syndrome; liver and kidney damage, depression of red blood cell metabolism leading to megaloblastic anemia, depression of platelets and white blood cells. The deaths reported for this combined pill were eight times greater per million prescriptions than those linked to the antibiotic ampicillin.[376]

This predictable disruption of cellular metabolism as a result of oxidative and nitrosative stress caused by this drug combination resulted in an inhibition of the enzyme cytochrome oxidase in the respiratory chain, decreased

---

376. Brian Deer, Ibid.

ATP production, DNA damage and disruption of protein synthesis, to increased cell disintegration—Type 1 overregulation of cell dyssymbiosis— or to cellular transformation to tumor cells that switch to the less efficient cytoplasmic glycolytic energy production—Type-II counterregulation of cell dyssymbiosis.

The mitochondrial stress effects of this drug are analogous to the effects of nitric oxide (NO) radicals as well as the nitroso groups of the azothioprine and azidothymidine (AZT). [377] Each of these Wellcome drugs acts to disrupt oxidative energy metabolism in the mitochondria, therefore it is not a surprise that they can cause so many problems including AIDS diseases and death.

The most amazing situation occurred when Dr. Henrich Kremer corresponded to the companies that produce the T/S drug combination— Wellcome, now GlaxoSmith Kline, Hoffman LaRoche, and Bayer. He raised the issue of a pathogenetic causal link of mitochondrial damage from the combined inhibition of folic acid metabolism in human cell systems and the subsequent appearance of acquired immune deficiency disease (AIDS) depending on dose and duration of medication and the disposition of the patient. He also inquired if they had done research in this area. The companies responded: "There were no clinical studies about the mitochondriotoxic effects of the single substance Trimethoprim or the combination substance T/S." These companies had introduced these toxic drugs for human use without having done the necessary toxicology studies. Had they even bothered to ask the question?

But just as azothioprine had been shown to create immune suppression in transplant patients resulting in increased incidence of Kaposi's sarcoma and opportunistic infections, a decade before the sudden appearance of opportunistic fungal infections and Kaposi's sarcoma as AIDS indicating diseases in homosexual men, it was already recognized that long-term medication with folic acid inhibitors could provoke neutropenia (low white blood cell count) and systemic fungal infections. It was also known that long-term inhalation of nitrite gases had an intoxicating effect, which also favored fungal infections. It was known that homosexual men with opportunistic fungal infections (AIDS) were habitual trimethoprin/sulfamethoxazol abusers and chronic nitrite gas consumers.[378] So one must logically ask, what was the rationale for inventing a virus to blame on the predictable outcome of chronic self-abuse with a virtual pharmacy of cyto-toxic AIDS causing substances?

---

377. Kremer, The Silent Revolution, 292–93.
378. Ibid., 287.

Along with the political and commercial reasons already stated, it was also a way to hide the fact that the great miracle drugs touted by the pharmaceutical industry were a disaster and that the hierarchy of the medical establishment had chosen to ignore biological realities. Microbes and humans possess the same type of eukaryotic cells. If a drug attacks the metabolism of the microbe, it also has the possibility to attack the metabolism of the human, and a range of antibiotics have been shown to do just that. However, the microbes have a distinct advantage. Because of evolutionary biology and their short life cycles, they have the ability to adapt to hostile environments faster than humans. Many of the drugs humans create to kill microbes, end up killing themselves. In the meantime, the microbes have moved on and developed resistance.

It is now known that Trimethoprim, Azothioprine and AZT suppress the function of nitric oxide (NO) gas producing Th1 immune cells and after a few days cause a Th1/Th2 switch of cellular immunity. This is important because it is the NO gas producing Th1 cells that kill intracellular parasites. If the Th1 cells are prohibited from producing NO gas because of exhaustion from chronic overexposure to free radicals or because of malnutrition, then the ability to mount an effective response of what is called cellular immunity (as opposed to humoral or antibody immunity) is thwarted, and this gives rise to the overgrowth of opportunistic microbes. It also gives rise to a Th2 counterbalance with an increase in antibody production. This is why HIV patients respond positively to the HIV test. Not because there is a virus, but because the organism is responding in an evolutionary biologically programmed way to environmental stressors.

A study funded by Burroughs Wellcome in 1970 looked at the effect of azothioprine, trimethoprim, and trimethoprin with a folate rescue in skin graft transplant white mice. The study showed that trimethoprim and azothioprine had the same immune suppressing effects (allowing the mice to keep the grafts), but the effect of trimethoprim could be overcome by the addition of folate (an antioxidant) to the transplanted mice (the graft was rejected).[379] Use of the folic acid vitamin overcame the toxicity of the drug. In spite of this knowledge, Burroughs Wellcome went on selling the products, the physicians continued to use the products, and in the context of the sexual and drug revolution of the 1970s, the doctors played a collusive role with the pharmaceutical industry in ignoring this science and going along with the new virus hypothesis.

---

379. M.W Ghilchik, A.S. Morris, O.S. Reeves, "Immunosuppressive powers of the antibacterial agent trimethoprim" Nature 227 (1970): 393–94.

It was also unconscionable that American researchers have withheld the knowledge from the people of Less Developed Countries that folic acid deficiency due to under nutrition or malnutrition (nutritional AIDS) or chemotherapy against tuberculosis and or the combination T/S or other antibiotics can cause exactly the same opportunistic infections and other AIDS-indicating diseases, which according to the AIDS theory is caused by a virus.

Finally, as someone who has spent a lifetime practicing reproductive medicine, a most important question must be raised to the possibility of irreparable mitochondrial genetic damage from toxic chemoantibiotics and chemotherapeutic agents over the maternal germline, as an inherited disposition for AIDS, cancer, and other chronic illnesses. When I began my practice, there was great concern among women whose mothers had taken the drug diethylstibestrol (DES) during their pregnancy to help prevent a possible miscarriage. There appeared to be no long-term effect on the mothers, but the daughters, in addition to having a higher than usual rate of infertility because of the mutagencity of the drug on the reproductive organs, also developed a rare vaginal cancer in their teen years. There are going to be so many problems in the coming generations from genotoxic effects of these chemoantibiotics that we are on the cusp of another created crisis.

The evidence on the use of AZT during pregnancy is not promising. In June 2000, researchers reported that "rapid disease progression" defined as occurrence of an AIDS-defining disease or AIDS-related death before 18 months of age was three times more likely to occur in babies born to mothers treated with AZT than when the mother was untreated. This was despite a halving in the purported infection rate in the AZT exposed babies.[380] An Italian study involving more than 200 HIV-positive children found that at 3 years of age, those born to mothers treated with AZT during pregnancy were significantly more likely to have developed severe disease and had a higher death rate than children whose mothers were not treated.[381] In France, researchers found mitochondrial damage in eight children exposed to AZT

---

380. R. S. De Souza, et al., "Effect of Prenatal Zidovudine on Disease Progression in Perinatally HIV 1 Infected Infants, J Acq Immune Def Syn & Human Retrovir 24 (2000): 154–61.

381. Italian Register for HIV Infection in Children, 28 May 1999. "Rapid Disease Progression in HIV 1 Perinatally Infected Children Born to Mothers Receiving Zidovudine (AZT) Monotherapy During Pregnancy," AIDS 13 (1999): 927–33.

in the womb and after birth. Two of the eight died, and the others had severe biological and neurological abnormalities.[382]

An article in the <u>American Journal of Medical Genetics</u> hints at the possibility of a potential mitochondrial genetic calamity in a study done by Chinnery and Turnbull. They found that in the last ten years, there has been a huge increase in the number of genetic defects found in patients with mitochondrial disorders and that the true impact of mitochondrial disease is only just becoming apparent. They noted that mitochondrial diseases are far more common than was anticipated.[383]

Evolutionary biology tells us that about 2 billion years ago new eukaryotic cells were formed by the combination of two cell types, one that did not need much oxygen to produce energy and the other bacteria that we now know as mitochondria that produced an enormous amount of energy by using oxygen. To this day, all eukaryotic cells get their main energy supply from these little organelles that retain many characteristics of their bacterial ancestors, including the ability to self-replicate. The mitochondria have their own mtDNA that is separate from the DNA in the nucleus. The survival of the cell and thus our survival depends both on an intact mitochondrial DNA and protein synthesis. Diseases associated with defects in mtDNA show that a large number of degenerative processes and cell death are caused by defects of mitochondrial oxidative phosphorylation which results in an ATP deficit. The rise in mitochondrial diseases is giving rise to a new specialty to treat such patients. Depending on the patient's disposition, different cells of the body will be maximally affected. Some recognized problems being seen in children and adults are: poor growth, loss of muscle coordination, visual or hearing impairment, developmental delays, learning disabilities, heart, liver, and kidney disease, gastrointestinal disorders, severe constipation, diabetes, increased risk of infection, neurological problems, seizures, thyroid dysfunction, and dementia. Although we are beginning to see a higher number of people with mitochondrial defects, there have been no broad-based epidemiological studies on the possibility that antibiotics can provoke congenital mutations of mitochondrial DNA, which could be passed down via the germline from mother to the following generations. After AIDS and Autism, this is the next great pharmaceutical disaster.

As long as the current medical mindset remains closed to the knowledge of the evolutionary biologically programmed cellular counterregulation

---

382. S. Blanche, et al., "Persistent Mitochondrial Dysfunction and Perinatal Exposure to Antiretroviral Nucleoside Analogues," <u>The Lancet 354</u> (1999):1084–89.

383. P.F. Chinnery, and D.M. Turnbull, "Epidemiology and Treatment of Mitochondrial Disorders," <u>Am J Med Genet 106</u> (2001): 94-101.

mechanisms and that life is characterized by the coupling of energy flows, they will remain blind to the fact that alterations in these flows lead to alterations in the redox control of metabolic processes. It is not a mystery why signal transduction, DNA and RNA synthesis, protein synthesis, enzyme activation, and regulation of the cell cycle are impaired in people who have AIDS. If allopathic medicine continues to work within a paradigm that thinks that a virus is causing the metabolic problem called <u>AIDS</u>, more people will continue to be harmed by genotoxic drugs. We will be sitting on top of another potential human catastrophe of unimaginable proportions. Given the population reduction fervor expressed often and openly in government documents, by think tanks and organizations such as the Club of Rome, perhaps that is the point.

So far on planet Earth, most of the species that have ever lived are extinct. If man, because of his own hubris, joins the ranks of the long gone, the bacteria will live on in a dance of ecological balance that they have had four billion years to perfect in the dance of dynamic disequilibrium of the biosphere of planet Earth.

> *A medical science that is no longer prepared to continue what it does or does not do on the basis of data and facts, which are available for all to verify, deserves no confidence and disqualifies itself as a guarantor of credibility.*[384]

Heinrich Kremer

---

384   Kremer, <u>The Silent</u> Revolution, 290.

Chapter 13

Why HIV is not Transmitted Sexually

○ ○

U.S. Armed Forces find that, just as in Africa, the distribution of HIV antibody is gender-neutral among the presumably fit adolescents wanting to enlist.

Harvey Bialy

As a matter of actual fact, research in the context of HIV/ AIDS has not revealed any racial differences in sexual behavior. Among drug users, no significant differences in behavior by race were found as to numbers of sexual partners, frequency of intercourse, numbers of sexual partners who were IDUs (intravenous drug users), numbers of non-IDU sexual partners, prostitution, or intercourse with people then or later diagnosed with AIDS. . . .another study found no significant racial differences in behavior among gay men in San Francisco and concluded that the black-to-white ratio of the frequency of HIV could not be explained by differences in major risk factors. . . .there was no difference found between the races as to anal intercourse, yet it was found that white Americans were less likely than black Americans to take protective measures during sex.

Henry Bauer, The Origin, Persistence and Failings of the HIV/AIDS Theory

Historical data from Zimbabwe records a higher incidence of venereal diseases among the white South Africa police and among the British Armed Services than among the Native Police or among Africans in general. Contemporaneous surveys have found that levels of sexual activity in general populations in Africa are comparable to those in North America and Europe.

Henry Bauer

Black Women and Green Monkeys

The 10th edition of the Merriam Webster Dictionary defines gorilla as "a tribe of hairy women mentioned in an account of a voyage around Africa." There is no mention of whose voyage or the accuracy of the observation. There is no indication of just where in Africa this tribe was located, and there is no evidence of authenticity of the observation. Yet, this not so subtle use of language conveys the message that Western culture is comfortable drawing black women into the world of subhuman primates. This type of racist innuendo is the essence of the common knowledge that early on in the AIDS debate claimed that it was a new sex and blood plague that must have originated in Africa. It was irrelevant that the first cases were identified in San Francisco, New York, and Los Angeles. After the homosexual community was first targeted, AIDS was positioned to be the new black plague.

Prestigious medical institutions and medical journals supported by the mainstream media created the impression by inference rather than evidence that AIDS originated in Africa. Against the known evidence that millions in Africa have long suffered from weight loss, chronic diarrhea, fever, and persistent coughs consistent with a hypercatabolic state brought on by a combination of infections and malnutrition, it was claimed that these symptoms were now caused by a new disease. In 1985, Western researchers suddenly redefined these symptoms as a distinct illness and declared that it was caused by a sexually-transmitted virus.

Webster's definition of gorilla was likely slipped into usage in the 19th century at a time when Europeans were attempting to justify enslavement and global commerce in trade of other human beings. It was also fundamentally necessary in this trade to create a belief in their human cargo that they were less than human and had neither history nor culture. References to Africans being little more than animals were quite common and openly expressed. There was a widely-held belief that Africans were languishing on the mother continent, living in the Stone Age, awaiting the enlightened arrival of Europeans to bring them civilization. Nothing could be further from the truth.

Unlike the variety of superstitious beliefs Europeans held of other peoples in previous centuries, European racism directed towards Africans was relatively systematic and internally consistent, and with time acquired a pseudo-scientific veneer that glossed over its irrationalities and enabled it to claim intellectual respectability. Many leading doctors and scientists of their day made their contributions to the pseudo-science of racism that became codified in the doctrine of eugenics.[385] The ideas from the eugenics movement have become so embedded in the culture that it persists in assumptions made by academicians—especially historians and anthropologists, politicians, jurists, and economists—and in the language and social manifestations of the culture.

This fear of Africa in Europe runs deep. This was not always so. The early people from the Northern Mediterranean area (before there was a Europe) who encountered Africa went there to study and learn philosophy, mathematics, and science. The high civilizations of the Nile Valley were already more than five thousand years old and past their prime when Alexander, the Macedonian, captured Egypt. However, one has to remember that Alexander depended to a major extent on the indigenous Africans for their aid in driving out the Persians under whom they had suffered greatly. The Africans despised the Persians for the barbarity of their rule more than they did Alexander.[386] This invasion was the beginning of major Greek enlightenment into the African Mysteries System of the Nile River Valley high cultures, and the center of major institutionalized learning for Greek students who were imported just for such a purpose by Aristotle.[387]

Several years after Alexander died mysteriously, one of his generals, Soter, proclaimed himself Pharaoh of All Egypt and took the title of Ptolemy I. It was the same Soter who, with Aristotle, sacked the libraries and lodges of the Mysteries System.[388]

According to history, Pythagoras underwent initiatic training for twenty two years in science, philosophy and symbolism in a *per ankh* (House of Life), probably in Thebes and is responsible for passing the number symbolism into Western culture.[389] He returned to his native island, Samos, where he established his order for a short time, after which he migrated to Croton.[390] What is now called Greek philosophy was a product of the Egyptian mystery schools. That the philosophy of the early Greek philosophers was foreign to Greece was born out by the fact that the Athenians sentenced Socrates to death in 399 B.C. and subsequently caused Plato and Aristotle to flee for

385. J. Ferguson, "The Laboratory of Racism," New Scientist 103 (1984):18–20.

386. Yosef Ben-Jochannan, Africa: Mother of Western Civilization (Baltimore, MD: Black Classic Press, 1971), 109.

387. Ibid., 110.

388. Ibid., 111.

389. Charles S. Finch III, M.D., The Star of Deep Beginnings" (Khenti, Inc. 2007), 9

390. George G. M. James, Stolen Legacy: Greek Philosophy Is Stolen Egyptian Philosophy (Classic House Books, 1980), 9.

their lives from Athens for teaching these new ideas.[391] According to George G. M. James in his volume Stolen Legacy:

> The Ionians and Italians made no attempt to claim the authorship of philosophy, because they were well aware that the Egyptians were the true authors. On the other hand, after the death of Aristotle, his Athenian pupils, without the authority of the state, undertook to compile a history of philosophy, recognized at the time as the Sophia or Wisdom of Egyptians, which had become current and traditional in the ancient world . . . later history has erroneously called (it) Greek philosophy, in spite of the fact that the Greeks were its greatest enemies and persecutors, and had persistently treated it as a foreign innovation. For this reason, the so-called Greek philosophy is stolen Egyptian philosophy which spread to Ionia, thence to Italy and thence to Athens.[392]

In 1324, when Europe was still in the throes of the Dark Ages, the great Mali King, Mansa Musa exited Timbuktu to cross the desert and to make his pilgrimage to Mecca with a caravan of 60,000 men. He was not going to war. He was going to worship. The caravan had a retinue of 12,000 servants dressed in brocade and Persian silk, and preceding Musa, who rode on horseback, were another 500 servants each carrying a staff of gold weighing about six pounds. King Mansa Musa had a baggage train of eighty camels each carrying 300 pounds of gold dust. The caravan made its way from Niani on the Upper Niger to Walata, then to Tuat, and then on to Cairo. Because he brought so much gold into Mecca, it led to the devaluation of gold in the Middle East for several years. On his return journey, Mansa Musa was accompanied by the celebrated Granada poet and architect, Es Saheli, whom he had met in Mecca. This fact testifies to the close links which even then existed between Africa and Spain.[393] It also testifies to the fact that many African states had a high degree of social organization and civil infrastructure before the civilizing forces of Europe arrived.

This brief incursion into a rich and maligned African history is to make this point: Africans, Arabs, Persians, and Europeans were interacting in a world in which the Europeans held no cultural superiority. Slavery had a long history in Europe before the African slave trade became a profit center. It was called

---

391. Ibid.,10.
392. Ibid., 10.
393. J.C. deGraft-Johnson, African Glory: The Story of Vanished Negro Civilizations (Baltimore, MD: Black Classic Press, 1954), 97--98.

feudalism, and it created a rigidly stratified and stagnant economic system for hundreds of years. Although the Arabs, Europeans, and Africans traded in slaves, slavery as an institution as practiced by Europeans, of systematic cultural destruction and dehumanization, was a new phenomenon.

After unsuccessfully attempting the colonization of the American continent, the Europeans, unable to supply their own labor needs profitably, sought a cheap and abundant labor supply. For this, they turned to Africa. There were not enough healthy Europeans to migrate, and the local Native Americans were exterminated by European disease and warfare and proved unsuitable for captive labor—they had a territorial advantage. Africans, who were healthy and skilled, would become a product of globalized free trade. Many of the Africans sought for capture were skilled in farming, animal husbandry, metallurgy, building, and sailing—all skills needed to make a go of the plantation system. To turn free men into slaves and make it stick in the psyche, a system of psychological dehumanization was begun. Part of the dehumanization process has been the heroic attempt to obliterate the African story from world history.

Because of the slave trade, African history has been distorted and misinterpreted in the justification of the foul business. When Europeans in greater numbers began to travel to Egypt, their intellectuals lost their bearings when they were confronted with the historical truth. The most ancient and advanced human civilization ever to have survived originated in the upper Nile Valley.[394] The meaning of the Negroid Sphinx hit Europe like a ton of bricks, and when they encountered themselves depicted by this highly developed black civilization as tattooed savages on the walls of the tomb of Sesostris I in the valley of Biban-el-Moluk at Thebes, the city of the gods[395] the reality of that information was too much to bear. It shattered their world view. Their court historians have twisted logic into an unrecognizable form, changed dates, deleted and destroyed information, called black red, surmised that there were extraterrestrials, called upon the lost continent of Atlantis and other fantasies, all in an attempt to refute the obvious ever since.

There are wealthy individuals both in Europe and the United States who have spent their fortunes attempting to convince other people and especially Africans of their inferiority and absence of historical significance. The ideals of the eugenics movement have been a consistent undercurrent in the culture, and millions of dollars are poured into private tax exempt trusts, such as

---

394. Graham Hancock and Robert Bauval, Message of the Sphinx (New York: Three Rivers Press, 1997).
395. Cheikh Anta Diop, The African Origin of Civilization: Myth or Reality? (Paris: Lawrence Hill Books, 1967), 43.

the Pioneer Fund that supports <u>scholars</u> who are willing to walk to the edge of rational thought in attempting to convince themselves of the inherent intellectual and social inferiority of blacks.[396]

The Pioneer Fund, a tax-exempt foundation, was incorporated in 1937 for the express purpose of research into "racial betterment." It is clear from the <u>research</u> that they produce that the Pioneer Fund <u>scholars</u> are pathologically devoid of rational thought on this issue. Their knowledge of African history, civilization, and culture is so obviously and profoundly lacking, that their attempts to establish racial hegemony are rather comical. Because they are so concrete and unimaginative, what they fear and project as African sexuality is in essence African vitality. It is unthinkable to these dour souls that a people that have been subjected to such persistent trauma are still filled with laughter, pride, and even optimism. So it was not surprising that J. Phillipe Rushton, a psychologist associated with the Pioneer Fund, and fellow psychologist Anthony F. Bogaert wrote "Population Differences in Susceptibility to AIDS: An Evolutionary Analysis," which appeared in a leading British Journal <u>Social Science and Medicine</u>. The abstract is a follows:

> Previously we have reported population differences in sexual restraint such that higher socio-economic status>lower socio-economic status, and Mongoloids>Caucasoids>Negroids. This ordering was predicted from a gene-based evolutionary theory of r/K reproductive strategies in which a trade-off occurs between gamete production and social behaviors such as intelligence, law abidingness, and parental care. Here we consider the implications of these analyses for sexual dysfunction, including susceptibility to AIDS. We conclude that relative to Caucasians, populations of Asian ancestry are inclined to a greater frequency of inhibitory disorders such as low sexual excitement and premature ejaculation and to a lower frequency of sexually transmitted diseases including AIDS, while populations of African ancestry are inclined to a greater frequency of uninhibited disorders such as rape and unintended pregnancy and to more sexually transmitted diseases including AIDS.[397]

---

396. Grace Lichtenstein, "Fund Backs Controversial Study of 'Racial Betterment,'" <u>New York Times</u>, 11 Dec. 1977.

397. J. P. Rushton and A.F. Bogaert, "Population Differences in Susceptibility to AIDS: An Evolutionary Analysis," <u>Soc Sci Med 28</u> (1989):1211–1220

To spend more time discussing such tripe is to give it more energy than it deserves, except to note that this is the type of pathology that passes for scientific observation in some of the most prestigious journals, especially as it relates to AIDS research. Suffice it to say, that articles such as this were strategically placed in the public domain to give the impression that intellectually inferior, sexually depraved, impulsive heterosexual Africans were the source of this new homosexual sex and blood plague.

Max Essex of Harvard first declared in the mid-1980s that the HIV virus had jumped species to man from the "African green monkey." Years later, it was proved that the first AIDS-like viruses in monkeys had been found by Max Essex in macaques, a monkey species primarily from Southeast Asia, not Africa. Essex, shamed by having his false theory found out, recanted, and admitted that the HI virus and the monkey virus were so different from each other that none of them could have been the ancestor of the other in a historical past. The damage was already done. Essex had succeeded in linking the African continent to the origin of this new disease pattern. The image was firmly implanted, and yet more was to come.

Nigel Hawkes, science editor for the Times (of London) said that if it was not the green monkey then it must "certainly" be the African chimpanzee, which being butchered for food, gave the virus to the man doing the butchering. It did not matter that most Africans have little contact with monkeys,[398] and among those who regularly hunt monkeys (for example, the pygmies of the equatorial rain forests) AIDS is notable for its absence.[399] Hawkes went on to claim, based on the thinnest of evidence of one positive antibody test from twenty-five year old frozen plasma, that "the disease was established for decades in Africa before it was recognized as a worldwide threat." It did not occur to him to ask for samples of stored blood from the United States and Europe to see if any of that blood was antibody positive before making this baseless pronouncement.

The first "positive" probes in Africa were found from more than 7,000 serum samples that dated only after the beginning of the eighties (1981–1982), well after the syndrome had shown up in the West.[400] It never occurred to the learned gentlemen of science and the press to posit the other question. Not how the disease got from Africa to the West, but how the disease got from the West to Africa? A monograph on HIV/AIDS from the National Institute of Allergy and Infectious Diseases indicates that studies of previously stored

398. R.J. Bigger, "The AIDS Problem in Africa," Lancet (1986): 72–82.
399. F.I.D. Konotey-Ahulu, "Group Specific Component and HIV Infection," Lancet (1987):1267.
400. Interview with Prof. G. Hunsmann. Monkey Business. Channel 4 Television, London 23:05 GMT, Jan. 22, 1990.

blood samples indicate that the <u>virus</u> entered the U.S. population sometime in the late 1970s. Further, why was it primarily in one very limited risk group in the U.S. and Europe but was an equal opportunity disease in Africa? Since the disease pattern was first identified in the United States, why were not researchers looking at stored blood in U.S. depositories for evidence of early viral presence in the population? The fix was in. It was going to be a blood and sex plague from Africa. That had to be the image that the world must have seared into the collective psyche and thus far, it has worked.

The syndrome was first recognized as a clinical entity in 1981 in the United States, but the case had to be made for Africa. An absolute cacophony of racial stereotypes spewed from the AIDS camp that clearly demonstrated that the pedigree of this <u>science</u> was the demon seed of past eugenicists. Before the monkey business, one of the first stories floated was the theory of the "lost tribe" who was said to have harbored the virus for centuries.[401] This made as much sense as the <u>Webster Dictionary</u> definition of <u>gorilla</u>. It was clear that these guys had grown up watching too many Tarzan movies. When the lost tribe story did not pan out, the monkeys were put into play.[402] When the monkey story fell apart, it was next blamed on the Haitians (but no one else) working in central Africa. It was posited that the Haitians must have acquired it by heterosexual sex, but on returning home to Haiti spread the disease to homosexual American tourists.[403] Luc Montagnier, the French virologist from whom Gallo swiped his original specimen piped in that the practice of female circumcision facilitates the spread of AIDS. He never accounted for the fact that Somalia, Ethiopia, Djibouti, and Sudan where female circumcision is most widespread, are among the countries with the lowest incidence of AIDS.

The CDC began to claim that Haitians as a group were at risk for AIDS along with homosexuals, intravenous drug users, and hemophiliacs. It was not until 1985 that the CDC, faced with overwhelming evidence that Haitians per se were no more at risk for AIDS than anyone else, conceded the point.[404] Again, more damage was heaped onto the Haitian community. Many had been dismissed from their jobs, evicted from their homes, and housed in separate prisons.

---

401. K. M. DeCock, "AIDS: An Old Disease from Africa?" <u>Br Med J, 289</u> (1984): 306–08,

402 V. M. Hirsch, et al., "An African Primate Letivirus (SIVsm) Closely Related to HIV-2," <u>Nature 339</u> (1989):389–92..

403. C.F. Farthing, et al., <u>A Colour Atlas of AIDS and HIV Disease 2nd ed.</u> (London: Wolfe Medical Publications, 1988).

404. A.E. Pichenik, T. J. Spira, et al., "Prevalence of HTLV/LAV Antibodies Among Haitians," <u>NEJM 312</u> (1985):1705.

Professor Nathan Clumeck of the Universite Libre in Brussels of all places had the temerity to claim in an interview with <u>Le Monde</u> that "sex, love and disease do not mean the same thing to Africans as they do to West Europeans because the notion of guilt doesn't exist in the same way as it does in the Judeo-Christian culture in the West."[405] Of course in this he is correct. Historically, before the installation of African puppets like Mobotu Sese Seku in Zaire, now the Congo, in thrall to the IMF and World Bank, no self-respecting African would think of turning his religion into a murder cult to justify the slaughter of half of his population and the enslavement of the rest as did the Belgium King Leopold II in the Congo in a period of about fifteen years.

In point of fact, there is little evidence to support Western obsession with the notion of African sexual promiscuity except as a projection of their own sexual habits. Widespread modesty codes for women, whose sexuality is considered a gift to be used for procreation, make many African societies seem chaste compared with the West. No one has ever shown that people in the so-called AIDS-belt of Rwanda, Uganda, Zaire, and Kenya are more active sexually than people in Nigeria or Cameroon, two countries with very low AIDS case rates.

In 1991, researchers from Médecins Sans Frontières and the Harvard School of Public Health conducted a survey of sexual behavior in the Moyo district of northwest Uganda. Their findings revealed behavior that was not very different from that of the West. On average, women had their first sex at age 17, men at 19. Eighteen percent of women and 50 percent of men reported premarital sex; 1.6 percent of the women and 4.1 percent of the men had casual sex in the month preceding the study, while 2 percent of women and 15 percent of men did so in the preceding year.[406] No national sex surveys have ever been carried out in Africa, yet AIDS researchers have assumed, based on the flimsiest of evidence, that heterosexual HIV transmission in Africa parallels the dynamics for HIV among homosexual men in the West. There is no scientific basis for this—NONE. Much of this work published in <u>reputable</u> journals was speculative, inflammatory, and overtly racist. And, as will be shown from multiple studies, HIV has never been shown to be transmitted sexually.

By 1985, the prevalence[407] of HIV began to decrease in all tested populations: military cohorts, the Job Corps, people tested at publicly

---

405. Charles L Geshekter, "Myths of AIDS and Sex," <u>New African,</u> October 1994.
406. Ibid.
407. The current number of people suffering from an illness in a year. Includes those diagnosed in prior years.

funded sites, and blood donors. The decrease was seen not only for those in disparate social groups, but also within them in both sexes and for all racial sub-categories.[408] This was rather curious because under the currently accepted view of HIV/AIDS, signs of infection by HIV—the antibodies detected by the HIV tests are irreversible. Therefore, the seroprevalence in a given population at a given time documents the cumulative infection among members of the population up to that time. Since the claim is that there is no way of curing the infection or of eliminating the virus, it follows that the total number of infected people can only increase, unless the numbers infected who die exceed the number being newly infected. Among the low risk population who test HIV positive, death from AIDS is quite rare. So a new trick was employed to keep the scam going and to dim the knowledge that for some who were HIV positive, it was a reversible condition. Just as AIDS was peaking, new categories were added to the catalogue of diseases.

As the symptom complex began to calm down among gay males in the mid- 1990s and classical AIDS was clearly on the decline, in 1993 the CDC began to tack on more diseases to keep the industry in business. That the predicted epidemic was declining would have been a financial disaster for the AIDS industry and the drug companies and their various propaganda organs. In 1993, they began to claim that a positive HIV test as well as recurrent bacterial pneumonia, pulmonary tuberculosis, recurrent pneumonia, invasive cervical cancer, and a T-cell count of less that 200 were now indicators for AIDS.

A low T-cell count is common in many syndromes and could result from pneumonia, kidney infections, infected wounds, malaria, sepsis, mononucleosis, tuberculosis, viral infections, diurnal variation, and normal pregnancy among other things. Asymptomatic HIV positives with a low T-cell count were now officially told that they had AIDS. Many of these new categories were also the same problems that cross reacted with the HIV antibody test and were now the diseases that were being added to the AIDS roster of indicator diseases. The CDC would brand people who had reversible diseases or were asymptomatic into their AIDS net as new antiretroviral drug customers. The pharmaceutical industry was ecstatic. Just as AIDS mortality was declining, the HIV antibody test began to rope more people into this trap. This speaks volumes to the intended iatrogenic nature of the problem.

As the projected AIDS pandemic was not materializing and the numbers began to rapidly decline among homosexual men, by the CDC adding these

---

408. D.S. Burke, et al., "Human Immunodeficiency Virus Infections in Teenagers—Seroprevalence among Applicants for U.S. Military Service," JAMA 263 (1990): 2074–77.

new categories, black women became a target group for the AIDS trap. The absurdity of claiming that cervical cancer was an HIV disease at the same time that they were claiming that it was an HPV disease (human papilloma virus) was idiotic. The CDC mounted another perception management campaign by claiming that black women were now the fastest growing group of AIDS patients—conflating HIV with AIDS. What the CDC did not say was that young black women were also one of the fastest growing groups of people using crack cocaine, and crack cocaine use just happened to be an independent variable for the development of many of these additional diseases they were now claiming were also caused by the elusive virus.

It has been shown that smoking crack damages the respiratory tract. This finding in crack smokers is even referred to as <u>crack lung</u>. Studies have also indicated that smoking crack cocaine is an independent variable for the development of tuberculosis.[409] Crack cocaine users are significantly more likely to have a positive Tb smear test than other drug users. Tuberculosis is one of the seventy other entities that cross react with the HIV antibody test. In addition, there are numerous reports of crack cocaine users developing interstitial pneumonitis, diffuse alveolar hemorrhage, and pulmonary edema.[410] Clearly, developing recurrent bacterial pneumonia is a consequence of chronic crack use and should indicate that the patient needs drug rehabilitation rather than anti-retroviral drugs.

Crack cocaine use has also been shown to be independently associated with an increased risk of having a Human Papilloma Virus infection associated with a high-grade squamous intraepithelial lesion (SIL) of the cervix.[411] Such SIL lesions are considered precursor lesions for cervical cancer. The rate of HPV clearance from the cervix was not related to cocaine use, but the clearance of any SIL abnormality was significantly lower in those who had recently used crack/cocaine compared with those who did not use. Again, this study showed that crack cocaine use is independently associated with cervical cancer precursor lesions, which are less likely to resolve with persistent use. The treatment of a crack cocaine user with a high-grade cervical lesion or invasive cervical cancer is an appropriate surgical procedure and metabolic compensation and detoxification, not antiretroviral therapy.

409. Alister Story et al., "Crack Cocaine and Infectious Tuberculosis," <u>Emerg Inf Dis,</u> September 2008

410   A.E. O'Donnell, et al., "Interstitial Pneumonitis Associated with 'Crack' Cocaine Abuse," <u>Chest</u> <u>100</u> (1991): 1155–57.

411. Howard Minkoff et al., "The Relationship Between Cocaine Use and Human Papilloma Virus Infection in HIV Sero-Positive and HIV Sero-Negative Women," <u>Inf Dis in Obs Gyn 2008</u>, Article ID 587082.

Both human and animal studies document that cocaine alters the function of natural killer (NK) cells, T cells, neutrophils and macrophages, and alters the ability of these cells to secrete immunoregulatory cytokines.[412] It was shown that cocaine has a direct immuno-suppressive effect on T and B lymphocytes, natural killer cells, and macrophages.[413] Here again, if appropriate studies were performed without a bias toward HIV anticipation, it might be made abundantly clear that crack cocaine independently has an adverse effect on the immune system and the suppression of CD4 T helper cells.

By inference and geographical origin it was not much of a stretch for the CDC to begin to sweep black women in the United States into their dragnet of the blood/sex plague. The work of planting the seeds to link the disease to primates and Africans had already been done. Because it is claimed that AIDS is a heterosexual problem in Africa, it was a small step to make the jump from AIDS being primarily a homosexual disease in the West to its becoming a heterosexual disease in black American women. If the disease was sexually transmitted, why was no one asking why white women who were equally, if not more sexually active, were not equally at risk? Because young black women in the AIDS category are another subset of the drug culture was simply more fodder to imply that because of the exchange of sex for drugs, it was sex and not drugs that was the cause of the problem.

Several other social phenomena also began to be floated as unique problems in black urban culture to explain the increasing number of black women being diagnosed with AIDS. One was the idea of the down-low male. Being on the down-low is descriptive of a man who pretends to be heterosexual while simultaneously having sexual relationships with other men. More will be said about this. Another factor was the number of black men who were incarcerated and were said to have contracted AIDS by having sex with other male inmates. However, this was another unfounded assumption, because in the mid-1990s only 16 percent of state prison systems had mandatory testing for HIV, and no major jail system had mandatory HIV testing. Furthermore, a review of studies done on the transmission of HIV while imprisoned did

---

412. G.C. Baldwin, M.D. Roth, D.P. Taskin, "Acute and Chronic Effects of Cocaine on the Immune System and the Possible Link to AIDS," J Neuroimmunology 83 (1998):133–38..

413   W. Xu, T.Flick, et al., "Cocaine Effects on Immunocompetent Cells: An Observation of in Vitro Cocaine Exposure," Int J Immunoopharm 21 (1999): 463–72. [Author, et al. is usually used with the first author's name only. I did not change it because I am not sure why you did not follow the rule}.

not confirm a high infectively rate.[414] Those going to prison, because of the high number of drug users in this population are, however, 5 to 7 times at greater risk of being HIV positive than the general population. This does not necessarily indicate sexual transmission because most of the excess prison increase is due to the increase in drug arrests.

The states that give the highest donations to presidential candidates are Texas, California, New York, and Florida. The states that have more drug money laundering and drugs flowing across their borders are Texas, California, New York, and Florida. The states that have the highest number of positive HIV tests and AIDS cases in correctional institutions are Texas, California, New York, Florida, and New Jersey.[415] The drugs–AIDS hypothesis is no mystery, but the importation of illegal drugs is a big money issue and is not going away in the near term.

Uncovering the reality of the drugs–AIDS hypothesis, as has been shown, uncovers the underbelly of the entire free trade globalization fiasco and its real consequences for real people. As has been well documented, the international drug trade represents 6 to 8 percent of the world economy. An investigation into the control of the drug trade starting at the top of the pyramid would uncover the deepest and darkest secrets of America's economic and political elite. Gary Webb paid for his exposure of the Iran-Contra affair with his life. Katherine Austin Fitts was physically and legally harassed to the point of losing a substantial fortune. Mike Ruppert, a Los Angeles detective, was drummed out of his job when he refused to participate in documented CIA drug running. AIDS has to be thought of as a sexually transmitted and blood born disease to protect this industry and the elite riff-raff who benefit from spreading misery to ordinary Americans who tolerate it.

It has not been difficult to associate black women with AIDS because the Western psyche had been prepared to accept black women as the new reservoir of a blood and sex disease. It was easy to make this leap. This obvious Freudian projection arose from the psyche of an earlier slave-holding society that sexually exploited black women at will. The political right portrays black women as <u>welfare queens</u> and crack <u>hos</u>. The political left portrays them as powerless victims of a patriarchal society. Both factions are paternalistically clueless. However, such notions are seared into the national consciousness by the portrayal of black women in the media.

414. Kate Dolan, "AIDS, Drugs and Risk Behavior in Prison: State of the Art," National Drug and Alcohol Research Center, Univ. of New South Whales, Sydney, Australia, [Date?].

415 National Research Council, <u>The Social Impact of AIDS in the United States</u> (Washington, DC: National Academies Press, 1993),180.

The music industry, controlled at the top by white males, has made millionaires of blacks who, willingly, in Rap videos and lyrics, portray black women in the most overtly sexual and degrading ways. Scantily clad, young and dumb black women gyrate to the disconnected and discordant rhythms of urban rappers who add to the viciousness by referring in their lyrics to young black women—their sisters and mothers of their children—as Bs and Hs. Many of the young women give tacit support to their animalistic portrayal in this obscene way by writhing wildly in music videos and on dance floors and by failing to mount any significant protest against the music industry which depicts them in this thoughtless and degrading manner. While the rest of the world makes the connection of easy sexuality that such images portray, many young black women remain willfully clueless as they listen and buy songs that diminish their humanity and their worth. The reference to black women as Bs and Hs became so customary that white disc jockey and television personality Don Imus casually used these terms in the national broadcast media to refer to black women. The situation finally exploded when Imus referred to the women of a winning Rutgers University basketball team in these demeaning terms and subsequently lost his job.

Max Essex had done his part. The damage was precise. The association of monkey with black women had been made when Gallo and Montagnier, the early creators of the HIV-causes-AIDS myth, started postulating that there was some connection between AIDS, and an African green monkey biting the butt of an African woman. The mindset and mental connection were already firmly planted in the Western psyche. It did not matter that there was no naturally occurring AIDS virus in monkeys,[416] or that no monkeys have died from what has been called <u>AIDS blood</u>. It did not matter that it would be statistically impossible for a single episode, such as a monkey biting some person, or some person eating a wild monkey, to have created a worldwide problem identified almost simultaneously in the United States, Europe, Africa, Brazil, and Haiti. It did not matter that 90 percent of the original cases in the United States were homosexuals, that the cases in Africa were heterosexual, and that the disease categories were quite different in different geographical areas.

The link was made between black women and AIDS, and so when the CDC claimed that young black women were being diagnosed with HIV, no one lifted an eyebrow in disbelief, and no one asked if a positive HIV test would always lead to AIDS. The leaders in the black community, right on cue, like Margaret Sanger's Negroes from her Negro Project, mouthed

---

416. Simian immunodeficiency virus, first identified in 1985 in laboratory rhesus monkeys.

the propaganda and ignored the science that was strongly against HIV being sexually transmitted and strongly for the HIV problem as a subset of the drug problem. They refused to make the connection between the toxicity of the drugs that were being dumped in their communities and the physiological damage created by the use of these poisons. They looked at the social and economic costs of these drugs. They overlooked the medical consequences and believed the tales of a medical system that was, once again, being used as a silent weapon against their community. It was easier to grab onto the illusion of an attack virus. This made sense because it was another slippery road out of self-responsibility. It was a way of not confronting the problems at the core of the opium/cocaine business and of the consequences of globalization and deindustrialization. It was a way of not looking at the crumbling infrastructure and the boarded up buildings and understanding their true cause. It was a way of not looking at the dumbing down that was taking place in crumbling prison-like schools. It was a way of avoiding the look of restless ennui on the faces of the overfed and undernourished children. Everything was connected. Unfortunately, the elite were thinking globally, and the black community was thinking locally. All politics had become global. National and individual sovereignty were meaningless words.

Black ministers, many of whom just a generation before had marched with Dr. King for the promotion of civil rights but turned fearfully from Dr. King when he began to talk about human rights, have become <u>confused</u> in their mission because of the influx of faith- based money. Many are uncritically accepting the HIV doctrine as truth. It gives them something to preach about at Sunday service. The black community has a plethora of grievances. Until the <u>faith-based</u> money started flowing, homosexuality was not one of them.

The idea that the down-low phenomenon was a uniquely black problem was promoted by Oprah on her daytime show when she hosted J.L. King, author of <u>On the Down Low: A Journey into the Lives of "Straight" Black Men who Sleep with Men</u>. The idea that this was somehow a specifically black phenomenon became linked to the rising tide of black women who were becoming HIV positive. Another cultural stereotype was being promoted on national television as uniquely specific to the black community. Oprah, however pure of heart, was doing her part in support of this cultural stereotype.

This cultural <u>aberration</u> was jettisoned into the mainstream in such a way that another viral meme infected the minds of the masses. A disease which was so pronounced in the largely Caucasian homosexual community was suddenly springing up in a new subpopulation— black woman. The number of black women in the early AIDS cohort was virtually zero but rose to 55/100,000 from 2000–2003. This was about a five- year lag time after the peak of the crack cocaine epidemic.

By ignoring lifestyle factors, the CDC has done such harm to medicine that it will take decades to recover from this damage. Just like that, the disease was divorced from lifestyle, antecedent risk factors, drug use, starvation, parasitic disease, mycoplasma, and vaccines. It has been an absolutely brilliant use of medicine for military, political, and economic purposes, but it has little if anything to do with medicine, except as another vehicle for the transmission of fear. The fact that the down-low phenomenon is not in any way a uniquely black sexual pattern [417] and that the original cohort of AIDS cases was predominantly white and male was conveniently forgotten. Why were white women not testing positive at the same or greater rate?

The supporters of the HIV theory posit that HIV is spread primarily through sex—vaginal and anal—or through tainted blood and shared needles. To understand that HIV is unlikely to be an infectious process, Roy Anderson, a professor of zoology in the U.K., has reviewed the characteristics of infectious disease epidemiology in an article, "The Spread of HIV and Sexual Mixing Patterns." According to Anderson, "The historical and epidemiological literature abounds with accounts of infectious diseases invading human communities and of their impact on social organization and historical events. We typically think of a new epidemic in a 'virgin' population as something that arises suddenly sweeps through the population in a few months, and then wanes and disappears. Indeed, the classical epidemic curve for many respiratory or intestinal tract viral and bacterial infections is bell shaped, with an overall duration of a few months to a year or so." (See figure below) This has not been the case for HIV. Infectious epidemics have a very different community spread pattern as opposed to chemical, physical, or non-contagious substances:

Characteristics of Viral and Microbial Epidemics

1. As originally described by William Farr in the early 19th century, infectious epidemics rise exponentially and then decline within weeks or months. The rise reflects the exponential spread of contagion, and the fall reflects the resulting natural immunity of survivors.
2. The epidemics spread randomly (heterosexually) in the population.
3. The resulting infectious diseases are <u>highly specific, reflecting the limited genetic information of the causative microbe</u>. As a consequence, viral diseases (viruses have much less genetic material

---

417. Senator Larry Craig and Governor Jim McGreevy of N.J. come to mind

than bacteria) are typically more specific than those caused by more complex bacteria or fungi. It is for this reason that the viruses and microbes are typically named for the specific diseases they cause. For example, influenza virus is called after the flu, polio virus after poliomyelitis, and hepatitis virus after the liver disease it causes. (There is not enough genetic information in a retrovirus to cause twenty-nine different diseases.)

4. Microbial and particularly viral epidemics are self-limiting and therefore typically seasonal, because they induce antimicrobial and viral immunity and select also genetically resistant hosts.

Characteristics of Diseases Caused by Non-Contagious, Chemical or Physical Stressors

1. The time course is determined by the dose and duration of the exposure to the toxin.
2. The spread accords with consumption or exposure to toxic agents, but not exponentially.
3. They spread either non-randomly with occupational or lifestyle factors, or randomly with environmental or nutritional factors.
4. They range from relatively specific to unspecific symptoms depending on the nature of the toxin.
5. They are limited by discontinuation of intoxication, but not self-limiting because they do not generate immunity.

The spread of HIV fits this latter pattern.

The pellagra epidemic of the rural South in the early part of the 20th century followed the pattern of a non-contagious disease. This scourge lasted decades, and no immunity emerged until a diet rich in niacin was recommended. The disease did not spread into the industrial North, nor was the disease seen in the doctors and nurses who cared for the malnourished patients. The eugenicists continued to pitch that pellagra was an infectious disease and hid the information that it was a nutritional deficiency for twenty years. The spread of pellagra was the typical pattern for a disease caused by an environmental stressor. In the case of pellagra, the environmental stressor was a niacin deficiency resulting from malnutrition. In the case of AIDS, it is largely a glutathione deficiency as a result of oxidative stressors.[418]

---

418. Freya Q. Shafer, and Garry R. Vuetner, "Redox Environment of the Cell As Viewed Through the Redox State of the Glutathione Disulfide/Glutathione

When speaking of Africa, the emphasis on underlying metabolic abnormalities becomes very important because AIDS existentialists claim that AIDS dissidents must be wrong because they stress the causative agent in the West is primarily drugs. Of course, drugs are not yet a widespread problem in Africa, ergo, they jump to the conclusion that the dissidents are wrong. This line of reasoning is easily rebutted. AIDS dissidents are targeting drugs as an environmental stressor, just as malnutrition, poverty, social disruption, and chronic recurrent infections are environmental stressors in Africa. The key is that the epidemiological pattern of HIV is explained by external toxins which may vary in nature from place to place and thus be the root cause of the variety of disease patterns under the rubric of AIDS. Neither epidemiology nor science supports the idea that HIV patterns demonstrate an infectious process.

Characteristics of the American AIDS Epidemic

1. It rose steadily, not exponentially, and plateaued at about a million cases over the course of twenty years.
2. It was biased 85–90 percent in favor of homosexual males.
3. It followed the onslaught of the overuse of recreational drugs and then the extensive use of antiviral AIDS drugs.
4. It does not manifest in one or a few specific diseases typical of microbial epidemics. It manifests as a spectrum of twenty-nine non-specific diseases.
5. It has not spread to the general population of non-drug users.

These are clues and rather strong ones at that for AIDS being a toxic rather than an infectious process.

Characteristics of Sexually Transmitted Diseases

Sexually transmitted diseases or STDs are caused by a variety of organisms that are transmitted from person to person primarily but not exclusively by sexual activity. The diseases can be irritating, debilitating, painful, the cause of infertility, and life threatening. More than twenty STDs have been identified. Such bacterial diseases include syphilis, gonorrhea, chancroid, and granuloma inguinale. Chlamydia, another bacterium, causes lymphogranuloma venereum. Infection with Chlamydia can be silent and without overt symptoms but can lead to scarring of the fallopian tubes and

---

Couple," Free Radical Biology & Medicine 30 (2001):1191–1212.

increased risk of ectopic pregnancy in the fallopian tube (a potentially life-threatening problem), and infertility.

Mycoplasma species are bacteria that are missing a cell wall and are the smallest of self-replicating organisms. Mycoplasma species are often found in women who are experiencing problems with conceiving. A pathogenic mycoplasma has also been patented (#5242820) by Dr. Shyh-Ching Lo, a United States government scientist, and filed on 6 June 1991, with the United States Patent Office. According to Lo's patent, this "novel pathogenic mycoplasma" was isolated from patients with AIDS and, in fact, can cause many of the symptoms associated with AIDS. It should be noted that it is this mycoplasma organism that the co-discoverer of the HIV antibody technique, Luc Montaganier of the Paris Pasteur Institute, now says is the co-factor that is necessary to produce the various diseases found in the AIDS complex.[419] He has stated, "There are too many shortcomings in the theory that HIV causes all signs of AIDS." The fact that one of the original proponents of the HIV/AIDS theory has begun to doubt the capacity of HIV to be the causative agent of such a plethora of diseases has not slowed the AIDS juggernaut.

There are several viral STDs: herpes simplex 1 and 2 and human papilloma virus HPV, which causes genital warts. Molluscum contagiosum is caused by a DNA virus, and finally, there is hepatitis B virus. Trichomonis is caused by a protozoan, and pediculosis pubis is caused by a louse. All of these diseases have a high rate of infectivity and vary from 30 to 60 percent infectivity after one contact. Studies have shown, as will be discussed below, that HIV cannot be easily transmitted by sexual activity.

Sexually transmitted diseases can usually be tracked to an epicenter. The disease spreads into the population from this center, rises rapidly, and then reaches a plateau or begins to decline depending on the effectiveness of therapy, the natural immunity of the population, and public health measures. The rate of growth is exponential, and if restricted by medication, the natural immunity of the population and/or public health measures resembles the graph below.

---

419. Michael Balter, "Montagnier Pursues the Mycoplasma–AIDS Link," <u>Science</u>, 1991.

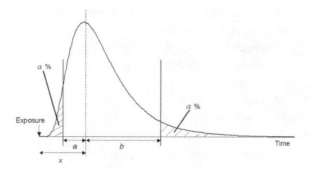

With this in mind, let us revisit the initial outbreak of what was termed AIDS in the United States. The original cases were all centered on three major urban areas: New York, San Francisco, and Los Angeles. Until recently, 90 percent of all AIDS cases were male and homosexual. The early population was also largely Caucasian males. It is estimated that 20 percent of the homosexual population is bisexual or on the down-low. It stands to reason from that information alone that if in fact HIV was a sexually transmitted disease, then the spread of cases should have been to white females in these three urban areas. This never happened. That the prevalence of HIV positives is now largely concentrated in communities of color in the North East and in wide areas of the South Eastern United States should raise some pertinent questions concerning the epidemiology of this problem. The spread outside the original contact areas but not inside the contact areas, except for New York, is simply not consistent with a sexually- transmitted disease or an infectious process.

Drug use is a greater predictor of female sex workers having AIDS than the consequence of their work. This has been true of studies done on female sex workers from Harlem to Holland and even China. From Russia, another study looking at the rate of HIV infection in prostitutes came to the same conclusion. In St. Petersburg, 48 percent of female sex workers are HIV positive, and 96 percent are IV drug users. By contrast, in Moscow, only 15 per cent of prostitutes are HIV positive, of whom 12 percent are IV drug users. In Moscow, the women are organized under pimps and madams who limit the use of drugs, whereas St. Petersburg is a freelance city.[420]

Prostitution is not even listed as an HIV risk category by the CDC because of the extremely low incidence of HIV transmission to clients who have no other risk factors, such as drug abuse. This underscores the observation that it is the content of the needles, not the sharing of dirty needles that is so

---

420. Simone Kozuharov, "Russia: Half of all Prostitutes in City Have HIV," St. Petersburg Times, 22 April 2004.

hazardous to health. This is further confirmed by observations on rehabilitated intravenous drug users (IDUs). Among those who had completed treatment and remained drug free, the frequency of HIV was less than half that among addicts who had just begun detoxification treatment. For those who had remained drug free for more than a year, the frequency of HIV was one-fourth of that among former IDUs who had remained drug free for less than a year.[421] This indicates that HIV positive status is a reversible condition.

Overall, sexually transmitted diseases have another characteristics pattern that the HIV pattern defies. STDs are more commonly seen in adolescents than in young and middle-aged adults. HIV is just the opposite. It is more common in young and middle- aged adults.[422]

Finally, like the medical workers who did not succumb to pellagra, medical workers who get multiple unintended needle sticks and exposure to blood and serum have not succumbed to HIV. Most medical workers who have been diagnosed with AIDS have risk factors that would explain their problems beyond any occupational hazard.

What sexually transmitted disease has a predilection for black females? The answer is none—until now. Whatever the HIV test is measuring, it is not sexually transmitted, nor is it necessarily lethal. Long-term non-progressors are often excluded from the conversation.

Other than being transmitted by sex—vaginal, oral, or anal—STDs have several other common characteristics: They are highly efficient in their transmission ratios—sometimes as high as 80 percent with one contact. STDs also cause the same disease from person to person. (Remember that there is no AIDS or HIV disease—there are twenty-nine already existing diseases, with various etiologies, that have been clumped together in people who develop symptoms of AIDS after testing HIV positive.) If any of such so-called AIDS diseases appeared in someone who was HIV negative, it would just be that disease. For example, Positive HIV test + tuberculosis = AIDS; negative HIV test + tuberculosis = tuberculosis. It is the same disease with a name change. In Robert Gallo's original research there was only a 36 percent correlation between so-called AIDS patients and the test to prove that they were HIV positive. MOST OF THE AIDS PATIENTS IN THE ORIGINAL RESEARCH WERE NOT HIV POSITIVE. With this new definition of AIDS, there is now conveniently a virtual one to one correlation—rather like a self-fulfilling prophecy. Only those people who

421. Moss, A. R., et al., "(1994) "HIV serconversion in intravenous drug users in San Francisco, 1985-90," AIDS, 8, 223-231

422. Wendell, D. A. et. al., "Youth at Risk: sex, drugs and human immunodeficiency virus" American Journal of Diseases of Children (1992) 146; 76-81

have a positive HIV test will be said to have an <u>AIDS</u> disease, whereas those with a negative HIV test will have whatever the diagnosis happens to be—even though in reality they both have the same disease.

Because of the virus hype by the CDC and the drug industry, flummoxed physicians will overlook the metabolic status of the patient; continue to pump the drugs that compromise the patient's metabolic status further until the patient has a serious complication, or death ensues. The doctor will then write on the death certificate, not death by medicine, arrogance, and ignorance, but death by AIDS. <u>Ego te absolvo.</u> (I absolve myself from any sense of duty or responsibility).

Although some STDs produce different symptoms in men from those in women, when investigated, there is a fairly equal carrier status distribution among the sexes. The diseases do not vary in a regular manner with age, race, and geography as does HIV.

It was claimed that the transmission was heterosexual in Africa and had something to do with African women and green monkeys. The green monkey story is a clue to the trademark and archetypal energy that promoted the infectious pellagra theory by the eugenics movement long after it was proven to be a vitamin deficiency. From the beginning, HIV was a construct, an idea that the original eugenics crowd would have been proud to propagate just as their reincarnate energy has done with great success. HIV/AIDS plays on every racist and sexist stereotype in Western culture. It was a propagandist's dream disease—a plague on homosexuals and now blacks.

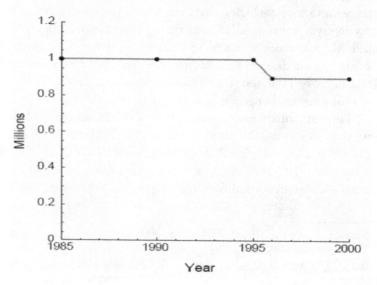

Prevalence of HIV in U.S. population

Padian Study: Why HIV Has Been Shown Not To Be Sexually Transmitted

Nancy Padian and a research group from the University of California at San Francisco published a ten-year prospective study in the <u>American Journal of Epidemiology</u> in which they looked at the rate of transmission of HIV in serodiscordant heterosexual couples—one partner was positive and the other negative—(82 infected women and their partners and 360 infected men and their partners). Her findings have turned the AIDS establishment into defensive name calling and sputtering idiocy in their attempt to reinterpret the findings from this well-designed study. This long-term prospective study provides no evidence that HIV is sexually transmitted. The study, in fact, provides convincing evidence to the contrary. The Padian group found that the efficiency of HIV is so low by sexual means that one must find another reason to question why any HIV test is positive.

The Padian study was done in Northern California and most of the participants were white and aware of their HIV status. Condoms were used but not consistently. Padian found that the male to female transmission was seven to nine times more efficient than the female to male. The male to female contact infectivity was .0009 or 1 in 1000 contacts. If sex occurred every three days with this transmission rate, it would take from six to twenty-four years to be transmitted from male to female. That also means that the female to male efficiency would be approximately 1 in 9000 contacts and take from 51 to 222 years to transmit this disease! The female to male infectivity was so low as not to be statistically significant. This is not the characteristic of a sexually transmitted disease. Even the CDC has commented that "the transmission probabilities are so low that it becomes difficult to understand the magnitude of the HIV-1 pandemic." One must question why they persist in their belief that HIV is a sexually transmitted disease when confronted with facts to the contrary.

Another study looking at the sexual partners of hemophiliacs from the <u>Archives of Internal Medicine</u> concluded: "The most likely value of the probability of infection within 26 months for this group of sexual partners is <u>zero</u>." (Emphasis added) Accordingly, hemophiliacs who are HIV positive are not transmitting the HIV positive status to their partners.

The simple mechanics of viral infection is a distinct improbability in hemophiliacs. The clotting factor that they use to prevent bleeding is cell free. The identified cell-free viruses are without knobs on their outer coat. The lack of knobs, according to current theory, leaves these <u>viruses</u> without a mechanical means of attaching to any cell surface. Attaching to the cell surface is the necessary first step for the virus to enter the cell to infect it. Furthermore, the clotting factor comes as a dried powder—an environment in which, according to virology studies, the virus could not survive. Clearly, hemophiliacs are not getting infected with the clotting factor blood product. They are, however, through chronic use of clotting factors, getting large doses of foreign protein. The humoral immune system naturally responds to foreign proteins with an elevated antibody response. Because hemophiliacs have much higher circulating antibodies than normal individuals, they are more likely to have cross-reacting antibodies on the <u>HIV</u> antibody test.

In a longitudinal study of HIV transmission done for the European Study Group on Heterosexual Transmission of HIV, Isabelle De Vincenzi conducted another prospective study of HIV negative subjects whose only risk of HIV infection was a stable heterosexual relationship with an HIV-infected partner. Like Padian, De Vincenzi found that the rate of transmission per contact was 1 per 1000.

A <u>meta</u> analysis is a collection and comparison of data from a range of studies that concentrate on a single topic. A meta analysis of data from North American and European studies of heterosexual couples substantiates the per sex act of 1 transmission of approximately 1 in 1000. A paper, "Viral Burden in Genital Secretions Determines Male to Female Transmission of HIV 1: A Probabilistic Empiric Model", states that "the probability of per-partner sexual transmission has been examined in 11 different studies, whereas the per sex act probability of transmission has been reported in 13 studies. The probability of transmission of HIV-1 from male to female during an episode of intercourse has been examined in seven of these studies. Analysis of data from North American and European studies of heterosexual couples provide estimates of per sex act of HIV-1 transmission of approximately 1 in 1000 (0.0001, ranging from 0.0008 to 0.0002), although the magnitude of the HIV-1 epidemic would argue that these estimates might be unreasonably low."[423] An alternative conclusion that HIV was not a sexually transmitted virus, but a marker for oxidative stress was never entertained.

In simple terms, the absurdity of stating that HIV is a sexually transmitted virus amounts to this:

- Having sex every day for three years would not be enough to ensure a single transmission;
- Co-habiting couples who engage in sex twice a week would take 10 years;
- If they had 10 sex acts a day it would take 100 days;
- If they had sex 50 times a day it would take twenty days

---

423. H. Chakraborty et al., <u>AIDS</u> 15 (2001): 621–27.

Even by European fantasies about African sexual prowess, this is a bit of a stretch to justify calling the situation a sexual pandemic. Perhaps the African males whom a Council on Foreign Relations report claim engendered the global AIDS pandemic and will plunge the world into wars, famine, and devastation are a godlike breed who have Olympian sexual powers far beyond their American and European counterparts. More likely, however, the global AIDS pandemic is another delusional fantasy emanating from the fetid minds and the ghosts that haunt Cold Spring Harbor.

AIDS Transmission In Africa

The WHO has promoted the idea from the very beginning of the AIDS scare that the so- called African AIDS epidemic was a matter of heterosexual transmission. Yet again, a study from Uganda, the African epicenter, found the probability of HIV transmission per sex act comparable to other populations, suggesting that HIV infectivity of subtypes cannot explain the explosive epidemic in Africa. The idea that sex explains 90 percent of African HIV does not fit the facts. Sexual practices in areas with the highest rates of infection were no different from those with low rates of infection. Infants of HIV negative mothers tested positive for HIV as did individuals with no sexual exposure. The AIDS existentialists have no explanation for these findings.

Heterosexual couples in Africa were found to be no more likely to transmit the virus to each other than their European and American counterparts. Given this information, whatever is being tested for cannot possibly be the result of a sexually transmitted disease. Thus, other possibilities must be considered.

What is being called HIV in Africa is what is known in the marketing trade as rebranding. It is the medicalization of poverty. A 1994 study from central Africa reported that the microbes responsible for tuberculosis and leprosy were so prevalent that over 70 percent of the HIV positive test results are false. The study also showed that HIV antibody tests register positive in HIV free people whose immune systems are compromised for a wide variety of reasons, including chronic parasitic infections and anemia brought on by malaria.[424]

---

424. O. Kashala, et al., "Infection with human immunodeficiency virus type 1 (HIV-1) and human T cell lymphotropic viruses among leprosy patients and contacts: correlation between HIV-1 cross-reactivity and antibodies to lipoarabinomannan", J Infect Dis 1995 Feb;171(2):502-4

Africans are dying of poverty, treatable infectious diseases, and the social disruption brought on by the very people who run guns and mercenaries into the continent and have a stake in making the world believe that Africa is dying from AIDS and not the result of the Washington Consensus.

Social disruption cannot be underestimated as a factor in disease causation. There are seven negative emotional states of the human mind that interfere seriously with oxidative metabolism, immune function, and digestion. They are fatigue, grief, disappointment, fear, anger, hate, and frustration. Psychoneuroimmunologist Candice Pert has coined the term molecules of emotion. Her research has shown that negative emotions can act as toxins by producing neuropeptides, little messenger proteins, that correspond to these feelings. Her radical discovery was that every neuropeptide receptor found in the brain is also on the surface of the human monocyte, one of the white blood cells of the immune system. Emotion-affecting peptides appear to control the routing and migration of monocytes, which are pivotal to the overall health of the organism. They communicate with other lymphocytes, called B cells and T cells, by interacting through peptides called cytokines, lymphokines, chemokines, and interleukins and their receptors. They thus enable the immune system to launch a well-coordinated attack against disease. When environmental toxins or toxic thoughts are presented to the human system, the oxidation energy system is usually able to neutralize the oxidants by means of the thiol/glutathione network. Over time, bombardment of the system with mental and physical stressors, the cellular respiratory process and then the immunity process becomes overwhelmed and impaired. This is the process that the medical establishment calls disease, and some of the diseases have been defined as acquired immunodeficiency syndrome.

Thabo Mbeki, former president of South Africa, knew what was really killing his people. When he questioned the HIV paradigm, he was blasted into silence by the medical priesthood and their spies from the Epidemic Intelligence Service who masquerade as journalists. Most of Africa also knows that AIDS is just another gift from white men with imperial aspirations. They have seen this before.

The 16th International AIDS Conference was held in Toronto, Canada, in August 2006. The theme of that year's conference was "Time to Deliver." Not surprisingly, since so little has been delivered to the African continent, not one African leader, according to the New York Times, attended this session. President Ellen Johnson Sirleaf of Liberia canceled her scheduled talk a week before the conference. This quiet boycott marked a turning point and a pivotal juncture for Africa in the wholesale acceptance of the HIV causes AIDS paradigm. It is the equivalent of Rosa Parks not moving from her seat in the back of the bus. It was revolutionary!

The HIV/AIDS construct is the fulfillment of Henry Kissinger's NSSM 200 and The Project for a New American Century document "Rebuilding America's Defenses." The signers of this document, in addition to calling for open warfare on the people of the Middle East, called for the use of "advanced forms of biological warfare that can 'target' specific genotypes . . . which may transform biological warfare from the realm of terror to a politically useful tool." In other words, they are seeking to commit another reign of terror on an unsuspecting civilian population. Intentions are causative and precede action. They already have.

Whatever <u>HIV</u> is, it is not a sexually transmitted disease, but it is just business.

Chapter 14

What You Don't Know About the HIV Antibody Test Can Kill You

o o o o o o o o o o o o o o o o o o o o o o o o o o o o o

But, under the Roosevelt aegis, a half dozen agencies of the Federal Government were turned over to the Rockefeller Drug Trust to do with as they willed. . . .The FDA . . . is very assiduous in putting out of business any and all vendors of therapeutic devices which increase the health incidence of the public and thus decrease the profit incidence of the Drug Trust. . . . The American Medical Association is the front for the Drug Trust.

Morris A. Bealle, <u>Super Drug Story</u>

The quacks who peddle worthless cures for profit kill thousands of people. The quacks who peddle pseudoscientific myths about the causes and cures of medically and socially preventable disorders kill and maim millions...The only difference between both groups of quacks is in their motivation. The peddlers of fake "cures" do it, in most instances, to make a dishonest if comfortable living. They know they are crooks, and would never dream of using any of their own "remedies." The peddlers of pseudosciences spread their propaganda because, as a rule, they are true believers in eugenics and/or related other branches of scientific racism.

Allan Chase, <u>The Legacy of Malthus</u>

Most importantly, to date nobody has proven the existence of the whole HIV genome in fresh, uncultured lymphocytes from AIDS patients. Furthermore...the finding of novel RNAs in human cells, especially those of AIDS patients and those at risk, is not proof that the RNA has been exogenously introduced by HIV or any other infectious agents.

The Perth Group, Mother to Child Transmission of HIV and Its Prevention with AZT and Neviriprine

In 1972, Congress established the OTA (Office of Technology Assessment) to serve the legislative branch as an independent source of information and analysis about complex scientific and technical issues. OTA construed health technology broadly, including "all elements of medical practice that are knowledge-based, including hardware (equipment and facilities) and software (knowledge skills) . . . the set of techniques, drugs, equipment, and procedures used by health-care professionals in delivering medical care to individuals and the systems within which such care is delivered."[425]

By 1978, the OTA produced a shattering report on the state of scientific medicine, Assessing the Efficacy and Safety of Medical Technologies. The report concluded that only 10 to 20 percent of what is done in modern American medicine has any scientific underpinning, and technologies are constantly being introduced to the market without proof of merit. That 20 percent may have been an underestimation, but the point was brought home that the business interests of the medical industrial complex were skyrocketing the costs of healthcare by the introduction of advanced technology that had lots of bells and whistles at inflated costs but offered little in the way of measurable improvement in patient outcomes.

In 1960, healthcare costs represented 5.2 percent of the Gross National Product (GNP). By 1978, when this report was completed, that number had risen to 9 percent. Today it is at 16 percent and expected to climb to 20 percent by 2015. In the span of about 15 years from when the HMO boondoggle was unleashed on America, the cost of health care almost tripled from $750 billion a year to $2.6 trillion. Not only is this acceleration unsustainable, there is a growing inverse relationship between total healthcare expenditures and the general heath status of the population. The more money we pay, the worse the health parameters are becoming. Something is very wrong.

Some of the new technologies and inventions introduced to the market after little or no scientific evaluation have had disastrous effects. This certainly

---

425. Office of Technology Assessment, "Development of Medical Technology,". 4.

has been true with the HIV tests and drugs. The leading cause of death today among HIV positive people is not one of the AIDS defining diseases, but end stage liver disease that is caused by the anti-retroviral drugs.

As discussed previously, Gallo never isolated a distinct virus HIV and as will be shown, it is not surprising that the glyco-proteins that are claimed to be HIV proteins have all been shown to identify cellular components or parts of other infectious agents commonly found in these patients. Dr. Matthew Gonda, head of the Electron Microscopy Laboratory at the National Cancer Institute unequivocally told Gallo before he published his papers in <u>Science</u> that became the basis for the HIV causes AIDS theory, that the specimens he sent for identification were nothing more than cellular debris without an identifiable virus. Gallo even admitted at a 1994 meeting sponsored by the U.S. National Institute of Drug Abuse: "We have never found HIV DNA in T-cells."[426]

Being forewarned that he had not demonstrated viral isolation, Gallo nevertheless rushed the HIV antibody test to patent <u>before</u> his four papers claiming that HTLV-III (HIV) was the <u>probable</u> cause of immune deficiency were published in <u>Science</u>. What is not as well known is that in previous papers, he had stated that similar retroviruses HTLV-I and HTLV-II were causing rare forms of leukemia—a cellular proliferative disease. They turned out not to be cancer viruses but benign passenger viruses. Gallo initially called HIV, HTLV-III and claimed that it was the same type of virus as HTLV I and HTLV II except this time, instead of causing cells to multiply it was said to be causing cells to die.

Before the HTLVs there was the HL23V saga. In the mid 1970s, Gallo's lab reported the isolation of the first human retrovirus, HL23V. The evidence for HL23V was more substantial than that which he would later produce for HIV. However, by using "viral glycoproteins," several independent research groups found that antibodies present in human sera, which reacted with these proteins, were "directed against carbohydrate structures" and concluded that "the results are consistent with the idea that the antibodies in question are elicited as a result of exposure to many natural substances possessing widely cross-reacting antigens and are not a result of widespread infection of man with replication of competent oncoviruses" (retoviruses).[427] This is why Gallo was likely chosen as the AIDS messenger. His behavior pattern indicated

---

426. J.L. Lauristen, (1995) NIDA meeting calls for research into the poppers-Kaposi's sarcoma connection. In: P.H. Duesberg, <u>AIDS: Virus or Drug Induced</u>, (Kluwer Academic Publishers, London), 325-330.

427. Snyder, HW., et al, 1980 "Specificity of human antibodies to oncovirus glycoproteins: Recognition of antigen by natural antibodies directed against carbohydrate structures" Proc Natl Acad Sci;77:1622-26

that he was wedded to proving an idea that was scientifically irrational: that benign passenger viruses that function as messenger particles in cellular metabolism were pathogenic. So when the drug-immune deficiency crisis broke into national consciousness he was primed to step into the limelight to receive his accolades. Whether a virus was causing the problem was irrelevant. The media would be the message.

Three years before the HIV pronouncement, Gallo accepted the evidence that the antibodies, which reacted with the presumed viral proteins of HL23V, were not virus specific, but were directed against normal human cellular material. This setback did not stop him from speculating because timing is everything, and so when young gay men began to turn up with a variety of opportunistic infections and Kaposi's sarcoma, Gallo was ready to declare a retrovirus the enemy. The same evidence that debunked HL23V has been produced for HIV and been ignored.

Gallo's claim that <u>HIV</u> kills T-helper lymphocytes could not be substantiated despite changing the theories[428][429]and despite his own admission that the HIV could not be found in T cells. This certainly negated the theory of how HIV was postulated to work—that HIV was a killer virus to the CD4+T cells. Just as in a court of law, if there is no evidence there should be no conviction. But just as some juries are hanging juries no matter the evidence—big Pharma wanted a sex and blood plague and they knew they had the power to make that illusion a believable reality for millions of people once the compliant government bureaucrats made their pronouncements and the controlled media parroted the party line.

The claims about the specificity and sensitivity of the antibody test have been specious at best. The only way to know if an antibody test that is introduced to clinical practice and on which life and death decisions are based and is actually specific for a unique virus is to have isolated the virus by traditional known protocols—protocols that had been in place since the early 1960s and were conveniently sidestepped by Gallo. Any other effort or short cut that has the effect of doing harm is not only bad science it is also unethical. But in this silent war, nothing takes precedence over profits.

Viral isolation is the proverbial <u>gold standard</u>. It is patently absurd to claim that an antibody/antigen reaction can be used to prove the existence of

---

428. Y. Rosenberg et al., "HIV Induced Decline in Blood CD4/CD8 Ratios; Viral Killing or Altered Lymphocyte Trafficking?" <u>Immunol Today;19</u> (1998): 10–17.

429. K.G. Wolters et al., "Rapid CD4+ T cell Turnover in HIV 1 Infection: A Paradigm Revisited," <u>Immunol Today 19</u> (1998) : 44–48.

a new virus without having isolated the virus first.[430] This was never done by Gallo or his French rival Luc Montagnier.[431] Montagnier like Gallo has even admitted publicly that the virus was never isolated.

The Office of Technology Assessment began to ring its own death knell when a 23 November 1987, US News and World Report article exposed some serious problems with the HIV test: "With public health officials and politicians thrashing out who should be tested for HIV, the accuracy of the test itself has been nearly ignored. A study last month by Congress' Office of Technology Assessment found that HIV tests can be very inaccurate indeed. For groups at very low risk—people who do not use IV- drugs or have sex with gay or bisexual men—9 in 10 positive findings are called false positives, indicating infection where none exists." That warning was conveniently ignored and the test was put into wide use.

The OTA was eventually disbanded in 1996 during the Clinton (D) administration under the strong urging of the House of Representatives run by (R) Newt Gingrich. The OTA from 1972 to 1995 provided Congress and the public with critical analyses and reports of the difficult issues interfacing science, technology, and society before Congress. The OTA had to tackle subjects that were very controversial, especially in corporate lobbying circles. They did studies on: defensive medicine that the hospital–medical lobby did not like; on access to public buses by people with disabilities that Greyhound did not welcome: on the auto industry that displeased General Motors: climate change that the fossil-fuel industry (oil, coal, and gas) did not approve. Newt, as part of his K Street Project designed to bring most of the lobbying money to the GOP, brought the ax down on a low-budget item that was giving the American people too much information with which to make informed choices. This paved the way for the development of medical knowledge

---

430. H. Caton The AIDS Mirage (Sydney, Australia: Univ. of New South Whales Press, 1994).

431. On 17 July 1997, French investigative journalist Djamel Tahi interviewed Professor Luc Montagnier in camera at the Pasteur Institute in Paris. Montagnier was asked, "Why do the EM (electron microscope) photographs published by you [in 1983] come from the culture and not the purification?" His reply was: "There was so little production of virus it was impossible to see what might be in a concentrate of the virus from the gradient ["pure virus"]. There was not enough virus to do that. Of course one looked for it, one looked for it in the tissues at the start, likewise the biopsy. We saw some particles but they did not have the morphology typical of retroviruses. They were very different. Relatively different. So with the [unpurified] cultures it took many hours to find the first pictures. It was a Roman effort! . . . . I repeat we did not purify."

monopolies that should rightly be called Frauds R Us. By cherry picking data that only shows their products in a positive light and suppressing information that gives evidence to any deleterious effect, the pharmaceutical industry has been given carte blanche in producing products that kill thousands annually. What other legitimate business could kill 100,000 people a year and still have the highest profit margins for any American industry and nobody ever goes to jail?

This knowledge monopoly has become so powerful that the general public is not even aware that expert molecular biologists, scientists, physicians, and informed citizens' groups have for years been contesting the theory of HIV/AIDS with detailed scientific and logical arguments. The HIV/AIDS case also offers a cogent illustration of the all too common willingness in the medical community to accept indications of correlation as proof of causation. But more than anything, it has been an exercise in how preconditioning of the public mind can create a mass hysteria similar in nature to the Salem witch hunts. That a new sex and blood plague would reign down on homosexuals and blacks was not a mistake. Both groups have long been outside the mainstream of American culture, and the myths surrounding the wanton sexuality of both groups have become part of what is called common knowledge.

A vacuum of reliable information has predictably created a power advantage for the producers of medical devices, drugs, and new technology and has led to "technology run wild" that has as its primary purpose the enrichment of patent holders. Selling this technology is done by frightening people into taking extravagantly overpriced drugs they do not need. As a result of such laissez-faire medicine, costs have spiraled out of control, the importance and reliability of many of the new products and drugs introduced are of questionable usefulness, and the overall health of the population is in general decline.

Pharmaceutical companies have acknowledged that HIV tests are not specific for HIV. The box below contains a typical disclaimer from an HIV-test manufacturer. What is so disturbing is that the FDA approved and licensed a blood test for HIV in 1985 (shortly after the test was developed), but did not approve it for human diagnostic purposes until 1990—a full six years after the ELISA test was developed.[432] The public was led to believe that the test was approved for human use as a diagnostic test and that it was reliable. The warning in the <u>U.S. News and World Report</u> was conveniently ignored.

---

432. Jon Rappoport, "The Massive Fraud behind HIV Tests," 2006. <u>www.areyoupositive.org/aidshoax.pdf</u>

There are currently two major categories of tests that are commonly used for the diagnosis of HIV infection: two are antibody tests, the ELISA and Western Blot (WB), and one is a genetic test, the Polymerase Chain Reaction (PCR), better known as the <u>viral load</u>. The antibody tests supposedly detect antibodies against what are claimed to be HIV proteins or antigens. As will be shown, the proteins in the antibody test are cellular in origin and are not HIV specific. The PCR test for HIV only detects copies of fragments of RNA genetic material that have been arbitrarily regarded as the nucleic acid of HIV. None of these tests detect the HIV virus itself, nor do they detect HIV particles because HIV HAS NEVER BEEN ISOLATED AND ANALYZIED BY STANDARD VIROLOGY PROTOCOLS.

Typical Disclaimers from HIV Test Manufacturers

"EIA testing alone cannot be used to diagnose AIDS, even if the recommended investigation of reactive specimens suggests a high probability that the antibody to HIV-1 is present. [...] **At present there is no recognized standard for establishing the presence and absence of HIV-1 antibody in human blood.** Therefore sensitivity was computed based on the clinical diagnosis of AIDS and specificity based on random donors"[1]

"Do not use this kit as the sole basis of diagnosing HIV-1 infection"[2]

"The Amplicor HIV-1 Monitor test is not intended to be used as a screening test for HIV or as a diagnostic test to confirm the presence of HIV infection"[3]

1. Abbott Laboratories, Diagnostic Division, 66-8805/R5; January, 1997
2. HIV-1 Western Blot Kit, Epitope, Inc., Organon Teknika Corporation PN201-3039 Revision #8

The corruption that began to engulf the discipline of virology can be traced directly to the accelerated corruption of the Nixon–Kissinger era. Prior to the arrival of the enormous funds that were dropped into Nixon's "War on Cancer," scientists who studied viruses had developed rigorous criteria by which they could judge if a virus was pathogenic. The isolation and characterization of viruses was done in the laboratory by the use of the electron microscope and a procedure called density gel centrifugation that was used to separate viruses from cell contaminants. The electron microscope was used extensively in this field of endeavor because the subject matter is so tiny and not visible with traditional light microscopes. Thus, these techniques were part of the standard methodology of the isolation procedure. By employing

EM of specimens that had been spun for hours at high speeds scientists were able to identify an isolate of viruses from a contaminated specimen. These researchers were able to tell if a virus was infectious, oncogenic (cancer causing), or simply a benign passenger. These techniques were also used to differentiate between true viruses and "virus-like particles." This is why the letter from Dr. Gonda to Gallo denying that there were identifiable viruses in his submitted specimens is a smoking gun.

Retroviruses characteristically had a diameter of between 100-120 nm[433]; had condensed inner bodies that were called the core and had an outer envelope imbedded with surface projections called knobs or spikes. However some particles with these characteristics were considered to be "virus like particles" and for this reason, following standardized rigorous protocols for ultrastructural characterization was essential for adequate differentiation between viruses and "virus-like particles." The nuclear material of viruses can be either DNA or RNA. HIV is considered an RNA virus.

Viruses replicate by using the machinery of the cells in which they reside. RNA viruses exhibited a particular characteristic: it appeared that the assembly of such RNA viruses took place at the cell surface. The surface membrane of the infected cell directly contributed to the future viral envelope by a multiple-step mechanism called <u>budding</u>. After budding, the viruses acquired knob-like structures on their surface. Such knob-like structures will become important for two reasons. First, it was claimed that the knobs are a necessary feature that allow the virus to become infectious by allowing the virus to attach to a new cell, and secondly, because the <u>knobs</u> were claimed to be one of the <u>HIV</u> proteins known as p160. It has never been shown that there are knobs on what they are calling <u>cell free HIV</u>—meaning what they are calling <u>HIV</u> has no infectious capacity by their own rules. Further, HIV proteins p160 and p120 have been shown to be oligomers of gp41[434]. Gp41 has turned out to be a cell structural protein, <u>actin.</u> Actin is a ubiquitous protein found in <u>all</u> cells, including bacteria and several viruses. It is part of the cytoskeleton that helps the cell maintain its shape. Actin filaments are also part of what has been described as a cellular highway system along which vesicles that contain packets of information are transported. Actin also contains S-H bonds that make it an important part of maintaining cell redox status.

---

433. Since 2000 the diameter has changedt o 80-100 nm with a spherical shape.

434. A. Pinter, W. J. Honnen, S. A. Tilley et al., Oligomeric Structure of gp41, the Transmembrane Protein of Human Immunodeficiency Virus Type 1," <u>J Virol</u> <u>63</u> (1989) : 2674–79.

Viruses are said to be released into the intercellular spaces by this budding process. This characteristic of infectious particles helped to eliminate the thousands of "virus like particles" observed in human malignancies. Budding of retroviruses also has the advantage of allowing the EM to identify what was thought to be infected single cells and to observe that such cells were perfectly viable, with absolutely no ultrastructural evidence of any cytolytic effect. The RNA viruses were not killing the cells! The cells containing these viruses maintained excellent viability. Trying to make the case for these tiny elements as destroyers as opposed to helpers again speaks volumes about a mind set that first identifies a thing as a foe before its true function has been assessed.

By ignoring this science, the promoters of the HIV theory made the claim that HIV, a retrovirus of the category that was never shown to be cytotoxic in man, was killing CD4+T lymphocytes. Moreover, the early electron microscopists were able to observe that typical viruses were frequently seen in cells undergoing mitotic division, and this did not indicate abnormality.

It is now known that many traveling viral elements, renamed exosome vesicles, transposons and retroransposons not only play a roll in removing plasma membrane proteins they are involved in the adaptive immune responses to pathogens and tumors. They also have the ability to suppress cellular immunity,[435] and they play a central role in communication between lymphocytes and dendritic cells[436], by mediating the development of cellular responses or suppressing excessive activation. They also have been shown to help regulate our genes. Essentially, they are packets of information that travel within and between cells. Because their function is generally helpful and it does not reconcile with the belief in HIV infectivity, they have begun to call these particles "Trojans".

Viruses, by definition, are packages of genetic information enclosed in a coat which consists of proteins. They can reproduce themselves only by infecting a suitable host cell and taking over the chemical constituents of that cell. The proteins making up the viruses are characteristic for each species of virus. The composition of proteins on a given virus results in a specific shape of the virus particle. The difficulty in virology is distinguishing a true virus from virus-like particles that are commonly found in the placenta and in the artificial environment of laboratory cell cultures. This has been the confusion

---

435.   D.D. Taylor and P.H. Black, "Inhibition of Macrophage Ia Antigen Expression by Shed Plasma Membrane Vesicles from Metastatic Murine Melanoma Lines," J Nat Cancer Inst 74 (1986): 859–67.

436.   Dendritic cells are sentinel immune cells. Their main function is to process and present antigens to other cells in the immune system.

with HIV because it appears that what are really <u>virus-like particles</u> are being called <u>HIV</u>. How could such a blunder occur?

By1970, the War on Cancer virus hunters were having great difficulty proving the notion that RNA tumor viruses were the cause of human cancers when two researchers, Temin and Baltimore, discovered an enzyme, reverse transcriptase (RT) that reoriented ideas on how RNA tumor viruses might work. Enzymes are proteins that speed up chemical reactions in a living organism. Temin and Baltimore incorrectly claimed that this enzyme was unique to retroviruses, which, they theorized, could be the link that transformed normal cells into cancer cells. This was nothing more than a hypothesis, a working supposition for which there was no concrete evidence, but they began to call what they thought were oncoviuses (RNA tumor viruses) retroviruses. Because of the largesse of the American taxpayer, these seekers of the absurd, continued the business of trying to prove the hypothesis that retroviruses caused human cancer. They failed in this quest, but the research effort changed in a very deleterious way the field of viral oncology.

It was later discovered that RT is not unique to retroviruses and is a DNA construction and repair enzyme that can be expressed under various cellular conditions. Forty percent of DNA is reversed transcribed from RNA. That RT was neither unique nor specific for the identification of a new retrovirus was known in virology circles. So, when Gallo claimed that by identifying RT in his stimulated cell cultures that he could use the expression of this enzyme as a distinct marker to establish his discovery of a new retrovirus, HTLV-III, later called <u>HIV</u>, he was committing scientific fraud.

According to Etienne de Harven, a well known electron microscopist, the years from 1970–1980 were dominated by a series of ideas that would never have withstood scientific scrutiny ten or twenty years before. This is how money directed to the War on Cancer ended up as the AIDS scam because this is the standard story of how money has corrupted science. Only those who were willing to follow the party line have access to significant funding grants. This is how Rockefeller interests hijacked allopathic medicine 100 years ago and this is how it is still controlled.

Generally accepted and recognized procedures for isolating and purifying retroviruses were established as early as 1964.[437] The word <u>isolation</u> is derived from the Latin <u>insulatus</u> [made into an island]. It refers to the act of separating an object from all matter that is not that object. <u>Webster's Dictionary</u> defines <u>to isolate</u> as "to set apart from others, to quarantine, to select from among others; to separate from another substance so as to obtain pure or in a free

---

437. T.E. O'Connor et al., "Density Gradient Centrifugation of a Murine Leukemia Virus," <u>Science</u> <u>1441</u> (1964): 144–47.

state." Even using the most liberal of definitions, combinations of phenomena described by Gallo including transcription of RNA to DNA (RT), retroviral-like particles, or antigen/antibody reactions in cultures or co-cultures cannot be considered proof of isolation of a retrovirus. They can be used for the detection of a retrovirus only if they are shown to be specific, and this can only be done by isolation.

There were rigorous procedures put in place to attain viral isolation. The most frequently used technique for isolation and purification of retroviruses includes the following primary and secondary steps:

<u>Primary</u>

1. Retroviruses are commonly removed from purified blood, tissue homogenates, and supernatant fluids from infected cell cultures. The cultures generally take several days or weeks. The viral particles are then concentrated by centrifugation. Retroviruses are known to band at a certain level in a sucrose gel density gradient. (1.16 gm/ml). However, other cellular constituents can settle at this same level. Therefore:
2. Electron microscopic photos are taken of the concentrated viral particles to make sure that there is true isolation and not cellular debris.
3. Biochemical and genetic analysis is performed on the purified viral particles. Verify that the particles contain a protein that causes reverse transcription.
4. A control experiment is run to avoid misinterpreting endogenous retroviruses as exogenous infectious retroviruses, and
5. Biological tests are done to ascertain if the isolated retrovirus is indeed potentially pathogenic and virulent.[438] [439] This is done by introducing the isolate into an uninfected culture.

<u>Secondary</u>

> After purification, the authors of these studies were then able to employ selected chemicals to disrupt the purified whole viral particles and release the internal components for further identification to make sure that the particles consist of proteins and RNA that are unique to them.

---

438. Ibid.
439 Etienne. De Harven "Viremia in Friend murine leukemia: the electron microscope approach to the problem. <u>Pathologie-Biologie 13</u> (1965a): 125–34.

In the decade prior to the appearance of AIDS, before excess money began to flow into the "War on Cancer" virus hunt, in order to identify viral proteins and to extract "viral RNA" samples, this method was successfully used to achieve purification of a typical virus. It was rapid, inexpensive, and reproducible.[440] <u>This has never been done with HIV!</u>

Because researchers <u>believed</u> that viruses could cause cancer during the period of the Nixon "War on Cancer," they began to take scientifically illogical shortcuts and the corruption began to set in. It became acceptable to postulate that when viruses cannot be seen by EM in cancer cells, biochemical or immunological methods "claiming" to be viral "markers" were enough to demonstrate viral infection of cells under scrutiny. Such markers were claimed to be reverse transcriptase, an antigen, various proteins, or some RNA sequences. In this Neverland fantasy world, not ever seeing the viral particles was conveniently explained by claiming the integration of the viral genome into the chromosomes of the alleged infected cells. These guys just made stuff up. Of course, anyone can see that this is not <u>isolation.</u> This is when the science moved out of reality and began to behave as if the years of prior rigorous research were no longer relevant.[441]

Neither Robert Gallo, nor French researcher Luc Montagnier adhered to the more rigorous techniques when they claimed to have isolated the <u>AIDS</u> virus. They did not concentrate the isolated particles, and they did not provide electron microscopic evidence that particles from the "infected" culture supernatant, sedimenting at 1.16 gm/ml of sucrose were composed primarily of concentrated viral particles. Further, in Gallo's lab the "infected" cells were pooled from several patients, they were co-cultured with cancer cells, and then this mixture was stimulated with highly oxidizing material and corticosterone. Anything could have happened in this witches brew.

Their experiments were not controlled. In laboratory science it is mandatory to run a control sample that has many of the characteristics of your study sample. This is done to assure that the results you attain are true results and not artifacts. These original papers on HIV contained no evidence of either the Paris Lab or Gallo's lab running controls.

The EM photographs were not of purified viral particles from the 1.16 gm/ml density band, but from stimulated cultured lymphocytes that were releasing particles similar to retroviruses. However, it has been shown that these same particles can be released by <u>non- infected</u> stimulated lymphocyte

---

440. Ibid.

441. Etienne,De Harven, "Retroviruses: The Recollections of an Electron Microscopist," www.virusmyth.com/aids/hiv/edhrecol.htm

cultures as well.[442] This was the control experiment that should have been done by Gallo and the others, but was not done until 1993 by an entirely different group of researchers. Working on "HIV 1 infected T-cell" culture supernatants, other researchers found that it contained primarily cellular debris and cell membrane vesicles that could not definitively be identified with HIV particles and rare virus-like particles.[443] In short, they confirmed Gonda's original EM findings that Gallo chose to ignore when he published in Science.

In the letter Gonda wrote to Gallo concerning the micrographs that were published in Science that Gallo claimed were HTLV-III (HIV), Gonda told Gallo, "I would like to point out that the 'particles' . . . are in debris of degenerated cells and at least fifty percent smaller than they should be if they were retroviruses." He concluded, "I do not believe any of the particles photographed are HTLV-I, HTLV-II or HTLV-III...No other cellular 'virus- like' particles were observed."[444] Nevertheless, Gallo submitted the micrographs to Science, and they published them. Science has been notified of this deception in a letter dated 1 December 2008, signed by numerous prestigious and senior scientists with attached documentation. To date the publisher and editor of Science have not retracted or corrected the Gallo papers that are the false foundation for the whole AIDS mess. Given the huge liability that this confers on the industry, it is wishful thinking to anticipate a mea culpa.

The upshot of this shoddy science was that Gallo was used by the drug running Reagan administration to claim the isolation of a new virus based on the identification of some non-specific proteins, a universal enzyme--reverse transcriptase activity, and RNA gene fragments that were found, not in the density gradient, but in the culture supernatants. Gallo never purified. He never isolated. NEVER. Therefore, there is no scientific data validating the contention that what is currently referred to as HIV is, in fact, a virus![445]

So in reference to HIV in the AIDS literature, it becomes a matter not of science, but of semantics. In the AIDS literature, HIV, HIV isolation,

---

442. R. R. Dourmashkin et al., "Small Virus-like Particles Bud from the Cell Membranes of Normal as well as HIV-Infected Human Lymphoid Cells," J Medcal Virology 39 (1993): 229–32.

443. P. Gluschankof et al., "Cell Membrane Vesicles Are a Major Contaminant of Gradient Enriched Human Immunodeficiency Virus Type 1 Preparations," Virolog; 230 (1997) :125-33.

444. Janine Roberts, Fear of the Invisible, (Impact Investigative Media Productions, 2008), 129–30.

445. Roberto Giraldo and Etienne De Harven, "HIV Tests Cannot Diagnose HIV Infection," 2006. www.robertogiraldo.com

pure particles, virus particles, virions, and infectious particles have a variety of meanings and include all of the following, but are without proof of the presence of an isolate of pure HIV:

- "RNA wrapped protein"
- Material from the cell culture supernatants which passes through tight filters but through which organisms such as mycoplasma may pass
- Detection in cultures from AIDS patients of a protein p41. P41 has been shown to be a cytoskeletal protein actin. Actin is the most abundant protein in typical eukaryotic cells accounting for up to 15 percent in some cell types. The protein forms a huge variety of structures in the cell in concert with a huge number of actin binding proteins—one of which is another so- called HIV protein, p24, which is most likely myosin. Myosin is important to cell motility, muscle contraction, and phagocytosis.[446]
- The pellet obtained by simple ultracentrifugation of the culture supernatant.

But whether or not HIV was actually isolated and the proteins belonged to HIV was not the point. Gallo was forthwith in the patent office to obtain a patent for the proteins that became the basis for the HIV antibody test. The goal was perception management, and it was the job of the Epidemic Intelligence Service to position stories in the mainstream media to do just that. Given the depth and breadth of the drug epidemic in the West and the structural adjustment, private military contractor and poverty epidemic in Africa, the world had to believe that HIV was the cause of AIDS and that this antibody test had some predictive value.

Research has shown that at least 40 to 50 percent of mammalian DNA is composed of repetitive sequences that are referred to as nonsense genes, parts of which were also described as retroviral genes. They exist in the thousands. Some can even replicate independently and jump within and between chromosomes. In the laboratory, they can be made to migrate and when this happens, reverse transcriptase is invariably detected, which underscores the

---

446. Cellular process of engulfing solid particles by the cell membrane.

fact that reverse transcription activity has nothing to do with retroviruses as such.[447] [448] [449] [450] It is a ubiquitous enzyme.

The task of authenticating a diagnostic test in clinical medicine requires that there is an independent method of establishing the presence of the condition for which the test is to be employed. This method is referred to as the gold standard and represents the tenet on which the scientific proof of validity rests. In HIV medicine, all of this science has been disbanded, and the HIV antibody test has been established as the measure of its own reliability.

Antibodies are proteins that that are found in the blood that detect and destroy invaders like bacteria and viruses that are called antigens (antibody generating). There are multiple problems with the claim that antibody tests are indicative of a specific viral infection. Besides the fact that the HIV virus has never been adequately isolated, the proteins claimed to be specific for HIV are universally present in everyone. In fact, it turns out that the HIV proteins are all likely to be cytoskeletal, bacterial, and fungal proteins that are reacting to the patient's own auto-antibodies. Antibodies are notoriously promiscuous and can mate with a variety of antigens, and even purified antibodies known as monoclonal antibodies can cross-react with other substances.

There is poor correlation among the three major tests and even between the same test run in different laboratories. Studies have indicated that the same blood run in the same laboratory can give different results, which underscores the lack of standardization that is the sine quo non of laboratory tests—reproducibility. The criterion for predicting a positive HIV antibody test change from lab to lab and country to country. A positive test in Africa is a negative test in Australia. In the early years, many people who had AIDS tested HIV antibody negative. In Gallo's original study, only about a third of his patients had antibodies to what he claimed was HIV. Today that poor correlation has changed, because the definition of AIDS now includes an HIV antibody test. This makes little clinical sense. If someone has tuberculosis and is HIV negative, they are said to have tuberculosis. If they are HIV positive,

447. L. Dixie et al.., "Identification of a Retrovirus-like Repetitive Element in Human DNA," PNAS 81 (1984): 7510–14.

448. C. O'Connell et al., "ERV3, a Full-length Human Endogeneous Provirus: Chromosomal Localization and Evolutionary Relationships," Virology 138 (1984): 2225–35.

449. D. Baltimore, "Retroviruses and Retrotransposons: The Role of Reverse Transcription in Shaping the Eukaryotic Genome," Cell 40 (1985) : 481–82.

450. A. M. Weiner et al., "Nonviral Retrotransposons: Genes, Pseudogenes, and Transposable Elements Generated by the Reverse Flow of Genetic Information," Ann Rev Biochem 55 (1986):631–61.

they are said to have AIDS. They have the same disease, but because of this faulty test, the AIDS patient is more likely to die, not because of an HIV infection, but because the patient will likely be treated more aggressively with toxic anti-retroviral therapy and his underlying metabolic dysbiosis will be ignored.

The pharmaceutical companies that manufacture and commercialize the test kits acknowledge the inaccuracy of the tests, which explains the warnings contained in the kit inserts:

- "Elisa testing alone cannot be used to diagnose AIDS, even if the recommended investigation of reactive specimens suggests a high probability that the antibody to HIV-1 is present" (Abbott 1997).
- Insert for the Western Blot warns, "Do not use this kit as the sole basis of diagnosis of HIV-1 infection" (Epitope Organon Teknika).
- The insert that accompanies the genetic test, the PCR viral load warns: "The Amplicor HIV-1 Monitor test is not intended to be used as a screening test for HIV or as a diagnostic test to confirm the presence of HIV infection" (Roche 2003).

Again, the only valid method of establishing the sensitivity and the specificity of a diagnostic test in clinical medicine is to compare the test in question with its gold standard. Sensitivity is a measure of how often a test is positive when you already know what you are testing is present. Specificity is how often a test is positive when the patient really does not have the condition. For example, if a thousand women are pregnant but the test only identifies 980, then it has a 98 percent sensitivity rate. If, on the other hand, there are a thousand women who are not pregnant, but there is one positive test, then the test is 99.9 percent specific. If you are not pregnant, but your test is positive, you can see how that may present a dilemma. This is even more so with HIV since people are told that the condition is irreversible and will end in death.

The only possible gold standard for the HIV test is the human immunodeficiency virus itself. Since HIV has never been isolated as an independent, free, and purified viral particle, it is not possible to define either the sensitivity or specificity of any of these tests. Currently, sensitivity is computed based on the clinical diagnosis of AIDS, and specificity is based on random donors. (Abbot 1997).

There are multiple indications that HIV antibody tests may be the result of antigenic stimulation other than HIV:

- HIV antibody levels are higher in blacks than in whites, which makes blacks five times as likely as whites among all risk groups and age and socioeconomic categories to have a positive test.[451] Blacks are known to produce more antibodies to the same antigenic stimulus than whites.

- HIV is thought to be transmitted by infected needles, yet a higher percentage of prostitutes who use oral drugs (84 percent) than IVs (46 percent) test positive.[452]

- A European study found that prostitutes who did not use drugs showed an HIV level of only 1.5 percent, whereas those who did use drugs showed a level of 32 percent.[453]

- Mice of certain autoimmune strains make antibodies against <u>HIV</u> proteins.[454]

- Recipients of negative blood seroconvert and develop AIDS, whereas the donors remain healthy and sero-negative.[455]

- In healthy individuals, partners of HIV-positive individuals, organ transplant recipients, and patients with lupus, a positive Western Blot antibody test may revert to negative when exposure to semen, immunosuppressive therapy, or clinical improvement occurs.[456] This indicates the reversibility of HIV.

- Although the frequency of positive HIV antibody tests in healthy blood donors and military applicants is low, patients with tuberculosis, including those with TB localized to the lungs, both in the U.S. and Africa, have high frequency (up to 50 percent) of positive Western Blot antibody tests.[457]

451. H. H. Bauer, "Demographic Characteristics of HIV: III. Why Does HIV Discriminate by Race?" J <u>Scientific Exploration</u> 20 (2006) :255–88.

452. C. Sterk, "Cocaine and HIV Seropositivity," <u>Lancet I</u> (1988):1052–53.

453. C. Fiala, "Epidemiological Evidence Against Heterosexual Transmission of HIV and Against Prevention Campaigns." www.virusmyth.net 25 June 2000f.

454. T. A. Kion et al., "Anti-HIV and Anti-Anti-MHC Antibodies in Alloimmune and Autoimmune Mice," <u>Science 253</u> (1991) : 1138–40

455 L. J. Conley and S. D. Holmerg, "Transmission of AIDS from Blood Screened Negative for Antibody to the Human Immunodeficiency Virus," <u>NEJM 326</u> (1992):1499.

456. J. S. Drummer et al., "Infection with Human Immunodeficiency Virus in the Pittsburgh Transplant Population," <u>Transplantation 47</u> (1989):134–39.

457. A.E. Pitchenik, et al., "Human T Cell Lymphotrophic Virus III (HTLV III) Seropositivity and Related Diseases among 71 Consecutive Patients in Whom Tuberculosis Was Diagnosed," <u>Am Rev Respir Dis 135</u> (1987): 875–79.

- Amazonian Indians who have had no contact with individuals outside their communities and have no AIDS have a 3.3 to 13.3 percent HIV Western Blot antibody seropositivity rate.[458]
- There are at least seventy conditions documented to cross-react with HIV proteins. (See chart: "Factors Known to Cause False Positive HIV Antibody
- Tests") [459]
- In a study of 1.2 million applicants for U.S. military service considered low risk, 1 percent or 12,000 had a first-time positive HIV ELISA. Only 2000 were also ultimately shown to be Western Blot positive and thus, according to the authors, HIV positive. That left 10,000 positive ELISAs, which must have reacted for other reasons than "HIV antibodies,"a prime example of cross-reactivity. Also note, that when an antibody test is done in Africa, the less accurate ELISA is likely to be used.
- The 30 October 1994, Sacramento Bee reported that "HIV tests are notoriously unreliable in Africa. A 1994 study published in the Journal of Infectious Diseases concluded that HIV tests were useless in central Africa where the microbes responsible for tuberculosis, malaria and leprosy were so prevalent that they (cross reacted) and register over 70% false positive (for HIV)."
- And of interest was a study out of UC Davis Veterinary Medical Teaching Hospital that reported in the Journal of Cancer Research that 50 percent of dogs' blood samples "reacted with one or more HIV recombinant proteins." Assuming that California dogs are not infected with HIV (as did the authors), one must conclude the data are further proof of antibody cross-reactivity to many of the HIV proteins.

What this means is that you are not necessarily infected with what your antibodies appear to tell you. The above examples are persuasive for the existence of non-specific and/or cross-reacting HIV antibodies. If this is not the case, then it must be considered that HIV infection has been acquired by unknown or unusual means. However, since dogs, laboratory mice, and healthy blood donors or humans receiving HIV negative blood or even their own blood are not believed to be at risk from HIV infection or the

458. L. Rodriquez et al., "Antibodies to HTLV-III/LAV among Aboriginal Amazonian Indians in Venezuela,"Lancet,II (1985): 1098–1100.

459 C. Johnson, "Factors Known to Cause False Positive HIV Antibody Tests Results," Zenger's ,(San Diego, Calif.), 8–9.

development of AIDS, then HIV cannot be regarded as either the necessary or sufficient cause of AIDS.

A positive HIV test must be placed in the context of a thorough clinical evaluation. Without an accurate evaluation of the patient's social history, toxic exposure, and economic status, this test is meaningless. However the HIV test can be used in the context of a thorough anemnesis as a reversible indicator of physiological stress. This test is not an excuse to practice lazy, mindless parrot-like medicine. But like other non-specific tests, such as the Erythrocyte Sedimentation Rate and the C - reactive protein, this test may be another marker of cellular dysbiosis and the need for treating any real infections and initiating reparative therapy with appropriate biological compensation.

Proteins Considered to Be HIV Antigens

HIV WESTERN BLOT STRIP	AFR	AUS	FDA	RCX	CDC 1	CDC 2	CON	GER	UK	FRA	MAC
ENV — p160 / p120 / p41	ANY 2	ANY 1	ANY 1	ANY 1	p160/p120 AND p41	p160/p120 OR p41	p160/p120 OR p41	ANY 1	ANY 1	ALL 3	ANY STRONG BAND
POL — p68 / p53 / p32 · **GAG** — p55 / p40 / p24 / p18	ANY 3 GAG OR POL		p32 AND p24	ANY 1 AND ANY 1			AND p24	p32 OR p24	ANY 1 GAG OR POL	p32 AND p24	OR 3 WEAK BANDS · ANY 1 OR ANY 1

AFR–Africa, AUS–Australia, FDA–Food and Drug Administration, RCX– U.S. Red Cross, CDC–Centers for Disease Control, CON–U.S. Consortium for Retrovirus Serology Standardization, GER–Germany, UK–United Kingdom, FRA–France, MAC–U.S. Multicenter AIDS Cohort Study, 1983–1992.

This Western Blot diagram is read as follows: The left axis has three words—env (envelope proteins), pol (polymerase enzymes), and gag (group specific antigens). These correspond to the genetic area of the virus claimed to code for the adjacent sugar containing proteins called glycoproteins; for example, env codes for gp160 and gp120, or pol codes for p53 and p 32, etc. At the top of the diagram are the abbreviations for countries or labs such as the CDC (Centers for Disease Control) followed by the criteria they use to identify a positive test. As can be seen, it only takes 2 env proteins to be positive in Africa. If that same person had the same test result any place else on the planet, they would be negative.

The immunogenic HIV proteins are thought to be coded by three genes displayed above: gag, pol, and env. The gag gene codes a precursor p53/55, which is then cleaved to p24/25 and p17/18. The pol gene codes for p31/32, and the env gene codes the precursor protein p160, which is cleaved to p120 and p41/p45.[460] None of these are HIV specific.

Proteins in the env Region

The components visualized in the 120–160 region do not correspond to gp 120 or its precursor, but represent oligomers of gp 41. An oligomer is a polymer that consists of two, three, or four small molecules called monomers. P41 is one of the proteins detected by both Gallo and Montagnier in the first HIV identifiers. Montagnier's group observed that p41 protein was found in HIV, HTLV-1 as well as non-infected cells. They concluded that the p41 band was likely due to contamination by cellular actin.[461]

Actin has numerous cellular functions as noted above. It is known that oxidation of cellular sulphydryl (S-H) groups (which is a consistent metabolic abnormality in AIDS patients) is correlated with assembly of polymerized actin [462] and that the level of actin antibody binding to cells is determined by the physiological state of the cells.

Platelets from healthy individuals also contain a p41/45 protein that reacts with sera from homosexual men with AIDS and immune thrombocytopenic purpura (ITP) and "represents non-specific binding of IgG to actin in the platelet preparation."[463]

---

460. L. Ratner et al., "Complete Nucleotide Sequence of the AIDS Virus, HTRLV III," Nature 313 (1985): 277–84.

461. F. Barri-Sinossi et al., "Isolation of a T-Lymphocyte Retrovirus from a Patient At Risk for Acquired Immune Deficiency Syndrome (AIDS)," Science 220 (1983): 868–71.

462. D.B. Hinshaw et al., "Actin Polymerization in Cellular Oxidant Injury," Arch Bioxhem Biophy 228 (1991): 311–16.

463. R.B.Stricker et al., "Target Platelet Antigen in Homosexual Men with Immune Thrombocytopenia," NEJM 313 (1985) :1375–80.

Normal human serum contains antibodies capable of recognizing the carbohydrate moity of the HIV glycoproteins gp 160, gp 120 and gp41.[464]

Other researchers have shown that antibodies to carbohydrate containing antigens (such as lipoarabinomannan and phenolic glycolipid) that constitute the cell wall of mycobacterium leprae, a bacterium, which "shares antigenic determinants with other mycobacterial species" and causes "significant cross-reactivities with HIV–pol and gag proteins"[465] The researchers warned that there is "a very high rate of HIV-1 false positive ELISA and WB results," and that the tests should be interpreted with caution when screening individuals infected with M. tuberculosis or other mycobacterial species. For this reason, they cautioned that the ELISA and WB may not be sufficient for HIV diagnosis in AIDS endemic areas of Central Africa where the prevalence of mycobaterial diseases is quite high.

Another major problem with these tests is that one hundred percent of AIDS patients even those with "no candida clinically" have Candida albicans antibodies. In addition to the mycobacteria, the walls of fungi (C. albicans, Cryptococcus neoformans, Coccidioides immitis, Histoplasma capsulatum, including Pneumocystis carinii) contain carbohydrate mannans.[466] This has led other researchers to state," It is possible that candida may act as a cofactor in the development of overt AIDS in HIV infected individuals."[467] This is incorrect. In the presence of chronic cellular acidosis, fungi will be expressed because this is a state in which there is a high turnover of cells, and fungi appear to clean up dying tissue.

It is also important that in gay men, the only sexual act that is a risk factor for seroconversion is passive anal intercourse. Because of the thin walls of the rectal mucosa, this makes an easy entrance into the blood stream for

464. T. Tomyama et al., "Recognition of Human Immunodeficiency Virus Glycoproteins by Natural Anti-Carbohydrate Antibodies in Human Serum,"Biochem Biophys Res Commun 177 (1991):279–85.

465. O. Kashala et al., "Infection with Human Immunodeficiency Virus Type 1 (HIV-1) and Human T Cell Lymphotropic Viruses among Leprosy Patients and Contacts: Correlation between HIV-1 Cross-Reactivity and Antibodies to Lipoarabinomannan," J Infec Dis 169 (1994):296–304.

466. O.A. Hoffman, et al., "Pneumocystis Carinni Stimulates Tumor Necrosis Factor Alpha Release from Alveolar Macrophages through a Beta-Glucan Mediated Mechanism," J Immuno; 150 (1993) :3932–40.

467. R. Matthews et al., "Candida and AIDS: Evidence for Protective Antibody," Lancet II (1988) :263–66.

semen. Not only is semen highly oxidizing, mannose is present in both the sperm and seminal plasma.[468]

Since antibodies to mannans react with HIV proteins and with mycobacterial infection in Africa, one would expect the sera of all people infected with fungi and mycobacteria to cross-react with the HIV-1 glycoproteins as well as to cause significant cross-reactivities with HIV-1 pol and gag proteins.[469]

Another study done at the University of Rome found that mice antibodies raised against a lipopolysaccharide from the common gut bacteria E. Coli reacted with gp120 and gp 41.[470] The group from Perth Australia with lead reaseacher Eleni Papadopulos-Eleopulos raised this very important issue: "Given the fact that individuals with fungal and mycobacterial infections have antibodies which may react with 'HIV proteins' in the absence of 'HIV' and that E. Coli is an intestinal commensal and a potential bacterium in all of us," how can one then assert that reactions between antibodies in the sera of AIDS patients are proteins present in cultures derived from the tissues of AIDS patients? Because these proteins react with the common opportunistic infections diagnosed in AIDS patients, it is more likely that patients diagnosed with AIDS have other reasons than an HI virus for being ill. In other words, the antigenic determinants of the opportunistic infections that plague people with immune deficiencies are what are really being tested in the HIV test.

The p32 Protein and why and how a major HLA-DR histocompatibly has been used as a "race specific bioweapon."

The human leukocyte antigen (HLA) test, also known as HLA typing or tissue typing, identifies antigens on the white blood cells (WBCs) that determine tissue compatibility for organ transplantation (that is, histocompatability testing). There are six loci on chromosome 6, where the genes that produce HLA antigens are inherited: HLA-A, HLA-B, HLA-C, HLA-DR, HLA-DQ, and HLA-DP.

Unlike most blood group antigens, which are inherited as products of two alleles (types of genes that occupy the same site on a chromosome), many different alleles can be inherited at each of the HLA loci. These are defined

468. T. Mann and C.Lutwak-Mann, Male Reproductive Function and Semen (New York: Springer-Verlag, 1981).
469. Kashala, Infection with Human Immunodeficiency Virus Type 1 (HIV-1) . . .
470. Eleni Papadoulos-Eleopulos, et al., "HIV Antibodies: Further Questions and a Plea for Clarification," Current Med Res Opinion 13 (1997): 627–34.

by antibodies (antisera) that recognize specific HLA antigens, or by DNA probes that recognize the HLA allele. Using specific antibodies, 26 HLA-A alleles, 59 HLA-B alleles, 10 HLA-C alleles, 26 HLA-D alleles, 22 HLA-DR alleles, nine HLA-DQ alleles, and six HLA-DP alleles can be recognized. This high degree of genetic variability (polymorphism) makes finding compatible organs more difficult than finding compatible blood for transfusion.

HLA typing, along with ABO (blood type) grouping, is used to provide evidence of tissue compatibility. The HLA antigens expressed on the surface of the lymphocytes of the recipient are matched against those from various donors. Human leukocyte antigen typing is performed for kidney, bone marrow, liver, pancreas, and heart transplants.

It was discovered that when transplant patients who were given immunosuppressive drugs, including the Burroughs Wellcome drug azothioprine, that 6-7 percent of these patients developed Kaposi's sarcoma, lymphomas, or opportunistic infections (transplantation AIDS). Because these people had been tissue typed before hand, it was noted that these problems more often developed in those of Jewish (Sephardic), Italian, or African descent who expressed an HLA-DR antigen. This is one of the connections between the HIV antibody test and the finding of increasing numbers of AIDS patients among African Americans. The p32 protein appears to be identical to the class II histocompatability DR proteins. In a 1987 study in the Journal of Virology, Henderson isolated p30-32 and p34-36 of "HIV purified by double banding" in sucrose gradients and found that they had the same sequence as these HLA proteins.[471] In a study done on the Venda in South Africa, it was found that HLA class II complex were associated with protection from malaria and hepatitis B/C, but predisposed the Venda to tuberculosis. This makes sense because tuberculosis was introduced to South Africa by Europeans at the end of the 19th century when miners hoping to strike it rich flocked to the gold mines.[472] This is why Tb is still one of the greatest killers in Southern Africa. It was not an indigenous disease. It is a testament to the strength of the Africans that they were able to survive the European onslaught better than some indigenous people of the Americas. It is also ironic that pulmonary tuberculosis has been reclassified as AIDS.

Including the p32 protein in the antibody test increased the likelihood that those of African descent would test positive more often than other racial groups, all other environmental characteristics being constant. This was the

---

471. L Henderson et al., "Direct Identification of Class II Histocompatibility DR Proteins in Preparations of Human T Cell Lymphotropic Virus Type III," J Virology 61 (1987) : 629–32.

472. Sally-Anne Jackson, "Peter Abraham's Mine Boy: A Study of Colonial Diseases in South Africa", 22 December 2007 Research in African Literatures.

answer to the question raised by Henry Bauer in his article, "Demographic Characteristics of HIV: Why Does HIV Discriminate by Race?" In his broad based review of HIV epidemiology he found that racial ancestry influences the frequency of positive HIV tests as an independent variable and that the variable has nothing to do with aberrant sexual behavior in the black community, but indicated a physiological response to stress "whose strength is modified by somatic race-associated factors."[473] HLA haplotypes are inherited en bloc as ancestral haplotypes that vary considerably between races. On 21 October 2009 there were 3126 citations in the PubMed database when searching for "HLA race".

The other link making those of African ancestry more likely to test positive is that Africans and even healthy African American blood donors have a higher IgG antibody level than Caucasians [474] One study from Israel in fact came to the conclusion that hypergammaglobulinemia (increased antibodies in blood) is a predictor of seropositivity.[475]

With control solidly in the hands of an information monopoly, by use of these sophisticated technologies, specific genotypes can be targeted by advanced medical technology—no virus need apply and very few the wiser. It is quite clever.

Pregnant women are also at risk of developing anti HLA-DR auto antibodies, long recognized as causes of anti-<u>HIV</u> cross-reactivity.[476] Is it simply a <u>mistake</u> that the CDC has advised that HIV testing be done as routine prenatal screening in obstetric clinics? Because HIV has not been isolated and it has not been proven to be infectious, the idea of mother to child transmission has to be re-examined.

Eleni Papadopulos-Eleopulos and the group from Perth, Australia produced a critically important paper that should be required reading for every obstetrician and pediatrician: "Mother to Child Transmission of HIV and Its Prevention with AZT and Nevirapine: A Critical Analysis of the Evidence." Their critique gives sufficient scientific evidence that immune deficiency was

---

473. H Bauer, "Demographic Characteristics of HIV: III Why Does HIV Discriminate by Race?, <u>J Scientific Exploration</u> (2006) 20:2; 255-288

474. D. Lucey et al., "Racial Differences in Anti p24 Antibody Titers and Total Serum IgG Levels in North American Persons with HIV 1 Infection," VII International AIDS Conference, 1991, Florence, 362.

475. B. Brenner et al., "The Prevalence and Interaction of Human Immunodeficiency Virus and Hepatitis B Infections in Israeli Hemophiliacs," <u>Israel J Med Sci 27</u> (1991): 557–61.

476. M. Proffitt, B. Yen-Lieberman, Laboratory Diagnosis of Human Immunodeficiency Virus Infection," <u>Infectious Disease Clinics of North America 7</u> (1993): 203–19.

being described in the U.S. in infants well before the AIDS era, mostly in children from drug-addicted mothers. They also present evidence that the altered redox status of AIDS patients is a result of oxidative stress, and this is likely sufficient to explain the development of the immune deficiency syndrome. In the West, it has been associated with maternal drug use, and in Africa it has been associated with widespread nutritional deficiencies and with well-known infections.

Another important study concerning maternal-infant transmission of HIV proteins from the British Lancet medical journal found that 85 percent of infants who were HIV positive at birth, were HIV negative by 18 months,[477] which supports the fact that HIV antibodies in the newborn represent passive transfer of maternal antibodies rather than an infection. This study was confirmed by another investigation in the British Medical Journal that followed 1,954 women who were screened at delivery. They concluded that "HIV-1 serology is unreliable among children less than 18 months of life."[478] Finally, the fact that newborns test HIV positive about four times more often than do children from about 1 year of age to pre-teens argues against a mother to child transmission of an infection and in favor of a passive transfer of maternal antibodies.[479]

It is well known that newborns receive passive immunity in the form of antibodies from the mother by way of the placenta as well as breast milk. This makes prenatal therapy with AZT or Neviripine or any of the so-called anti-retroviral drugs an act of criminal battery to both the unborn and to infants of HIV positive mothers especially since the AIDS establishment has chosen to institute these drugs before there is a full assessment of the underlying metabolic and nutritional deficiencies. Unless there is an acute infection, compensatory therapy should be initiated before any drugs are given. Children are born with a cellular mediated immune system (Th1 cells), a humoral immune system (Th2 cells), and a regulator immune system (Th3 cells) as major pieces of their overall immune systems. These three arms are immature when babies are born, and begin to mature as children are exposed to their environments through their nervous systems, skin, airways and intestines. Antibiotics, poor nutrition, stress, exposure to heavy metals and other environmental toxins including maternal use of narcotics, and the

477. "European Collaborative Study. Mother to Child Transmission of HIV Infection,". Lancet 5 (1988):1039–43.

478. S. K. Hira et al., "Perinatal Transmission of HIV-1 in Zambia," BMJ 299. (1989) :1250–52.

479. H. H. Bauer, "Demographic Characteristics of HIV: II. What Determines the Frequency of Positive HIV Tests?" J Scientific Exploration 20 (2006): 69–94.

use of vaccines, may interfere with the proper maturing process of these three arms of children's immune systems. In theory, if the Th system is allowed to mature, and is not interfered with, children will develop a mature, balanced Th1, Th2 and Th3 immune system by age three.

P24/25 protein

To date nobody has proven that p24 is an HIV protein even though the CDC claims that this is the most indicative HIV protin. There is considerable evidence that p24 is a cellular protein. Two of the best known experts of HIV and HIV testing, Jorg Schupbach, the principle author of one of Gallo's 1984 Science papers where isolation of HIV was claimed, and Philip Mortimer, director of the UK Public Health Laboratory Service, do not consider the reaction between the p24 antibody and antigens in cell cultures as HIV specific. Using cultures of unfractionated blood and defining detection of p24 as virus isolation, HIV has been isolated from 82 percent of presumably uninfected but serologically indeterminate individuals and 5/5 seronegative blood donors."[480]

According to Mortimer, "Experience has shown that neither HIV cultures nor tests for p24 antigen are of much value in diagnostic testing. They may be insensitive and/or non-specific."[481] Of great concern, because use of these tests in pregnant women, using monoclonal antibody to p24, the p24 protein (as well as the p120 and p18 HIV proteins), has been identified in normal, non-HIV infected placentas, especially "in (chorionic) villi with immunopathological evidence of villitis."[482] Villitis is an inflammation of the placenta. On the basis of these tests, the unborn and newborns are being given genotoxic anti-retrovirals.

Antibodies to p24 have been detected in 1 out of 150 healthy individuals, 13 percent of randomly selected otherwise healthy patients with generalized warts, 24 percent of patients with cutaneous T-cell lymphoma, and 41 percent of patients with multiple sclerosis.[483]

---

480. J. Schupbach et al., "False Positive HIV 1 Virus Cultures Using Whole Blood," AIDS 6 (1992): 1545–46.

481. P. Mortimer et al., "Towards Error Free HIV Diagnosis: Notes on Laboratory Practice," Public Health Laboratory Service Microbiology Digest 9 (1992): 61–64.

482. W. P. Fault and C. A. Labarrere, "HIV Proteins in Normal Human Placentae," Am J Repro Immunology 25 (1991): 99–104.

483. A. Ranki et al., "Intepretation of Antibodies Reacting Solely with Human Retroviral Core Proteins," NEJM 318 (1988): 448–49.

Genesca et al. found that the p24 band was the predominant band in 70 percent of the case samples of healthy blood donors screened with the Western Blot test. They were considered Western Blot indeterminate (WBI). Among recipients of WBI blood, 36 percent were WBI 6 month after transfusion, but so were 42 percent of individuals who received WB-negative samples. Both donors and recipients of blood remained healthy. They concluded that WBI patterns "are exceedingly common in randomly selected donors and recipients and such patterns do not correlate with the presence of HIV 1 or the transmission of HIV 1."[484]

In another study, "In half of the cases in which a subject had a positive p24 test, the subject later had a negative test without taking any medications that would be expected to affect p24 antigen levels. . . . The test is clinically erratic and should be interpreted very cautiously."[485]

P17/18 protein

In addition to the p24 band, the p17/18 band is the most often detected in WB of healthy blood donors. When lymphocytes are stimulated with mitogens (oxidizing agents) but are not infected, the AIDS sera bind to a p18 protein in the non-infected lymphocytes.[486]

AIDS patients and those at risk have high levels of antibodies to the ubiquitous protein myosin, which has two subunits of molecular weights 18,000 and 25,000.[487]

In view of the above evidence, it is difficult to defend the perspective that bands p41 (and therefore p160 and p120), p32, p24 or p18 represent specific HIV proteins. Even if it could be shown that all these proteins are HIV specific, it cannot be automatically assumed that the antibodies that react with each of these proteins are specific to HIV infection.

In the final analysis, the question remains: Can the <u>HIV</u> antibody test give usable information about the health status of the patient and the condition of the immune system? Because, as has been demonstrated, the test substrate contains human, bacterial and fungal proteins, it can only indicate

484. J. Genesca et al., "What Do Western Blot Indeterminate Patterns for Human Immunodeficiency Virus Mean in EIA Negative Blood Donors? <u>Lancet II</u> (1989): 1023–25.

485. G. Todak et al., "A Clinical Appraisal of the p24 Antigen Test," <u>Abstracts VII International Conference on AIDS I</u>, Florence, Italy, 326.

486. R. B. Stricker et al., "An AIDS Related Cytotoxic Autoantibody Reacts with a Specific Antigen on Stimulated CD4+ T Cells," <u>Nature 327</u> (1987): 710–13.

487. P. Matsiota et al., "Detection of Natural Autoantibodies in the Serum of Anti-HIV Positive Individuals," <u>Ann Inst Pasteur/Immunol 138</u> (1987): 223–33.

the degree to which the patient will react to these proteins, and therefore, its predictive value for the current or future health status of the patient is limited. At the very least, the test might indicate a Th2 dominance with an increased antibody production, but the issue here is the condition of the Th1 cell mediated immune system. As will be discussed in the chapter on therapeutic considerations, there are more pertinent tests to assess the status of cell mediated immunity that would also suggest a clinical approach to therapy.

The Polymerase Chain Reaction (PCR) Test

If virologists followed the above protocol outlined by de Harven for viral isolation and identification of viral elements, there would be no need to invest in the absurdity of a gene amplification test. Why would there be a need to amplify a virus that is said to cause so much damage? Was it in hiding or was it a figment of some very over active imaginations? One of the reasons that HIV is unlikely to be the cause of AIDS is that the virus is never found in a quantity sufficient enough to have any pathogenic significance. Typically viruses that cause disease are found in very high titre when the disease is active. But HIV was claimed to be incubating for ten years and even in the presence of full blown AIDS the virus can hardly be found. Just as these cogent arguments were being made by prominent virologists, especially Peter Duesberg, HIV theory was twisted into another mind bending exercise trying to rationalize why a snippet of non-specific HIV RNA had to be multiplied with this new technology in order to not find direct evidence, but only inference that HIV was present.

It is not exactly clear in 1995 what David Ho and Xiping Wei might have been thinking when they came up with the idea of using the polymerase chain reaction technology to "amplify" this elusive virus that was said to be killing people. But what was clear is that he and his colleagues must have been overdosing on fluoridated water. One critique of his work observed that," No-one spotted the absurdity that if there were that much virus present in the blood you would not need to amplify it by PCR in order to detect it. To claim to have found so much cell-free virus by using sequence amplification is as ludicrous as 'finding' a previously invisible inflatable elephant with a bicycle pump.[488]

In 1996, David Ho was named Time's Man of the Year because of his radical misuse of PCR technology. Ho, a long-time HIV researcher, concocted

---

488. Michael Verney-Elliott, "Virtual Viral Load Tests, Seeing is Believing, its Time to Call Their Bluff", Continuum Midwinter 1998/1999

a rather impossible mathematical model that he claimed explained how HIV replication leads to AIDS. As it turned out, the model was a dazzling mathematical flight of fancy that explained nothing and was considered in more ethical scientific circles as dead on arrival. However, it was a useful tool for the pharmaceutical industry as the justification for selling more products to people who were dazzled by the numbers. Its accuracy for the prediction of disease status or outcome was irrelevant. The model was another strategy in the AIDS propaganda war. It was more Houdini magic to wave in front of the fearful tranquilized masses. According to Ho's "run-away hypothesis," an uncontrolled cycle of T cell activation, infection, HIV replication, and cell destruction eventually culminates in AIDS.[489]

Ho's model was a dream for big Pharma. The irony of using this mathematical manipulation to explain the rapid and massive replication of what was claimed to be a "slow" virus was lost on the public, but was used to justify early administration to those pronounced "HIV positive" with toxic and expensive retroviral drugs The idea of "hitting early and hitting hard," even when a patient was asymptomatic and had a satisfactory blood count, became the rationale for the current therapy protocol in which anti-retrovirals (ARVs) are prescribed at the time of confirmation of a positive-HIV antibody test when combined with the PCR. According to Ho, the "slow" HIV virus replicates rapidly from the time of the initial infection, at a rate that is just faster than the body's ability to mass produce the CD4+ cells. As a result, he claims that viral replication outpaces the immune system until the immune system collapses. To prevent this hypothetical destruction, Ho's model calls for immediate treatment of all newly identified HIV positive patients with a continuous cocktail of anti-retroviral drugs. This was a significant deviation from standard medical practice that had heretofore sought to improve the quality of a patient's life. Recognizing the serious toxicity of cancer therapy drugs, physicians had always used these drugs in a judicious fashion. In this instance, the laboratory parameters as defined by this erroneous test became more important as an end point than a patient's life. As a result, the complications, including death, from the early introduction of these drugs has risen sharply, and the touted benefits have come as a result of giving these drugs to people who may not have needed them in the first place.[490] Because of a false HIV/AIDS/DEATH construct, it was assumed that patients were going to die anyway, so that using them as subjects for human experimentation became socially and medically acceptable.

---

489. D. D. Ho, "Viral Counts in HIV Infection," Science 272 (1996):1124–25.
490. David Crowe, , "Concerns about HAART," 2001. www.virusmyth.com.

It was not long after Ho released his mathematical model that multiple researchers debunked his theory. One of these was Mark Craddock from the University of Technology in Sydney, Australia who pointedly commented that if Ho's theory were correct, over the 10 years that AIDS usually takes to develop in untreated First World HIV positives, they would each "produce more particles of HIV than there are atoms in the universe."[491] Craddock raised further poignant questions about the Ho et al., assumptions when he observed: "The logic [of Ho and Shaw] here is remarkable. It is claimed that HIV sends the immune system into overdrive as measured by a supposedly accelerated production of T4 cells . . . But where are the healthy controls? How can this production of T cells be ascribed to HIV if there is no comparison made with healthy people? And even if there were a comparison, how can the production be unambiguously attributed to the 'battle' with HIV? The patients in both study groups were being treated with new drugs such as nevirapine (we are naturally told nothing of possible toxic side effects of these drugs) whose effects are largely unknown. So how can these results be extrapolated to HIV positive people who are not taking these drugs? It must surely be admitted that the system they are trying to study, namely the interaction of HIV with T4 cells, might behave substantially differently in people who are not being pumped full of new drugs, in addition to 'antiretrovirals' like Zidovudine [AZT]? Yet HIV 'science' has declined so far that these elementary questions are addressed neither by the research groups themselves, nor the referees at <u>Nature</u> where Ho's work was published, whose job it is to critique the papers before publication."

Another group of researchers from Emory University in Atlanta and Imperial College, London evaluated Ho's model. They concluded that if the model were correct, then the body's CD4+T cells would decline to very low levels in months, not years.[492] Dr. Benigno Rodriguez of Case Western Reserve University in Cleveland, Ohio observed, "In an individual with advanced disease, if you look at the number of cells that are actually infected (with HIV), we are talking less than 1 percent . . . but . . . that person may have lost 20, 30, 50 percent of his immune cells."[493]

However, timing is everything. It seems that Ho's paper was published in <u>Nature</u> as a way to counter heavyweight Peter Duesberg, a highly respected scientist, who was presenting very strong arguments that the AIDS epidemic

---

491. M. Craddock, cited in C. Farber, "Serious Adverse Events: An Uncensored History of AIDS," (Hoboken, NJ: Melville House Publishers, 2006).

492. A. Yates et al., "Understanding the Slow Depletion of Memory CD4+T Cells in HIV Infection," <u>PLoS Med 4</u> (2007): e177.

493. E. J. Mundell, "Scientists Probe How HIV Infection Turns into AIDS," <u>Washington Post</u> 3 August 2007.

was a subset of the drug epidemic. It was also a way to increase the sales of protease inhibitor drugs that are claimed to reduce "viral load." Duesberg pointed out in his paper "Retroviruses as Pathogens and Carcinogens: Expectations and Reality," that one of many reasons why <u>HIV</u> could not be the cause of AIDS is that the virus is never found in sufficient quantity to have any pathogenic significance in those supposedly infected. Typically, viruses that cause disease are found in high titer at the time the disease is active. This was not the case with HIV—either in those said to be incubating AIDS for years or those with full blown AIDS. If <u>HIV</u> was detected at all, it was only ever 'found' in trace amounts and only then by stimulating cultures with oxidizing agents and co-culturing with cancer cells. According to Duesberg, this is one of the chief characteristics of a persistent harmless passenger virus.

Paul Philpott and Christine Johnson raised these issues in their 1996 article "A Viral Load of Crap." They found that the most troubling part of the Ho research was that most of the AIDS patients in the studied cohorts were also infected with a wide array of known and identified infectious viruses: cytomegalovirus (present in 40 percent of all Americans); Epstein-Barr virus (50 percent), hepatitis B virus (5 percent); herpes simplex virus type 1 (65 percent) and type 2 (40 percent). All of these viruses are cytotoxic and can be shown to infect at least one third or more of their target cells. HIV is not cytotoxic and has never been shown to be present in any more than a small fraction of cells, if it could be found at all without co-culturing with cancer cells and adding strong oxidizing agents and corticosterone to the mixture.

The fact that the early AIDS patients were infected with all of these real viruses would certainly account for the rise in their antibody titers and make it more likely that an HIV antibody test would turn positive. It is the simple law of probability. However, the idea of having to use a sophisticated state of the art and totally inappropriate amplification technique to find this terrible invader only proved that either the invader was smarter than the scientists using the test, or the invader is a figment of overactive imaginations—the latter being the most likely conclusion.

At any rate, the viral load PCR test only measures fragments of genetic material claimed to be HIV. The test is not able to distinguish infectious fragments from non-infectious genetic fragments and is incapable of measuring an actual virus. In the final analysis, this test also has been shown to poorly correlate with the antibody tests.

If the virus is not there, amplifying some extraneous RNA or DNA gene segments is not going to make it so—which is what Ho and Shaw did with the PCR gene amplification technique. It is not surprising, that with all of that amplification and gee whiz technology, there has still been no centrifugation, purification, and production of an electron micrograph of purified HIV that has settled at 1.16 gm/ml in sucrose gel, and there never will be because, it is just business.

Chapter 15

What Is Causing Immune Deficiency?

The Liquid Crystalline Organism, the Evolutionary Biology of Cell Symbiosis, The Dual Strategy of the Immune System

o o o o o o o o o o o o o o o o o o o o o o o o o o o o o o o o o o

The HIV hypothesis ranks with the 'bad air' theory for malaria and the 'bacterial infection' theory of beriberi and pellagra [caused by nutritional deficiencies]. It is a hoax that became a scam.

> Bernard Forscher, former editor,
> U.S. Proceedings of the National Academy of Sciences,
> in <u>Sunday Times</u> (London), 3 April 1994

Big Pharma and the World Health Organization are killing machines and the cemeteries of the world are full of their victims. Gullibility can indeed be lethal.

> David Ickes

Changes in the cellular redox environment can alter signal transduction, DNA and RNA synthesis, protein synthesis, enzyme activation, and even regulation of the cell cycle. Activities such as ligand binding, DNA binding, and nuclear translocation have been shown to be under redox control. Most eukaryotic transcription factors have been found to be under redox control...Thus, the redox environment of the cell might determine if a cell will proliferate, differentiate, or die. . . .We suggest that the redox environment may be the final determinant for the execution of apoptosis (programmed cell death). This is supported by the finding that <u>a decrease in glutathione levels correlates with apoptosis in lymphoid cells</u>.[494]

Freya Q. Shafer and Garry R. Buettner

The Liquid Crystalline Organism

Liquid crystals have become a constant feature of modern living. Liquid crystal displays (LCDs) found in electronic watches, calculators, and TV and computer screens have become a common technology familiar to most. LCDs offer some real advantages over other display technologies because they are thinner, lighter and draw less power. Their picture definition is impressive. However, much less is known about the function of these displays and the fascinating scientific background of the liquid crystalline state.

Liquid crystals combine the properties of both solid crystals and liquids and amazingly optical and non-linear physicists have found that the structural properties of living organism behave much like liquid crystals. This not only has enormous exciting possibilities for the future of medical therapy, but for the possibility of tapping into expanded awareness beyond the five senses ranges into other vibratory frequencies at will.

What makes crystals unique in the electrical world are that their atoms and molecules are packed in a three dimensional regularly ordered repeating pattern. Because the molecules in crystals are aligned in this way they have a resonance capacity that can amplify a vibration when exposed to an external force whose frequency is equal or close to the natural vibration frequency of the system. The liquid crystalline state retains much of this function.

The liquid crystalline state was discovered more than 100 years ago in 1888 when Fredrick Reinitizer, an Austrian botanist and chemist, synthesized several esters of cholesterol. He discovered a phenomenon that he called "double melting": At certain temperatures the compound changes from crystalline solid phase to an opaque liquid that transforms at a defined higher temperature to an optically clear liquid. A colleague of Reinitizer's, Otto

---

494   F. Q. Shafer and G. R. Buetner, "Redox Environment of the Cell as Viewed through the Redox State of the Glutathione Disulfide/Glutathione Couple," <u>Free Radical Medicine</u> 30 (2001): 1191–1212.

Lehmann, quickly discovered that the optical anisotropy of these liquids was the result of elongated molecules which are oriented parallel with the long axis. An example of anisotropy is light coming through a polarized lens. In the field of computer graphics, an anisotropic surface will change in appearance as it is rotated about its geometric normal. Liquid crystals have been found to assume other than elongated shapes, but the property of orientation along an axis is particularly important to the usefulness and diversity of their functions. Unlike solid crystals liquid crystals have the unique ability to be flexible, malleable and responsive.

George Gray, who has studied liquid crystals for many years, refers to them as "tunable responsive systems", and as such, ideal for making organisms.[495] It is already widely recognized that all the major constituents of living organisms may be liquid crystalline-- lipids of cellular membranes, DNA, possibly all proteins, especially cytoskeletal proteins, muscle proteins, and proteins in the connective tissues such as collagens and proteoglycans. Recent nuclear magnetic resonance (nmr) studies of muscles in living human subjects provide evidence of their "liquid-crystalline-like" structure. However, very few workers have yet come to grips with the idea that *organisms* may be essentially liquid crystalline. If these finding are true, and this has been confirmed in the laboratory, then it means that living organisms are not only receivers of vibrational energy, they are senders of information as well. And it does not matter if the information to be understood is in the same room, or on the same planet.

This has been confirmed by experiments that the United States government engaged in at the Cognitive Sciences Lab that involved what is called remote viewing. Remote viewing is the ability to produce information that is correct about a place, event, person, object or concept that is located somewhere else in time/space, and which is completely blind to the remote viewer. This was confirmed to me by Joseph McMoneagle whom I met at the Monroe Institute in Virginia. McMoneagle became expert at remote viewing in the U.S. Army and was Remote Viewer #001 in the Army's Stargate program. This liquid crystal property of living organisms may be the observable link explaining psychic ability.

The importance of liquid crystals—molecular orientation along an axis-- for living organization was actually recognized a long time ago. However, direct evidence for that has only recently been provided by Mae-Wan Ho a trained geneticist and her co-workers who successfully demonstrated that light and living matter are intimately linked in such a way that their research pushes

---

495   Mae-Wan Ho, The Rainbow and the Worm, 2006 (The World Scientific Publishing Co.) 173

the frontiers of quantum optics and other nonlinear optical phenomena in condensed matter physics and is one of the most exciting areas of endeavor in the biophysical sciences. They found that all organisms emit light (a vibratory frequency) at a steady rate from a few photons[496] per cell per day to several hundred photons per organism per second. Biophoton emission is universal to living organisms. They found that it is not specific to organelles but it is strongly correlated with the cell cycle and other functional states of cells and organisms. This will become pertinent to the discussion of AIDS and cancer. Importantly, the coherent energy of emitted photons is not lost completely and is coupled back coherently or reabsorbed by the system. Mae-Wan Ho goes on to say that, "...These observations are consistent with the idea that the living system is one coherent 'photon field' bound to living matter. This photon field is maintained far from thermodynamic equilibrium, and is coherent simultaneously in a whole range of frequencies that are nonetheless coupled together to give, in effect, a single degree of freedom. That means energy input to any frequency will become readily delocalized over all the frequencies..."[497] This vibratory energy can be transferred through large distances, theoretically infinite, if the energy is radiated, as electromagnetic radiations. It can travel though space at the speed of light, though in practice, it may be limited by nonspecific absorption in the intervening medium.[498] Variation from the single degree of freedom may arise because some parts of the system may be temporarily or permanently decoupled from the whole, as appears to be with malignant cancer cells.

This light emission property allowed the imaging of live embryonic organisms using a polarizing microscope and an interference color technique that amplifies weak birefringence typical of biological liquid crystals. They have discovered that all organisms so far examined are polarized along the anterior-posterior axis, so that when that axis is properly aligned, all the tissues in the body are maximally colored; the colors changing in concert as the organism is rotated from that position.

Another fascinating observation has been that connective tissues that function to give the body shape and form and that most have considered in simple mechanical terms, because of their liquid crystalline properties may also be largely responsible for the rapid intercommunication that enables our body to function effectively as a *coherent* whole, and are therefore central to our health and well-being.

---

496   A photon is a discrete bundle of quantum energy emitted as light when electrons change energy potentials.

497   Mae-Wan Ho, Ibid, 152

498   Mae-Wan Ho, Ibid, 32

Much of the connective tissue is made up of collagens that form a triple helix pattern that aggregates into long fibrils and bundles of fibrils that further assemble into fibers and sheets or other more complex three dimensional liquid crystalline forms. Recent studies have shown that collagens are not just mechanical fibers and composites. They have dielectric and electrical conductive properties that make them very sensitive to mechanical pressures, pH, and ionic composition[499] as well as electromagnetic fields. The electrical properties depend, to a large extent, on the bound water molecules in and around the collagen triple helix.

According to Mae-Wan Ho, all the evidence from physical measurements points to the existence of an ordered network of water molecules, connected by hydrogen bonds, and interspersed within the protein fibrillar matrix. The significance of the water bonds and their alignment with this helical configuration is that it supports rapid jump conduction of protons—positive electric charges—which has been confirmed by dielectric measurements. This jump conduction is a kind of semi-conduction and is much faster than ordinary electrical conduction or conduction through nerve fibers. That is because it does not actually require any net movement of the charged particle itself. It is passed rapidly down a line of relatively static, hydrogen-bonded water molecules. Based on mathematical calculations it is estimated that conductivity along the collagen fibers is at least one-hundred times that across the fiber.

It has been found that even the structure of the cell is highly ordered. This information has enormous potential for a total paradigm shift in medicine because of the amplification properties of aligned molecules vibrating in unison and coherently and emitting and reabsorbing light biophotons. These vibrational patterns and wave emissions carry coherent instantaneous information throughout the organism. This means that the living system only needs small inputs to create a cascade of change and rapid transmission over the entire organism. In humans, as in other living organisms, conductive circuits link the entire body in such a way that the whole system recognizes injury instantaneously and is able to respond. This has profound implications not only for consciousness being delocalized throughout the liquid crystal continuum but also the dominance of quantum and electrical forces as drivers of the much slower biochemical mechanisms.

Living systems are entirely electrodynamical. According to the great Hungarian physiologist Sznt-Györgi, "...life is driven by nothing else but

---

499   S. Leikin and D.C. Rau, et. al., "Temperature Favored Assembly of Collagen is driven by Hydrophilic not Hydrophobic Interactions"; Structural Biology 2 (1995): 205-210

electrons (and protons), by the energy given off by these electrons while cascading down from the high level to which they have been boosted up by photons.[500] An electron going around is a little current. What drives life is thus a little electric current."[501] The molecules in living organisms are largely dielectric or dipolar that are packed tightly together in coherent clusters. As a result, thermal energy arising from metabolism can be retained in the system by the excitation of these molecules creating an enormous electric field. Small signals will be greatly amplified because whole populations of cells will act in concert to set off a train of macroscopic coherent reactions. The excited molecules vibrate at various characteristic frequencies involving the coupling of electrical displacements and mechanical deformations. This builds up into collective modes of both electromechanical oscillations (sound waves) and electromagnetic radiations (photons) that extend over macroscopic distances within the organism and perhaps outside as well.[502] These excitations, like lasers, are coherent. And just as the solid state laser results from a quantum phase transition, biological organization is largely a quantum rather than a classical phenomenon. Coherent excitations can then account for most of the characteristic properties of living organisms: long range order and coordination; rapid and efficient energy transfer and extreme sensitivity to specific signals.[503]

If the organism is indeed a liquid crystal able to amplify frequencies at quantum speeds then it follows that the form of the organism will follow this bio-electric function. Until fairly recently it was thought that the cell had a central nucleus and was surrounded by a bag of enzymes and metabolites dissolved in solution bounded by a membrane. Because of the electron microscope and specific staining techniques it was discovered that the cell is highly structured. It is bound by a membrane which is comprised of a double layer of lipids with dissolved proteins which is supported by and attached to a membrane skeleton composed of contractile filamentous proteins--microtubules. The membrane skeleton connects with the three dimensional network of fibrous proteins called the cytoskeleton that form an interconnecting system with a terminus at the nuclear membrane. The chromosomes in the nucleus are anchored to the nuclear membrane. There

---

500   Photons—in quantum mechanics an elementary particle that exhibits the wave-particle duality dependent on the observer. It is the force carrier for electro-magnetic force.

501   A. Szent-Györgi, Light and Life , (W.D. McElroy and B. Glass, Eds.), Johns-Hopkins Press, Baltimore, 1961.

502   Mae-Wan Ho, The Rainbow and the Worm, The Physics of Organisms , 2006 (World Scientific, New Jersey) 113-114

503   Mae, Wan Ho, Ibid, 115

are even three dimensional canals and spaces believed to be involved in intracellular transport. Much of the volume is taken up by organelles such as the mitochondria. The microtubule roads are linked to a finer network of actin threads. Both networks constantly carry thousands of moving particles.

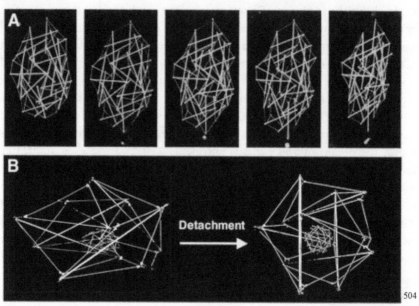

Tensegrity cell models composed of sticks-and-strings. (A) A model was suspended from above and loaded, from left to right, with 0, 20, 50, 100 or 200 g weights on a single strut at its lower end. Note that a local stress induces global structural arrangements (B) A tensegrity model of a nucleated cell when adherent and spread on a rigid substrate (left) or detached and round (right). The cell model is composed of large metal struts and elastic cord; the nucleus contains sticks and elastic strings. In this cell model, the large struts conceptually represent microtubules; the elastic cords correspond to microfilaments and intermediate filaments that carry tensional forces in the cytoskeleton.

The word tensegriy has been transferred from the language of the brilliant architect and social commentator, Buckminster Fuller to describe the structure of the cell and the living organism. A tensegrity system is characterized by a continuous tensional network supported by a discontinuous set of compressive elements--(the cytoskeleton to the organelles and protein complexes, connective tissue to bone, etc.). In the highly structured

504   Donald E. Ingbar, "Tensegrity I: Cell Structure and Hierarchical Systems Biology:, Journal of Cell Science 116, 1157-1173 (2003)

interconnected cell, electrical dipole interactions will be just as important as mechanical interactions in determining metabolic function. That is because mechanical deformations automatically generate electrical disturbances, and *vise versa*. The cell is an electromechanical continuum as is the entire organism. Successive enzymes and substrates in a metabolic pathway will move in a correlated fashion, which accounts for the characteristic rapid and efficient catalysis in living organisms.[505]

Because of this dynamic cell configuration, the membranes and the chromosomes can all be remodeled within minutes subject to appropriate signals from the environment. The entire cell acts as a coherent whole[506] and is an electro-magnetic continuum. It follows that electrical fluctuations, whether cyclical as those that drive mitosis or instantaneous as those responding to environmental stimuli (food, oxidative stressors) are translated into chemical energy.

All movement is based on the principle of alternating energy differentials. " 'Work' is performed solely because the electric current, which divides a motionless condition into two unbalanced conditions, sets up two oppositely straining tensions of unrest which must move to release those tensions."[507]

In the cell, this electric differential is measured in millivolts and is called the redox potential. The alternating change in this potential drives the function of the genomes and thus the anabolic reactions, including the transcription of DNA into RNA, and RNA into proteins, and proteins into enzymes. This fact became abundantly clear when researchers began performing cloning experiments. Workers observed that there appeared to be elements in the cell cytoplasm that drove the expression of the nuclear genome. It turns out that the genome is not a static hierarchal controller, but is adaptable to stimulations from the environment and is a continuously changing population of sequences. The genome also contains many relict viral sequences that have lost their ability to move independently and are present in all genomes including the human genome. About fifty percent of the human genome is now known to consist of virus-like sequences and transposons (virus like messenger particles), many with reverse transcriptase.[508]

This understanding of the physics of liquid crystals and the knowledge of organized coherence in living organisms gives credence to the reduction/oxidation theory of cellular function proposed by Eleni-Papadopulos-

---

505 Mae-Wan Ho, Ibid., 124

506 Mae-Wan Ho, Ibid., 121-122.

507 Walter Russell, A New Concept of the Universe (Waynesboro, VA: The University of Science and Philosophy, 1953), 22.

508 Mae-Wan Ho, Living with the Fluid Genome, (Third World Network, Penang, Malaysia 2003) 49

Eleopulos. By design, this theory wisely steps back from the minutiae of genes, DNA, RNA and proteins and considers the cell acting as a whole within its particular environment. The theory is based on the facts that for a cell or organ to perform any function, requires energy; the cell must be able to transform its energy into work; and all cellular (organ) functions are cyclical.

According to Papadopulos-Eleopulos cellular cycles are controlled by a periodic charge exchange in the thiol (sulfhydral S-H bond) moieties . Cell signaling involves the interaction of redox chains (S-H bonds), involving initiation, propagation, and termination. The messengers are mainly radicals and electrons that are generated during electron transfer and hydrogen atom abstraction reactions.

I will return to this function of cell signaling further on, but first it is important to understand why and how AIDS patients may present with a   CD4+T cell deficit. To do this, we must consider how living systems developed energetically and how and why they respond to energetic inputs as an organized result of evolutionary endosymbiotic relationships. It is becoming clearer that evolution did not take place by the neo-Darwinian mechanism of "selfish" selection of the fit, but by response and adaptation to environmental changes which are ongoing.

Evolution of the Eukaryotic Cell

Lynn Margulis, an evolutionary biologist, developed the theory of cell endosymbiosis. Endosymbiosis is a symbiotic relationship in which the symbiont takes up permanent residence in the host cell, and the two cells begin to function as one. This theory is germane to the development of many diseases, including immune deficiencies, because what is observed in the development of the disease process is a deficiency of energy production in the mitochondrial symbiont that leads to a dissociation of the cooperative function of the two genomes in the eukaryotic cell. Margulis postulated that life on planet Earth has been successful not because it is naturally Darwinian, but because those life forms that have survived have learned how to cooperate with other life forms for their mutual benefit and survival. The eukaryotic cell, which is defined by an enclosed nucleus, is an example of the successful symbiosis of two ancient bacteria that usually work together to maintain the redox environment, but can separate their functions if the cell's survival is threatened. This is called dyssembiosis. This also confirms Mae-Wan Ho's observation that parts of the living system can temporarily or permanently decouple from the whole.

Why life occurs on Earth and not on Mars or Venus is no longer a mystery, thanks to the NASA space program. The understanding of the organization of life processes in the Earth's planetary and atmospheric system that came from questions raised as a result of space exploration opened a way for microbiologists to reevaluate how life developed and sustained itself on the microscopic level. This NASA research gave evolutionary biologists a way to understand how life ultimately became more complex and sustained in the biosphere by being able to use energy in such a way that it organized away from thermodynamic equilibrium. Life has the ability to not only respond to but change its environment in a dance of mutual benefit. It appears not to be the genome but the energy flow through the entire living system that keeps it organized.

Space is not electrically neutral. More than ninety-nine percent of the observed universe exists in the form of plasma. Plasma consists of charged particles—negative electrons and positive ions (an atom missing one or more of its electrons). These charges create an electromagnetic force that has the potential to collapse the energy into what appears to be a solid state that we recognize as matter. At some point matter began to organize into a liquid crystalline state that we recognize as life. By ignoring the electric nature (redox potential) of living organisms and focusing on the biochemical, we have made life more complicated than it is. The change of focus to energy flows rather than static genomic architecture (that is anything but static) and slow biochemical reactions in turn is leading to incredible research into the identifiable causes of illness as primarily altered electrical and quantum processes that lead to alterations in coherence resulting in altered cell cytosociology and functions.

By understanding the nature of these processes, the physician can then initiate logically appropriate biological compensatory therapies. This new, scientifically validated understanding of the mechanisms of subtle energies gives a new understanding of how therapies such as reiki, acupuncture and homeopathy work. It also helps to explain why pharmaceutical drugs have so many untoward effects and must be used sparingly and judiciously.

Lynn Margulis came to understand that the micro-gaian energy fluxes of the cell responded to the macro-gaian environment in such a way that it created opportunities for evolutionary events to occur and allow the development of ever more complex organisms. From this idea, Margulis developed the theory of cell endosymbiosis.

The Darwinian model of evolutionary biology postulates that natural selection occurred as the result of genetic mutations and that new lineages and adaptations only formed by branching off from old ones and by inheriting the genes of the old lineage. Margulis has a different perspective on evolution. She states, "Life did not take over the globe by combat, but by networking. Life forms multiplied and complexified by co-opting others, not just by killing them."[509] This has been borne out by cloning research that has shown that the structure of genes and genomes are both subject to small and large changes in the course of normal development, and in response to feedback from the environment. The forms that survived did so because of symbiosis—the relationship that develops between two different species of organisms that became interdependent in response to an environmental crisis, with each gaining benefits from the other.

These ideas were absolutely revolutionary to both the medical and social institutions that had premised their beliefs on hierarchical supremacy. In the cell, they thought it was the central nucleus that controlled cell dynamics and genetic inevitability. The eugenics movement was and the human genome project is based on this erroneous assumption of genetic determinism. As it turns out, it was the cooperation between the central nucleus, the A nucleus, and the B nucleus of the endosymbiont—the mitochondria responding to external changes in the environment—that allowed for the evolutionary organizational development of more complex structures. It was the co-operation of these two ancient bacteria that created the micro-gaian environment of alternating redox potentials that were responsive to intracellular and extracellular environmental events that created the opportunity for complexity.

Margulis's theory contends that ancestors of eukaryotic cells (cells that have a nucleus and are the cell type of bacteria, fungi, protozoa, and humans) are a combination—a symbiotic consortium—of at least two or perhaps more bacterial species (endosymbionts). Because of the changing composition of the Earth's atmosphere and the oxygen catastrophe that occurred, bacteria that were able to use oxygen invaded anaerobic amoeba-like bacteria (prokaryotes that developed in an oxygen-free environment), and each was able to survive the environmental changes by performing mutually beneficial functions. The bacteria would make use of the oxygen rich environment and breathe for the anareobic amoeba-like bacteria, and the amoeba-like bacteria would navigate through new oxygen-rich waters in search of food. This way, each of the organisms would benefit from their symbiotic relationship as the waters and atmosphere of the Precambrian Earth were changing. This was life co-operating rather than killing, by adapting to external forces in order to survive—the antithesis of the neo-Darwinian paradigm.

---

509   Lynn Margulis and Dorion Sagan, ,Microcosmos: Four Billion Years of Microbial Evolution (Berkeley, CA: University of California Press, 1986), 29.

In support of the idea of the internalization and co-operation of two functionally different species of bacteria, it has been recognized that oxygen began to accumulate between the first fossil records of Prokaryotes and Eukaryotes. Because life existed (prokaryotic organisms) before the Earth's atmosphere contained free oxygen gas, these early prokaryotic cells obtained energy from a process known as glycolysis or fermentation. Energy from this process was produced in the form of a molecule of adenosine triphosphate (ATP).

It was only when free oxygen appeared in the atmosphere as a waste product—about two billion years ago—that the higher development of life was possible. The drive for greater complexity was able to occur because the symbiotic consortium now included bacteria that could utilize oxygen to make many more of the energy molecule ATP. Instead of getting only 2 ATP from a glucose molecule during fermentation, 38 ATP could be manufactured by these bacterial endosymbionts using the energy supplied by oxygen. This process is called oxidative phosphorylation—OX/PHOS. Oxidative phosphorylation is the metabolic pathway that uses energy released by the oxidation of nutrients to form the energy molecule ATP (Adenosine triphosphate). However, this more efficient energy mechanism also created more reactive oxygen species that required more reducing agents to restore the redox balance. These reactive oxygen (and nitrogen) species are known as free radicals. Free radicals are molecules that have an unpaired electron and are therefore unstable and highly reactive. They can be damaging to the cell because they alter the redox balance and if they are not able to be reduced because of an over supply of oxidizing agents or an under supply of anti-oxidants, they may alter the efficient functioning of the metabolic processes. This results in disease and aging.

The uptake of an electron (as well as a positively charged hydrogen ion—proton) by a receiving molecule is called reduction. The donation of an electron (as well as a hydrogen ion) is called oxidation. In living cells, the effective proportion of reduced substances to oxidized substances is called the redox balance. Because electrons cannot remain as entities on their own, electrons are always transferred from one compound to another so that the reduction–oxidation reaction or the electron donation–electron acceptance reactions always operate as couples. These coupled reactions known as redox reactions are a principle energy mechanism that drives the cells slower biochemical processes including the upregulation of chemical messengers. It can therefore be understood that radicals and electrons can operate in a dual manner, producing favorable influences, or unwanted results.

Every eukaryotic cell still has the capacity given the redox status to use predominantly both or one of these energy functions inherited from the two ancient bacteria. In a normally functioning cell, energy production is about 86 percent from oxidative phosphorylation and 14 percent from glycolysis. The ratios change during cell division when the energy requirement is met exclusively by aerobic glycolysis. The change in energy production during cell division allows the A nucleus to be protected from the risk of oxidative damage that occurs with oxidative phosphorylation. The fluctuations in redox status are the signals that initiate cellular chemical reactions. Oxidative signals are necessary in the early division phases, while reductive signals are needed in the later phase. This switch in energy usage is a simple yet brilliant strategy to minimize oxidative stress on proliferating cells.

Mitochondria still have their own DNA separate from nuclear DNA. Nuclear DNA (A nucleus) is inherited from both parents, but mitochondrial DNA (B nucleus) is inherited solely from the maternal germ line and traces back 200,000 years to what noted molecular biologist Rebecca Cann called the "mitochondrial mother" (i.e. the 200,000 year old East African Khoisan woman whose genes survive in all six plus billion of her present descendants).[510] The DNA of the A nucleus, however, codes for some of the proteins required for mitochondrial function, whereas the mitochondria produce the major source of energy needed for total cell function. The evolutionary cooperative transition of these two uniquely different bacteria permitted a massive increase in available energy production. This in turn allowed these simple early bacteria to develop into more complex forms. Over time, both the prokaryotic host as well as the bacteria endosymbionts developed a mutually satisfying or beneficial existence, and both entities lost their ability to function without the other.

An important facet of this cooperative endeavor is the ability under conditions of chronic oxidative stress for more and more dissociation of cooperation as the energy production transfers to the less efficient glycolysis produced in the cytosol at the expense of the more efficient oxidative phosphorylation of the mitochondria. Whether the cell is able to use the more efficient OX/PHOS energy metabolism of the mitochondria or switch to survival mode by using the less efficient glycolytic pathway in the cytoplasm is controlled by the cellular redox potential responding to local and external stressors (toxins, infectious agents, catabolic hormones, nutritional deficiencies, etc.).

The redox potential is also important for the transport of nutrients across the membranes of the cell organelles and from cell to cell and for the integrity of the vital molecules such as proteins, nucleic acids, fatty acids,

---

510   R. L. Cann, M Stoneking and A.C. Wilson, "Mitochondrial DNA and Human Evolution", January 1, 1987, <u>Nature</u>. 352

and many other biological substances. The cell that is producing too little energy has only three options depending on the speed and the duration of the oxidative stress. It can die, it can work less efficiently, or it can dismantle the cooperation of the two nuclei and de-differentiate. Too much sudden oxidative damage can give rise to sudden cell death known as <u>necrosis</u>. Chronic oxidative damage can lead to an increase in the rate of apoptosis or organized cell death. The increase in cell turnover above and beyond the daily turnover of cells becomes an important pathological mechanism for heightened autoimmune reactions that occur in AIDS patients and in many other disease processes. If the cell does not have the energy available to differentiate after mitosis, it can continue to replicate. Because it lacks the normal markers for down regulating the division cycle, it continues to proliferate. This is called <u>cancer</u>.

The idea that cancer cells have disassociated from the normal cell signaling process is further confirmed by Mae-Wan Ho when she observes that, "The electromagnetic signals may be involved in intercommunication is suggested by the photon emission characteristics of normal and malignant cells. While normal cells emit less light with increasing cell density, malignant cells show an exponential increase in light emission with increasing cell density. This shows that long-range interactions between the cells may be responsible for their differing social behavior: the tendency to disaggregate in the malignant tumor cells, as opposed to attractive long range interactions between normal cells. The difference between normal cells and cancer cells may lie in their capacity for intercommunication, which in turn depends on their degree of coherence...The inability of the system to re-absorb emitted energy coherently...is shown to increase with increasing cell density in malignant cells, and to decrease with increasing cell density in normal cells. These results are consist with the suggestion that cancer cells have a diminished capacity for intercommunication"[511]

The Redox Theory of Cellular Functioning

This new research coming out of the laboratories of physicists who study non-equilibrium thermodynamics, quantum optics and liquid crystals from people who dare to seriously inquire into Schrödinger's question, "What is life?" gives great support to the oxidative stress theory of AIDS as proposed by Eleni Papadopulos-Eleopulos. The redox theory of cellular functioning has not only been predictive of the AIDS crisis in a way the HIV/AIDS

---

511   Mae-Wan Ho, Op. cit, 154

theory has not but it has also suggested a reasonable approach to congruent biological compensatory therapy. Papadopulos has argued:[512]

- AIDS would remain in the restricted risk groups.

- The only sexual act leading to AIDS or a positive antibody test is a very high frequency of receptive anal intercourse in either sex. In 1986, Gallo, the proponent of the HIV/AIDS theory wrote, "Data from this and previous studies have shown that receptive rectal intercourse, for example, is an important risk factor for HTLV-III [HIV] infection. Yet, at the time of entry into this project, nearly half of the participants still practised this technique. We found no evidence that other forms of sexual activity contributed to the risk."[513]

- Both antibody positive and antibody negative drug users will develop AIDS and that not only individuals who use dirty needles but also those who use clean needles or even non-parenteral drugs will develop positive antibody tests. That both intravenous and oral drug users develop positive "HIV" antibody tests was shown as far back as 1988 when Sterk reported that a higher percentage of prostitutes who use oral drugs (84%), than IV (46%), test positive."[514]

- In Africa there was neither a new disease AIDS nor a new virus HIV. When <u>Reappraisal of AIDS: Is the oxidation caused by the risk factors the primary cause?</u> as finally published was written in 1984/85, Africa was not considered an important issue. Thus, Africa is only briefly mentioned. Following the 1986 Paris AIDS conference, AIDS in Africa became the defining example of heterosexual transmission.

This has been the pattern of the AIDS crisis. Even Luc Montagnier, one of the proponents of HIV/AIDS, is attempting to backtrack into the oxidative metabolism theory of AIDS. He rejected the notion when presented with the idea by the Perth Group, but now he is reportedly writing articles about

---

512   Eleni Papadopulos-Eleopulos, "Looking Back on the Oxidative Stress Theory of AIDS," Continuum Magazine 5 (1998/99): 30–35.
513   C. E. Stevens, P. E.Taylor, E. A. Zang et al., "Human T-Cell Lymphotropic Virus Type III Infection in a Cohort of Homosexual Men in New York City," JAMA 255 (1986) :2167–72.
514   C. Sterk, "Cocaine and HIV Seropositivity,". Lancet I (1988):1052–53.

oxidative stress in cancer and AIDS as if he had thought of the idea on his own.

In the cell, reductive potential energy is stored in sulfur-hydrogen bonds of amino acids known as thiols. Thiols are found throughout the cell in the cytoskeleton structure in the redox couplets, the proteins actin and myosin. The mitochondria appear to also play a central role in controlling the fluxes needed in the redox potential for initiation of the various cell functions of differentiation, proliferation, or apoptosis (programmed cell death). This is accomplished primarily but not exclusively by using thiol containing proteins and thiol containing couplets [and NADPH/NADP+], one of the most important thiols couplets being glutathione/reduced glutathione [GSSG/2GSH].

A consistent finding in both HIV positive and AIDS patients has been a low glutathione level. The finding of glutathione deficiency in HIV positives was established as early as 1989. Writing in the Lancet, Buhl et al., found that total and reduced glutathione concentrations in the plasma of HIV-infected subjects were about 30 percent of those in normal individuals. Concentrations of these substances in the epithelial lining fluid of the lung of HIV-infected subjects were about 60 percent of those in the controls.[515] These researchers commented on previous studies that had shown that depletion of intracellular glutathione was found to inhibit lymphocyte activation by mitogens (oxidizing agents that can induce cell division), and that glutathione is critical for the function of natural killer cells and for lymphocyte mediated cytotoxicity. It was shown that in vivo administration of glutathione enhanced activation of cytotoxic T cells, while exposure of lymphocytes to extracellular oxidants caused breaks in DNA strands and suppression of the ability of lymphocytes to proliferate—the pathological conditions observed in AIDS patients. After the release of this very important study, an enlarged study should have been done to compare the effects of anti-retroviral protocols to the replacement of glutathione and other known nutritional deficits in HIV positive and AIDS patients. However, this was not imperative for the commercial interests that control science and the application of that science to medical practice.

The Buhl study also found that depletion of intracellular glutathione in addition to inhibiting activation of lymphocytes, increases susceptibilities of human lymphoid cells to radiation, and suppresses cell-mediated cytotoxic functions, all of which suggest that intracellular glutathione can modulate the function of immune cells. Finally, the authors commented that to their knowledge, the HIV sero-positive state is the only known condition in

---

515   R. Buhl et al., "Systemic Glutathione Deficiency in Symptom-Free HIV-Seropositive Individuals," Lancet (1989):1294–98.

which there is a generalized deficiency in extra-cellular glutathione levels. Subsequently, low glutathione levels have been found to occur in many diseases.

As a result of glutathione deficiency, that represents an overall energy deficit, the cell symbiosis theory explains why eukaryotic cells become diseased or cancerous under conditions of prolonged oxidative stress. Because eukaryotic cells have two genomes—the nuclear DNA inherited from both parents and the mitochondrial DNA inherited from the maternal germ line—the symbiotic relationship can disassociate under conditions of oxidative stress. By assigning the energy of cell division between these two genomes, this separation permits a high degree of differentiation and controlled orderly division of the cell cycle. When the energy deficit, due to electron availability because of thiol deficiency occurs, the orderliness is diminished or lost. Because of the energy reversal, the cell can get trapped in the division cycle. And because of the altered redox status the cell is then unable to exit the division cycle. This is what is being called cancer.

The low-energy producing A genome dominates the late cell division while the high-energy producing B genome drives the early cell division phase and functions of the various differentiated cell types. From these fundamental cellular biological facts, the cell symbiosis concept leads to the following conclusions: 1. There is a controlled toggle switch between the mitochondria and both nuclear subgenomes; and 2. Transformation to cancer cells is a functional (not structural) failure of this toggle switch—after the division phase, the cells are no longer able to switch back to the differentiated cell performance phase; 3. The cause of the permanent functional failure is the gradual deficiency of one of the central functions of the mitochondria— to supply about 90 percent of the energy storing and energy transporting molecule ATP. When the mitochondrial functions are disturbed, alteration of the redox milieu occurs, and cancer cells intermittently or permanently revert to the archaic form of ATP synthesis, or glycolysis, which takes place in the cytoplasm. This is a much less efficient form of energy production, and this decrease in energy cannot sustain the high degree of differentiation and coherence which leads to a permanent alteration in the functioning of a normal cell. The less efficient energy production process causes up to a 20-fold increase in glucose turnover. As a result of the hypercatabolic metabolic state and increasing cell breakdown, patients can develop increasing numbers of immune complexes and the muscle wasting of cachexia seen in cancer (and AIDS) patients.[516]

---

516   Heinrich Kremer, "The Secret of Cancer: Short Circuit in the Photon Switch," The Silent Revolution in Cancer and AIDS Medicine (Bloomington: IN: XLibris Corporation, 2008).

This is why feeding cancer and AIDS patients high caloric diets without supporting the underlying metabolic deficiencies is fruitless.

As early as the 1920s, German biochemist Otto Warburg, M.D., proposed that cancer was caused by altered metabolism—a change in cellular energy production from oxidative phosphorylation to glycolysis. Warburg won a Nobel Prize in 1931 for his findings, but, like many who are ahead of their time; his cancer theory fell on deaf ears.[517] Today, Warburg's theory is enjoying a resurrection as prominent cancer biologists are finally beginning to understand that the so-called Warburg effect is a fundamental property of cancer cells and not a byproduct of the cells' transformation. In a prescient lecture Warburg presented at a meeting of Nobel-Laureates on 30 June 1966, at Lindau, Germany, he stated, "Impairment of respiration (oxidative-phosphorylation) is more frequent than impairment of fermentation because respiration is more complicated than fermentation. The impaired respiration can easily be replaced by fermentation, because both processes have a common catalyst . . . the consequence of the replacement of respiration by fermentation is mostly glycolysis, with death of the cells by lack of energy . . . cancer arises because respiration, but not fermentation, can maintain and create the high differentiation of body cells." Clearly, Warburg understood the evolutionary biological principle that was at issue in the development of cancer.

It was this insight and knowledge that led the Rockefeller-dominated cancer industry to focus away from the knowledge of this natural causal phenomenon to a reasoned but dead-end debate about genetic mutation and viruses. Genetic mutation is the effect. Altered energy metabolism is the cause.

The Dual Strategy of the Immune System

In addition to developing strategies for coping with oxygen deficits, cells developed methods of immune protection as part of the evolutionary survival process. As these eukaryotic organisms became more highly organized into colonies, they had to design methods to protect themselves from invaders. The first multicellular complexes of eukaryotic cells that developed (such as sponges) only had to contend with protecting themselves from harmful intracellular invaders (fungi, parasites, mycobacteria, and some virus species).

---

517   The early work on the energetics of life was done at the Dahlem Institute and funded by the Rockefeller Foundation. This is another choke point for suppressing vital information that threatens the lucrative business of cancer chemotherapy.

These cells used a cloud of the poison gas, nitric oxide (NO) to kill the invading organisms. NO gas works by oxidizing metallic compounds such as ferrous proteins and enzymes. Too much NO gas, however, can damage the cell by the production of free radicals, especially if it is not able to be neutralized with a reducing agent. To carry out the function of neutralizing intracellular organisms with lethal NO, these early cell colonies developed what we now call <u>cell mediated immunity</u>. This ability to kill intracellular parasites was notably absent in AIDS patients.

Cell mediated immunity involves lymphocytes binding to the surface of other cells that display an antigen (foreign or self) that triggers a particular cytokine or messenger response. Clinically, cell mediated immunity is involved in Delayed Type Hypersensitivity (discussed below), contact sensitivity, such as skin rashes that many people develop following contact with chemicals (for example, poison ivy), graft rejection in transplant patients, and pertinent to the AIDS issue, the killing of intracellular parasites.

As organisms became more complex and differentiated and developed circulatory systems, there was now a need to develop another way of neutralizing larger invaders, including worms. Larger invaders could no longer be held in check solely by inflammatory T cells because of the resulting oxidative and nitrosative damage. The secondary immune response that developed used protein molecules called <u>antibodies</u> to neutralize larger invaders. Today, this is known as <u>humoral immunity</u>. The T lymphocytes that participate in humoral immune response do not produce cytotoxic NO gas, and they respond to a different set of cytokine messengers from lymphocytes that participate in cell-mediated immunity. The distinct division of labor of lymphocytes and the immune system—a dual strategy— arose as an evolutionary biological necessity for the survival of complex organisms.

In the 1980s, Mossman and Coffman were able to understand the evolutionary biologically programmed dual strategy of the immune systems of complex organisms, including man. They identified the two parts of the immune system as Th1 (cell-mediated immunity) and Th2 (humoral immunity)[518]. They discovered that a corresponding stimulation of the inflammatory T4 cells is answered with a corresponding counter-regulation: a balance shift to increased stimulation of antibody synthesis. It takes about seven days for the shift to balance out. If redox homeostasis is not regained, then cellular immunity is weakened, and there is an evolutionary programmed strategy that increases antibody production of the humoral

---

518   The immune system has been shown to be more complex, but understanding the balance between Th1 and Th2 will give an approach to metabolic compensation therapy.

system. Depending on the cytokine profile responding to alterations in redox cell signaling, immature Th0 cells mature either to Th1 lymphocytes able to produce NO gas, or to Th2 lymphocytes that migrate to bone marrow and communicate with B cells to produce more antibodies.

This means that there are two functionally different types of CD4+ T cells that are morphologically identical. The dual function of morphologically similar CD4+T cells explains the finding of low blood CD4+T cells with increased antibodies in the initial AIDS patients. The patients had a prolonged alteration in their redox status from environmental stressors that had initiated a cascade of events and had changed the balance shift of the immune system to Type 2 predominance.

The Th2 cells migrated to the bone marrow (and out of the blood stream) where they communicated with the B cells the need for increased antibody production. Because of the oxidative stress there was an increase in cell turnover. Cleaning up the body's daily turnover of cells is part of the function of the immune system. This increased cell turnover also increases the level of immune complexes leading to the production of a higher antibody count. At the same time, the Th1 cells, because of severe and chronic oxidative stress, had lowered their redox potential because of depleted thiol pools and were no longer able to mount a cytotoxic NO gas response to kill intracellular invaders. This condition allowed for the overgrowth of opportunistic infections.

These are the common findings in AIDS patients: increased immune complexes, increased antibody counts and a decrease in circulating CD4+T lymphocytes. Even if there were a causative virus, the mechanism of altered cell metabolism would still have to be considered to institute appropriate compensatory therapy. Killing a virus without compensating for altered changes in cell metabolism cures nothing. People who are healthy or relatively so are able to heal from infections after chemotherapeutic intervention because they have not reached a cellular tipping point. Thus, they are able to take in enough anti-oxidants to maintain function and, therefore, cell differentiation as well. This was not the case for AIDS patients who had multiple metabolic deficits, a severe glutathione deficiency being a primary one. The energy deficit accounts for the numerous deaths of the original cohort who were treated with AZT, a very strong oxidizing agent, that not only aggravated an already energy deficient status but also directly attacked the mitochondrial endosymbionts that produce the most ATP.

The initial AIDS patients presented with opportunistic diseases indicative of a deficiency of cell-mediated immunity. Many of them also developed Kaposi's sarcoma that arose from the chronic diminished oxygen carrying capacity of hemoglobin to the capillaries from long-term nitrite use. The AIDS protagonists have argued that it is not the nitrites but the factor of repeated contacts with rectally deposited semen. The argument against their epidemiology is the decrease in the number of Kaposi's sarcoma cases in the gay community which correlates with a decrease in the use of poppers. However, rectally deposited semen is highly oxidizing and would strongly support this alternative hypothesis. Another factor in support of this thesis is the nitroso chemical profile of inhaled nitrates and their known carcinogenic effects.

These patients also presented with a corresponding compensatory counter-regulation of the Th2 system that manifested as a heightened antibody response. It is the heightened antibody response that is being measured with the HIV antibody test. These characteristics should have been a clue to the nature of the problem. The meaning is clear. The patients were not fundamentally immune deficient. Immune deficiency was the effect. The cause of the balance shift in the immune response was an altered redox status that allowed the expression of a Th2 response and created an unfavorable disposition for blocking intracellular pathogens. The patients had an altered bioterrain that permitted overgrowth of opportunistic organisms. One of the most common infections was pneumocystis carinii in the lung. This particular fungus is found colonized in at least 20 percent of healthy people without causing ill effects.[519]

The discovery of the dual strategy of the immune system by Mossman and Coffman answered the conundrum of a low CD4+T cell count in the presence of a high antibody count. To this day, the viral hypothesis has no plausible explanation for how the virus attacks solely the Th1 cells while sparing the Th2 cells. Because they are morphologically the same although their functions are quite different, how does the virus choose one over the other?

The Dual Role of Nitric Oxide (NO) gas

Another discovery important to the AIDS issue was made by researchers Furchgott, Ignarro, and Murad and illuminated the various functions of nitric oxide (NO). Their research gives another level of understanding the cell dyssembiosis theory of cancer and AIDS. NO can function as a cytotoxic gas. It kills intracellular organisms, but it must be quickly reduced to limit cellular damage. However, if it can no longer be produced through overuse by constant ingestion of oxidizing chemicals, or is undersupplied because of

---

519   Alison Morris et al., "Epidemiology and Clinical Significance of Pneumocystis Colonization," JID 197 (2008): 10–16.

malnutrition, the ability of the Th1 immune cells to restrain or kill microbial agents is compromised.

NO also has another important role in cell signaling as a regulator of the redox potential, both within cells and between neighboring cells, for example, between immune cells and microbes, local mucous membrane cells and microbes, normally differentiated cells and cancerously transformed cells. Nitrogen oxide is a small molecule effective as an ancient principle for communication within and between cells. The molecule interacts with metal ions and sulfur-hydrogen bonds (thiols, glutathione, etc.), in order to adjust redox potentials. As important as its cytotoxic function the role NO plays as a signaling molecule in the regulation of redox potentials and various bodily functions, such as the regulation of blood pressure, is equally if not more important.

As a result of this knowledge, there has been an explosion of research in numerous medical fields affected by the new nitrogen information, including but not limited to research in Immunology, Infectious Diseases, Hematology, Oncology, Cardiology, Diabetes, Hepatology, Sepsis research, Lung research, Tuberculosis, Organ Transplant research, Rheumatology, Multiple Sclerosis, sleep research, and sexual medicine.

The universal function of cytotoxic NO gas and of metabolites derived from this pervasive bio-molecule, as an archaic regulatory principle in human cell systems, has placed into question all previous disease theories, particularly those of AIDS and cancer. However, in light of a dynamic evolutionary view of these disease phenomena, an abundance of findings can be integrated into a revised holistic conceptual understanding.[520]

Given this background, the AIDS problem can be understood in light of the historical context of mass poisoning from a plethora of immune stressors that have resulted from "civilization," from the choice of commodities sold on the free market for mass consumption and the pharmaceutical drugs that operate to compound the problem, especially in those who are more predisposed to reacting to such toxins. We know that long-term use of chemotherapeutics and chemo-antibiotics are not only dangerous to the health of the current generation but also the health of future generations because of the damage inflicted on mitochondrial DNA by such products.

Since the polio scare of the 1950s, the American public has been programmed to accept that viruses cause disease and that vaccinations developed by the pharmaceutical industry can offer protection and thereby reduce certain infectious diseases. However, it is becoming increasingly clear

---

520 Kremer, "The Secret of Cancer," The Silent Revolution in Cancer and AIDS Medicine, 39–40.

that this is one of the great myths of modern medicine and that the epidemic rise in allergies and autoimmune diseases can be traced to the numerous vaccines children are coerced into receiving. The pharmaceutical companies have hijacked state authorities and school systems to demand that children receive 33 doses of 10 vaccines by the time they are 5 years old. If these vaccines are so wonderful and work as promised, why do the free market gurus at the drug companies use the state apparatus to enforce the sale of their products as they did during the Opium Wars with China? This has nothing to do with protection of community health and everything to do with protection of pharmaceutical profits.

The hypothetical idea of viral infection was taken up by the pharmaceutical industry for several reasons. The pharmaceutical industry was an outgrowth of chemical and petroleum industries that possessed knowledge of the toxicity of the products they were producing for the mass market. Looking for viruses instead of toxins as the source of disease outbreaks was an astute business move that allowed for the development and sale of profitable vaccines as a public health safety need. Unfortunately, this has been another medical myth created for profit because the promotion of vaccines as a public health measure came at a time in most Western countries when the outbreak of contagious diseases was falling precipitously, even before the massive and widespread intervention of antibiotics and vaccines. Neither of these marvels actually contributed to the acceleration of the slope of the downward trend of infectious diseases.

Ivan Illich has written in his book Limits to Medicine, "But two things are certain: the professional practice of physicians cannot be credited with the elimination of old forms of mortality or morbidity, nor should it be blamed for the increased expectancy of life spent in suffering from the new diseases. For more than a century, analysis of disease trends has shown that the environment is the primary determinant of the state of general health of any population. Medical geography, the history of diseases, medical anthropology, and the social history of attitudes towards illness have shown that food, water, and air, in correlation with the level of sociopolitical equality and the cultural mechanisms that make it possible to keep the population stable, play the decisive role in determining how healthy grown-ups feel and at what age adults tend to die. . . .In contrast to environmental improvements and modern nonprofessional health measures, the specifically medical treatment of people is never significantly related to a decline in compound disease burden or to a rise in life expectancy.[521]

---

521   Ivan Illich, Limits to Medicine, Medical Nemesis: The Expropriation of Health (London: Marion Boyars, 2002).

In the African AIDS belt countries of Uganda, northern Tanzania, Rwanda, Burundi, Congo, and part of Kenya, it has been reported that if people refuse to vaccinate their children, the World Health Organization and UNICEF have been able to mobilize the local army and/or the police and move from house to house grabbing children at gunpoint and vaccinating them.[522] Thousands of people, during what are called National Immunization Days in the months of July and September, go into the bush and stay there for weeks to hide from the vaccine police. While the army is looking for children to vaccinate, diseases that kill children like malaria, cholera, and stunted growth because of illness and poor nutrition and lack of infrastructure are completely ignored.

Putting all of this information together and for purposes of simplification, we can summarize that the human immune system is composed of two functional branches that, depending on a number of factors, may either work together in a mutually cooperative way, or in a mutually antagonistic way. One branch of the system is identified as Th1 and is the effector system. It controls what is called cell-mediated immunity (CMI). Cell- mediated immunity is the function of cells found mainly in the thymus, tonsils, adenoids, spleen, lymph nodes, and systemic lymph system. CMI is primarily responsible for destroying, digesting, and discharging foreign antigens from the body. This work usually takes place inside the cell, and the cell uses nitric oxide (NO), a poisonous gas, in carrying out this function. The Th1 function of destroying, digesting, and discharging foreign antigens is called the acute inflammatory response and is familiar to anyone who has had the classic signs of inflammation: fever, pain, malaise, mucus or purulent discharge, skin rash, or diarrhea.

The other branch is the humoral immune system or Th2, which primarily has a sensing function. Th2 cells interact with B cells in the bone marrow to produce large proteins called antibodies. Antibodies act as sentinels in the bloodstream to identify and neutralize foreign objects. An overreaction of the humoral system can produce allergies and autoimmune diseases.

A growing number of scientists are beginning to realize that the alarming rise in allergies and asthma (Th2) are likely triggered by the lack of stimulation of the Th1 cell- mediated immunity branch in childhood. This is happening because childhood infections that would normally activate the evolutionary biologically programmed response of the Th1/Th2 immune system is

---

522 "Polio Genocide in Uganda." Transcript of a talk given by Kihura Nkuba at the National Vaccine Information Center, Third International Public Conference on Vaccination, 7–9 November 2002, Arlington, Virginia, and aired on C-Span 2 on 7 November 2002.

suppressed by the onslaught of numerous vaccinations that may contain live attenuated viruses. The WHO was aware of the potential damaging effects of vaccines as early as 1972 when they produced a *Memoranda* that stated, "Viruses have long been suspected of contributing to the pathogenesis of autoimmune diseases. Antibodies directed against normal cell constituents have been reported in several viral infections." Further the *Memoranda* stated that "studies are now in progress to search for an association between HLA phenotype and susceptibility to diseases with a suspected viral etiology…" Vaccines contain either parts of viruses or attenuated viruses that are claimed to be less harmful. This confirms the hunt for biological weapons that can "target specific genotypes.

The T-helper cells of pregnant women switch to Th2 dominance between mother and embryo in the contact areas of the placenta, but the T-helper cells of the newborn child are imprinted with the Th2 type. After birth, a regulated Th1/Th2 balance has to be trained.[523] The vaccinations given during the first days of life are training the system to Th2 predominance, thus accounting for the alarming rise in allergic and autoimmune diseases in children since WWII. The exposure of mothers to drugs, foodstuffs, contaminated drinking water (nitrosamines, pesticides, hormones, antibiotic residues, cigarette consumption, environmental poisons, exposure to natural and artificial radiation, heavy metals, contraception pills, and so on) are likely to produce the same unbalanced shift to the Th2 profile.

Vaccines are antigens that are designed to stimulate the production of antibodies, the (Th2) response, without eliciting a digesting and discharging function of the cellular immune system (Th1). The repeated use of vaccines shifts the immune system balance from the Th1 (acute inflammatory discharging response) to the Th2 antibody producing side (chronic autoimmune or allergic response).

It appears that vaccinations do not strengthen the whole immune system. Vaccinations, unfortunately, over stimulate the humoral Th2 part of the system while simultaneously suppressing the Th1 cell-mediated immunity system. The vaccine- stimulated unbalancing of the system so early in life serves to weaken its CMI response. This in turn does not prevent disease but impairs the ability of our cellular immune system to manifest, to respond, and to overcome disease.

---

523   G. Delespesse, L. P. Yang et al., "Maturation of Human Neonatal CD4 and Cd8+ T Lymphocytes into Th1/Th2 Effectors," <u>Vaccine 16</u> (1998):1415–19.

Delayed Type Hypersensitivity

The Th1/Th2 unbalancing phenomenon and glutathione deficiency explain three decisive findings of the immune response of the T helper cells in AIDS patients who came down with massive fungal infections and other opportunistic infections: a depletion of T helper cells in the blood serum while at the same time exhibiting an increase of certain classes of antibodies; an unsuccessful or unsatisfactory maturing response (of lymphocytes) to stimulation with antigenic and/or proliferation factors; the anergic response of immune cells in the skin after provocation with recall antigens in delayed type hypersensitivity (DTH) tests. The retrovirus theory cannot be used to explain these immunological anomalies.

The DTH skin test is used to elicit information about prior exposure to an antigen. It has been recognized for 200 years and was first described by Jenner when he observed redness, hardening, and blistering at the location where he had injected smallpox. Reactivity is an indicator for the competence of cell-mediated immune response of the Th1 immune cells.

In current practice, a small quantity of antigen is injected intradermally, and a characteristic response is elicited that includes induration, swelling, and inflammatory cell infiltration into the site of the lesion within 24 to 72 hours. This reaction has been shown to be absolutely dependent on the presence of Th1 memory cells. Both CD4+ and CD8+ fractions of lymphocytes have been shown to modulate the response. Experiments have shown that Th2 cells may be involved, but the response is largely a Th1 phenomenon. If the DTH reaction is positive, then a successful defense and elimination of intracellular microorganisms (bacteria, viruses, fungi, and protozoa) can be expected. If the DTH reaction is negative (anergic), then a successful elimination of intracellular pathogens is less probable. Chronic, opportunistic, or highly acute infections could possibly develop. Therefore the DTH skin test has a higher predictive value of a possible negative outcome in potential AIDS patients than the HIV antibody test.

Since the mid-1970s, research studies in surgical patients have shown that those who remained anergic beyond several days post-op had higher post-operative infectious morbidity and mortality than those patients who were able to mount and maintain a DTH response. In addition, surgeons noted that an anergic DTH reaction as an expression of depressed cell-mediated immunity before admission to the hospital was significantly linked to sepsis in spite of the use of massive doses of antibiotics. A high percentage of these patients had significant adverse events, including a higher death rate.

According to German physician Heinrich Kremer who has written extensively about both cancer and AIDS, the surgical studies indicate, "The significant fact still remains that a long-lasting T-helper cell imbalance under pressure from heavy stress (as found in AIDS patients) is not altogether uncommon in the population as a whole . . . data from the findings [on surgical patients indicate] a high variability of the regulation of the immune response between the cell-mediated and humoral immunity manifested either in a stable immune balance, a flexible immune balance, or a fixed immune cell imbalance . . . a long-lasting immune cell dysbalance (sic) under profound stress loads (acquired immunodeficiency = AID) with or without an infectious syndrome is by no means a rare or 'puzzling' occurrence."[524]

In other words, acquired immune deficiency with or without the syndrome of infectious disease had been noted many times before in the medical literature before the current AIDS era.

This information was known and significant when the early AIDS patients presented with an anergic DTH skin response. Because the immunological disturbances of the AIDS patients mimicked those of the anergic surgical patients, a connection should have been made about the underlying metabolic disorder. Part of the art of medicine is to be able to observe phenomenon and connect the dots. The finding of an anergic skin response in AIDS patients was a clue to altered cellular immunity, not from a virus that could not be found, but from external oxidative stressors that were present in abundance and should have been known from the intake anamnesis.

What is called AIDS or acquired immune deficiency, is a severe depletion of the available potential energy stored in the electrons of the thiols, especially glutathione. This in turn leads to an altered redox state that favors the cytokine profile that preferentially selects for the expression of Th2 lymphocytes at the expense of Th1 lymphocytes. Because Th1 constrain the growth of intracellular parasites using the poisonous nitric oxide gas, in their absence, opportunistic infections proliferate. Simultaneously, Th2 cells initiate the proliferation of antibodies. Some of the environmental toxins associated with AIDS, such as amyl nitrites, also create a condition known as methhemaglobinemia, in which less oxygen is carried to the small blood vessels. Because of the reduced oxygen level, the mitochondria have less of this energy substrate, and this in turn leads to de-differentiation and cell proliferation—Kaposi's sarcoma—and to increased cell turnover leading to hypercatabolism and muscle wasting.

AIDS is not a mystery. AIDS is not an infectious disease. AIDS is not transmitted sexually—except to the anal receptive partner because of the

---

524   Kremer, Silent Revolution in Cancer and AIDS Medicine, 106.

oxidizing capability of sperm. AIDS is an energy deficit condition leading to immune system disturbances, and it does not have to be a death sentence.

Chapter 16

Overcoming the HIV/AIDS paradigm by using "The Secret"

○ ○

We are so used to this darkness that we mistake it for reality. We cannot recognize light because we believe the darkness is light. This makes for a very upside-down world. People who exploit separateness are called successful; those who make war are immortalized in bronze or marble. This is living in pitch darkness . . . and calling the darkness day. Those who really see are those who forget themselves completely in living for the welfare of all.

Eknath Easwaran, The Bhagavad Gita for Daily Living

There is nothing more powerful than a human mind determined to think and act for itself. Such a phenomenon is a manipulator's nightmare and, like everyone on this planet, you have that power. . . .You only have to use it.

David Icke, And the Truth Shall Set You Free

Operation Gladio was an intelligence network under NATO (North Atlantic Treaty Organization) auspices that carried out bombings across Europe from the 1960s until the 1980s. Operation Gladio's specialty was to carry out what is termed false flag operations—terror attacks against innocent civilians that were blamed on their domestic and geopolitical opposition.

In March 2001, Gladio agent Vincenzo Vinciguerra stated, in sworn testimony, "You had to attack civilians, the people, women, children, innocent people, unknown people far removed from any political game. The reason was quite simple: to force the public to turn to the state to ask for greater security."[525]

The existence of Operation Gladio was revealed by former Italian President Francesco Cossiga. Cossiga was elected president of the Italian Senate in July 1983 before winning a landslide election to become president of Italy in 1985. He served until 1992. Cossiga also revealed in one of Italy's major newspapers that the 9/11 terrorist attacks were false flag attacks, and this was common knowledge among global intelligence agencies. Morgan Reynolds, former director of the Criminal Justice Center at the National Center for Policy Analysis, made the same claim. Reynolds stated in a speech at the Wisconsin Historical Society that everyone in the worldwide intelligence community knew that 9/11 was an inside job as soon as it happened, with the obvious stand-down of U.S. air defenses, controlled demolition of the World Trade Center (and building 7), and lack of protection of the President in Florida as the biggest tip-offs. The head of the Russian equivalent of the Joint Chiefs of Staff, the former head of German intelligence service Andreas Von Bulow, former National Security Agency official Wayne Madsen, former MI-6 agent David Schayler, and former Pakistani ISI chief Hamid Gul have all openly called 9/11 an inside job. In 2009, 9/11 Commission member John Farmer, in The Ground Truth: The Story behind America's Defense on 9/11, claimed that "the public had been seriously misled about what occurred during the morning of the attacks . . . at some level of the government, at some point in time . . . there was an agreement not to tell the truth about what happened."

For those who study significant historical events as evidence of deep politics rather than the propaganda of elite chroniclers, the revelations by high-placed bureaucrats was not news but evidence of a long-standing pattern of using terrorism against soft targets by the global criminal class for achieving a desired end. The idea of employing strategic deception against the American public was detailed by a Council on Foreign Relations member Richard N. Gardner in 1974 in the journal Foreign Affairs: "The Hard Road to World Order". Part of the strategy he outlined is to create the illusion of incompetence and disorder as a method of confusing opponents of this plan. The stand down on 9/11 and the destruction of New Orleans post Katrina are recent examples of planned incompetence. In the parlance of the internet: LIHOP (Let it happen on purpose)

The technique of shocking civilian populations by use of terror was perfected by the Mossad in subduing the Arabs and driving the British out of Palestine after WWII. It has been used extensively by U.S. covert agencies

---

525. www.americanfreepress.net/html/9-11_solved118.html

during the last century in Africa, in Central America, and South America. Now, in the final drive for global financial consolidation, it is being used as an existential threat against the populations of Europe and the United States. The Project for the New American Century document, "Rebuilding America's Defenses," released in 2000, actually stated that "the process of transformation, even if it brings revolutionary change, is likely to be a long one, absent some catastrophic and catalyzing event—like a new Pearl Harbor."

In the case of 9/11, it was a catalyzing event to induce high levels of fear and panic in the population, similar to operation Gladio, in order to engage the world in a war against various nations in the Middle East and Afghanistan (to increase the opium supply and oil revenues) and to institute draconian measures in democratic countries to make the curtailment of rights, domestic spying, and torture acceptable to the public. It was also used to hide a $2.3 trillion heist from the Pentagon that occurred under the watch of Dov Zakheim, a dual Israeli/American citizen that was announced on 9/10/2001, on national news by Donald Rumsfeld, Secretary of Defense at the time. And as always, it was a way to destabilize civil society through financial manipulation in order to consolidate more power into fewer hands with the goal of advancing the final phase of global economic consolidation. During the period 1983 to 2004, of all the new financial wealth created in the U.S., 42 percent went to the top 1 percent of the population. That the very people who created the financial crisis are now running the Treasury Department, the Federal Reserve, and are acting as presidential financial advisors underscore this view.

In sworn testimony, according to Sibel Edmonds, a State Department translator who has been muzzled by both the Bush and Obama administrations, Douglas Feith, Paul Wolfowitz, and Richard Perle, (all neocon signers of the PNAC document that also called for the use of bioweapons that target specific genotypes as a politically useful tool) in the summer of 2001, four months before 9/11, were negotiating war plans with the Turkish ambassador to Washington, whereby the U.S. would invade Iraq and divide the country. The U.K. would take the south; the rest would go to the U.S. They were pre-arranging what Turkey would require in exchange for allowing an attack from Turkish soil. She also noted that there were 'bin Ladens' under our management being helped by the Pakistanis and Saudis, under the direction of Marc Grossman, who was the third highest ranking State Department official and former ambassador to Turkey. Edmonds claims to have translated documents that showed that this aid continued up to 9/11. The U.S. was financing the taliban (al Qaeda)!

John M. Cole, a former FBI counterintelligence and counterespionage manager, confirms the FBI's decade long surveillance of Grossman in connection with numerous cases of Israeli spying. Edmond's allegations also claim that Grossman worked closely with the Turks and Israel in obtaining and selling nuclear weapons technology on the worldwide black market and that it was Grossman who tipped off Turkish diplomatic colleagues about the true identify of then-covert CIA operative Valerie Plame. Plame was an undercover operative working for a CIA front company, Brewster Jennings, who was tasked with tracking the sale of weapons of mass destruction on the black market. Her cover was blown by now deceased journalist Robert Novak. No affirmative action was taken by the FBI against Grossman despite mountains of evidence collected.

According to Edmonds, under Grossman's direction, they were bringing people from East Turkistan into Kyrgyzstan, from Kyrgyzstan to Azerbaijan, from Azerbaijan some of them were being channeled to Chechnya, some of them were being channeled to Bosnia. From Turkey, they were putting all of these 'bin Ladens' on NATO planes. People and weapons went one way, drugs came back. The drugs were routed to Belgium with NATO planes. After that, the drugs went to the U.K., and a lot came to the U.S. via military planes to distribution centers in Chicago, Illinois and Paterson, New Jersey. Turkish diplomats who were never searched were coming in with suitcases of heroin.[526] Since the United States invaded Afghanistan and restored opium production, which the Taliban had prohibited, there has been a drop in price, an increase in potency, and a steep rise in heroin deaths in the U.S. and world wide.

In his 1957 book Battle for the Mind: A Physiology of Conversion and Brain-Washing, William Sargant, a psychiatrist with the British Tavistock Institute, exposed the threat of mind control: "Various types of belief can be implanted in people after brain function has been deliberately disturbed by accidentally or deliberately induced fear, anger or excitement. Of the results caused by such disturbances the most common one is temporarily impaired judgment and heightened suggestibility. Its various group manifestations are sometimes classed under the heading of 'herd instinct,' and appear most spectacularly in wartime, during severe epidemics, and all similar periods of common danger, which increase anxiety and so individual and mass suggestibility. . . .We would be advised not to underestimate the effect on the collective psyche in terms of fear and a desire for the authorities to 'protect

---

526. Sibel Edmonds and Phillip Giraldi, "Who's Afraid of Sibel Edmonds?" The American Conservative, 1 November 2009.

people' from that fear."[527] Creating external fears through terrorism, claims of phony pandemics, manipulated financial crisis, and recurring Emmanuel Goldstein bogey men are the barking sheep dogs herding the masses passively into a state of total complicity with their warders. However much on the surface this use of terror seems to be growing, the fact of the matter is that it is the only weapon these people have, and, globally, as more and more ordinary people become aware of the rules of this game, it is becoming less and less effective. This is the reason staged terror has become more frequent and more spectacular.

The pattern used to manipulate behavior is rather predictable:

1. Create a crisis of some sort that leads to suffering among the people who then desire that something must be done.
2. Influential people are duped into supporting the cause without realizing the real agenda; such people are subsequently dumped after they have served the purpose;
3. The use of mass propaganda to exploit the public's natural sense of injustice, to disinform, and to lead opinion in the desired direction.
4. Lies are told about opponents of the plan coupled with assassination of their character to the point where people have great hatred for them.
5. The organization of 'rent-a-mob' to cause agitation and encourage others to overthrow the established order.
6. The installation of a phony democracy or alternative dictatorship.[528]

How did this model work in the creation of the AIDS crisis?

1. The crisis of immune deficiency was created by a combination of widespread mass poisoning that occurred after WWII and a concentrated release into the population of legal and illegal drugs during and after the Vietnam War.. In Africa, it was the result of widespread social and economic disruptions as a result of World Bank and IMF imposed "Structural Adjustment Programs." The environmental assaults resulted in those so disposed: a maladaptive hormonal response combined with an acute inflammatory process and displacement of the individual's metabolism with a hypercatabolic state that engendered energy and immune problems. Those of

---

527. Sargant, William, The Battle for the Mind: A Physiology of Conversion and Brainwashing, (Lewisville, TX: Major Books, 1997).
528. David Icke, ". . . And the truth shall set you free" (Cambridge, U.K.: Bridge of Love, 1995), 56.

African descent were specifically targeted because the HIV antibody tests were designed to identify particular genomic polymorphisms, such as those used to track the course of human migration of the last one hundred thousand years. Since the 1970s the WHO had been tasked with studying the association between HLA phenotype and susceptibility to diseases with a suspected viral etiology.

2. Robert Gallo was the scientist used to create the illusion of a new viral infection because he had particular personality characteristics that made him a useful tool. Many others came on board because they agreed with the manipulation, or because this was where the money and accolades were.

3. Massive propaganda campaigns were mounted based on epidemic fabrications and scientific falsifications to make the public believe this oxidative hypercatabolic state induced by environmental toxins was a sex and blood plague that originated in Africa and would soon envelope the globe in an uncontrollable pandemic. Many Hollywood and television stars jumped on the bandwagon. The repetition of the false mantra HIV/AIDS and sex and blood plague created a mass hypnosis in the public to accept such unfounded assertions.

4. Peter Duesberg was at the top of his game in virology research. He knew that HIV science was flawed and spoke openly of this early on and stated that AIDS was a subset of the drug epidemic. Although he had been published in major scientific journals, they began to refuse to publish his rebuttals of this flawed theory. He lost status, his funding, his laboratory, and his graduate students. President Thabo Mbeki of South Africa simply called a conference to hear all sides of the AIDS argument when the <u>New York Times</u> began to call him "irresponsible" for being hesitant about poisoning his population with ARVs. People who held alternative views were deemed "AIDS denialists," and reasoned scientific arguments never made it into the major trade journals or the public debate. There was an intentional information blackout.

5. The drug companies funded multiple front organizations, including the outspoken group "ACT UP" that were mobilized to crush any alternative views of the pathological process and healing modalities that could be used to reverse the toxicity. They specifically demanded fast action from the drug companies and a speed up of FDA drug approval—and they got it in the form of AZT, a mitochondrial toxic drug that finished off people who were in need of detoxification and biological compensatory therapy. The toxic therapy thus made HIV/AIDS a self-fulfilling prophecy in the public mind.

6. The CDC, with the aid of their Epidemic Intelligence Service, became the arbiter of all things <u>scientific</u> that related to AIDS. Any evidence that did not meet with their approval and was contrary to the HIV/AIDS dogma was roundly dismissed. Rebuttals from serious scientists were kept out of scientific journals and the mainstream media. The CDC established a knowledge monoply with absolute authority over life and death without accountability. The journal <u>Science</u>, in which Gallo's original articles were published, has been presented with uncontestable evidence retrieved from the National Archives and signed by thirty-seven reputable senior scientists that Gallo never isolated a virus and that the cause of AIDS could not be found, but the journal has refused to revise this serious scientific fraud.[529]

The classic pattern of counterinsurgency warfare is always predicated on an illusion. If the truth will set you free, the corollary is that a lie will enslave you. The consistent predictable pattern is that lies are promulgated as truths and hidden in the fog of confusion. Walking out of the fog requires something truly revolutionary—a change of consciousness. This persistent warfare used by the overlord class to get their way at the expense of other humans and the planet is at base, spiritual in nature. The real world war is not about financial control, or bioweapons, or bombs and drones, or drugs or terrorism. The real war is for the energetic destruction of the congruency of the heart and mind in an attempt to darken the light of the human spirit. There are 7 billion hearts and minds on the planet and, if as few as 10 percent were aligned in spiritual harmony, the war would likely be over immediately—the destructive energy Matrix that has taken hold of the minds of the masses with their created illusions and who are hell bent on world domination by monopoly control of credit and resources would not have enough psychic energy to power its base. To do what is being done, people must not only believe in the illusion based on fear, but they also must be taught to doubt their own abilities of perception and analysis. If the belief in the illusion falls away, it is no longer effective as a means of control. To believe the nonstop lying, whether they are direct or lies of omission is to give your energy to the Matrix system whose primary goal is to use your productive energy for the growth of their wealth and power. To hope that Matrix energy can produce anything that ultimately will not be more destructive than constructive is to believe in grifters and hijackers. It is what it is.

The battle of seeing through the fog of illusion is not at first self-evident but becomes easier with practice. We are all the confused Arjuna on the

---

529. Janine Roberts, <u>www.fearoftheinvisible.com</u>

field of battle with ourselves. In the <u>Bahagavad Gita</u>, Sri Krishna is Arjuna's true nature and higher self who speaks to him as a spiritual guide. This alter ego true self gives Arjuna, who is every man, many lessons in winning the battle over his own raging spirit. At one point, he states, "With your mind intent on Me, Arjuna, discipline yourself with the practice of yoga. Depend on me completely. Listen and I will dispel all your doubts; you will come to know Me fully and be united with Me." In other words, Arjuna's challenge and great battle of life in which he is engaging is to become aligned with his true spiritual nature which is other than the five sense world. The physician and spiritual guide, Deepak Chopra has often stated it succinctly, "We are spiritual beings having a human experience." Quantum physics tells us that we have the power to create the experience we want. The question that should be raised is: What discipline is required to learn how to calm the mind enough to dispel doubts and not to confuse the five senses world with the quantum nature of who we really are?

The great battlefield the <u>Gita</u> talks about is our own body/mind where there rages an unceasing battle between the forces of selflessness and selfishness, of light and darkness, love and hatred, unity and separateness, harmony and violence. The power of the Matrix energy is such that it has mastered the art of making selfishness appear to be selflessness, darkness appear to be light, and hatred and separateness appear to be love and unity. One of their great and useful mantras is: "We're here to help you." This help usually entails the restriction of some sovereign right and the aggrandizement of more power into fewer hands.

Because they have skillfully learned to use propaganda to raise passions, we self-sabotage and become a threat to the health of civil society and to ourselves. The worst threats to health come from anger, fear, greed, and self-will. These emotions sabotage our health, our security, and our capacity to love. This is why the news is constantly filled with the most horrendous stories and stories of love, hope and optimism are seldom addressed. In the midst of the planned confusion it is possible to find internal peace by learning the practice of empowerment through stillness. Through the practice of meditation, we can learn to quiet our Arjuna nature. Even the Bible advises, "Be still and know that I am God." The <u>I</u> being referred to is alignment with our higher spiritual self.

One of the most fundamental spiritual laws is that only right means can produce right ends. War cannot produce peace. Greed cannot produce satisfaction, dishonor cannot produce honor. Understanding this principle allows us the freedom from disappointment in the institutions and people we have been taught to admire and trust. Understanding that pharmaceutical companies are in business to make a profit and not to protect our health frees us from the illusion that they are incapable of creating epidemics to make more money and that they would not intentionally promote products that they know are harmful or deadly. It would allow us to understand that such companies have no problem using state authority to violate our inalienable rights to refuse their products and that they have usurped our fundamental rights by buying enough politicians to pass laws protecting them from the harmfulness of their products. But more than buying politicians, they have bought our belief and trust although they have consistently shown themselves to be untrustworthy. That fault lies not with the politicians or the drug companies, but with our willingness to be gullible even when we understand the principle of right means and see it being constantly violated. Holding two opposing views simultaneously is called "cognitive dissonance" and it is not only a mental aberration, it is indicator of spiritual turmoil.

The AIDS paradigm has created a universal belief system based not on science but on inference, innuendo, and association. Very few people will exercise the capacity to synthesize what on the surface may appear to be unrelated events. The assassination of President Kennedy, the prolongation of the Vietnam War, the War on Drugs, the War on Cancer, the rise of Kissinger and Iran-Contra, the de-industrialization of the United States and the strengthening of China as a world power, the genocide in the Congo and the current financial crisis are different acts of the same psychodrama.

The tendency, especially among allopathic physicians, will be to rely on public pronouncements and secondary sources furnished by the drug industry that filter and twist information until what is up appears to be down and what is down appears to be up. Many who do know better remain silent because, as social corruption swept in on the tidal wave of banker/drug/mob culture, there can be great personal or professional danger in becoming a whistleblower.

Sibel Edmonds is an anomaly. Her exposure of intrigue and treason at high levels of government has been deliberately suppressed. Her experience confirms that the person who exhibits integrity in a society ripe with corruption is not likely to be well received. However, by honoring people who take such risks, we can deconstruct Matrix energy. What if every town square in America had a statue erected to a whistleblower or a peacemaker in place of a war memorial? It is not warriors who have kept us free. That is a true looking glass concept. It is warriors who have made it safe for bankers to enslave us. It is warriors who do the bidding for a force that uses and forgets them if they are broken in service to the illusion. Major General Smedley Butler understood the principle when he wrote <u>War is a Racket:</u> "It is possibly the oldest, easily the most profitable surely the most vicious. It is the only one international in scope. It is the only one in which profits are reckoned in dollars and losses in lives."[530]

The ongoing physical and psychological terrorism and information manipulation projects designed to create some desired outcome make it very clear that the global overlords are aware of the human energy systems and of our spiritual nature and how and why they function in the creation of physical, mental, and spiritual health. By using Tavistock techniques of mass mind control, they have become expert at blocking these energy centers that, by natural inclination, must align harmoniously to allow us to understand our true nature, to extract ourselves from illusions, and to become unaligned with false reality. This is why there has been an onslaught of mercury- and aluminum- ladened vaccines, fluoride in the water, drugs that attack the cell's energy metabolism and spiritual will, genetically modified food, toxic chemicals, and toxic ideas. They are working very hard, but they still have not succeeded—and will never succeed in these efforts. The entire goal of this system is to keep us mired in the five sense world and to deny that there is a larger reality. AIDS is another dissonant note sent to disrupt universal harmonics and natural laws. Poisonings are being deliberately administered to diminish human intellectual and spiritual potential, especially our capacity to use our will. Without will, we have no freedom, and without freedom of choice, we become the automatons divorced from our spiritual potential.

Part of the control mechanism has been to misinform people about the nature of empowering esoteric knowledge, often referred to as occult.. The idea that esoteric knowledge is dark associates it with negative symbolism. Such knowledge is so powerful that it has been intentionally suppressed for over two thousand years. Yet, it has been misused to drive planetary energy to its lowest vibrational state by instilling fear as a control switch. It is used by religions, corporations, and governments that have all come under Matrix control.

As we cycle into the 21st century, it is clear that the suppression of this knowledge is becoming less effective and is at the core of what is driving the onslaught of ever more successive future shocks designed to create more fear with the hope that people will collectively give up their freedoms and free will and will willingly submit to more vaccines, more drugs, more cameras, more prisons, more police, more intrusion into privacy, and more economic deprivation. But in the end, it is being done to create the illusion of separation.

The knowledge being suppressed is fairly straightforward. It is that each individual has the ability to create his reality and has the potential to harness the energies of Creation not only for transformation but also for dispelling

---

530. Smedly Darlington Butler, War is a Racket, (August 2003, Feral House)

the illusion of separateness. We are not alone. Anyone who tries to stand on what is changing, who tries to cling to things that are slipping away, cannot help but get more desperate and insecure. The understanding that humans have access to received knowledge independent of external control and input means that the revolution that has to occur cannot occur by the creation of more fear and violence, but by nonviolent nonparticipation combined with the discipline of self-awareness and self-control. It is the Gandhi principle.

The revolution does not entail naiveté about the potential for overlord violence. They have one note, and this is all they can play, and they will play it. But even their carnal circus has to fall away in the face of massive nonparticipation—this is the secret and the power of the mob. This is why the Chinese government became so frightened when thousands of Falun Gong practitioners came silently to the streets and sat in quiet meditation doing nothing but seeking to align themselves with the universal harmonic principle in an ancient Chinese meditation practice known as qigong. Falun Gong emphasizes the fundamental principles of truth, benevolence, and forbearance. The reaction of the Chinese government was predictable—violence, killing, and jailing of this quiet group. The quiet meditative group energy not only frightened the Chinese elite but also caught them off guard. Ordinary Chinese people had reached back into their ancient past and found a spiritual practice that the Chinese ruling class clearly understood could destroy their dominance and control. The communist revolution killed so many people that they assumed the human spirit had been thwarted. The Chinese elite as the rest of the world's governing class will soon learn that you can kill thousands, even millions, but you cannot kill an idea when its time has come.

Those who are seeking to reach a higher consciousness in service to themselves and mankind will no longer give their energy and thoughts to the steady onslaught of manufactured villains and created wars of the controllers. They will no longer participate in magnifying intentional disharmony. They also will be, in their achieved wisdom, mildly bemused by the repetitive nature of immature, low energy, spiritually infantile, and manipulative gamesmanship. It is difficult to manipulate a person who has taken control and personal responsibility beyond what is deemed socially acceptable parameters as defined by the Matrix energy system.

Because AIDS was positioned as a sex and blood plague, this mental viral meme was used to deliberately attack the chakra energy system at its base. The base chakra is not only the energy pathway that needs to be strengthened for humans to reach their highest potential through the other six chakras; it is the seat of the archetype of the victim. The blockage of the base chakra and the exploitation of the victim archetype are the overarching characteristics of the HIV/AIDS paradigm.

There are seven main chakras in the human energy system that are aligned through the body's center from the area of the tail bone to the crown of the head. Chakras are non-anatomical vortices of energy that exist just outside and within the physical body. Their purpose is to filter energy through the human system so that we have enough vitality to live our lives. Each of the seven chakras relates to a ductless gland and to specific organs in its area and augments them with life energy that connects with the cosmos and the Earth. It is part of our gaian universe. If any chakra is blocked as the result of trauma or false belief, life energy is blocked, and physical problems can develop in that area. One of the points of the discussion of the living organism as a liquid crystal was to make the association between altered energetic states and disease. Before the body produces physical disease energy indicators such as prolonged lethargy and depression are telling us that we are losing our vitality. Each chakra relates not only to physical health but also to specific emotional issues.

In most human beings who have not made a disciplined effort to arouse spiritual awareness, evolutionary energy, or kundalini, circulates among the three lowest centers. These are the centers of physical consciousness that are connected with the functions of the body. It is only when kundalini rises to the higher levels of consciousness, the fourth center and beyond, can our vision be penetrated and give us a greater capacity to see life clearly. This is the discipline of meditation applied to daily life—the discernment to clearly perceive if something that we have chosen to participate in has a beneficial effect on our conduct and character. When we spend our time dwelling on ourselves, indulging ourselves more and more in eating what is not nourishing or too much, becoming addicted to alcohol or drugs or sex or gambling or one of the many vices the overlords profit by selling, our being becomes enveloped in darkness and disharmony. Health begins to wane, and because we lack the facility of discernment, we run to the very people who have created the problem for a solution, when the solution is in ourselves.

The degree of positive or negative energy within each chakra corresponds to the archetype we are presently living out in our lives. However, there are usually several archetypal themes and sub-themes playing out in our lives simultaneously. Both archetypes and chakras reflect a direct link between how well we love ourselves, and our levels of vitality, responsibility, and empowerment. They reveal the qualities we have that make us spectacular and those that are in need of greater awareness and development.[531] Most importantly, our thoughts and attitudes block or release the flow of energy

---

531. Ambika Wauters, <u>Chakras and Their Archetypes: United Energy, Awareness and Spiritual Growth</u> (Freedom, CA: Crossing Press, 1997), 21.

through chakras, which is why rulers, whether secular or religious, exercise control by creating boundaries of acceptable thoughts and attitudes and by creating situations that give rise to fear, panic, and hatred.

Our thoughts and attitudes also directly impact our immune system through the glandular hypothalamic–pituitary–adrenal axis. The persistent release of glucocorticoids and catecholamine from the adrenal glands because of psychic stress has an inhibiting effect on redox potentials and the resultant depression of immune system functioning. This is why it is so important for the "masters of the universe" to control our thoughts with viral memes sent overtly and subliminally through the controlled media and also with ever more massive future shocks. This is also why, as discussed in the chapter on the Flexner brothers, they seek control of both educational and medical systems. An independent and free thinker who can maintain intellectual and spiritual composure in the face of the onslaught of dissociative future shocks intended to induce fear and panic is a danger to this contrived system. If we understood that products such as vaccines, AIDS and many pharmaceutical drugs are more harmful than helpful, would we buy them?

By 2008, twenty-three published studies reported lowered IQs in people with high fluoride exposure.[532] More than sixty percent of drinking water supplies in the United States are fluoridated. A population subjected to a combination of future shocks that inhibit <u>chi</u> energy and toxins that decrease human IQs is a manipulator's dream population. This may be one of the reasons why fluoride is being dumped in the water supply. It has been shown that fluoride decreases the secretion of serotonin, which is a precursor for melatonin. These are the hormones that are excreted by the pineal gland.[533] Melatonin and serotonin are involved in sleep/wake cycles, immunity, cancer inhibition, anti-aging, and mood stabilization. Melatonin is a direct free radical scavenger and an indirect antioxidant. Many of the antidepressants currently marketed are selective serotonin reuptake inhibitors (SSRIs) which means they disrupt the necessary production of melatonin. Their use has skyrocketed over the last ten years, up 75 percent since 1996.[534]

The pineal gland is located in the area of the seventh or crown chakra, the chakra that activates and opens up to higher consciousness. Through the energy of this chakra, mystics have long learned to transcend the duality of our nature by becoming aware that we are spiritual beings having a human experience. Not only do we have the experience we create but we are also the

---

532. http://fluoridealert.org/iq.studies.html

533. J. Luke, Effects of Fluoride on the Physiology of the Pineal Gland, <u>Caries Research 28</u> (1994): 204.

534. "Antidepressant use up 75%," 3 August 2009, http://psychcentral.com/news/2009/08/03/antidepressant-use-up-75-percent/7514.html

observer of that experience. This chakra takes us beyond time and space—an option of realty that quantum physics has begun to confirm. Fluoride concentrates in the pineal hydroxyapatite crystals and forces a disconnection from our innate ability to perceive the vibratory patterns of the universe; that is, it prevents us from receiving perceived knowledge as mystics and prophets of times past could. What U.S. government experiments in remote viewing proved was that every person on the planet has the psychic ability that can be developed and extended.

The first chakra is the foundation for emotional and mental health, the connection to traditional familial beliefs and group identity. The emotional issues relating to this chakra revolve around essentials we need for survival and our sense of security in the world. This includes the shelter of a home to protect us, financial security, and adequate nutrition. It also includes good emotional ties with our family, friends, community, and country. According to medical intuitive Caroline Myss, "The sacred truth inherent in the first chakra is that *All is One...*We are all part of a spiritual community and as a part of our spiritual development and biological health, this sacred truth has physical expressions in honor, loyalty, justice, family and group bonds, groundedness, our need for a spiritual foundation, and the ability to manage physical power for survival."[535] She goes on to observe that, "Becoming conscious of the responsibility inherent in the power of choice represents the core of this journey" and that "While honor is not usually considered a component of health, I have come to believe that it may well be among the most essential, equal to love. A sense of honor contributes a very positive and forceful energy into our spiritual and biological systems, the immune system and our bones and legs. Without honor it is very difficult, if not impossible, for an individual to stand up for himself with pride and dignity because he lacks a frame of reference for his behavior and choices and thus cannot trust himself or others."[536]

This chakra becomes damaged when we lose our connection to the earth—when we become disconnected from the most basic human levels of existence. The organs associated with this chakra are the spine, legs, bones, bone marrow, feet, rectum, and the immune system. Problems associated with this chakra include depression, addiction, obsessive-compulsive behavior, and interestingly, immune disorders—the behaviors and symptoms associated with AIDS. The color associated with this chakra is red. It is not a mistake that much of the Matrix energy is directed at blocking the first chakra. Reiki

535. Caroline Myss, The Anatomy of the Spirit, (Harmony Books, New York, 1996) 104-105
536. Caroline Myss, Ibid., 119

therapy[537], gong and sound therapy, and acupuncture are helpful in opening blockages in energy flow.

A major premise of this book is how drugs have been used since the time of the British East India Company for profit and internal disruption of established social systems. One of the purposes of drugging people is to render them spaced out, unable to define their reality by living in a world of fantasy and conjecture. Drugs are used to disconnect people from their feelings and to induce in users a poor grasp on life so that they are unable to care for themselves properly. Drug users lose their will to the drugs and the only loyalty a drug addict has is to finding his next fix.

Drugs are also used to destabilize the most important social and functional unit—the family. America is Aldous Huxley's[538] dream come true. Americans use more mood- altering and mind-altering drugs per capita than any other people on the planet. Drugs have filled prisons with the unwitting, depleted the financial and mental resources of many families, and produced a breakdown in the family unit. This is not an accident. During the 1950s, '60s and '70s, the CIA/Pentagon ran multiple mind-control projects: MKUltra, Monarch, Bluebird, Artichoke, MKDelta, Project Chatter and MK Naomi, all of which had the goal of introducing a drug culture to America's youth as a way to destabilize and morally degrade the culture. It was a silent war directed at first chakra energy.

CIA psychologist José Delgado revealed in his book Physical Control of the Mind: Toward a Psychocivilised Society that "physical control of brain function is a demonstrated fact . . . it is even possible to create and follow intentions, the development of thoughts and visual experiences. By electrical stimulation of specific cerebral structures, movements can be induced by radio command, hostility may appear and disappear, social hierarchy can be modified, sexual behavior may be changed, and memory, emotions, and the thinking process may be influenced by remote control"[539] This book was written in 1971. The technology for mind manipulation is now much more advanced and can be controlled from a distance by tiny implanted microchips that are finer than a human hair. As usual, microchips are being sold to the public as a helpful device that can find a lost animal, a lost grandmother suffering from Alzheimer's, or as a way to remind forgetful seniors to take their

---

537. Reiki is a Japanese healing art that involves the transfer of energy from practitioner to patient. It brings about deep relaxation, destroys perceived energy blockages, and increases the frequency of vibrations in the body.

538. Huxley's works imagine a future world in which the state controls reproduction and people are so alienated they require a drug called soma to function.

539. J. M. Delgado, Physical Control of the Mind: Toward a Psychocivilised Society (New York: Irvington Publishers, 1991).

medicine. Once medical records are computerized, they will be promoted as a way to store personal data "in case of an emergency."[540]

VeriChip of Delray Beach, Florida, presented the idea to investors that the chip and its database could form the basis of a new national identity database linked to Social Security and NationalCreditReport.com.

Grounding means that all basic life support systems are maintained: food, clothing, shelter, a medium of exchange. When we lose our grounding either through the use of drugs or because of severe social or economic upheaval, our ability to maintain contact with reality is compromised and we can find ourselves relating to the world as victims. One of the most common methods used to keep people frozen in the victim archetype is through the use of future shocks to induce fear. The "War on Drugs," the "War on Terror," the "War on Cancer," the "War on AIDS," and economic upheaval are masterfully used fear models of disinformation to undermine meaningful attempts to solve such problems. The problems are intentionally created not to be solved. They have been used purposefully to create a numbed population whose group behavior can be predicted and controlled through the use of sophisticated war game theory developed on rapid fire high-end computers.

The victim archetype is the lowest level of energy and awareness. Victims suffer because they believe that choice has been taken from them and their fate is completely outside their control. Sometimes circumstances combine to put victims outside the mainstream of hope or help. To alter the perception of the victim archetype, a person must understand that the illusion of helplessness must first be overcome spiritually and psychologically before any constructive action can be taken. Indeed, not recognizing or being resigned to one's circumstances creates inaction. It is not coincidental that the groups that have been hardest hit with AIDS have been homosexual males, drug addicts, and people of African origin who have traditionally tended to be outside the mainstream of Western culture. People of the so-called first world countries remain willfully oblivious to the harm their governments and corporations cause other people. Even so- called enlightened European countries, such as Norway, have been caught dumping toxic waste off the coast of Africa. Although the first world claims to want to transition to green products and a clean planet, Africa has become the dumping ground for first-world garbage so that they can maintain the illusion of going green.

The victim archetype is a psychological and spiritual impediment that can and must be overcome to heal the AIDS paradigm—to heal the chaos being bombarded on the planet. African Americans must step up to their

---

540. Jin Edwards, "Microchip Implant to Link Your Health Records, Credit History, Social Security", 5 October 2009, www.bnet.com

responsibility to set the bar higher for themselves, the African continent, and Africans of the diaspora by understanding that the AIDS paradigm is based on created illusion and that the answers for healing will never come from the people who created and prosper from the illusion. While many African Americans struggle to identify with the African homeland, the overlords see the spiritual connection and claim that this so-called sex and blood plague, first seen among gays in New York, San Francisco, and Los Angeles, really originated in Africa.

Even in the most difficult circumstances some people have found a way to rise to the challenge. One of the people that I most admire is Harriet Tubman, a woman who refused the role of victim. She was born into slavery on a farm on Maryland's Eastern Shore. She became known as the "Moses of her people." Over the course of ten years and at great personal risk, she led hundreds who refused to remain victims to the slave system out of Maryland on the Underground Railroad. One of her observations relates to the idea that the first step out of victimhood is to recognize your situation. Tubman mused, "I freed a thousand slaves. I could have freed a thousand more; if only they knew they were slaves." Acceptance of the HIV/AIDS paradigm given to the world by the Center for Disease Control (CDC), the World Health Organization (WHO) and the major drug companies is to acquiesce to the condition of spiritual slavery. It is a choice.

Following the HIV/AIDS logic is a road to entrapment. To get out of the entrapment, you have to recognize it, acknowledge it, and create a plan of action. HIV/AIDS is first and foremost a spiritual crisis not only of the individual but also of the society that creates the conditions for such malignant ideas to flourish.

When you are able to change a state of fear for a state of unconditional love and acceptance, first and foremost of yourself, you become much more than a single separate person. You become a permanent force that is released wherever you go, to ameliorate the terrible conditions that threaten not only your health but the health of the entire planet. Your life is an investment for every creature. No bear market or contrived war can threaten this investment. It increases through good fortune and bad, and nobody has to buy shares to get the dividends: they are distributed to all. You are inexhaustible: the more you give, the more you receive in patience, endurance, security, resilience, and love. The most difficult choice is using the integrity of your will to change your state of consciousness. Only you have that power. That is the secret.

Chapter 17

Therapeutic Considerations for HIV Positive and Aids Patients

○ ○

Note: The information presented here is for educational purposes and is not a substitute for the advice of and treatment by a qualified professional.

Any treatment for HIV/AIDS must...include normalization of body levels of glutathione, glutathione peroxidase, selenium, cysteine, glutamine and tryptophan. ...Physicians involved in a selenium and amino-acid field trial in Botswana ...are reporting that this nutritional protocol reverses AIDS in 99% of patients receiving it, usually within three weeks.

H. D. Foster[541]

Death Prognoses (of HIV/AIDS) are an expression of limited medical knowledge, rather than justified as a biological fact.

Heinrich Kremer

The following treatment recommendations are based on the work of Dr. Heinrich Kremer from his work The Silent Revolution in Cancer and AIDS Medicine and from a review from the AIDS therapy study group and Felix A. de Fries in Zurich, Switzerland, and Alive and Well, San Francisco. Much

---

541. H.D. Foster, "How HIV 1 Causes AIDS: Implications for Prevention and Treatment," Med Hypothesis, 62 (2004): 549–53.

of it is based on research that can be found at www.virusmyth.com and at http://www.ncbi.nlm.nih.gov/pubmed/

What Does HIV+ Mean?

The HIV test cannot be the measure or the criteria for beginning any type of therapy. Unfortunately, this test is unreliable as a predictor of anything because neither the ELISA nor the Western Blot contains proteins from a "retrovirus HIV."[542] The proteins are from human cell cultures that were adjusted by laboratory manipulation to respond to a higher than normal level of nonspecific antibodies from a Th2 dominance generated against both self and foreign antigens (See chapter 14). The test also gives no clue as to when the antibody elevation happened. Because the major defect has been found to be in the function of cell mediated immunity, then it follows that tests specifically directed at determining the functional capacity of CMI need to be identified. The Delayed Type Hypersensitivity (DTH) skin test can be used to determine the effectiveness of the cell mediated response and flow cytometry can be used to measure the cytokine profile. The glutathione and the amino acids cysteine, glutamine, arginine and glutamate as well as trace mineral levels, especially selenium are important as well.

Prophylaxis for AIDS is indicated in those who manifest a persistent displacement in their CD4 cytokines profile from Th1 to Th2, have a depleted blood or pulmonary glutathione level, and are shown to be anergic by a DTH skin test or other laboratory measure of Th1 lymphocyte deficit. A history of drug use (both legal and illegal, especially certain antibiotics), malnutrition, chronic exposure to other oxidizing agents such as rectally deposited semen, recurrent infections, and prolonged psychic stress must be considered. In people of African ancestry, additional care must be exercised in determining their immune status based on the HIV antibody test. (See below)

The problem with a positive-HIV test or an AIDS diagnosis is that it allows the practitioner to ignore many underlying metabolic and nutritional disorders and to treat people as if they have a generalized nutritional deficiency. Each person who presents must be evaluated for specific nutritional and mineral deficiencies based on the anamnesis and the presenting symptoms as well as directed laboratory evaluations for nutritional deficiencies such as trace mineral and Vitamin D levels. In addition to testing for anergy, cytokine profiles, and glutathione, consideration has to be given to intestinal

---

542. Eleni Papadopulos-Eleopulos, F. Valendar Turner and John M. Papadimitriou, "Is a Positive Western Blot Proof of HIV Infection?" Bio/Technology 11 (JUNE 1993).

absorption patterns, liver health, hydration, pH, and displacement of the hypothalamic–pituitary–adrenal axis. It is essential that a holistic nutritionist who has managed such cases and has specific knowledge of specific nutritional deficiencies and how to balance them be called in as a consultant. AIDS patients have been shown to be deficient in a wide array of vitamins, amino acids, minerals, essential fatty acids, and other nutrients, including water. Some of this is due to poor intake and some to poor absorption and/or utilization. Knowing the differences and treating the underlying conditions is crucial, especially among those who may have intestinal parasites.

Is the patient anergic and thiol (glutathione) depleted?

The Delayed Type Hypersensitivity (DTH) skin test will give an indication as to whether or not cell-mediated immunity is intact. A weak or anergic response can identify those who likely already have Th2 immune cell dominance.

Because there are no reliable surface markers, measuring blood CD4+T cells does nothing to evaluate the balance between Th1 and Th2 cells. The balance can only be measured through levels of Th1 and Th2 cytokine profiles in the T helper cells. This is probably best done with a technique called flow cytometry.

The measuring of glutathione (GSH) values in the plasma and the intracellular GSH values in T4 cells is crucial for preventive and therapeutic intervention in HIV positives as indicators of the status of the redox balance and thus the performance capacities of the whole immune cell network. HIV positives' with normal GSH values in the plasma and in T4 cells and other peripheral blood cells, and normal cysteine, glutamine, arginine and glutamate values in plasma as well as other balanced readings of T4 cells, NK cells, neutrophils and eosinophils within normal fluctuations are not threatened by opportunistic infections. They require a detailed clarification about the clinical insignificance of an isolated 'HIV positive' test. Even orthodox HIV/AIDS medicine admits that 5% of the 'HIV positives' are . . . 'False positives'. [543] The Polymerase Chain Reaction (PCR) viral load test has been thoroughly discredited as a measure of HIV infectivity and appears to add nothing substantive but cost and anxiety to the patient or to illuminating the need for biological compensatory therapy.

For patients who have known or unknown pro-oxidative stress risks, whether they are symptom free or symptomatic, it is mandatory to treat a

---

543. Kremer, The Silent Revolution in Cancer and AIDS Medicine, 394–95.

proven glutathione (and other supportive amino acids) deficiency. These deficiencies, leading to an altered redox balance, is the key feature of Type 2 counter regulation of cellular dyssymbiosis which, if not biologically compensated, can lead to organ failure (AIDS), cancer, nerve and muscle degeneration and other systemic diseases.

Disposition Factors and the f(HIV) in people of African ancestry

In a review article published in the Journal of Scientific Exploration, Prof. Henry Bauer raised the question "Why does HIV discriminate by Race?" He noted that between 1981 and 2000, the ratio of black Americans to white Americans reported with AIDS trebled, although the ratio of positive-HIV tests in the two groups remained the same. In his examination of multiple epidemic studies of the distribution of HIV positive people, what he terms f(HIV) or the frequency of HIV, he found that among all groups, ages, sexes, drug users, military, job corps, homosexuals, etc. blacks were always five times as likely to have a positive-HIV test as whites.[544] The large studies always had this phenomenon: Asians had the lowest frequency, followed by whites, then Native Americans, Hispanics, and blacks the highest. If one follows the logic of the CDC and considers that HIV is sexually transmitted, then one would have to assume that blacks are more constantly engaged in carelessly unsafe sex and sharing infected needles than are other racial groups and that, among blacks, this is the accepted behavioral norm, on average five times as often as white people and in every sector of society. One would also have to assume that these behavioral differences would explain the same disparities seen within the high risk groups themselves, among men who have sex with men and intravenous drug users. Research in the context of HIV/AIDS has failed to find racial differences in sexual behavior. Therefore other factors must be considered.

The correlation between the f(HIV) and the racial categories used officially in the United States reflects not behavioral differences but **genomic polymorphisms** that are used to track the course of human migrations over the last few hundred thousand years. The human genome also contains certain patterns that parallel conventional racial classifications. Genomic patterns that influence skin color are linked to genomic patterns that modify the physiological responses to stresses. This disposes people of African ancestry to display the strongest response and people of Asian ancestry the weakest.

---

544. H. H Bauer, "Demographic Characteristics of HIV: II. What Determines the Frequency of Positive HIV Tests? J Scientific Exploration 20 (2006): 69–94.

This polymorphism corresponds to the inherited polymorphism of serum protein groups, of intracellular enzyme groups, and of the class-II human leukocyte antigen, locus A of (HLA) systems. The HLA systems are present in differing numbers as sugar proteins on the surface of the cells of almost all tissues. The HLA gene complex, the major histocompatibility complex (MHC) located on chromosome 6 provides a large number of HLA phenotypes that are divided into four main classes.

The pineal gland secretes melatonin, and melatonin increases the expression of MHC Class II molecules as well as being an antioxidant. Studies have shown that there are racial differences in the rate of pineal calcification, whites having considerably more calcification than blacks. However, there is scant literature looking at whether there are racial differences in melatonin secretion. However, finding a larger gland, one might infer that more melatonin is secreted. It has been shown that melatonin in the presence of antigen presenting cells promotes the production of Th2 cytokines.[545] Finding elevated melatonin secretion levels as well as increased antibody levels to a given physiological stress in those of African ancestry would make sense. Tropical regions near the equator not only have the same day night cycle the year round, they harbor a wide array of endemic bacterial, fungal, and parasitic diseases. It would be unusual if humans evolving in Africa had not acquired very strong immune responses against that wide range of challenging external oxidative stressors to health. What is criminal is that this heightened immune response is being used to claim immune deficiency.

Since the 1970s it has been known that kidney patients who developed opportunistic infections and Kaposi's sarcoma during immunosuppressive treatment with Azathioprine were disproportionately Jewish (Sephardic), Italian, or of African descent and that in these patients the HLA-DR5 locus was dominant. **It was assumed that as a result of genetic deviation of HLA-DR5 locus, even a relatively low immunosuppression could trigger Kaposi's sarcoma.** So one must certainly consider that the use of the p32 protein in the HIV antibody test that identifies the HLA-DR protein was not a mistake by the eugenic mindset that is claiming HIV to be sexually transmitted. The antibody test is rigged in such a way to make it appear that blacks are more often HIV positive than other racial groups. Physicians treating black patients who are HIV positive and in a low risk group must be aware of this and be vigilant in determining if this is a false positive test or

---

545. V Raghavendra, et al., "Melatonin provides signal 3 to unprimed CD4+T cells but failed to Stimulated LPS primed B Cells", J Translational Immun, 2001 June; 124(3): 414–422.

if there actually is a real or incipient problem with the patient's cell mediated immune status.

According to Bauer, after examining data from tens of millions of HIV tests on a disparate variety of sectors of the population of the United States, "racial ancestry determines the relative level of f(HIV) as an independent variable at all ages, in both sexes and in groups presumed to be at low risk for AIDS or HIV infection as well as those judged to be at high risk."[546] The CDC confirmed his results.

The black community must be aware as to HIV and AIDS—there is no connection between HIV and AIDS. The percentage of AIDS cases who are black almost doubled from the first appearance of AIDS to the present time; it increased from 25.5 percent in 1981–87 to 32.1 percent in 1988–92, to 38 percent during 1993–95, and to 44.9 percent for 1996–2000.[547] The percentage of AIDS cases that were white decreased correspondingly from 59.7 percent to 50.4 percent to 43.4 percent to 34 percent. The ratio of black percentage to white percentage changed overall by a factor of 3. However, there was no such corresponding trend in the ratio of the f(HIV). This indicates that physicians are over diagnosing and over treating African American patients with little consideration given to metabolic expressions of variable genomic patterns.

The CDC implies without directly stating that these trends are because of aberrant sexual behavior in the black population. However, research in the context of HIV/AIDS has failed to find racial differences in sexual behavior. Among drug users, no significant differences in behavior by race were found as to number of sexual partners, frequency of intercourse, number of sexual partners who were IV-drug users, number of non-IDU sexual partners, prostitution, or intercourse with people then or later diagnosed as AIDS.[548]

Samuel and Winkelstein found no significant racial differences in behavior among gay men in San Francisco and concluded that the black-to-white ratio of f(HIV) could not be explained by differences in major risk factors.[549] Another study from the San Francisco Department of Health found no differences between the races as to anal intercourse, as measured

---

546. H. H. Bauer, "Demographic Characteristics of HIV: III: Why Does HIV Discriminate by Race?" J Scientific Exploration 20 (2006): 255–88.

547. CDC, "HIV and AIDS—United States 1981–2000," Morbidity and Mortality Weekly Report 50 , (1 June 2001): 430–34.

548. Friedman, S. R., et al., "The AIDS epidemic among blacks and Hispanics", Milbank Quarterly;65 supplement 2 (1987): 455–59.

549. M. Samuel and W. Wilkelstein, "Prevalence of Human Immunodeficiency Virus Infection in Ethnic Minority Homosexual/Bisexual Men," JAMA 257 (1987):1901–902.

via the incidence of rectal gonorrhea.[550] Bausell et al. actually found white Americans <u>less</u> likely to take protective measures during sex than black Americans.[551]

It is clear that the HIV/AIDS problem has been positioned as a sex and blood plague to hide how the problem has been targeted to specific genotypes by the use of inherited polymorphisms of the HLA group as well as genetically determined antibody response.

The evolutionary-biologically programmed interplay between disposition and exposure explains much of what is puzzling in the risk groups of homosexuals and drug addicts and the racial disparities with the same risky behavior. Only a small portion of those with excessive pro-oxidative stress will go on to develop "HIV seroconversion." Patients have to be genetically predisposed in such a way that the average glutathione depletion of 30 percent apparent in <u>HIV positives</u> is sufficient to trigger a type 2 cytokine dominance that in turn stimulates an unusually high number of antibodies.[552] Therefore, besides pro-oxidative exposure, there must be a genetic disposition that activates the redox dependent genetic expression for the biosynthesis of type 2 cytokine proteins more quickly and for longer periods of time. It is also significant that multiple studies have shown that blacks have a higher antibody response to the same stimulus or in various autoimmune diseases than whites. The <u>HIV</u> antibody test, as a measure of increased antibody load, would also tend to find blacks more often positive than whites.

This is what the Project for the New American Century (PNAC) document was referring to when they envisioned the use of "bioweapons that target specific genotypes" as a politically useful tool. What was at one time an evolutionary advantage of a redox-sensitive sustained type 2 cytokine immune response has become a liability because of industrialization with the mass poisoning of the environment and because of modern medicine, especially the introduction of vaccination programs and antibiotics over the last fifty years. People with a particularly redox-sensitive disposition are now at a disadvantage because they respond to toxic influences faster and with a more sustained type 2 counterregulation that is more efficient in dealing with the inhibition of extra-cellular bacteria or multicellular parasites.

---

550. San Francisco Dept. of Public Health, Bureau of Communicable Disease Control, "Rectal Gonorrhea in San Francisco, October 1984–September 1986," <u>San Francisco Epidemiological Bulletin, 2, 12</u> (1986): 1–3; cited in [49].

551. R. B. Bausell et al., "Public Perceptions Regarding the AIDS Epidemic: Selected Results from a National Poll," <u>AIDS Research</u> 2 (1986):253–58.

552. Kremer, <u>Silent Revolution in Cancer and AIDS Medicine</u>, 420.

The HIV test is frontloaded to identify more people of African descent as positive because it is an antibody test and because the protein p32 has been shown to correspond to a major histocompatability locus HLA-DR that is more common in those of African origin. This is why a thorough history of not only drug use but also recent vaccinations, autoimmune diseases, allergies, and atopic problems as well as recent viral, bacterial and yeast infections must be accounted for because they may cross-react with the test.

Autoimmune Reactions

The processing of cell fragments resulting from the continuous cell metabolism is a permanent physiological task of the immune system. The human organism consists of about 10^{14} cells.[553] About 10^{12} apoptotic cell fragments that are produced daily are recognized by the cytotoxic T-cells originating from the Thymus and by the natural killer cells, and are transmitted to the macrophages, which process them without any signs of inflammation. Prolonged exposure to exogenous toxins will increase the daily turnover as well as initiate an inflammatory response.

Systemic autoimmune reactions can occur not only with chronic viral infections, but have been shown to occur as the result of toxins as well.[554] This stress induced adjustment to the autoimmune system to the elimination of non-self structures is always associated with an inflammatory activation of marcrophages. The stress induced hypercortisolism causes a reduction of Th1 cytokines. This reduction in Th1 cytokines reduces the ability of cells (macrophages and Th1 CD4+T cells) to respond to intracellular pathogens. There is also a corresponding activation of Th2 cytokines and an enhanced antibody response. As a result, endogenous proteins play a central role in that autoantibodies against cellular structures are what is being identified as HIV antibodies. This is why the HIV proteins have been shown to be cellular in origin. (see chapter on HIV antibody test)

Nucleoside analogs, protease inhibitors, and fusion inhibitors severely reduce the levels of thiol and thereby further aggravate the severe glutathione deficits in HIV positives. Chemoantibiotics (sulfonaminde/trimethoprim—(Bactrim, Septra) and insecticides (lindane used against crab lice) block production and release of folic acid and purines that are necessary for the

---

553. A. Hassig, et al., "HIV-Can You Be More Specific? Open Questions Concerning the Specificity of Anti-HIV Antibodies: Do They Belong to the Group of Autoantibodies Against Cellular Structures"

554. M. Goldman, et. al., "Th2 Cells in Systemic autoimmunity: Insights from Allogeneic Diseases and Chemically Induced Autoimmunity", <u>Immunol Today</u> 1991 Jul;12(7):223-7.

development of DNA in mitochondria. They block the iron and copper containing enzymes needed for cell respiration and block ion channels as do heavy metals. Both opiates and cocaine shift the immune system to the Th2 profile through the hypothalamic–pituitary–adrenal axis. Many currently used antibiotics have been shown to be cytotoxic because they directly damage the mitochondrial endosymbionts.[555] Cocaine cytotoxicity has been shown also to directly involve mitochondrial damage.[556] These mitochondrial toxins lead to decreased energy production and mitochondrial antioxidant function that play such a central role in detoxification and control of the cell redox environment.

Some chemoantibiotics (Bactrim, Septra) block the enzyme dihydrofolate reductase (DHFR) necessary for the production of tetrahydrofolate that is needed for the generation of glutathione in the liver and for the production of tetrahydrobiopterin necessary for the production of nitric oxide--NO. By choking cellular respiration as well as a decrease in the production of nitric oxide, these compounds promote fungal infestations in the mucosa, intestines, and skin. Long-term use of these antibiotics alters the genetic structure in bacteria. The bacteria exchange plasmids with each other and in this way become increasingly antibiotic resistant. Chemotherapeutics must be used judiciously and not without biological compensation.

Effects of Antiretroviral therapy

Nucleoside analogs inhibit the maturation of immune cells in the mucous membranes (B-cells, T-cells, macrophages, and dendritic cells). The disruption of the maturation of the B cells leads ultimately to a decrease in the production of antibodies and a further weakening of this antibacterial defense mechanism. If the Th2 CD4+T cells do not encounter any mature B cells, they continue to circulate in the bloodstream for 24 hours. This rise in CD4+ T counts gives a misleading sense of rebounding T cells, but these Th2 cells are not programmed to synthesize cytoxic NO and so will do little to improve cell mediated immunity. The rebound phenomenon actually is indicative of a weakened Th2 response as well because of the decrease in B cells.

---

555. N. Duewelhenke et al., "Influence on Mitochondria and Cytotoxicity of Different Antibiotics Administered in High Concentrations on Primary Human Osteoblasts and Cell Lines," <u>Antimicrobial agents and chemotherapy</u> 51 (Jan 2007): 54–63.

556. A. Zarogoza et al., "Mitochondrial Involvement in Cocaine Treated Rat Hepatocytes: Effect of N-Acetylcysteine and Deferoxamine," <u>Brit J Pharm132</u> (2001): 1063–70.

Both nucleoside analogs and protease inhibitors cause disturbances to the biosynthesis of proteins and enzymes and nucleic acids which are essential for the formation of new cells. Because the cells have been under prolonged oxidative stress, in attempting repair, there will be increased nuclear fragments that are measurable. This is what has been called the viral load.

When HAART (highly active antiretroviral therapy) is initiated, the massive increase in pro-oxidants causes genetic damage that initiates a heightened repair process, such that the consumption of RNA is increased. This initial increase in RNA consumption is why the plasma RNA (viral load) drops to low or undetectable levels. However, continued use of these drugs leads to the depletion of the repair enzymes. By impairing the production of nucleic acids, these drugs create damage in both the nuclear and mitochondrial DNA. This eventually leads to damage to brain cells, muscle cells (heart attacks and paralyses), and the internal organs, as well as to the formation of cancer. This also eventually leads to products of reverse transcription no longer being able to be adopted by DNA. Such metabolic exhaustion noted by a rise in RNA, is then interpreted as a rise in the viral load and an irrevocable resistance to combination therapy.

Short-term use of these drugs may be warranted in select cases for their anti-fungal and antibiotic properties, but the continued use of these drugs causes the cells to switch to an oxygen-free fermentation metabolism that creates more lactic acid and causes muscle wasting as the cells draw essential energy substrates directly from muscle proteins. With continuing damage to the mitochondria because of the blockage of their membranes, glutathione deficiency, and DNA damage, the symbiosis between mitochondria and the nucleus breaks down (Warburg Phenomenon). This assures the survival of the nuclear DNA by reverse transcription. It also can give rise to malignant transformation in some cells.

In 1996, the death rate from complications unrelated to AIDS was about 13 percent. By 2004, this figure had increased to 43 percent as a result of the early use of ARVs. Complications include bacterial sepsis, cancers unrelated to AIDS, intestinal diseases, kidney damage, and liver disease. Although the deaths from AIDS are going down, deaths from the complication of AIDS drugs are rising. This is unexceptable.

Compensatory Therapy

The goal of compensatory therapy is sixfold:

1. **Detoxification**–mental and physical, liver protection to relieve systemic thiol deficit
2. **Antioxidation**–balancing the thiol and micronutrient deficits, amino acid dysregulation. Strengthening of the extracellular matrix;
3. **Hydration**
4. **Alkalinization**, mitochondrial activation–treatment of fungal infestation
5. **Hormonal Balancing**
6. **Strengthening**–body–mind–spirit.

Detoxification

Over 250 years ago a German doctor, Samuel Hahnemann, who was exacerbated by the aggressive treatment methods of his profession began the practice of homeopathy. Patients at that time were treated with a variety of poisons including mercury and arsnic, were bled and purged until they were too weak to sustain an illness and often died at the hands of the physician. Homeopathy is based on the principle of "like cures like" and has more to do with the currently unfolding world of post-quantum physics of today than the Newtonian physics of his day. Treatment involves administration of very dilute doses of substances called "remedies" that produce similar symptoms of illness in healthy people if they were given in larger doses. Treatment is individualized, and practitioners select remedies according to symptoms, lifestyle, and emotional and mental states. In homeopathy, the ordering of priorities for the initiation of a remedy puts psychological symptoms at the top and presenting symptoms at the bottom. Medical intuitive Carolyn Myss has written extensively on the topic of energy medicine and how our energy fields show evidence of disease before it manifests. In her work with Dr. Norman Shealy, it became clear to her that healing the spirit is crucial to healing the disease.

One of the themes of this book has been the use of fear as a method of controlling us to make decisions that are contrary to our optimal well being. Since choice is the process of creation, if fear intervenes the choices that we make can turn our choices into the false gods of our addictions. Addictive behavior is an underlying theme in the AIDS story.

If there is a chronic use of drugs, legal or illegal, or alcohol; if there are toxic relationships with a loved one or family; if the living environment is filled with toxins, or there is a job that is ruining the health of your body–mind–spirit, your first thoughts must be to take the necessary steps to begin to detoxify your life. This will be a different process for each individual. The first step is to recognize that you are engaging in toxic behaviors or relationships and begin to alter the situation. All of the other advice in this section deals with physical detoxification and is secondary.

To detoxify your body and your immune system, it must be understood that it did not become toxic overnight and that the reversal of the imbalance must be viewed as a process. What I have tried to convey in this book is that the pollution of our bodies–minds–spirits has been done deliberately by the profoundly negative energy that manifests itself in the behavior and attitudes of a small group who have a passion to control everything on this planet, including each of us. Our goal is to be just as passionate about being free from manipulation to choose our own path. This means a leap of faith outside the matrix and into a life of your own imagining. The journey now beginning is to define your own needs in relationship to the life you want to lead.

The principles for therapeutic intervention in patients who are immune deficient must have the goal of re-establishing cellular symbiosis and redox harmonization. Because heavy metals are omnipresent environmental toxins and are known to block mitochondrial ion channels, removing such toxic chemicals is important. Heavy metals have been shown to disrupt the normal functioning systems in the body, including the nervous, immune, and cardiovascular systems. They exert toxic effects by binding to sulfur-containing groups in proteins and disrupting protein (enzyme) function. Heavy metals are also strong oxidizers that lead to the production of free radicals.[557] Heavy metal toxicity can result in damaged or reduced mental and central nervous function, lower energy levels, and damage to blood composition, lungs, kidneys, liver, and other vital organs. Long-term exposure may result in slowly progressing physical, muscular, and neurological degenerative processes that mimic Alzheimer's disease, Parkinson's disease, muscular dystrophy, and multiple sclerosis. Allergies are not uncommon and repeated long-term contact with some metals or their compounds may even cause cancer (International Occupational Safety and Health Information Centre, 1999). The most commonly encountered heavy metals are arsenic, mercury, lead, cadmium, iron, and aluminum. Mercury and aluminum have been used extensively in vaccines. Some cities such as Washington, D. C. have been found to have particularly high lead levels in the drinking water.

There are several methods to detoxify from heavy metals. Finding a reliable and trustworthy practitioner is part of the process. Removal of mercury from dental fillings is advisable. Reverse osmosis filters and water softeners can precipitate much of the lead from drinking water.

---

557. R. A. Goyer et al., Metal Toxicity (New York: Academic Press, 1995).

Chelation therapy is the process of removing from the body the undesirable ionic material by the infusion, or taking orally, of an organic compound that has suitable chelating properties. Simply defined, it is the process by which a molecule encircles and binds (attaches) to the metal and removes it from tissue. Depending on the drug used, chelating agents specific to the heavy metal involved are given orally, intramuscularly, or intravenously. Once the bound metal leaves the tissue, it enters the bloodstream, is filtered from the blood in the kidneys, and then is eliminated in the urine. The decision to chelate should be made only by professionals with experience using chelation therapy.

Chelation therapy is widely used for the treatment of atherosclerosis and other chronic degenerative diseases involving the circulatory system. It also has other benefits. The beneficial effect of chelation treatment is the removal of metallic catalysts that cause excessive free radical proliferation. This reduces the oxidation of lipids, DNA, enzyme systems, and lipoproteins. Research over the past thirty years has confirmed the benefits of EDTA. The protective influence of EDTA would be enhanced by an appreciable presence of antioxidant nutrients, such as vitamins A, C, and E, selenium, and amino acid complexes, such as glutathione peroxidase. Other commonly used chelating agents are Dimercaprol (BAL), Dimercaptosiccinic acid (DMSA), (Succimer), Dimercaptopropane- sulfonate (DMPS), and D-pencillamine. These agents not only mop up free radicals but also assist in reinforcing the stability of cell membranes.

EcoNugenics makes a series of detoxification products for oral use. **PectaSol® Chelation Complex** consists of polyuronides, such as pectin and alginates. These are naturally occurring complex polysaccharides. Citrus pectin is a soluble dietary fiber composed predominately of repeating galacturonic acid units. Alginate, found in seaweed, is made of linear chains of mannuronic and glucouronic. The structure and charge of these compounds make them excellent metal chelators. The use of modified citrus pectin results in a significant excretion of lead, arsenic, cadmium, and mercury. After at least one month of this gentle detoxification, a second product **Detox Complete®** can be introduced. The nutrients in Detox Complete in combination with **PectaSol Chelation Complex** help in removing heavy metals from tissues and body without side effects. This product contains garlic, cilantro, sulfur containing amino acids (glutathione, methylsulfonylmethane, cysteine, N-acetyl cysteine, and alpha lipoic acid). It also contains selenium, which is necessary for the normal functioning of the glutathione peroxidase enzymes.

The liver is the largest gland in the body and is import in considering a thorough detoxification process. The liver has multiple important functions, including detoxification, protein synthesis, and the production of biochemicals necessary for digestion. The liver is involved in carbohydrate, fat, and protein metabolism, in the storage of vitamins and minerals, and in many essential physiological processes. The liver helps control blood sugar and hormone levels. Glycogen is stored in the liver where red blood cells are decomposed, and plasma proteins, including albumin, are synthesized. Liver overload from alcohol intoxication, environmental pollutants, and hepatitis must be considered.

The liver has three main detoxification pathways: 1. filtering the blood to remove large toxins; 2. the use of enzymes to break down unwanted chemicals, and 3. synthesizing and secreting bile for excretion of fat soluble toxins and cholesterol.

The longstanding practice of using milk thistle for a variety of liver problems has been validated by modern research.[558] The active ingredients of milk thistle, **Silymarin** and its chief active ingredient **silibinin** help prevent toxic liver damage. If there is damage, both of these substances help the liver to regenerate faster. Silymarin and silibinin actually accelerate the rate of protein synthesis in the liver leading to faster cell regeneration. Silymarin and silibinin act in the ribosomes, special cellular organelles where protein synthesis takes place. It was discovered that silibinin can bind to the receptor for an important enzyme called DNA-dependent RNA polymerase I. This brings an increase in ribosomal RNA, which then leads to more protein synthesis.

S-adenosyl-methionine (SAMe) has been shown to be effective in the treatment of liver disorders. Healthy adults produce from six to eight grams of SAMe daily, with most of it being made in the liver where it works to detoxify the body of poisons, such as drugs, alcohol, heavy metals, pesticides and solvents. Beyond its function in liver detoxification, SAMe is a critical component in cartilage production, an important factor in brain chemistry, and a key element in methylation, one of the most important biochemical reactions--the transmission of gene expression states from parent to daughter cells involves methylation.[559]

One way the liver works to remove toxic substances from the body is to produce **glutathione**, a tri-peptide antioxidant composed of cysteine, glutamic acid, and glycine. When glutathione encounters a toxin, such as drugs or pesticides, it attaches to this entity and makes the substance become more water soluble. The toxin can then be excreted safely via urine without

558.   C. Dehmlow et al., "Scavenging of Reactive Oxygen Species and Inhibition of Arachidonic Acid Metabolism by Silibinin in Human Cells," Life Sci 58 (1996): 1591–1600.

559.   Momparler, R.L., et al., "DNA methylation and cancer" J Cell Physiology 2000 May;183(2) 145-54

causing any damage.[560] Damage occurs when the liver is so overwhelmed by toxins that it cannot produce enough glutathione. SAMe is a necessary component in the production of glutathione.

Cilantro as an ingredient in fresh green juice or as a pesto taken three times a week has been shown to be helpful in the excretion of mercury.

Other liver supports include: **probiotics** (Lactobacillus, acidophilus, Bifdobacterium biffidum); **Vitamin C** with mineral ascorbates, **N-acetylcysteine; lipoic acid, taurine; glycine; bioflavonoids (quercetin, grape seed extract, rutin).**

Foods that support liver health are **dandelion, broccoli, collard greens, kale, watercress, pomegranate, and green tea. Onions, broccoli, cabbage and garlic** contain thiocyanates that help activate liver detoxification enzymes. Glucuronic acid (in the fermented tea beverage kombucha, made from a symbiotic yeast/bacterial "mushroom" can support liver function in those with additional stress, such as hepatitis.

Colon cleansing and colonics, under guidance, should be part of the detoxification process. Colonics serve to break down toxic excrement that inhibits proper assimilation and elimination and can help to eliminate intestinal parasites. Because most of the lymphatic tissue is in the intestines, it is vital to maintain healthy functioning of this organ system for proper immune functioning. Foods that act as pro-biotics: plantain, chicory root, Jerusalem artichoke, and lacto-fermented food and beverages (for example, kimchee, unpasteurized sauerkraut, beet kvass (fermented beet, water and sea salt). N-acetyl-glucosamine, L-glutamine, aloe vera juice and oils of rice bran, olive, and sesame can also help soothe and rebuild the gut lumen after intestinal inflammation (for example, diarrhea, parasites, candida, etc.).

Mycosis, skin and mouth infections, and internal infections can be treated with **grapefruit seed extract**, neat or in cream; it is highly effective against many fungi, viruses, and both gram positive and gram negative bacteria. For external use, creams containing sulphur, tea tree oil, or acidophilus have worked well in practice.

Fungal infestations of the intestines (Candida albicans) can be treated with **caprylic acid** in capsules resistant to gastric acids or **undecylenic acid** derived from castor bean oil. Other effective treatments include biotin, whole leaf aloe vera juice, wormwood, herbal extracts containing berberine (goldenseal, barberry, Oregon grape root) and tannins (chamomile, Echinacea, black walnut, etc.), Pau d'Arco tea, essential oils of oregano, cinnamon,

---

560. R. Elkins, The Remarkable Substance That Promotes Detoxification, Relieves Arthritis, and Fights Depression (Pleasant Grove, UT: Woodland Publishing, 1999), 23.

clove, and garlic. Intestinal flora should be supported with pro-biotics during antifungal therapy. A diet that avoids all sugar and refined foods, including alcohol, refined grains, sweet fruits, as well as acid-forming foods, such as red meat, most dairy, and coffee is recommend. Avoiding moldy foods, such as leftovers and dried fruits and nuts is also appropriate.

Parasites, such as worms and flukes, are immunosuppressive and can cause inflammatory tissue damage and inactivate NO synthesis via inhibitory counterregulation. Herbs, such as a combination of wormwood , black walnut extract, and freshly ground cloves have been found beneficial in expelling parasites.

Antioxidation

Because some patients may have absorption problems, trace mineral replacement may need to be considered. Trace minerals are usually found in extremely small amounts in the parts per million range, and a minimum of sixty have been demonstrated to be vital in maintaining health and well being. Deficiencies of zinc, iron, copper, and selenium have been shown to lower resistance to disease. The glutathione enzymes need selenium to function properly. Studies have shown an inverse relationship between selenium intake and cancer risk. **Cracked cell chlorella, spirulina** and **kelp** are rich in trace minerals.

Glutathione (S-acetyl-L-glutathione 400-600 mg od of enteric coated capsules) has been repeatedly mentioned in this text. Glutathione is a selenoprotein, and so sufficient stores of selenium are necessary for its optimal functioning. In many areas of the world, the soils are depleted of selenium, and in patients who are glutathione deficient, whether because of oxidative stress or malnutrition, selenium must be considered a necessary supplement. Selenium can be taken as Se-methylselenocysteine, which is an essential co-factor of glutathione peroxidase. Nutrients that help stabilize glutathione levels include alpha lipoic acid, N-acetylcysteine (NAC), glutamine, Vitamin E and Vitamin C. Glutathione may also be increased by using whey protein concentrate.

Recancostat is a patented nutritional formula consisting of anthocyans, L-cysteine and reduced glutathione. The role of reduced glutathione in cancer is particularly important. The redox balance within cells is a major factor in the functioning of the p53 tumor suppressor protein. This protein helps to prevent and to destroy cancer cells. When nuclear DNA undergoes mutation, p53 tumor suppressor protein slows cell division to allow repair proteins time to mend the genetic damage.[561] This, in effect, results in the conversion of a premalignant cell back into a normal cell. If DNA sustains excessive damage, p53 tumor suppressor protein has a plan B. It induces apoptosis-programed cell death. It actually causes cancerous cells to self-destruct. This is the way cells function when the intracellular redox potential is normal. If there is a reduced glutathione deficit and a change in the redox potential, then, instead of acting as a tumor suppressor, p53 acts as a tumor promoter. Maintenance doses are 100 to 600 mgs. daily, in divided doses. Higher doses for serious conditions should be monitored by a clinician. Minerals should not be taken too close in time to taking Recancostat. Supplementing with additional antioxidants, such as vitamins C and E, carotenoids, and selenium can further enhance the efficacy.

Several substances listed under detoxification are powerful antioxidants as well (glutathione, N-acetylcysteine etc.). Others of importance are:

Curcumin – (500 mg. 2 three times a day). This is a spice derived from the plant Curcuma longa, an ingredient in curry powder known as turmeric. Curcumin acts on ultra violet light to inhibit the signals between cells that induce ongoing inflammation, the growth of opportunistic infections, and degenerative changes. Recent studies have shown that it can inhibit UV irradiation induced oxidative stress including induced apoptotic changes, loss of membrane potential and mitochondrial release of cytochrome C.[562] It supports cellular immunity (Th2 to Th1 switch that leads to detection and destruction of defective cells and of cells containing viruses, mycobacteria, and fungi). If there is a glutathione deficiency, curcumin should not be administered with high doses of vitamin C, E, beta-carotene or herbal mixtures, as curcumin is then transformed to a pro-oxidative substance without any anti-inflammatory capacity.

Curcumin is not only a powerful anti-inflammatory agent but also has anti-cancer properties as well. Carcinogenesis encompasses three closely associated stages: initiation, progression, and promotion. Curcumin has been shown to be beneficial in all three states of carcinogenesis.[563]

A new formulation of curcumin, **BCM-95®** has a higher absorption rate and half life. The formulators of this product went back to the roots,

---

561. J. B. Rotstein and T. J. Slaga "Effects of Exogenous Glutathione on Tumor Progression in the Murine Skin of Multistate Carcinogenesis Model," Carcinogenesis 9 (1988): 1547–51.

562. Wen-Hsiung Chan, et al., "Curcumin Inhibits UV Irradiation Induced Oxidative Stress and Apoptotic Biochemical Changes in Human Epidermoid Carcinoma A431 cells, 27 August 2003 J Cell Biochemistry:,(90)2 327-338

563. R. L. Thangapazham et al., "Multiple Molecular Targets in Cancer Chemoprevention by Curcumin," AAPS J 8 (2006): E443–49.

so to speak, reincorporating many of the components of raw turmeric root, which are normally removed during the extraction process. This has greatly enhanced the bioavailability of active constituents in the process. In essence, this reformulation relies on the inherent synergy of the turmeric rhizome's natural components to enhance bioavailability. As a result BCM-95® is six to seven times more bioavailable than the ordinary 95 percent extract. Just one 400 mg dose is equivalent to taking 2,772 mg. of standard 95 percent curcumin extract or 2,548 mg of plant bound curcumin extract with piperine.[564]

Co-enzyme Q10 (100 mg. daily) can improve electron transport in the mitochondrial respiratory chain. It facilitates the transformation of fats and sugars into energy. CoQ10 has the ability to restore mitochondrial function and has been shown to have a profound effect on one's overall health.[565] When CoQ10 levels diminish, the ability of cells to sustain even basic metabolic functions is impaired.

CoQ10, in addition to being a free radical scavenger, is necessary to maintain the redox potential of the mitochondrial membrane and by inhibiting depolarization is able to prevent apoptosis (cell death).[566]

For ubiquinone CoQ10 to be utilized, it first has to be reduced in the body to its active metabolite called ubiquinol. Although most ubiquinone is naturally reduced to ubiquinol in the body, the optimal way to supplement with CoQ10 is to ingest it in its ready-to-use ubiquinol form.

Other nutrients necessary for ATP synthesis include: folic acid (5–30 mg. daily), thiols, L-carnitine (6 gm. daily for 14 days), alpha lipoic acid (300–600 mg. daily), Vitamin B1 (150–300 mg. daily), B6 (250 mg.) and B12 (usually comes combined with folic acid) and low doses of chromium (100–300 mcg. daily), selenium (250 mcg. daily) and zinc (10–20 mg. daily. Uridine from sugar cane molasses (2 tbs. daily) also supports ATP synthesis and repair of damage to mitochondrial DNA.

L-carnitine plays an important role in the oxidation of fatty acids by their transport across the inner mitochondrial membrane. A deficiency of

---

564. D. Kiefer, "Novel Turmeric Compound Delivers Much More Curcumin to the Blood," www.lef.org

565. R. T. Matthews, L. Yang, S. Browne, M. Baik, and M. F. Beal,. "Coenzyme Q10 Administration Increases Brain Mitochondrial Concentrations and Exerts Neuroprotective Effects," Proc Natl Acad Sci USA 95. (July 1998); 8892–97.

566. L. Papucci et al., "Coenzyme q10 Prevents Apoptosis by Inhibiting Mitochondrial Depolarization Independently of Its Free Radical Scavenging Property," J Biol Chem 278 (July 2003); 28220–228.

L-carnitine impedes the energy-releasing process of glycolysis. L-carnitine also helps to prevent muscle wasting.

Beta-glucans are naturally occurring polysaccharides and can act as a biological defense modulator that nutritionally potentiates and modulates the immune response. Beta-glucans have been shown to increase host defense by activating the complement system and to enhance both macrophages and natural killer cell function, and have demonstrated anticarcinogenic activity. They have been shown to reduce tumor proliferation and to prevent tumor metastasis.[567]

L-glutamine—(40 gm. daily) Glutamine is normally considered to be a nonessential amino acid. However, recent studies have provided evidence that glutamine may become "conditionally essential" during inflammatory conditions, such as infection and injury. It is now well documented that under appropriate conditions, glutamine is essential for cell proliferation, that it can act as a respiratory fuel and can enhance the function of stimulated immune cells. Studies thus far have determined the effect of extracellular glutamine concentration on lymphocyte proliferation and cytokine production, macrophage phagocytic plus secretory activities, and neutrophil bacterial killing. Glutamine utilization has been linked to functional activities of cells of the immune system, such as proliferation, antigen presentation, cytokine production, nitric oxide production, superoxide production, and phagocytosis.[568] Glutamine helps prevent muscle wasting.

L-arginine (20-30 gm daily). L-arginine has been classified as a semi-essential amino acid. In addition to participating in protein synthesis, L-arginine has been shown to be a powerful mediator of multiple biological processes, including the release of several hormones, collagen synthesis during wound healing, antitumor activity, and immune cell responses.[569] Arginine plays a role as a substrate for the urea cycle, the production of inducible nitric oxide and as a secretagogue for growth hormone, prolactin, and insulin. Strong evidence suggests that dietary supplementation with arginine enhances immunocompetence in adults. It modulates the activities of the immune cells in several ways. Dietary arginine can increase the weight of the

---

567. D. Akramiene, A. Kondrotas, J. Didziapetriene, and E. Kevelaitis, "Effects of Beta-glucans on the Immune System," <u>Medicina (Kaunas) 43</u> (2007): 597-606. [Publication of the Dept of Physiology, Kaunas U of Medicine, Kaunas, Lithuania]

568. P. Newsholme, "Why Is L-Glutamine Metabolism Important to Cells of the Immune System in Health, Postinjury, Surgery or Infection?" <u>J Nutrition 131</u> (2001); 2515S–2522S.

569. L. Thomás-Cobos et al., "Arginine and the Immune System," <u>Proc Nut Society 67</u>,(2008): OCE, E3.

thymus, an effect that is directly correlated with an increase in the number of thymic T lymphocytes. Arginine enhances phagocytosis by neutrophils and adhesion of polymorphonuclear cells, activities that help produce nitric oxide for immunomodulation. This enhancement is protective and is different from the cytotoxic responses generated by macrophages that result in the production of superoxide.[570]

RM-10 is derived from medicinal mushrooms, such as shiitake and Maitake, and contains a mix of polysaccharides and amino acids. It is described as a combination of ten certified organic medicinal mushrooms, synergistically balanced with aloe vera and the healing herb Uncaria tomentosa (cat's claw). It acts as a booster of natural killer cell activity.

Olitipraz is a di-thiol derivative and has the ability to raise blood levels of protective "detoxification" enzymes that help ward off cancer. These enzymes resemble antioxidant compounds in broccoli, cabbage, and similar vegetables. It can act as a chemo-protective agent against liver toxins by increasing the levels of glutathione-S-transferase. It was originally developed by Johns Hopkins pathobiologist Ernest Buening as an antiparasitic drug to fight schistosomiasis. It exerts a protective function in the liver and many other cell systems, especially the intestinal mucosa. Besides the protective effects against opportunistic germs and endoparasites, it has been shown to have antiviral and anticarcinogenic effects.

Polyunsaturated Fatty Acids and Essential Fatty Acids—(primrose oil or fish oil)—Dietary sources of omega-3 fatty acids include fish oil and certain plant/nut oils. Fish oil contains both docosahexaenoic acid (DHA) and eicosapentaenoic acid (EPA). **Omega-3 fatty acids** are used in the formation of cell walls, thereby effecting membrane fluidity and the behavior of membrane-bound enzymes and receptors. The Omega-3s help to form lipid rafts that are dynamic microenvironments in the plasma membrane (cell wall) structure, which is a phospholipid bilayer. These rafts preferentially group proteins according to their function. Activation of the proteins within rafts can result in rapid clustering that appears to be important for signal transduction in both T and B lymphocytes.[571] The T cell receptor clusters within lipid rafts on contact with an antigen-presenting cell form an immunological synapse, or contact zone, where intracellular signaling is thought to be initiated.

---

570. J. K. Stechmiller et al., "Arginine Immunonutrition in Critically Ill Patients: A Clinical Dilemma," Am J Crit Care (January 2004).

571. Y.U. Katagiri et al., "A Role for Lipid Rafts in Immune Cell Signaling," Microbiology and Immunology 45 (2001): 1–8.

In addition to their roll in cell signaling and communication, fatty acids have been shown to **activate macrophages, neutrophils, and natural killer cells and induce generation of nitric oxide to bring about their tumoricidal, antibacterial, antiviral, and antifungal actions.**[572] Polyunsaturated fatty acids have been shown to augment the antibacterial actions of synthetic antibiotics against drug-resistant bacteria.[573]

Polyunsaturated fatty acids (arachdonic acid) have also been shown to exert anti-hepatitis C virus activity at physiologically relevant concentrations and exert a strong synergistic effect when combined with interferon-α.[574]

Padma 28 is a Tibetan herbal formula that has been shown to exceed Vitamins C, E, and Beta-carotene in counteracting oxygen and NO radicals and inflammatory mediators from activated macrophages.[575] According to these authors, treatment with Padma 28 is so effective in patients who have hepatitis that they survive as symptomless carriers.

Stabilization of the extracellular matrix

The extracellular matrix is composed of various negatively-charged macromolecules possessing polyanionic[576] character, for example, proteogylcans, lipid bilayer membrane surfaces, microtubules, microfilaments, and polynucleotides. Polyanions are important to assure proper protein folding for efficient functioning and as transport chaperones. Some of these polyanions also possess antimicrobial activity and are hypothesized to be a part of the innate immune system. They appear to be important in the ability of the cellular uptake and compartmentalization of proteins.[577]

For prevention and therapy, this matrix can be reinforced by supplying polyanions in the form of chrondroitin sulfates, shark cartilage, macroalgae

---

572. U. N.Das, "Antibiotic-like Action of Essential Fatty Acids," Can Med Assoc J 132 (June 1985): 1350.

573. E. J. Giamarellos-Bourboulis et al.; "n-6 Polyunsaturated Fatty Acids Enhance the Activities of Ceftazidime and Amikacin in Experimental Sepsis Caused by Multidrug Resistant Pseudomonas Aeroginosa," Antimicrob Agents Chemother 48 (2004): 4713–17.

574. G. .Z. Leu et al., "Anti-HCV Activities of Selective Polyunsaturated Fatty Acids," Biochem Biophys Res Commun 318 (2004): 275–80.

575. A. Hassig et al., "Pathogenesis of human suppression in hypercatabolic diseases: AIDS, Septicaemia, Toxic Shock Syndrome and Protein Calorie Malnutrition," Continuum 4 (June/July 1997).

576. Polyanions are any anion having more than one negative charge.

577. L. S. Jones et al., "Polyanions and Proteome," Molecular & Cellular Proteomics (3)8:746-69.

or agar-agar. The balance of the redox potential of the matrix synergistically supports the glutathione system and relieves cell symbiosis in states of pro-oxidative and systemic stress.[578]

Hormonal Balancing

Scientists are just now beginning to unravel the ways in which in the mind influences the body, and vice versa. The hypothalamic–pituitary–adrenal (HPA) axis plays a major role in both mind and body health. The intricate connection between the brain and endocrine system broadly influences our health, and many researchers suggest that our stressful, modern lifestyles are overtaxing the HPA axis.

The increased release of catecholemines and glucocorticoids from the adrenals elicits what is known as a flight or fight response. The metabolic process is designed to rapidly increase the energy supply for the possibility of flight or fight. The physiological function of glucocorticoids consists mainly of limiting life-threatening acute phase reactions by endogenous mediators of inflammation.[579] Cortisol is, in many ways, a paradoxical hormone. A certain amount of cortisol is needed to maintain optimal health, but too much or too little can be deadly. Chronically raised cortisol content has been shown to lead to permanent suppression of Th1 cellular immune reactions and to increase susceptibility to opportunistic infections.

The effects of elevated cortisol can be countered with daily exercise, Vitamin C 4gm daily, DHEA, ginko biloba and melatonin.

By taking time out each day to relax and meditate can bring psychic calm. Considerable scientific evidence has established that relaxation and meditation techniques are valuable therapeutics for optimal health.

A study evaluating the effects of consistent meditation practice over a four-month period found a significant drop in cortisol levels compared with controls who did not practice meditation. This study, as well as others, strongly suggests that meditation may help reverse the effects of chronic stress.[580]

Yoga and Tai Chi are more active meditation practices that have the additional benefit of improving body strength as well. What stress reduction

---

578. Kremer, The Silent Revolution in Cancer and AIDS Medicine, 444-45.
579. A. Munck and P. M. Guyre, "Glucocorticoid Hormones in Stress: Physiological and Pharmacological Actions," Endocrine Reviews 5 (1984). 25-44.
580. R. K. Maclean et al., "Effects of the Transcendental Meditation Program on Adaptive Mechanisms: Changes in Hormone Levels and Responses to Stress after 4 Months of Practice," Psychoneuroendocrinology 22 (May 1997):277-95.

techniques, whether body awareness, deep breathing, progressive muscle relaxation, biofeedback, or guided imagery all have in common is that they allow the development of focused attention using the alpha brain wave state. Fresh creative energy can begin to flow. Fears can vanish, and you can begin to experience a liberating sense of peace and well-being.

Melatonin not only acts as a powerful antioxidant, Zhang et al., reported that treatment with DHEA (dihydroepiandrosterone) or melatonin, alone or in combination, prevented the reduction of B and T cell proliferation and Th1 cytokine secretion in mice with induced AIDS. Melatonin also suppressed the elevated production of Th2 cytokines, reduced hepatic lipid peroxidation, and prevented loss of Vitamin E.[581]

Hydration

Modern medicine has almost completely ignored the healing power of water. In the discussion of living organisms as liquid crystals, the water molecule alignment with collagens as well as cellular proteins was discussed for their importance in cell signaling capability and speed. Hydrogen bonds form between water molecules, giving rise to supra-molecular aggregates or clusters. The clustering of water is a cooperative phenomenon. The clusters are dynamic flickering networks whose structure accounts for the many unusual properties that are essential for supporting life.[582]

Water is the most amazing molecule. It is the reason there is life on this planet; it is the substance that connects all of life. In a healthy adult, it comprises 70 percent of the body mass. As fetuses, we start out life being 99 percent water. When we are born, we are 90 percent water, and by the time of adulthood, we are about 70 percent—the same proportion of water to land as the Earth. Water is the basis of all life and that includes your body. The muscles that move your body are 75 percent water; the blood that transports your nutrients is 82 percent water; the lungs that provide your oxygen are 90 percent water; the brain that is the control center of your body is 76 percent water; even your bones are 25 percent water. If we die of old age, we will probably be about 50 percent water. In other words, throughout our lives we exist mostly as water. Yet there is hardly a mention of water in most biochemical textbooks. Water flows, and it allows the life force and the nutrients we need to maintain health to flow throughout our system. It is

581. Z. Zhang et al., "Prevention of Immune Dysfunction and Vitamin Loss by DHEA and Melatonin Supplementation during Murine Retrovirus Infection," Immunology 96 (1999): 291–97.

582. Mae-Wan Ho, op cit., 105

water that informs the power of the liquid crystalline state and coherency of living organisms.

The HIV/AIDS observation that I have put forward is based on the hypothesis that the rapid rise of environmental pollutants, whether chemical, psychic, or electromagnetic, introduced into our bloodstreams and energetic systems have overwhelmed the capacity of those who are disposed to be able to detoxify their organ systems. Just as these pollutants have poisoned about 80 percent of our waters, they have deposited these same poisons into our bloodstream. Our internal rivers and lakes are poisoned.

Dr. Jacques Benveniste, a French physician, discovered that when a substance is diluted in water, the water can carry the memory of that substance even after it has been so diluted that none of the molecules of the original substance remains. This is the basis of homeopathy. The molecules of any given substance have a spectrum of frequencies that can be digitally recorded with a computer, then played back into untreated water (using an electronic transducer), and when this is done, the new water will act as if the actual substance were physically present. That water has memory is an astounding characteristic of this molecule, and this phenomenon has been underscored by the work of Japanese researcher Masaru Emoto.

Masaru Emoto, using the camera to photograph water crystals, came to the same conclusion as Dr. Benveniste—that water has the ability to copy and store information. Water connects humans to the Gaian biosphere in such a way the rising tide of illness is not just an individual problem but can be viewed as a deformity of society as a whole. We must ask ourselves why we continue to tolerate the poisoning of our environment and ourselves as standard business practice. Emoto has shown in his amazing photographs of water crystals that not only does water carry the energy of electrical and chemical pollution and other toxins but it also carries the energy of sound as well as the energy of thoughts, good or bad. His experiments have shown in a very dramatic way, the power of polluting energy to deform.

Heavy metal music and thoughts of hate produced misshapen, deformed frozen water crystals. Mozart's "Symphony No. 40," Tchaikovsky's "Swan Lake," and Bud Powell's "Cleopatra's Dream" produced intricate delicate crystals. The most beautiful ice crystal was produced in response to words of love and gratitude. These are words that should be spoken, thought and felt throughout the day, every day. Symbolically, paste them on your forehead: **LOVE AND GRATITUTDE.** These are words that dispel fear, loneliness and despair.

In Fereydoon Batmanghelidj's book <u>Water: For Health For Healing, For Life</u>, he discusses his discovery that many people who experience pain, whether chronic or acute, are actually dehydrated. Dr. Batmanghelidj discovered that many chronic diseases are metabolic problems that have dehydration as a core element: This is what he observes about AIDS:

> [E]veryone assumes that AIDS is actually a viral disease, which is a fraudulent statement by those people who presented it, because the human body is the product of many, many years of having fought various viral diseases, and has survived. Smallpox, polio, measles, and all the other viruses that can kill very easily, and the body has an ability to mount a defense system against these hot viruses, viruses that actually very quickly can kill. But having survived those, how is it possible that the slow virus would kill us in the name of AIDS? I can't understand it.
>
> I have researched this topic extensively, and I have shown in fact that AIDS is a metabolic problem, when the body begins to cannibalize its own tissue because of certain missing elements in the raw materials that it receives through food or beverages, and the body of a person who gets AIDS, actually, is short of quite a number of building block amino acids. They're short of tyrosine, they're short of methionine, cysteine, they're short of histidine, and they've got a whole lot of others in excess. So how can we expect a body that depends on the other amino acids to survive?[583]

Given the known healing properties of water, it should come as no surprise that one of the biggest businesses on the planet is the sale of sweetened, chemically laden, caffeinated, adulterated water known as soft drinks? Caffeine is warfare chemical for the plant. Anything that would eat it will lose its art of camouflage, its alertness, good reaction, good response, and becomes easy prey to its own food-chain predator. Caffeine is technically an insecticide. So is morphine, and so is cocaine. They are the same family of drugs—neurotoxic substances. High fructose corn syrup used in soft drinks has been shown to have suppressive effects on the immune system. A recent study by the Institute for Agriculture and Trade Policy found increased levels of mercury in 31 percent of 55 products (other than soft drinks) tested that listed corn syrup on the label.

---

583. Interview at www.naturalnews.com

Alkalinization

A healthy body functions best when it is slightly alkaline. The ideal blood pH is 7.365. The American medical establishment accepts 7.4, but this is too alkaline and indicates the body is collecting and storing alkaline minerals to dampen excess acidity. A change in pH can bring about changes in the reduction potential for the thiol pool by increasing or decreasing the redox potential of the cell, thus making energy production less efficient and thereby creating the antecedent conditions for disease formation. Fungal overgrowths are common in acidic states.

PH can be tested in a doctor's office or at home using pH strips which can be purchased at most pharmacies or on line. More information on pH balance can be found in The pH Miracle, Balance Your Diet, Reclaim Your Health, by Robert and Shelley Young.

Love and Gratitude

In the end, in the world of unconventional warfare, free markets, Darwinian ethics, globalization, structural adjustment programs, and population control, the words love and gratitude are absent. Information Operations have displaced informed decision making with an undisclosed agenda. Yet each of us individually has the power to change that dynamic. It is a choice. The words gratitude and love form the fundamental principles of the laws of nature and the phenomenon of life.

What I have learned from the exercise of writing this book, which at times was overwhelming, is that there is not a system—political, economic, medical, religious—that has not been designed as a form of mass control and a way to separate us from our fundamental nature and each other. More than anything, if we are to survive as a species, we can no longer be dominated by this destructive force. We have the power to harness the energy of the universe to be creative beyond our wildest imaginations. If we did not, the masters of the universe would not work so hard to separate us from that knowledge.

Everything in the universe is energy and so are we. We have the capacity to resonate with every plant, every animal, and every thought that ever existed. We can send energy into the world, and we can receive energy in return. If we want to continue to live in a world we think is essentially stingy, then we will perpetuate greed. If we think we live in a world of abundance, then we can begin to live from gratitude and love and create that world. If we find ourselves in constant conflict with our friends and loved ones, then that conflict will be reflected in continuous hot and cold wars. So many of us harbor wounds and hurts that are covered with the thinnest tissue of emotional veneer, but the wounds have never fully healed. If we learn how to love unconditionally and forgive with passion, then those energies will be drawn into our world.

Constant greed and grasping for dominance serve to destroy the harmony of the planet. So much so that some feel comfortable proclaiming that the only solution is to kill 90 percent of mankind. The people who are leading us, who function in the world of shadow and mystery do not honor us or our spirits. So we must honor our own spirits by turning away from their synthetic promises. They can bring us nothing but fear, war, plagues, and pollution. It is inevitable. Someone once stated that a healthy society is one in which the citizens demonstrate a high moral character and collective discipline. We seem to have lost the ability as a society to demonstrate either of these characteristics.

Long ago, we used to ask, "What if they had a war and nobody came?" Everything that comes from greedy energy is war—finance—medicine—education—media. HIV/AIDS is war. You have the power to say, "Thank you, no." Claim your place on the planet and do something really revolutionary. Sing your own song; vibrate in harmony with life, and every day that you are physically present on this planet, wake up to the words: <u>love</u> and <u>gratitude</u>. The ripple that you send into the universal ocean will create a tidal wave so powerful that you will be amazed that the power comes from you!

Index

oxidative stress theory and
AIDS in, 193, 194n298
pan-Africa union, 12
people imported, to U.S., 104,
107
PMCs in, 157
poverty, impact of, 13, 24,
24n32, 157–158
resources in, 5
sex and blood plague in, 268,
273, 370 (*See also* sex and
blood plague)
sex surveys in, 275
silent wars in, 188
slaves from (*See individual
entries under slaves*)
studies on HIV in, 291–293
West view of history in, 212
Africa-America Institute, 150
African American Health, on pellegra
deaths, 236
African American women (black
women), 8, 48, 60, 87, 229,
277–280, 287
African Americans (blacks)
AIDS, myths about increase of,
278–280
antibody levels in, 310,
310n451
apartheid system in Southern
U.S. and, 236
AZT and, 248, 316
communities as targets, 228
crack cocaine and, 195
drug dealing, 113
drug use, 172, 180–181,
181n285–286
environmental sensors and, 52,
52n74
"eugenic discrimination" for,
230

HIV testing results for, 374,
375–376
increasing number of, 215
infant mortality of, 89
Iran-Contra and, 203
as IV-drug users, 8
literacy figures for, 26
lose homes in Los Angeles,
202–203
The Negro Project and, 229,
231
prison system and, 182
radiation experiments on, 226,
226n338
and sex, taking protective measures, 267, 377
slavery and (*See* slavery)
state of, 87
victim archetype and, 369–370
African ancestry, and f(HIV),
374–375
African green monkey, 273, 280
African Mysteries System of
Nile Rive Valley, 269
African National Congress
(ANC), 117
African Slave Trade, 182,
182n287
African Union Government,
152, 152n225
agriculture, financial warfare on, 4
AIDS (Acquired Immune
Deficiency Syndrome)
about, 4–6, 8–10, 44
in Africa (*See* Africa)
anti-retroviral drugs and, 58
AZT and, 7, 220
Burroughs Wellcome as winners
in, 246–247
as business model, 148

Barri-Sinossi, F., 313*n*461

Barron, Frank, 166

Baruch, Bernard, 128

Bateson, Gregory, 167–168

Batista, Fulgencio, 134*n*191

Batmanghelidj, Fereydoon, 394–395

The Battle for the Mind (Sargant), 357–358, 358*n*527

Bauer, Henry, 267, 310*n*451, 317, 317*n*473, 374, 374*n*544, 376, 376*n*546

Bausell, R.B., 377, 377*n*551

Bauval, Robert, 271*n*394

Bay of Pigs (Cuba), 134–135, 135*n*193

Bayer, 262

Bayh-Dole Act, 2*n*7

BBC, on MIBA, 143, 143*n*205

BCCI, drug bank, 104

Beal, M.F., 388*n*565

Bealle, Morris A., 27*n*35, 41*n*60, 294

Becker, Loftus E., 105

Behavioral Science Teacher Education Project (BSTEP), 37

BEIC (British East India Company) about, 42, 42*n*63, 43–44
ascent to power, 95–96, 95*n*123, 96*n*124
China, ships opium to, 94–95, 94*n*120, 246
drug epidemic and, 24–25
expansion of opium market, 98–99
free trade movement and, 97, 123–124
in South Africa, 119
trade with Hong Kong, 177
Vietnam War impact on, 13

Beisel, W.R., 238*n*353

Belgian, 150–151

Belgium, 357

Bellow, Saul, 1

Bengal (India), 95, 98, 99, 123

Benin, 212

Ben-Jochannan, Yosef, 269*nn*386–388, 270*nn*291–292

Bennett, John Wheeler, 161

Benveniste, Jacques, 394

Berlin Wall, 83

Bernays, Edward, 71, 169

Bernhard, Prince, 170

Bernstein, Carl, 177*n*276

Bess (researcher), xxi

Beta-glucans, 380

Between Two Ages (Brzezinski), 167, 167*n*256

Bhutto, Benazir, 111

Bialy, Harvey, 267

Biddle, Mary Duke, 232

Bigger, R.J., 273*n*398

Bihar (India), 99, 123

Bilderberg Group, think tank, 165, 170

Bin Laden, Osama, 111

bio-energetic system, 64

biological compensatory therapy, 77

Biological Warfare Division, of U.S military, 226

BIS (Bank for International Settlements) (Switzerland), 27–28, 207, 207*n*323

Black, Erick, 121*n*165

Black, P.H., 302*n*435

black ops funding, 112

Black Panther Party, 165

black women (African American women), 8, 48, 60, 87, 229, 277–281, 287

blacks (African Americans), 369–370

British Medical Journal, on HIV-1
  serology in children, 318
British MI6, 104
British Research Council, 254
British Round Table Group, 28
British Tavistock Institute, 357–358
Browne, S., 388n565
Brush, Charles Francis, 232
Brush, Dorothy H., 232
Brussels, diamonds traded in, 141
Brzezinski, Zbigniew, 78–79,
  78n104, 84, 122, 161, 165–166,
  167n256
BSTEP (Behavioral Science Teacher
  Education Project), 37
Buchalter, Louis "Lepke," 101, 107
budding, 301
Buenos Aires (Argentina), 126
Buettner, Garry R., 219n330,
  326–327, 327n494
Buhl, R., 341, 341n515
Bundy, McGeorge, 133–134n190
Bureau of Narcotics and Dangerous
  Drugs, U.S., 101n137
Burford, Ann, 195
Burke, D.S., 276n408
Burma (Myanmar), 102, 106,
  106n145, 108, 111
Burroughs Wellcome
  about, 6
  azathioprine, as producer of, 6
  AZT, falsifying toxicology find-
    ings, 258–259
  AZT, marketing of, 253, 255
  becomes Glaxo Smith Kline,
    246
  FDA and, 254
  immune deficiency drugs, creat-
    ing, 248
  immune suppressing drugs,
    6–7, 251, 316

study funded by, 263
supplies missionaries, 246
T/S study, 263
T/S used to treat AIDS by, 260
Burton, Hersh, 133n189
Burundi, 154, 349
Bush, George H.W., xvii
  about, 196
  birth control in budget, 231
  donors to campaign, 153
  drug trade and, 113, 181
  father of, 199n309, 223
  "Infrastructure Privatization"
    and, 32n45
  Iran-Contra and, 90–91,
    150n221 (*See also* Iran-
    Contra)
  in Skull and Bones Society, 112
Bush, George W.
  China admission to WTO,
    85–86
  consentration of wealth, shift
    of, 84
  as economic conservative, 88
  economic decline, 65–66
  economic issues, federal collec-
    tion data on, 211
  FBI transfer of agents after 9/11
    to terrorism, 121
  grandfather of, 29, 29n41
  loss of jobs, 79
  presidential campaigns, 90
  as signer of PNAC, 356
  at Yale, 112
Bush, Prescott, 29, 29n41, 199n309,
  223
Bush Pioneer and Ranger, 90
Butler, Smedly Darlington, 362–
  363, 363n530
Bybee, Henry, 224
Byrd, D. Harry, 133

Ebola, 47, 240
economic
    hit men, 141, 141n200
    models, 44, 97, 204, 206, 223
    viruses, 211
Economic Mobility Project, 238
Economists, on production *vs.* safety
    in mines, 143
EcoNugenics, 383
Ecoscience (Erlich and Holdren), 172
ectopic pregnancies, 285
Edmonds, Sibel, 356–357, 357n526,
    362
Edwards, Jim, 167n258, 369n540
Egypt, 160, 174, 179, 269, 271
Eisenhower, Dwight, 69, 104,
    134–135, 139, 178, 178n277
Electron Microscopy Laboratory,
    19, 296
Eli Lilly, xi, xvii
ELISA, antibody test, 19n21, 145,
    146–147, 299, 309, 311, 314,
    372
Elizabeth I (queen), 123
Elkins, R., 385n560
Elliot, T.S., 166
Elliott, William Yandell, 161
Ellison, Keith, 85
EM (electron micrograph), xvi, xxi,
    298, 301–302, 305–306
Emaform (clioquinol), 216, 217–
    218, 218n327, 219
Emoto, Masaru, 394
empire
    of debt, 50
    international, Onassis, 136
    Tempelsman, 141 (*See also* Tem-
        pelsman, Maurice)
    United States, 126
    Zionist, 28
empire system, 86

endowments, 104, 112–113
Engdahl, F. William, 170n266,
    171n267
England *See* Great Britain
Enron, 203, 203n317, 210
Entero-vioform (clioquinol), 216,
    217–218, 218nn327–328, 219
Environmental Protection Agency
    (EPA), 195
environmental stressors
    in Africa, 284
    compound toxins as, 65
    cumulative external, 64
    diagnosis and, 252, 263
    overload of, 21
    oxidizing, accumulation of, 14
environmental toxins
    abuse of, 5, 13
    creating oxidative stress crisis,
        109
    disease, rise in, 65
    fluoride as, 73
    long-term exposure to, 20
    mitochondria, damage to, 3
Environmental Working Group
    (EWG), 74
enzymes
    about, 19n22
    functioning of, 257
    human DHFR, 260
    inactivating cell respiration, 258
    microbial, 260
    natural nuclear, 256
    poison of, 72
    retroviral, 19
    reverse transcriptase, 50–53, 54,
        109
EPA (Environmental Protection
    Agency), 195
Epidemic Intelligence Agency, 191
    creation of, 13

Friedman, S.R., 376n548
Friedreich ataxia, 57–58
Friends Committee on National
    Legislation Report (2008), 173
Friendship Bridge, 111
Frist, Bill, 150
fructose corn syrup, 66
Fuller, Buckminster, 332
Furchgott, Robert F., xxi, 346

G
Gallo, Robert "Bob"
    and Gallos "virus" (HTLV-III),
        10–11, 78
    HIV, antibody test for, xvii, 9,
        287, 296, 307
    HIV, characteristics of, xxi
    HIV, isolation of, xvi, xxii,
        9–10, 298
    HIV, kills T-helper lympho-
        cytes, 297
    HIV proteins, 19n24
    HIV virus, isolation of, 304
    human retrovirus, isolation of,
        xiv, xv
    lab tests showing AZT effect on
        HIV, xviii
    proteins detected by, 313
    research findings, 17–22,
        49–51, 51n73, 55, 55n80,
        56, 259
    retro virus, discovery of, 303
    on sexually transmitted virus,
        47
    theory of HIV/AIDS causation,
        340
    viral cause of cancer, 185–186,
        305
    viral infection, creating, 359
    See also HIV (Human
        Immunodeficiency Virus)

Galton, Francis, 226
Gamble, Clarence J., 230, 230n341,
    231, 231n342
gangsters (mob), 101–102, 107, 117,
    128, 131, 133, 134, 134n192,
    136, 364
Gardner, Richard N., 84, 355
Garrett, Robert, 232
Garrison, Jim, 178n277, 179n281
Gates, Jeff, 45
Gates, Robert, 105
GATT (General Agreement on
    Tariffs and Trade) See General
    Agreement on Tariffs and Trade
    (GATT)
Gatto, John Taylor, 26, 35n48,
    37–38, 38n54, 39n56
gay community, 109
    See also homosexual com-
        munity
Gbedemah, Ghana finance minister,
    152
Geir, D.A., 245n356
Geir, M.R., 245n356
Geithner, Timothy, 122
Gemstone File, 127, 127nn175–176,
    136n197
Gemstone Thesis, 127n173
General Agreement on Tariffs and
    Trade (GATT), establishment
    of, 30
General Aniline & Film
    Corporation, 41
General Education Board, 45–46
    Occasional Paper Number One,
        38–39, 39n55
General Electric, 184, 184n290
Genesca, J., 320, 320n484
genocide
    in Africa, 12, 44, 140–141,
        150, 153, 349n522

grounding, 369
guanosine, 247
Guinea, 158
Gul, Hamid, 355
Gulf War (first), 169, 169n264
gum disease, use of fluoride and, 72
guns. in neighborhoods, 182
Guyre, P.M., 392n579

H

HAART (anti-retroviral l therapy),
xxi, xxiii, 8, 194, 379–380
Hahneman, Samuel, 5n8, 381
Haig, Alexander, 33
Haiti, 212, 274, 280
Halliburton, 154
Hamer, Fannie Lou, 229n339
Hamilton, John, 254
Hamilton, Lee, 200
Hamilton Securities, 202–203, 205
Hancock, Graham, 271n394
Hanoi, 175
Harriman, E.H., 233–235, 236–
237
Harrit, N.H., 122n169
Hartmann, Florence, 156n235
Harvard AIDS Institute, 140, 146
Harvard Corporation, 203
Harvard Endowment Fund, 182,
203
Harvard Management Corporation,
182
Harvard Psychedelic Drug Research
Institute, 166
Harvard School of Public Health,
275
Harvard School of Public Health's
AIDS Initiative, 66, 118–119,
148, 159

Harven, Etienne de, 184–185,
185nn291–292, 303, 304n439,
305nn440–441, 306n445, 321
Hassig, A., 378n553, 391n575
Hassig, Alfred, 192
Havana (Cuba), 134
Hawkes, Nigel, 273
Hayes, Rutherford B., 236
health care
cost of (U.S.), 40n58, 40nn57–
58, 41
industries, organized in 20th
Century, 39
records, 369, 369n540
treatment for poor, 68,
68nn93–94
Health Education and Welfare
(HEW), Dept. of, 39–40
Health Freedom Protection Act, 42
health rate decline, 66
health records database, 46n65
Hearst, William Randolph, 129
heart disease, 66n90
heath care
costs, 295
delivery system, 2
Heckler, Margaret, 47, 49
hedge funds, 80, 205
Hekmatyar, Gulbuddin, 110n153
Helliwell, Paul, 128, 198, 198n307,
199n309, 203–204
hemophiliacs, 7–8, 48, 78, 191, 274,
289–290
Henderson, L., 316, 316n471
Hepatitis B, 285
Heritage Foundation, think tank,
165
heroin
addiction of GIs to, 176
Afghanistan trade, to Europe,
110, 110n152

Honnen, W.J., 301n434
Honnold, Lincoln William, 142
Hoover Institution, think tank, 165
Hopkins, Harry L., 22–23, 22n29, 61
Hopsicker, Daniel, 90, 91n119
hormonal balancing, 381, 392–393
hormones, 4, 64, 231, 338, 350, 366, 389, 392
House, Edward Mandell, 171
Housing and Urban Development
    See HUD (Housing and Urban Development)
Housing and Urban Development (HUD), 202, 205
HPA (hypothalamic-pituitary-adrenal) axis, 392
HPV (human papilloma virus) vaccine, 36, 37n51
HUD (Housing and Urban Development), 182, 182n287, 202, 205
HUD (Housing and Urban Development) forecloses, 125
Hudson Institute, think tank, 165
Hughes Commission, 197, 197n306
Hull, Cordell, 33
human experimentation, 7, 9, 255
    See also eugenics
human genomes, 51, 51n71, 53, 228, 333, 336, 374
    See also genomes
Human Immunodeficiency Virus (HIV) See HIV (Human Immunodeficiency Virus)
Human leukocyte antigen (HLA) test, 315–317
human metabolic system. poisoning of, 3
human papilloma virus, 277, 285

Human Rights Division, of State Department, 195
humoral immunity, 344
Hutus Rwandan exiles, 150n222, 154, 155
Huxley, Aldous, 368, 368n538
Huxley, Julian, 223, 223n335
Hyde Amendment, 227
hydration, 393–395
hypertension, 4, 46, 77

I

Icke, David, 354
ICTR (International Criminal Tribunal for Rwanda), 156, 156n239
identification number issued at birth, 37–38
Ignarro (researcher), 346
illegal drugs
    addiction to, 89
    and infant mortality, 89–92
Illich, Ivan, 41, 41n61, 47n66, 348n521
Illinois (IL)
    Chicago Democratic convention (1968), 136
    as drug distribution center, 357
    nursing care in, 68
    opium trade influence in, 112
IMF (International Monetary Fund)
    See International Monetary Fund (IMF)
IMF riot, 130
Immigration and Naturalization Services, 195, 195n303
immune deficiency drugs, 248
immune suppressors, 6–7, 13, 244, 347
    See also AZT (azidothymidine)

immune system
  branches of, 349–350
  opiate receptors in, 99–100,
    100*n*131
  parts of, 344, 344*n*518
Immunological synapse, 390
Imus, Don, 280
Income Tax law, 171, 171*n*268, 243
India
  globalization and, 87
  imports from New England,
    104
  opium growing regions, 123
  opium trade, 99, 111
  opium war, 95
  risks in, 174
  slave labor of, 97
  textile markets in, 98, 98*n*129
Indonesia
  international white crime net-
    work and, 31
  risks of, 174
Indonesia, Dutch pacified, 94
infants
  chemical contaminants in, 74
  mortality of, 67, 89–90
  See also children
infections
  opportunistic (*See* opportunistic
    infections)
  transmitted, 11
infectious diseases, isolating
  organisms for, 10
informed consent, 244
"Infrastructure Provatization,"
  32*n*45
Ingbar, Donald E., 332*ill*, 332*n*504
Institute for Social Relations, think
  tank, 165
Institute of Pacific Relations, 83
insurance industry

denying standard care, 67–68
organized in 20th Century, 39
intelligence agencies (U.S.), 106
    See also CIA (Central Intel-
    ligence Agency); FBI
International Advisory Council
  (Harvard), 146
International Bank for
  Reconstruction and
  Development, 30
    See also World Bank
International Criminal Tribunal for
  Rwanda (ICTR), 156, 156*n*239
International Federation of
  Eugenicists Organizations, 124
International Monetary Fund (IMF)
  allopathic medical profession,
    control of, 61
  bailout of Wall Street, 205
  creation of, 13, 25, 30, 81
  drug trade and, 207–208
  free trade and, 130
  impact on democracy, 31–33,
    31*n*43, 32*n*45, 33*n*46
  imposing "Structural Adjust-
    ment Programs," 358
  population control programs
    and, 173–175
  riot, 130
International Occupational Safety
  and Health Information Centre,
  382
*The International Problem of
  Governing Mankind* (Jessup),
  83, 83*n*110
International Strategic and Tactical
  Organization (ISTO), 154
International Symposium on AIDS,
  xv, xvii
intestines, 71, 318, 379, 385

L

Labarrere, C.A., 319*n*482

Labor Party Investigating Team, U.S., 107*n*146

Lake, Anthony, 150, 150*n*222, 153–154, 153*n*228–229

Lamberti, M.R., 127*n*174

Lamour, C., 127*n*174

Lancer, on infant HIV positive, 318

Lancet (researcher), xxiii

Lang, G.H., 72*n*97

Langmuir, Alexander, 59, 245

Lanka, Stefan, 54*n*78, 61, 192

Lansdale, Edward, 178

Lansky, Meyer, 101, 107, 127–128, 128*nn*177–179, 134

Laos, 102, 108, 180

L-arginine, 389–390

Las Vegas (NV), cancer treatment in, 68

Latin America, 180, 193

Lauristen, J.L., 296*n*426

Lauristen, John, 250*n*362, 253*n*366

law and order campaign, 172, 180–181

Lazare Kaplan International (LKI), 141, 144, 148–149

L-carnitine, 388–389

Le Monde, on sex and love to Africans, 275

Lean, Geoffrey, 65*n*88

Leary, Timothy, 166

Lechner, Bruce, 11*n*14

Lee, Janet, 116, 118, 118*n*162

Legrand, Bernard, 155

Lehman Brothers, 80*n*106

Lehmann, Otto, 327–338

Leikin, S., 330*n*499

Leitner, Michael, xxi

Leon Commision, on occupational health published, 143, 144

Leon Tempelsman & Son, 140, 141, 149

Leopold II (king), 150–151, 151*n*224, 275

leprosy, 291

Less Developed Countries (LDCs), 173, 175, 209–210, 232, 264

Leu, G.Z., 391*n*574

Levey, Noam, 68*n*94

Levine, Michael, 199, 201

Lewin, Kurt, 164–165

L-glutamine, 385, 389

Li, X.S., 72*n*97

Liberia, 158, 292

Lichtenstein, Grace, 272*n*396

life expectancy, 47*n*66
 of Americans, 40, 40*nn*57–58, 66
 rise in, 47

Limitation Law (1933), 127, 127*n*174

Limits to Medicine (Illich), 348, 348*n*521

Lincoln, Abraham, 107

Lippman, Walter, 40

liquid crystal displays (LCDs), 327

liquid crystal organisms, 327–334

Lite, Jordon, 2*n*5

Litton Biometrics, 9

liver, 261, 265, 316, 379, 382–384, 385, 390

liver disease, 296, 380

Living with the Fluid Genome (Ho), 51*n*71, 333*n*508

Livingston, David, 246

LKI (Lazare Kaplan International), 141, 144, 148–149

Lo, Shyh-Ching, 285

lobbying, 36, 36*n*49, 39

London, City of (England),
financial instruments as acts of
terror, use of, 80
Los Angeles (CA), 202, 204, 268,
370
CDC report of pneumonia in,
xvi
first diagnoses of AIDS, 286–
287
"lost tribe," theory of, 274, 274n401
Lows, Abriel Abbott, 112
Lows family, 111
LSD (lysergic acid)
distribution of, 168
flooding market with, 7, 109,
136, 208
impact of, 168–169, 168n261
MK-ULTRA and, 163n250,
167
research of, 69, 102
teachers and, 166–167
Lucey, D.R., 52n74, 317n474
Luciano, Charles "Lucky," 101, 107,
128n177
Ludlow massacre (CO), 224
Luke, J., 366n533
Lumumba, Patrice, 135, 135n195,
139, 150, 151–153, 159
Lutwak-Mann, C., 315n468
Lutzenburger, José, 210
lymphomas, 248, 249, 252, 253
lysergic acid See LSD (lysergic acid)

M

Maclean, R.K., 392n580
macrophages, 278, 302, 378, 379,
389, 390, 391
The Mad Cow News
on Bush's (G.W.) presidential
campaigns, 90n117

on seizure of American planes,
90
made man, 196n305
Madison, James, 160
Madoff, Bernie, 121
Madsen, Wayne, 153n229, 154,
154n233, 355
Magaysay, Ramon, 178
Mail and Guardian (South Africa),
on scramble for Congo wealth,
139–140
Makhijani, Arjun, 64n87
maladaptive response, 114
malaria
affects of, 222
in Africa, 211, 316, 349
antibodytesting and, 9
control of, 221, 221n332
deaths from, 174
ELISA testing and, 145, 146
HIV and, 291, 311, 326
impact of, 230
pellagra and, 239
T-cell count and, 276
Malawi, 158
Malay Peninsula, impact of opium
trade on, 99
Malcolm X, 165, 180, 203–204
Mali, 158
malnourishment, and poverty,
239–240
malnutrition/starvation, deaths
from, 33, 33n47
Malthus, Thomas, 120, 123–124,
130, 227
Malthusian economics, 237, 238–
239
Malthusian marketing strategies,
246
Man the Unknown, (Carrell), 226
Manhattan Project, 69, 70

National Council for Mental
Hygiene, 163–164
National Drug Strategy Network,
181
national electronic vaccine tracking
registry, 46n65
National Endowment for
Democracy (NED), 149
National Institute of Allergy and
Infectious Diseases, 273–274
National Institutes of Allergy and
Infectious Diseases (NIAID),
255
National Institutes of Health
(NIH), 6, 40, 60, 255
as control agent, 40
National Research Council, 61,
279n415
National Security Act (1947), 104
creation of, 13
National Security Agency, 355
creation of, 13
National Security Council (NSA),
196, 201
National Security Council, U.S.,
173
NationalCreditReport.com, 369
NATO (North Atlantic Treaty
Organization), 354, 357
natural food markets, and FDA, 42
naturopathy, 45
medicine's impact on, 36
Nazi Party (Germany), 226
Nazification, of Germany, 41, 98
necrosis, 339
NED (National Endowment for
Democracy), 149
The Negro Project, 229, 231,
280–281
Negroes *See* African Americans
(blacks)

Nevada (NV), medical care in, 68,
68n93
New Deal, 22n29
New England, opium lords, 104–
106
New Jersey (NJ)
as drug distribution center, 357
farmers, lawsuit on effects of
fluoride on livestock, 69,
70, 72
New Orleans, 202, 355
New Scientist, on diseases signifying
AIDS, 146n212
New York (NY)
drug importation to, 111,
111n154
families, trading in opium, 111
first diagnoses of AIDS, 268
fluoride research, 69, 71
New York City (NYC), 141, 204,
220, 286, 370
See also sex and blood
plague
New York Social Register, 105
New York Times
on cocaine use and Mexican-
U.S. border, 90
on heroin addiction, 176n273,
179n283
on international AIDS conference, 292
interview with Justice Ruth
Ginsburg, 227
on Mbeki, Thabo, 359
on prescription drugs, 242
New York World, on making perfect
race, 234
Newburg (NY), water fluoridation
study, 71
Newell, G.R., 250n361
Newsholme, P., 389n568

glutathione and, 342
HIV antibody test, results of, 20
indirect surrogate markers and, 19
nitrosamines and, 6
pro-, 50, 373, 387
redox potential and, 338–339
selenium and, 386
sulfamethoxazole and, 261
UV irradiation induced, 387
oxidative stress theory, 193–194, 194n298, 194n300, 339, 340n512
oxidative stressors, 8, 65, 193, 283, 333, 352, 375
Ozalid Corporation, 41

P

Packer and Sen (researchers), xx
Padian, Nancy, 289–290
Padma-28, 391
Pakistan, 108, 111, 174
Palast, Gregory, 129n184
Palimpsest (Vidal), 116–117
Palmisano, Samuel, 88n114
pan-Africa union, 12, 152
Panama, 226
Papadopulos-Eleopulos, Eleni
  on AIDS in Africa, 148n216
  on HIV positive patiens, 48n67
  on HIV proteins, 315, 315n470
  "Mother to Child Transmission of HIV" (article), 317–318
  oxidative theory of AIDS, 55, 55n81, 194n298, 339–340, 340n512
  on redox potential, 192–193, 192n297
  reduction/oxidation theory, 333–336
  on Western Blot test, 371n542

Papucci, L., 388
parapolitics *vs.* deep politics, 119–120, 120n164
Paris AIDS conference (1986), 340
Paris peace talks, 108, 162
Parkinson's disease, 382
Pasteur, Louis, 76
Pasteur Institute, Paris, xiv, xv, 10–11, 285, 298n431
  See also Montagnier, Luc
Paterson (NJ), 357
Paterson, Graham, 89n116
Pathfinder International, 231
Patriot Act, 165
Paul, Ron, 42, 80, 85
PBS Frontline (television show), on opium, 177
PCP (Pneumocystis carinii pneumonia), xvi, 103, 208, 260
PCR (Polymerase Chain Reaction)/ viral load, genetic test, xvi, xx, xxiii, 300, 309, 321–325, 373, 380
Peabody family, 111
PectaSol® Chelation Complex, 383
Peebles, J. M., 225
Peking (China), 103
pellagra
  about, 221–223
  cause of, 235–237
  eugenicists and, 234–235, 283
  as niacin deficiency, 219, 220, 237
Pentagon, 122
  See also 9/11 attack
Pentagon heist, 356
Pentagon projects, 73, 73n101
Penthouse, on Mena, 201, 201n314
People's Republic of China *See* China
Perkins, John, 141

Russia
as a diversion, 83
eugenics adherents in, 227
fluoride, use of, 71
HIV infections, rate of, 286,
286n420
industrial assets, 129–130
infant mortality in, 89
money laundering, 205
October Revolution in,
195n302
privatization, 210
Rwanda, 150, 156, 159, 275, 349
Rwandan genocide, 138, 154–155,
155n235–155n236, 158
Rwandan Patriotic Army, 154,
154n233
Rwandan Patriotic Front (RPF),
154–155
Ryan White CARE Act, 60

S
Sachs, Jeff, 32
Sacramento Bee, on HIV testing in
Africa, 311
Sagan, Dorion, 336n509
SAIC (Science Application
International Corporation), 158
SAMe, 385
SAMe (S-adenosyl-methionine), 384
Samual, M., 376, 376n549
San Francisco (CA)
Alive and Well in, 371
first diagnoses of AIDS, 268,
286–287
sex and blood plague and, 370
(*See also* sex and blood
plague)
San Francisco Examiner
on attitudes of *Washington Post,*
129

on guerrilla leader in Columbia,
190*ph*
on sale of old ships, 131n186
on staying out of WWII,
129n183
San Jose Mercury News, on Iran-
Contra scandal, 196, 201
Sanger, Margaret, 59, 215, 229,
229n340, 230, 230n341, 233,
280
Sargant, William, 357–358,
358n527
SARS (Severe Acute Respiratory
Syndrome), 14, 14n17
Sasson, David, 96, 96n126, 104
Savings and Loan (S&L) scandal,
195, 198–199
Schacht, Hjalmer, 28, 136
Schayler, David, 355
Schering & Company, 41
Schreiber, S.L., 58n84
Schripps, E.B., 232
Schrödinger's question, 339
Schultz, George, 32
Schultz, T.J., 57n83
Schupbach, Jorg, 319, 319n480
Science
on cause of AIDS, 9–10, 17–18
as evidence center for AIDS,
360
on HIV, 20, 20n25
Science Application International
Corporation (SAIC), 158
scientifically based medical training
model (Germany), 39
scorecard of daily deaths, 33
Scott, Peter Dale, 106n144, 115,
115n156, 119–120, 127–128,
197–198
Sea Supply, 198
Seager, Ashley, 40n49

Nicaraguan Contra, 195 (*See also* Iran-Contra)
organizations in South (U.S.), 223–224
See also 9/11 attack
Texas (TX)
Dallas Book Depository, 133
drug importation to, 111, 111*n*154
Texas Academy of Science, 240
Texas Mexican Railway Company, 112
Thailand, 108, 174, 231, 231*n*343
Thangapazham, R.L., 387*n*563
T-helper, 14, 255, 350
T-helper lymphocytes, 297
think tanks, 24, 61, 122, 124–125, 150, 165, 170, 238, 266
See also Tavistock Institute of Human Relations
thiols
about, 14*n*16, 341
ATP synthesis and, 388
charge exchange in, 334
depletion of, 373
electrons of, 192, 352
HIV positives and, 378
proteins containing, 14
redox potentials and, 347
Thomas, L, xix
Thomas, Lewis, xvii, 220–221
Thomás-Cobos, L., 389*n*569
thought control, in eugenics, 227–228
thyroid medications, 72, 72*n*98
Thyssen, Fritz, 105
Tiananmen Square (China), 83, 177
Tibet, 83
Tiffany's diamonds, 141
Tilley, S.A., 301*n*434
Timbuktu, 212, 270

Time Magazine
Man of Year (1996), 321
on most influential people, 2009, 156
on Rhoades work, 226
on supply of weapons to Vietcong, 83
Times (London), on AIDS in monkeys, 273
Tiranti, Dexter, 218*n*329
T-Lymphocyte Retrovirus, 313
Todak, G, 320*n*485
Tomyama, T, 314*n*464
Toronto (Canada), 292
Toronto Star, on drug trade, 111, 111*n*155
Tragedy and Hope (Quigley), 27–28, 122
transplant patients
AZT for, use of, 6, 6*n*9
immune suppressing drugs, given, 316
renal, 7, 11
The Trials of Henry Kissinger (documentary), 162, 162*n*249
Trilateral Commission, 84
trimethoprim, xiii, xiv, xv, 247, 260, 262, 263
See also sulfamethoxazole
Trocki, Carl A., 42*n*63, 93, 97*n*127, 104*n*142
"Trojans," 302
Trotsky, Leon, 195, 195*n*302
Trout, Robert, 95*n*121
Truman, Harry, 129, 131, 179
T/S (Trimethoprim/ Sulfamethoxazole), 7, 250–351, 378
See also sulfamethoxazole; trimethoprim
Tsugane, Dr., 217

tuberculosis
    Christmas Seal campaign,
        22–23
    crack lung variable for, 277,
        277n409
    HIV antibody test and, 9, 308
    incident rates for, 147,
        147nn214–215
    microbes responsible for, 291
    pulmonary, 5, 144–145,
        145n211
    scrrening for, 314
    in South African mines (*See*
        South Africa)
    in Southern Africa, 316
Tubman, Harriet, 370
tumor growth, 249
"tunable response systems," 328
Turkey, 111, 127, 174, 356–357
Turnbull, D.M., 265, 265n383
Turner, Val, 192
Tutsi Rwandan exiles, 155

U
Uganda, 147, 147n214, 150, 154–
    155, 275, 291, 349, 349n522
U.N. Drug Control Program, 111
Unabomber, 166
UNDP (United Nations
    Development Program), 174
unemployment rate, 79, 79n105
UNESCO (United Nations
    Educational, Scientific, and
    Cultural Organization), 223,
    228
UNFPA (United Nations Fund for
    Population Activities), 174
UNICEF (United Nations
    Children's Fund), 349
United Fruit Company, 105, 112

United Kingdom (U.K.), 80, 104,
    119, 357
United Nations (UN), 84–85, 93,
    110, 173–174, 174n271
United Nations Children's Fund
    (UNICEF), 349
United Nations Development
    Program (UNDP), 174
United Nations Educational,
    Scientific, and Cultural
    Organization (UNESCO), 223,
    228
United Nations Fund for Population
    Activities (UNFPA), 174
United Nations Population Fund,
    228
United States (U.S.)
    Africans brought to, 104, 107
    AIDS epidemic in, characteris-
        tics of, 284
    AIDS in, first termed, 274,
        286–287
    cultural revolution, 169
    as debtor nation, 12, 33, 86
    decade of unrest, 135–136
    de-industrialization of, 24
    drug epidemic in, 102–103,
        103n141
    drug smuggling in, 104–108,
        104n142, 107n147
    economy and drugs, 183,
        184n290
    empire, 126
    enters World War I, 28
    fascist/socialist state, rise of, 78
    fiscal crisis (2008), 34
    health rate decline, 66
    heroin addiction in, 176,
        176n273–176n274
    heroin market, 102, 102n140,
        107

Bretton Woods agreement (*See* Bretton Woods Agreement (World War II))
British colonial empire after, 112
China, after, 85–86
development of atomic bomb, 69
drugs after, release of, 358
impact on Africa, 12
push to enter, 129, 130
rationing, during WWII, 137
reparations from Germany, 28
revival of drug trade, 102, 102n138
silent weapons, development of, 16–17
smuggling of heroin during, 101, 101n137
Versailles Treaty, 44
winners of, 34
    See also atomic bomb; Hitler, Adolf
World Zionism, 28
WTO (World Trade Organization) *See* World Trade Organization (WTO)

X

Xu, W., 194n301, 278n412

Y

Yale Skull and Bones society, 112, 196, 196n304, 236
Yamani, Sheikh Ahmed Zaki, 170–171, 171n267
Yang, L., 388n565
Yates, A., 323n492
Yen-Lieberman, B., 317n476
Yiamouyiannis, John, 71, 72n99

Young, Owen D., 28
Young, Robert, 396
Young, Shelley, 396
Young Plan, 29
Youngstown (OH), 98
Your Life Is Their Toy (Josephson), 22, 22n30
Yunnan Province (China), 100, 108

Z

Zaire, 147, 147n214, 153, 155–156, 275
Zakheim, Dov, 356
Zang, E.A., 340n513
Zang, Z., 393n581
Zarlenga, Stephen, 30n42
Zarogoza, A., 379n556
zero population growth, 232
Zhou Enlai, 175
Zimbabwe, 147, 147n214, 149, 154, 158, 159, 211, 212, 267
Zimmerman, Seth, 238n352
Zionists
    cause, 118
    delegation at Versailles (WWI), 28
    pressure group, 149